Kamala Joyce Platt
Environmental Justice Poetics

Kamala Joyce Platt

Environmental Justice Poetics

Cultural Representations of Environmental Racism from Chicanas and Women in India

DE GRUYTER

ISBN 978-3-11-221496-1
e-ISBN (PDF) 978-3-11-104157-5
e-ISBN (EPUB) 978-3-11-104206-0

Library of Congress Control Number: 2023943400

Bibliographic information published by the Deutsche Nationalbibliothek
The Deutsche Nationalbibliothek lists this publication in the Deutsche Nationalbibliografie; detailed bibliographic data are available on the Internet at http://dnb.dnb.de.

This volume is text- and page-identical with the hardback published in 2023.
Cover image: © Mary Agnes Rodriguez

Printing and binding: CPI books GmbH, Leck

www.degruyter.com

Acknowledgements

This book has been in the making since the early 1990s and there have been phases of fecundity and rest to the project. Each stage brought inspirations, solidarity, contributions, and synthesis, and I acknowledge the value of it all. Initially, stimulation from peers and professors in UT, Austin's Comparative Literature and related graduate programs and departments in combination with acquaintances and kindred spirits in community organizing around Austin, Texas, offered grounding. They are behind these pages in elemental ways.

What became this book was originally a cultural studies dissertation project that was honed down to a solely literary focus for the dissertation. My dissertation director José E. Limón's staunch, firme support buoyed my project through two high-powered dissertation committees—without him neither the graduate degree nor the expanded project that followed would have happened. Though the first committee dissolved, I am grateful for the hard questions they raised and the groundwork I completed under their guidance, especially for their mentorship in Resistance Literature, Third World Feminisms, and Chicana Literature and Cultural Studies. I am indebted to my subsequent committee for interdisciplinary guidance from Chicana/o and Middle Eastern, Feminist and Ethnic & Third World Literary & Cultural Sqweruqwerutudies, and from Geography and Anthropology. Craig Calhoun's workshop, a generous gathering of orphan multidisciplinary/sociology scholars at NYU was more than a godsend of solidarity and wisdom while I was in NYC teaching at NCC. Colleagues from institutions and communities, where I have taught and/or held fellowships have honoured me with exchanges over many of the poetics in this book. I am happily beholden to all those along the way who offered ideas and introduced me to scholars, activists, artists, and all the above, alike.

Recommencing the broader cultural work I'd set aside to complete my PhD, I benefitted from making a home during teaching and fellowship work in several places—in New York City metro area while I taught at Nassau Community College; in Eugene Oregon with support from University of Oregon's Women in Society Studies program as a fellow in their Women, Science and the Sacred Program; in Albuquerque, New Mexico, with support from UNM's Feminist Research Institute, teaching an environmental justice literature course through their Women's Studies Program, and living at Kalpulli Izkalli; and in San Antonio, TX while teaching at numerous schools and working with many community groups on environmental justice and related organizing, often spreading the word through expressive poetics, and further south while teaching at University of the Incarnate Word and researching environmental justice cultural poetics

https://doi.org/10.1515/9783111041575-202

along both sides of the Texas-NE Mexico border with my colleague Irasema Coronado for the Guadalupe Cultural Arts Center's Gateways Project.

After this fruitful time, during which I completed a full manuscript and had hopeful correspondence with several publishers, I moved into contingent teaching and my completed manuscript mostly sat on a shelf, even while I continued other less extensive environmental justice poetics research, activist, and creative projects. In the 21st Century, colleagues, peers, neighbors, and kin have added to my understanding and fed the persistence that kept *Environmental Justice Poetics* alive and dreaming through its long slumber. Over the years, I sent applications to grant programs in hopes of buying time to revive and reframe the project in the face of epoch-defining events such as 9-11-2001 and the wars and divisions that followed, and, subsequently, the intensifying Anthropocene climate chaos and injustice, and the concurrent destruction of habitat, and ecological and cultural systems, and the mass extinction of species, languages, and stories. Those who were writing and speaking about these existential crises, the "inconvenient truths," inspired me with their mandates—the moral imperatives of mapping sustainable, earth-and-her-kin-honouring, futures built on reciprocity. Those reviewers who identified my project as significant and excellent supported my belief in rekindling it, myself. However, by the time I submitted my manuscript to De Gruyter's 10th Open Access Book Anniversary contest, my goal was to simply publish the work online as a record of its existence. Shorter articles from which I'd developed some chapters had contributed to early environmental justice cultural studies scholarship, but virtually none of my teaching positions came with much interest in my scholarship or service in environmental justice cultural studies/ humanities.

When I heard from Maxim Karagodin that De Gruyter might be interested in publishing my book, I was elated and felt the worth of my project was finally being acknowledged, again. I am grateful to De Gruyter's anonymous reviewer for recommending publication and for their suggestions that drew my attention to a few of the most noteworthy of the plethora of environmental justice literary poetics that has been created since the turn of the century, especially in South Asia. As I prepared the book for publication, the dimensionality of the intervening decades came into focus. While I was not reframing, I was filling in (especially in footnotes) the sometimes-transformative passage of time since the original. I am honoured to have Mary Agnes Rodriguez, sister in struggle and expressive poetics, to paint the collaged, murals-inspired cover art. Everyone at De Gruyter has offered kind and friendly assistance and advice, and I especially thank Elisabeth who as Production Manager has guided my preparatory work with patience even in light of my sometimes-obstinate laptop.

My Preface makes clear the importance of the North Star orientation of both the more than human, natural world, and the justice, peace/nonviolent resistancia and Satyagraha orientations from my parents Dwight and LaVonne, our small, extended family, and interconnecting spheres of kin, colleges, and communities. I wish to acknowledge their contributions to my part in this circle and its steady source of strength, a foundation for my bookmaking. I take responsibility for the errors, herein, as well as the complicity of my study in an unjust and ecologically and culturally disastrous world headed into climate cacophony. Nevertheless, this book is the result of a great many world kin who have shared their visions, art, struggle, scholarship, and hope—my appreciation, and my pledge to not give up hope and to move y/our work forward.

Table of Contents

Part II: Women Write Environmental Justice: The Literary Tradition in India and Greater Mexico

Preface

Environmental Justice Poetics: Representations of Environmental Racism from Chicanas and South Asian Women investigates the issues and icons of resistance and self and community representation in India and Greater México by examining how the social issue environmental justice operates in selected instances of literature and other cultural production. I began this comparative study of women's poetics of environmental justice in Chicana/o and South Asian communities in the fall of 1992 shortly after the commemorations of 500 years of European domination in the Americas had drowned out the celebrations of the anniversary of Columbus's arrival. Five years later, people throughout the Indian Diaspora celebrated 50 years of India's independence from British colonial rule, and the year after that, Chicana/os commemorated one hundred and fifty years under the Treaty of Guadalupe Hidalgo, which took from México a landmass that on contemporary maps extends from Texas through California and north into Colorado, Kansas, and Oregon. In India, as in many other formerly colonized nations, the end of a foreign colonial presence has not meant the end of domination or its effects. Over decades, India and Pakistan, like the US and the USSR, have rehearsed nuclear cold war threats. In Chicana/o homelands, like in South Asia, the effects of multiple layers of domination continue. In both South Asia and the Americas, the practice and effects of environmental racism that date back to European colonization (Kerr & Lee; Omvedt 1993) increase with the expansion of multinational corporations. In response to the increasing devastation, a swelling of protest, centered in rich poetic expression, grows and diversifies, demanding more equitable relations between peoples and more responsible treatment of the environment.

Internationally and intra-nationally, an environmental justice movement has linked environmental injustice with structural racism and patriarchy, identifying environmental racism as the outcome of colonialism and imperialist capitalism. In the last decades of the Twentieth Century, calls for environmental and ecological justice became rallying cries in many parts of the world. The cultural poesis of this movement reveals community struggles against what Vandana Shiva, "the South's best-known environmentalist," according to the *New Internationalist*, has named "green imperialism." Those who take part in these struggles proclaim that environmentalism is incomplete if it does not address the implicit justice issues that impact human communities, and furthermore, "mainstream" environmental thought must be examined for its complicity with domination of communities of color and economic disenfranchisement and of the "Third World" or Global South, more broadly.

https://doi.org/10.1515/9783111041575-204

In 1992, only one of the major literary texts under consideration in this study had been published (in English), but the People Organized in Defense of the Earth and her Resources (PODER) was forcing the relocation of 43 oil tanks belonging to six national oil companies that were polluting the Govalle neighborhood in East Austin, Texas, the Chipko movement had forestalled deleterious development in the Himalayan foothills, Bhopal gas survivors had presented their case before the Voices of the Victims of Industrial Disasters Tribunal in Bombay, and farm worker campaigns, building on the earlier successes of boycotts in support of workers' rights, were again urging a grape boycott to curtail dangerous pesticide usage by growers. As this chronology suggests, literary texts follow the lead of activists on themes of environmental justice. I consider this sequence important and have used it in organizing this book.

Generally, grassroots communities are ahead of academic communities in having thought through the implications of the human impact of environmental destruction. That communities in the U.S. that are the targets of environmental racism might have something in common with South Asian communities in the same position has seemed clear to community activists, who spread the word that the damaging results of corporate globalization are right here in "our town," and *not only* across the border or overseas.

When I first began talking about environmental justice, the most common question asked of me was "environmental what?" By the turn of the century, although I often needed to reiterate that environmental injustices directly impact the basic rights and eco-systemic survival of human communities, most people demonstrate some familiarity with the term, environmental justice. A second question, which I continue to answer frequently, is, Why compare India and Greater Mexico? For me, the comparison between the two sites never seemed odd, but that probably has to do with my own history.

I was less than three years old when I attended my uncle's and aunt's wedding festivities in her family's hometown south of Juarez in Chihuahua, México. I have an early memory—though surely from a later trip—of my mother giving me her explanation of class/social structure in the U.S. and Mexico. This conversation involved the comparison of countries and communities, family and lifestyles, and—albeit not discussed as such, at the time—environmental impacts, even as my mother explained that though we lived in different national contexts and regions, both my aunt's family and my own family were lower middle class.

The first decade of my life spanned the 1960s, but my family's involvement in racial justice, civil rights, international peace, and environmental struggles was not so much a reflection of the times as a continuation of family concerns that go back generations. Like many with European ancestry in the Americas, my ancestors traverse a spectrum of political and cultural affiliations that shape a contradictory personal history vis-á-vis social justice struggle. My paternal grandfather's family gave me not only my surname, but a family legacy of abolitionist beliefs expressed in actions such as offering stations on the underground railroad, settling Kansas as a free state, and teaching in Freedmen's Schools. My paternal grandmother inherited a Mennonite tradition of pacifist resistance and a belief in social equity and carved her family's life accordingly. Her solidarity work with the civil rights movement in Kansas in the 1940s and 1950s and her interest in and connections to international peace struggles, shared with her children, eclipsed Mennonite Anabaptist tradition of the time. In the early 1950s, my father, and later my mother, joined an American Friends Service Committee (AFSC/Quaker) Village Project in Barpali, Orissa (now Odisha), in India; they were married in India, later returning to teaching in Kansas. When I was eleven, my family returned to India, to spend a long-anticipated year in Sambalpur, Orissa, where my dad, on sabbatical from teaching at Bethel College, a small, Mennonite-affiliated, liberal arts college, taught at Sambalpur University.

I became aware of the international inequities of environmental standards largely through my father's work. As a biology teacher with growing environmental concerns, he was interested in the changes wrought in village ecosystems in the interlude since my parents' years in Orissa over a decade earlier. In much of India, that timespan was marked by increasing use of pesticides in agriculture and public health, driven by "Green Revolution" models. As the negative effects of many pesticides were discovered, their use was often banned in Western countries, but corporate production and marketing continued in so-called developing countries. For example, DDT was used extensively in India long after it was banned in the U.S. in 1972.

My learning about the inequities of environmental standards—based on ethnicity and national heritage, and vis-à-vis the pesticide DDT—came full circle, when I was teaching at University of the Incarnate Word (UIW) in the late 1990s. In teaching a composition course I had designed with an umbrella topic of environmental justice, I learned about DDT in Shiner, Texas, from a Chicana student. Her paper describes her Spanish-speaking grandfather, a *mexicano* farmer in South Texas, purchasing the chemical up into the mid-1980s—at the recommendation of a local hardware store. His sons and daughters became alarmed when they read the fine print in English on the pesticide packaging and described the implications of using DDT, in Spanish, to their father. My student describes how her family subsequently realized that in uncovering the decades of DDT use on their family farm, they had discovered the potential cause of minor deformities with which half of her cousins had been born. Previously, the family had wondered why half of their youngest generation had small birth defects that had never appeared in previous generations.

If a cross-cultural childhood initiated my thinking about environmental justice poetics in India and Greater Mexico, my classroom experiences—as teacher (as illustrated above) and as student—furthered it. My interest in Chicano literature and cultural poetics was raised during classes with Ramón Saldívar, and sustained by later coursework with José E. Limón, and with Lora Romero, who taught the only class that focused on Chicana literature I had the opportunity to take at University of Texas, Austin. My interest in South Asian literature was nurtured in the classroom of the esteemed Indian fiction writer R.K. Narayan. Graduate coursework for my PhD in Comparative Literature that included interdisciplinary work in the social sciences and in the humanities more broadly also provided me with theoretical frameworks through which to think out my longstanding engagement with various forms of cultural poetics—predominantly creative writing, visual and performance art, photography, and film. However, much of my learning about the poetics of environmental racism took place off-campus.

In the summer of 1991, Resistencia Bookstore, home of Red Salmon Press and "Native American/Chicana/o/x/Latina/o/x-based cultural arts organization with a history of working within indigenous communities of Austin since 1983" (https://www.resistenciabooks.com/2023) was located "east of the freeway." I spent many days there, helping Raúl R. Salinas, proprietor and Chicano poet to prepare for exhibits, canto libres, and benefits, and meeting his wide variety of visitors. Salinas was working on a collection of poetry, entitled *East of the Freeway*. The geographic delineation is also a socio-political and cultural one—East Austin is made up of predominantly Chicana/o and African American communities, communities at greater risk for environmental racism, communities who have introduced the concept of environmental justice to what may be Texas's most environmentally conscious city. At Resistencia, where I eventually defended a dissertation on environmental justice literature, at other politically progressive art venues in Austin's communities of color, and at gatherings and conferences, such as The Other Economic Summit (TOES) in Houston, Texas in 1990, where I met rising luminaries such as Luiz Inácio Lula da Silva from Brazil and Winona La Duke from Anishinaabe community in Minnesota, I was beginning to hear more and more about people coming face to face with environmental toxins, about struggles for environmental justice. Around the same time, I began to read about Indian women's ecological justice actions that utilized poetry, cultural traditions, legend, and religious ritual in protecting the forests from outsider logging and deleterious land use.

These conversations crossed conventional university-community divides. In preparing a panel response for Public Radio's *Asian Communiqué* to a Union Carbide representative's visit to the University of Texas, Austin, I had learned about the continuing effects of transnational environmental racism. For affected communities in Bhopal, Madhya Pradesh, after a Union Carbide pesticide plant leaked a toxic mixture of gases into the surrounding city, effects would be permanent. A fellow student and panel member from Bhopal suffered from chronic eye damage from gas exposure—he had arrived in his hometown by train that night and was exposed to the gas getting home from the railroad station. The same spring, in a rally at UT's West Mall in honor of a visit by the United Farm Worker (UFW) president, Cesar Chávez had addressed the links between toxic conditions for farm workers in the U.S. and corporate pesticide production and use in the "Third World." The screening of the UFW film *Grapes of Wrath* and discussion from Texas UFW Director Rebecca Flores Harrington solidified the statistics and trends noted at the rally, by documenting the voices, fears, and tears of farm worker families, the "canaries in the mines," as Cesar Chávez described them. In doing so, it revealed the permanent effects of pesticides on the human body. These experiences—particularly hearing survivors' stories—mark the beginnings of my involvement with, and theorization of, the issues and poetics of environmental justice narrated in this book.

A frequently asked question in conversations about my interest in environmental justice is "Why *women* and environmental justice?" Environmental justice issues internationally are often issues in which women have taken the lead, with or without the support of men; this is true in the activism as well as literary production. A primary reason for this is that in societies where women are discriminated against structurally (in other words, globally), environmental damage impacts people in gender-related ways. Often these social ramifications of environmental damage are more severe for women. Furthermore, the biological effects of environmental toxins often target women's reproductive systems, affecting the women, and their children, for whom they are most often primary caregivers. Because of their experience with environmental destruction, and because environmental justice impacts the home, as well as the larger community and world, women have sometimes used environmental justice as a steppingstone into grassroots political realms that were previously primarily men's terrain. Mary Pardo describes this in her studies of the work of the Mothers of East Los Angeles (MELA), as do Vandana Shiva and Gail Omvedt, in speaking about Indian women's social environmentalism. Ana Castillo and Nina Sibal describe the same process in fiction. Critical gender analysis of such environmental justice issues raises questions about the interconnections of social identity and social transformation. I hope that this book will provide a platform to begin to address further trans-gender identities and cross-cultural dialogue on these issues.

Deciphering the role of gender in environmental justice poetics is important to me. By centering my study in work done by women, I seek to establish a polemic that works against the conventional patriarchal assumptions entrenched in academic investigation. Similarly, focusing on the work of organizations in India and a U.S. movement led by people of color, intervenes in institutionalized racism, internationally and intra-nationally. My subject-matter is transcultural—women's texts, that while not necessarily represented as feminist, are creating *women-centered* theory based in the work of people of color and people of the "Third World." My focus encourages vigilance against a patriarchal structure that permeates across political spectrums. These are the complex, subtle answers to the question on women and environmental justice. The more straightforward answer is that, as a woman involved in her own activism, art, and scholarship, I want to find the texts to which academia is not necessarily going to guide me, texts created by all genders who would be my mentors, models, friends, colleagues, and compañer@s. I am interested in finding answers to the question: How is environmental racism portrayed by those who support this growing movement for environmental justice that is at once local and international? The work of striving for environmental justice is not just community work, is not merely academic, is not simply trendy art, performance, or literary works; environmental justice work demands interdisciplinary, transnational, trans-community sharing, multiple border crossings, and solid alliance-building. These activities have generated a rich body of cultural poetics that have in common a transformative vision of environmental equity. *Environmental Justice Poetics: Representations of Environmental Racism from Chicanas and South Asian Women* presents my study of the process and products of this environmental justice work.

Introduction

> You can't really separate issues of ecology from feminism or from human rights or from development, or from issues of ethnic and cultural diversity.
>
> Vandana Shiva

New Titles On An Old Story: Whose Justice? Whose Environment?

> To be a social environmentalist is to be a person who is concerned about humanity and also about all living things in our world.
>
> Gilberto Rivera

In winter 1993–1994[1], the Austin, Texas-based environmental justice organization People Organized in Defense of the Earth and her Resources (PODER) produced a T-shirt that proclaims, "As people of color, we must redefine environmental issues as social and economic justice issues, and collectively set our own agenda to address these concerns as basic human rights." In creating this shirt, PODER transposed a part of its mission statement into an expressive form of popular culture (up for market exchange) and created a means of transmitting a message of social transformation across classes, and generational and ethnic boundaries. When combined, the words "environment," and "social justice," raise a set of contemporary issues that expand the territories of both terms. Defining environmental justice leads to a re-evaluation of race, gender, class, and related issues considering the degradation of the habitats of human and non-human communities. The coined term poses the questions: Whose environment is protected? Whose environment is neglected? Who makes these decisions? "Environmental Justice" challenges those with narrow definitions of environmentalism to reconceptualize their concerns for environmental "protection," extending it to *humans*. For those involved primarily with social justice concerns, the term signals the necessity for more extensive inclusion of environmental issues in their agendas. For those who do not separate the two concepts, "environmental justice" names, and thus underscores, the importance of their dialectical work.

PODER's T-shirt suggests that at the crux of "environmental justice" is the act—initiated by people of color in the U.S.—of expressively *revising* social defi-

---

1 Parts of the introduction were adapted from my paper "Pedagogies of Environmental Justice" published in *Greening the Campus Conference Proceedings*, Ball State University, Indiana: Spring, 1996.

https://doi.org/10.1515/9783111041575-001

nitions. As the popular form of dissemination of this social message marked distinct complexities at the end of the 20th century, so the message issued a burgeoning demand from grassroots communities of color for revision of social power. Thus, at the nexus of environmental and social justice concerns is the reworking of social institutions and relationships. This process is, by definition, transformative in its praxis and its theory. And it is a process that leaves in its wake, expressive culture sculpted by the conveyor and context, as well as the content. Such cultural acts create the poetics at the heart of this book.

Environmental Justice Poetics: Cultural Representations of Environmental Racism from Chicanas and South Asian Women investigates the activist, artistic, and academic texts that make up a portion of this poetics of environmental justice. Focusing on Chicana/o communities and communities in India, *Environmental Justice Poetics* examines images that seek to promote environmental justice and eradicate environmental racism through representations of self and community. While all the women I discuss may not name their goal "environmental justice," they all address issues in which the impact of environmental degradation directly affects human health and wellbeing. If some activists inflect their struggles differently, they nonetheless identify themselves as part of a grassroots community that is expanding previous environmental and social justice agendas; they are mostly based in communities of color and/ or the "Third World" and many are led by women.

Their images are part of a body of poetics, or "cultural poesis" that has generated the foundational concepts of environmental justice around which I have organized my study. Its diverse iconography addresses environmental justice issues that are often ignored by the mainstream media. Such concerns include the destruction of forests that provide villagers' subsistence, the uneven distribution of toxic waste dumps, dangerous pesticide use by agricultural growers, dam projects that displace communities and irrevocably destroy their land, livelihoods and sense of place, industrial "accidents" and resulting holocausts, and the environmentally-related health concerns of women in the industrial/high-tech work place, in maquiladoras, farmworker labor, and indentured servitude; whether rural or urban, the setting is most often in economically disenfranchised communities, in places such as borderlands or neighborhoods within metropolitan areas to which rural women have been displaced.

The mushrooming impact of environmental devastation on "Third" and "Fourth" World or indigenous communities (especially on women and infants), within both the global North and South has given rise to vital discussions of environmental justice. This growing international movement links environmental injustice with structural racism and patriarchy, identifying "environmental racism" as the outcome of colonialism and global capitalism, and critiquing "mainstream" environmentalism.[2] This has occurred even as in literary studies, the category of "literature" has undergone radical revision into the broader realm of cultural poetics, and in the social sciences, new social movement theories and participant-observer ethnographies and host verification directives have revised (though not replaced) earlier, modernist readings of culture and exclusively quantitative strategies for performing critical analysis. In all these fields, scholarship has been broadened to include more facets of experience that were previously ignored; these include perspectives of women, people of color, indigenous peoples, immigrants, gay and lesbian and economically and educationally disenfranchised peoples, among others.

Contemporary cultural narratives that expose environmental racism and demand environmental justice have been presented in a variety of genres including novels, creative nonfiction, short stories, poetry, songs, manifestos, testimonios, theory, philosophy, film, video, drama, performance art, street theater, radio programs, poster art, community flyers, graphic art, political cartoons, sculpture, installations, murals, and other public art. Groups like PODER, the Mothers of East Los Angeles (MELA and Las Madres), the United Farm Workers (UFW), the Chipko Andolan, Bhopal Gas-affected Survivors groups, and Stop the Narmada Dams organizations have promoted environmental justice in press conferences, demonstrations and rallies, padyatras, pilgrimages, marches for protest or protection, radio programs, toxic tours, galleries, lectures and cultural celebrations. Activists, artists, and academics have worked side by side, often in different but mutually supportive roles, to confront neighborhood and international, environmental issues impacting human communities.

Within the United States, much of the work done under the rubric "environmental justice" centers around the disproportionate use of toxins in the neighborhoods and at the worksites of people of color. Internationally, race and ethnicity are also pivotal points in constructions of environmental justice politics and suggest that environmental racism exists intra-nationally within the South, as well as the North. In the Afterword to *Imaginary Maps*, a collection of Mahasweta Devi's short stories translated and discussed by Gayatri Chakravorty Spivak, who evokes racial, economic, and national issues involving "ecological

---

2 The movement is international in that people across the world have organized various means towards promoting the rubric of "environmental justice on local terms;" no formal coalition, platform, or mass international framework for mutual support of struggle exists (circa 2000), although certainly a growing informal network is in place.

justice." She foregrounds her critique on the attack manifested against the Fourth World or, in common Indian parlance, *Adivasis* or *Tribals* through the appropriation of the Fourth World's ecology.

> Here kinship can be felt through the land grabbing and deforestation practiced against the First Nations of the Americas, the destruction of the reindeer forests of the Soumis of Scandinavia and Russia, and the tree felling and eucalyptus plantations on the land of the original nations, indeed of all the early civilizations that have been pushed back and away to make way for what we call the geographic lineaments of the map of the world today (198).

In India and in the US, a similar spectrum of environmental oppression affects the lifestyles, livelihoods, and life spans of various groups differently. The formula, in both countries and possibly universally, is nearly identical: being poor, a person of color, an indigenous person, a woman, LGBTQ+ and/or an immigrant work against one's chances of an ecologically and economically sustainable lifestyle in a relatively unpolluted, non-carcinogenic environment.[3] Thus, along with race and ethnicity, other social identity issues including class and gender identities are vital for study in order to understand strategic depictions and resistance to corporate or government sponsored destruction of communities, livelihoods, cultural traditions, and personal health—destruction that can lead to ecocide, and even genocide. Activists' and artists' representations interlink these issues, producing strategies for education, resistance, and community empowerment. Hence, the practice of resisting environmental racism exists in dialectic relationship with the theory; in other words, it both utilizes and generates the theory—a fact often missed when academics study social movements or culturally attentive art.

The term "environmental racism," applied predominantly in the U.S., refers to environmentally related discrimination based on race, but not divorced from other social identity issues such as class and gender. The term was first used in the U.S. in 1982 when African Americans fighting the environmental degrada-

---

3 That the influence of these factors is not predictable in all cases is demonstrated by, for example, the high rate of breast cancer among women in wealthier neighborhoods outside of New York City, which surpassed the inner-city rate due to a more contaminated source of water for those outlying areas (NPR 4-7-94, Rosalie Bertell). Long Island, for instance has had one of the highest rates of breast cancer in the country; the NYC rate has been lower. Such exceptions to the formula may demonstrate how underdeveloped is our ability to systematically detect environmental health problems. To the extent to which repressive systems in power have control of environmental factors, toxins are generally kept away from the neighborhoods of those in the dominant race and class.

tion of their community recognized a familiar pattern of racial discrimination in the environmental issues they faced (Chavis in Bullard 1993, 3).[4] Since the early eighties, individual communities of color fighting against localized environmental injustices, usually without support from mainstream environmentalists, have led the environmental justice movement in fighting environmental racism. In comparison to middle class NIMBY (Not In My Backyard) demands for protection of their communities, social justice environmentalists demand that toxic waste *not be in anyone's backyard*, that corporations clean up their acts at home and abroad, and that governments work against structural racism in all arenas (Chavis in Bullard 1993, 5).

Environmental poetics shows environmental racism to be part of postcolonial conditions and a legacy of colonialism. Thus, focusing on environmental justice includes understanding postcolonial conditions and decolonizing strategies. Much work in postcolonial studies addresses the concerns of continuing colonialisms that plague both those groups who have achieved political independence and those still under direct political domination from another nation. "Post" has been discussed and redefined repeatedly, so that for many theorists, the term "post" indicates that societal, cultural, and literary representations are still shaped by the vestiges of colonialism —even when countries have (in name) gained "independence." Alternatively, studying decolonialism—initially drawing on the work of France Fanon and Aimé Césaire—foregrounds community resistance to domination; the resulting cultural poetics may link with environmental justice discourse.

The fact that postcolonial comes after colonialism does not suggest that domination does not continue. Indeed, new forms such as "biocolonialism" (to use Vandana Shiva's term) have evolved. Cultural scholars have shown that

---

4 Readers may notice variance in citation style between humanities and social science style guide protocol and between different national styles. I have attempted consistency in style, while respecting context, quotation, language, needed information for clarity, and disciplinary variances in tradition. Admittedly, determining a consistent style of citation and reference, and even punctuation, capitalization, and spaces, for this book has been discombobulating. Developing consistent elements of style in an interdisciplinary study with quotations from authors in multiple registers, dialects, and languages, especially when the writing and revising span 30 years, is a more multifarious project than is initially apparent. Working with an international publisher added complexity to the final editing. It turns out there are a myriad of differences in rules to follow (right down to where to put dots and spaces), between U.K. English and U.S. English. I am grateful for the editorial team's generosity in helping me work out the most rational compromises. Hopefully, the stylistic solutions to retaining consistency in this idiosyncratic book don't befuddle readers from any continent.

literary postmodernism is dependent on literary modernism, building upon modernism rather than breaking with it. In the image my college English professor used in my first literary theory course, the poststructuralists stand on the shoulders of structuralists, while pulling their feet out from under them. Likewise, the postcolonial builds on the foundation of colonialism even as it interrogates and—in multiple senses—deconstructs it. The colonialisms faced today are sometimes more lethal than 19th Century European colonialism, and new kinds of environmental destruction are endemic in postcolonial situations.

While writers and theorists, those with "lived experience" involved in postcolonial situations or progressive activism, have pushed the envelope on the significance of post coloniality, in U.S. academic culture, literature from or about previously colonized countries is often taught here with inadequate historical or political context. Literature professors often fail to teach the consequences of U.S. imperialism, consequences that are brought to light in "Third World" cultural poetics from both within and outside of the "first world." [5] Environmental justice poetics critically examines such depoliticized misrepresentations and reinserts the work of art into the frame of environmental racism. It thereby closes the geopolitical gap between colonizer and colonized, bringing postcolonial studies closer to "home" in the Americas and mapping the close links between (post)colonialism and (present) globalization, neocolonialism, and "biocolonialism."

In May 1992, in her keynote speech at the National Conference of Indian Activists, in Chicago, Vandana Shiva constructed a polemical relationship between "green imperialism" and "environmental justice" (IPAG 2). The polemic represents a decision *for* or *against*—respectively—the imperialist land grabbing of the "Fourth World," (First Nations in Canadian parlance) of indigenously settled lands that Gayatri Spivak describes, the toxification of working class/communities of color described by U.S. social environmentalists, and in essence, any situation of outside domination that affects a community through degradation of its environment. The choice between the two, Shiva said, is a

5 In choosing to use title case for "Third World" and leave "first world" in lower case letters, I follow the custom used in Black and white, in reference to race; this practice foregrounds and upturns the power deferential and underscores the vigilant struggle to change skewed power relations. When I use quotation marks for both terms, it is to remind us that both are geopolitical markers that must be constantly brought into question, even as the terms may be the most adequate to date. In the 21st Century, "Third World" has fallen from usage, but is retained in the names of organizations, and caucusing groups, and in establishing a long-standing political identity with its cultural capital claimed from struggle. For these reasons, I've continued using the term.

choice "between a common future for all or continued economic and environmental apartheid" (IPAG 3). Shiva clarified her use of the term "apartheid" with the rhetorical question: "Are we going to move into a[n] era of environmental apartheid, where the North becomes clean and stays rich while the South stays poor and becomes the toxic dump of the world?" (IPAG 3). Like her activist and academic peers have observed in communities of color in United States, Shiva's language reiterates that, in the "Third World," environmentalism, when it is being transported from the "first world," may merely re-inscribe structural violence.

Ecopolitical Histories

> When Columbus landed in America for the second time he brought with him stalks of sugarcane.... Planted in the West Indies and north-east Brazil, cane became the basis of the infamous 'triangular trade' linking the West Indies and New England, Britain and Africa in the production of sugar and rum, through the labor of slaves. It was also the beginning of ecologically destructive agriculture, for after flourishing for about a century in northeastern Brazil sugar plantations rendered the land so unproductive that the region has remained the most impoverished in the country ever since.
>
> Gail Omvedt (in CtH 99)

The recent naming of "environmental racism" does not suggest that the phenomenon is likewise recent. As Gail Omvedt notes, environmental injustices have been occurring in much of the world for centuries. In the following passage, Omvedt links such racism to the European colonizing of several continents.

> Even before industrialization took hold, the rise of capitalism entailed the transformation of agriculture throughout the world. Some regions were turned into plantation colonies; in others, small peasants were forced through high taxes or other forms of bondage to produce crops for the European market; still others became sites of subsistence agriculture that functioned to reproduce the labour power of low-paid migrant workers in mines and factories. The forms varied, but there was a common thread. The extraction of surplus from the land, its forests, its plant and mineral wealth, was crucial to capital accumulation on a world scale. And it was accompanied by the exploitation, both direct and indirect, of the women and men of peasant and forest-dwelling communities throughout the world. (Omvedt in CtH 99)

The nexus of environmental racism, colonialism, and capitalism that Omvedt identifies, is crucial for my study. For many, this juncture functions as a historicized foundation from which to produce theory and advocate action. The connections between slavery and environmental degradation resonate in Mahasweta Devi's characters from Bihar and Bengal, India; they see themselves bonded into indentured servitude and the land they work is held by landowners, who abuse both workers' human rights and the land, itself. Within the U.S., as the concept of environmental justice is defined and situated historically, earlier examples of environmental racism, and its resistance, are identified. The title of an article by Mary Lee Kerr and Charles Lee, "From Conquistadors to Coalitions: After Centuries of Environmental Racism, People of Color are Forging a New Movement for Environmental Justice," asserts the historical extent of environmental racism in the Americas. Kerr and Lee map the colonial beginnings of environmental racism in the Southern United States: "[t]he first Southerners to experience environmental racism were Native Americans. Cherokees, Choctaws, Chickasaws, Creeks, Tuscaroras, Catawbas, Seminoles, Natchez, and other Southern Indians who inhabited the region long before Columbus lived in complex, self-sustaining communities" (10). Yet while the institutions and attitudes that create environmental injustice have been developing for centuries, the material effects—due to unregulated proliferation of new industrial and technological processes—have become more pervasive and more lethal in recent years. These effects materialize in conjunction with gender, race, class and other differentials of power and disenfranchisement.

In the U.S., starting in the last decades of the 20th century, social environmentalists point the way to identifying and countering environmental racism regardless of the context. They distinguish themselves from many previous social movements by retaining relatively equal emphasis on the group's goals and the subject identities that group members hold in common. Through interrogation that uncovers the ramifications of environmental racism, they expand the agendas of the environmental and the social justice organizations that preceded them. Thereby, they consistently articulate the relevance of the interconnections between "who they are" and "what they want." They emphasize their foundation as working-class people of color attempting to live harmoniously in their "natural" environment without negative intervention from dominant societal power structures.

Work studied in *Environmental Justice Poetics* may be the vanguard of postcolonial studies, because like in decolonial studies, its creators link a colonial past with a present that is dominated by capitalist imperialism; they have taken their lead in this analysis from environmental justice activists. Progressive, grassroots communities are consistently more advanced than universities in thinking through the implications of environmental justice vis-á-vis societal landscapes of domination; the postcolonial landscape is no exception. Their environmental justice poesis brings to the surface the complicated interactions between race, gender, class, and other social identity issues as they intersect with culture and politics. Unexamined essentialist categories can create an impasse for scholar-theorists when identity politics erase different creases within social identity categories. Examining environmental justice activism may help disaggregate this for scholars, especially when the activists' motivations are to create both practical and *transformative*, social change—change, which not only rectifies an unjust situation, but also begins to reshape the unjust structure of society. The activist's/artist's roots in praxis and/or politicized aesthetic production may both filter and broaden the academic's ways of seeing. The activist/artist conceptualizes the global wheels on local hubs and mediates problems to account for contextual local instances while simultaneously proposing transformations of culture and politics.

Several rough parallels exist in the experience of the groups in the two geographic areas under study. Common to both India and Greater Mexico—the self-described homelands of Chicana/o communities in the U.S.—is the degradation of the environment under the guise of development. This is a process that predictably displaces agricultural workers into economically disenfranchised communities, urban communities of color that are often the industrial toxic dumping zones for the metropolis. In both India and Greater Mexico, the complexities of social disenfranchisement and displacement have sometimes pitted communities against each other. However, local alliances between immigrant and indigenous, rural, and urban, and other socially disenfranchised communities have been a means of strengthening resistance to exploitation. Environmental justice poetics has aided these struggles for freedom and self-determination. It extends and sometimes revives traditions as it speaks out against colonialism, imperialist capitalism, and racism. Women are key players in conceptualizing and disseminating this cultural work in which artistic practices propose that environmental justice be a central part of local, and ultimately global, equity and enfranchisement.

Vandana Shiva has consistently focused on the ways in which environmental devastation has affected women's lifestyles and the subsequent roles women have played in fighting for environmental justice. Inherent to her gender critique is a consistent analysis (historically, largely missing from much conventional women's studies in the U.S.) of how class, nationality, region, and ethnicity shape the issues as well. In other words, a woman's standing in the place she lives affects her experience of environmental degradation. Shiva defines environmental justice based on her support for and interaction with rural India's struggles for environmental justice.[6] Although she has a Ph.D. in physics, she

---

6 Shiva received some criticism soon after *Staying Alive* was published for overemphasizing the roles of women and the role of environmental concern in the Chipko Andolan. While some

credits "the peasant women of rural India" with teaching her "[e]verything [she has] learned about environmentalism" (IPAG 2). In so doing, she demonstrates that in this arena academics have much to learn from those less formally educated. Although Vandana Shiva has been distinctively prolific in her writing about environmental injustice internationally, little attention has been paid to how women with (largely unpublished) concerns that resonant with Shiva's, have represented their perspectives on the struggles for environmental protection and social justice.

Women of color have often taken leadership roles in social environmentalism. To consider social identity dynamics in this discourse from their standpoints, I focus primarily on their work. As mentioned in the preface, women in general suffer different, and often more severe, biological and sociological effects from environmental toxins than men. For instance, in the Himalayan foothills, women are affected more adversely by deforestation because their daily work depends on a forest-based subsistence economy that is being destroyed, while men are more likely to benefit, at least in the short term, from the intruding cash economy. Thus, women are discriminated against structurally. When such structural discrimination impacts daily family life, women have often emerged into the public sphere, initiating grassroots politics, and bringing with them a poesis based in cultural tradition and individual creativity. In some cases, earlier struggles against colonialism set a precedent for women's activism that was rekindled in the contemporary environmental justice movement. The Chipko Andolan's history with Gandhian Satyagraha workers in the Himalayan foothills is an example of this.

The groups and individual artists who are the focus of my project can lay claim to a lineage of local victories that is impressive in grassroots organizing and in artistic production. Many of the activists have a substantial history of organizing, and their organizations have successfully evolved over the years to meet new situations and demands. The writers and visual and performance artists who have addressed issues of environmental injustice have presented them in a range of venues—their fiction has been published with major publishing companies and with small presses; their poetry and songs appear on the pages of books published as zines and by university presses, and in demonstrations in the foothills of the Himalayas, and in cantinas and taquerias in Austin, Texas. Visual art has been produced on T-shirts in the southwestern U.S., on postcards in Bhopal, Madhya Pradesh, and in murals on the walls of a tribal

---

feminists felt she misrepresents Indian women and uses the subaltern to voice her own concerns, much of the criticism is tied to a patriarchal, even misogynist, world view that seeks to erase women from India's ecological activism.

development office in the Kalahandi District of Odisha, India, a school in the Mexican border-town of Ciudad Acuña, and near a waste dump site on "el otro lado," near Del Río, Ciudad Acuña's sister city.[7]

Cultural texts generated in solidarity with environmental justice are not limited to organizationally sponsored work. Individual artists have described environmental racism and community resistance, thereby demonstrating alliance with organizational stances on environmental justice. Such work includes Marsha Gomez's sculptural *Madre del Mundo* series and Ester Hernández's screenprint entitled "Sun Mad," transmedia performance art such as Belinda Acosta's piece, "Objects in Mirror Are Closer than they Appear," and performance poetry such as "FALSIES and the new way to reclaim information about your/my/our body" by Tammy Melody Gómez.

Some of the most extensive treatment of environmental justice issues has been in literary genres—fiction, drama, poetry, and testimonio. Such literary works by women who promote the struggle for environmental and economic justice present productive continuities and discontinuities with the visual images, political tracts, and other types of cultural production. These writers often recount theoretical concerns and social analyses drawn from the broader realm of cultural poetics, thereby furthering grassroots environmental justice projects. Newly published novels that address environmental justice are increasing. Early examples in English include Ana Castillo's *So Far From God*, in which a weapons industry worker fights industry over deadly exposure to carcinogens. In Castillo's novel, mother and daughter protagonists face a variety of social ills, (including cancer caused by handling industrial toxins); the descriptions replicate environmental racism described by activists and journalists in New Mexico, where the novel is set. Furthermore, the mother's creative, proactive response to the domination of her town is comparable to the work of Chicana organizers in the Southwest.

Another early novel is Nina Sibal's *Yatra (The Journey)*, which describes a cosmopolitan Indian woman's *padyatra*, or foot journey, to the Himalayan villages that, since the seventies, have been involved in the Chipko movement against deforestation. Somewhat like Vandana Shiva suggests about herself, Krishna, the protagonist of *Yatra*, turns to the women of the Chipko movement for a model of personal and political growth.

Helena María Viramontes' *Under the Feet of Jesus: a novel* narrates in poetic prose the deadly health effects of pesticides for a young farm worker as it de-

7 The Odisha mural and the Del Rio mural provided inspiration for the painting by Mary Agnes Rodriguez used in the book's cover. For more about Mary Agnes' artwork, see https://www.artists-at-work.org/mary-agnes-rodriguez

scribes a California farm worker family who adopts an adolescent worker who has been poisoned by pesticides. This environmental justice fiction tells the stories of continuous "real life" struggles—the struggle for the basic rights of food, shelter and health, and the struggle against those whose domination make these basic rights nearly unattainable. Against this backdrop of struggle, *Under the Feet...* is, like *Yatra*, a bildungsroman of both personal and political transformation.

The novels examined in *Environmental Justice Poetics* are only a sampling of the novels addressing environmental racism in the last two decades of the 20th Century. In Leslie Marmon Silko's *Almanac of the Dead*, indigenous peoples from the South lead an ecological justice revolution that has had prophetic parallels in the subsequent "real life" Zapatista uprising in Chiapas, Mexico. Many of Rodolfo Anaya's books, most notably the Chicano classic *Bless Me, Ultima*, expose the environmental racism of the nuclear industry in the southwest, and Salman Rushdie briefly addresses environmental justice issues that Indian women workers and activists face in *The Moor's Last Sigh*. Latinas such as Julia Alvarez have addressed environmental justice issues in the Americas repeatedly in their writing. With the increase in fiction, collections of literary criticism focusing on women and men of various ethnicities involved in writing about environmental justice are proliferating as well.

Short stories that address the topic include much of the work of Mahasweta Devi that has been translated from the Bengali/ Bangla. For example, "Dhowli" and "Paddy Seeds" are stories that map the effects of bonded slave labor on the lives and lands of disenfranchised peoples in Bihar and Bengal; Mahasweta Devi's short stories of ecological justice struggles, from *Imaginary Maps* (in translation by Gayatri Chakravorty Spivak) and *Of Women, Outcastes, Peasants, and Rebels: A Selection of Bengali Short Stories* (translated by Kalpana Bardhan), address land, forest, resource, gender, ethnicity, and caste issues in the context of rural and indigenous (tribal) communities in Bihar and Bengal (previously West Bengal). Mahasweta's[8] depiction of tribal communities is, arguably, the most extensive in 20th Century Indian literary writing in English. Her extensive body of nonfiction and drama, as well as interviews with her, along with Gayatri Spivak's theoretical commentaries on Mahasweta's work, provide a grounding for my own analysis of these stories as exemplary, environmental justice prose,

---

8 To sustain consistency with my practice of retaining the author's policy on the italicization of "foreign" words, I keep with "the Indian custom of referring to thoroughly public figures by their first name as a sign of recognition of their stature" (Spivak 1995, 208), as do Spivak and Bardhan. Devi is not a surname, but a title of respect taken on by many Indian women. Bibliographical and Index citations are organized by first names as well.

prose that exposes the structural basis of environmental racism and demands global social transformation.

Complex structural domination that revokes environmental rights is also portrayed and protested in Chicana drama. Such plays include María Elena Lucas's "Flor Campesina" (Farmworker Flower), a *teatro campesino* pageant that uses Mexican Catholic metaphor to document the aerial pesticide spraying of farm workers and their subsequent decision to seek out Cesar Chavez and join the United Farm Workers. "The Hungry Woman" presents queer Chicana -centered contemporary mythology that builds on Cherríe Moraga's earlier, socially, and environmentally concerned plays that include "Watsonville" and "Heroes and Saints," that like "Flor Campesina" dramatize the effects of pesticides on farm worker families, as well as farm workers' continuing resistance that demands from growers environmentally safe working and living conditions.

Environmental Justice Poetics analyzes the interrelationship of local and global social environmentalism that responds to such lived experience, at points contrasting it with representations of environmentalism from outside the environmental justice movement. Comparisons with corporate environmental representations reveal that outsiders with vested corporate interests often undermine the interests of environmental justice, even while claiming to support ecological wellbeing. Juxtaposing comparable representations of "the forces of domination" made by media, commercial interests, and mainstream groups broadens the landscape of environmental rhetoric; the comparison places narratives and icons of environmental justice on a spectrum demonstrating contemporary boundaries of environmental discourse. A further goal, one that extends current research in women's studies, is to examine how the images generated in discussion of environmental justice contrast with the ways in which women's texts have been represented in, or ignored by, popular culture and media. My work situates environmental justice geopolitically by asking the question, "how do the issues voiced by environmental justice groups, and in the literary and cultural texts that support them, clash or connect with mainstream environmental organizations, ecofeminists, corporate environmental advertisers, green consumerists, governmental environmentalists, climate activists and mainstream peace and justice organizations?"

Surveying the artistic methods by which cultural discourses expose environmental racism, reveals the theoretical groundwork that orients the "new directions" taken by the work executed under the rubric of environmental justice. This work generates iconographies and figurative language that provide a rich symbolic resource for environmental activists. These conceptual and epistemological resources expose the many, subtle ways that environmental racism is linked to other forms of social domination as well as to other forms of environmental degradation. This theoretical complexity contributes to the work of civil rights, mainstream environmental and social justice organizations, and contemporary cultural theories.

Much environmental justice literature extends into a realm I call "Virtual Realism," a mode of presentation that presents social issues from experiential and culturally specific foundations that historicize rather than falsely naturalize reality through literature. The investigation of literature in Part Two, read in comparison to Part One's investigations of less "traditional" cultural texts, allows me to differentiate and draw out likenesses in the various types of cultural poetics involved in creating theoretical and practical resistance against environmental racism. Such analysis is useful in understanding the political ramifications of the cultural products of social movements. The analytical focus on a project-in-common allows my study to break down the critical division between "literary" and popular/grassroots cultural texts and suggests that symbiotic relations between the two also take place.

Cultural theory, such as sociology's new social movement theory and Third World Feminisms (who largely work on social identity from women of color theorists), resonates with the theoretical perspectives in the poetics, thus contributing to an increased depth and breadth to investigations of social movement and identity questions. My discussion of social environmentalism and social identities is informed by theoretical offerings of predominantly "Third World" scholars such as Chandra Mohanty, Cherríe Moraga, Gail Omvedt, Mary Pardo, Laura Pulido, Vandana Shiva, Gayatri Spivak and Lourdes Torres. Engaging arguments from literary and cultural theorists such as Norma Alarcón, Antonio Gramsci, Gayatri Chakravorty Spivak, Jenny Sharpe, and Edward Said who work from cultural studies, postcolonialist, Marxian, and/or "Third World" perspectives, I argue that intrinsic to the struggle to attain environmental justice is the discernment of the complex involvement of post/de/colonial, gender, class, race, and nation status. With this foundation, I chart an overarching methodology by which to examine the cultural production of environmental justice.

In utilizing the rich field of sociological study that followed the conceptualizing of resource mobilization in the 1970s, I concentrate on late 20th Century investigations of structural inequality and social identity formation in social movements. New social movement theory has broadened its range of vision as it has developed. Yet, I know of no studies in the field that examine social movements primarily through investigation of the literary and artistic representations of activists and movement allies using a measured, interdisciplinary approach. Thus, my approach to environmental justice cultural poetics through interdisciplinary theory may enhance academic work in several fields that productively converse. Mary Pardo and Laura Pulido are among the first to study Chicana environmental justice organizing; my work is indebted to theirs.

Organizational Structure

This book is divided into two parts consisting of thirteen chapters based on thematic and formal considerations. *Environmental Justice Poetics: Cultural Representations of Environmental Racism from Chicanas and South Asian Women* follows a sequence that iterates the global context of environmental justice organizing and then details issues through investigation of local and individual expressive culture. Initially, my book raises prominent rhetorical questions that environmental justice practitioners ask about government and corporate environmentalism: Whose Justice, Whose Environment is to be protected? Whose will be neglected? What changes might make environmental destruction minimal and equitably distributed? I address these questions by examining the roles of "context" and "actors" in mapping the geopolitics and poetics of representing injustice.

"Part One: New Social Movement Poesis: Environmental Justice, Transformative Culture" uses sociological and cultural theories of new social movements and social identities to examine narrative, expressive, and iconographic texts—primarily poetic, educational, journalistic, philosophical, and aesthetic treatments of environmental racism and resistance—texts that have been generated by environmental justice movement organizations. In Chapters One through Seven, I investigate a wide range of textual representations from activists and artists who define and promote the actualization of environmental justice. In applying new social movement and cultural studies theories to the cultural poetics produced in environmental justice organizing I am able to investigate the social resonances of self-representation and identity issues inherent in this environmental justice discourse; these include the roles of race and nation in corporate and government toxin regulations, the relationship of indigenous groups to other disenfranchised groups, and the role of social identity issues in creating "environmental vulnerability."[9]

9 While I present the historical beginnings of British cultural studies to distinguish an important contribution to later work, the broad category of contemporary cultural studies theory comes from a broad base of theorists, who are related through their interests in the relations of social identity, culture, and power relations of various kinds. Not all the theorists I include have been part of the cultural studies collections, some may not align themselves with cultural studies, and some may have been excluded by discriminatory considerations in the field itself. While the work in this category, which this study considers, makes valuable contributions to cultural studies theoretical conversa-

In the second and third chapters, drawing on cultural studies theories and the work of new social movement and social identity theorists such as Craig Calhoun, Myra Marx Ferree, Hank Johnston and Bert Klandermans, Alberto Melucci, Aldon Morris, Carol McClurg Mueller, Verta Taylor, and Nancy Whittier, I establish my methodological framework. I use this framework to examine narrative, poetic and visual texts of social environmentalism for their transformative critiques of structural oppressions rooted in experiential realities. I apply my methodology to cultural production generated primarily for education and *conscientização*, by and/or about grassroots organizations such as the Narmada Dam opposition groups, People Organized in Defense of the Earth, and her Resources (PODER of Austin Texas), and the United Farm Workers (UFW). These groups set out issues that are picked up again in more extensive treatments of The Mothers of East L.A and Las Madres, the Chipko Movement, and the Bhopal Gas-Affected Victims Support Groups in subsequent chapters.

Part Two reiterates the concerns and contexts of Part One while focusing on literary texts that examine environmental justice struggles in contemporary fiction and other literary work by Chicanas and women in India, again situating environmental justice issues in relation to the larger fields of race, class, and gender justice. These chapters focus on fictional representations of environmental and economic justice struggles from Chicana and South Asian women novelists, short story writers, poets, playwrights, and performers. These writers' texts suggest theoretical and social analysis, which often reiterates the issues found in the organizational poesis. Arguing that such literary representations further the project of the social justice organizations, I find a pedagogical impulse in the literature that continues the purposes of *conscientização*—Paulo Freire's concept for learning "social, political, and economic contradictions, and to take action against the oppressive elements of reality."[10]

"Chapter Eight: So Close to the United States: Environmental Injustice and the Death of Fe in the 'Land of Enchantment'" examines environmental racism in the workplace and neighborhood as portrayed by Chicana activists, by Tammy Melody Gómez and Belinda Acosta in performance art, and in the fiction of Ana Castillo. "Chapter Nine: India's Forests and the Interconnected Legacies of Environmental Degradation and Colonialism" establishes the intersections of colonialism and environmental justice in an eco-historiography of Indian forest politics, in the

---

tions, I do not wish to elide the other theoretical categories with which these cultural critics identify, particularly those women of color theorists whose work offers most crucial insight for my study.

10 See *https://www.peace-ed-campaign.org/quotes/*. Unless another date is referenced, this and all links have been assessed and checked in July, 2023.

Chipko Andolan's poetry and in Nina Sibal's fiction. "Chapter Ten: Chicana/o Poetics: Farm Workers United Against Pesticides and City Dwellers Organized Against Toxins" explores environmental racism at work and home portrayed in United Farm Worker socio-poetics, the fiction of Helena María Viramontes, and in drama, testimonio and other genres produced by Cherríe Moraga and María Elena Lucas. "Chapter Eleven: A Farmworker's Blue Cape: Testimonio and Teatro examines the expressive arts and organizing of María Elena Lucas. Chapter Twelve and Thirteen investigate gendered ecojustice in the fiction of Mahasweta Devi, using the theoretical writing of Vandana Shiva and Gayatri Chakravorty Spivak. "The Epilogue: Local Hubs, Global Wheels: Future Implications of Studying Environmental Justice Literature" brings together the work under investigation in a discussion of the pedagogical implications of women's environmental justice poetics. I draw on examples of environmental justice work from global contexts and from within the college classroom to anecdotally, but also more globally, substantiate the premise I study through Chicana and South Asian poetics. Afterward: Environmental Justice Cultural Poetics, a Blueprint for Climate Justice proposes that these 20th Century poetics and environmental justice mobilizations offer much needed counsel to our 21st Century communities calling for climate justice. The Afterward notes a few examples of the plethora of poetics from Chicana and South Asian communities offering representations of struggle against environmental and climate racism in the 21st century.

Part I: **Cultural Poetics in Environmental Justice Movements: Organization, Theories, and Resistance in India and Greater Mexico**

1 Building Movements, Building Theory: Organizing, Resistance and Social Environmentalism

> ... even though subaltern groups "think" according to the terms of hegemonic discourse, their philosophy manifests itself in the contradiction between thought and action. Rather than being at the forefront of social change, academic knowledge lags behind—which is why Gramsci insists that theory not be separated from politics.
>
> Jenny Sharpe (1993, 16)

> Many of these movements share with contemporary literary theory a distrust of easy binary oppositions: they seek to get beyond static dichotomies like reform/revolution, culture/politics, public/private, symbolic/real, black/white, gay/straight, male/female. Virtually all these struggles are concerned with the redistribution of social and cultural as well as economic capital. Virtually all raise questions about social representation, identity and difference, hierarchy and equality, centralization and decentralization. They suggest the possibility of new movement strategies aimed at creating multiple, semiautonomous, decentralized nonhierarchical political units.
>
> T.V. Reed (1992, 14)

1.1 Context: The Geopolitics of Naming

The introduction has sketched out the terrains in which environmental justice poetics is produced; Chapter One offers extended discussions of the key contexts, geopolitical concepts, and the nexus of issues brought forth in the Preface and Introduction. Doing so grounds subsequent chapters' discussions of specific stories of the empirical and fictional realities of environmental desecration, as nuanced by the subject positions and social identities and perspectives of the authors and storytellers. Few extensive studies compare South Asian women's work with work from Chicanas, so I envision this work as an original contribution to comparative studies. In the past, much postcolonial literary and critical theory primarily focused on areas that had experienced British colonialism. By the end of the millennium, this theory had been extended to Chicano/a literature by scholars such as José David Saldivar; their studies are part of the forefront of a shift to more international perspectives in Chicana/o Studies.[11] However, in millennial, literary studies, more broadly, Indian literature falls under the rubric of postcolonial studies, while Chicana/o literature is still largely con-

11 José Saldívar in *The Dialectics of the Americas* and *Border Matter; Remapping American Cultural Studies* and Mary Louise Pratt are among those initiating such comparative emphasis in the early 1990's.

https://doi.org/10.1515/9783111041575-002

textualized within the larger rubric of multicultural or U.S. ethnic literature. My study acknowledges both areas as post- and de-colonial sites of ethnically identified poetics, relevant in global, national, and regional contexts.

Both Indians and Chicana/os live in countries shaped by "post-war"/colonial partition: U.S.-México treaties separated much of what was subsequently termed Greater Mexico from the rest of México several decades after México had gained independence from Spain in 1821. The main vehicle for division was the Treaty of Guadalupe Hidalgo in February of 1848.[12] Nearly 100 years later, in August 1947, the Indian subcontinent was divided, even as it gained independence from England. More recently, immigration from the "post-colonized" country to the colonizer country has created an expatriate Diaspora of Indians/South Asians in England, and has increased the communities of people of Mexican descent in the U.S.

Common to both India and Greater Mexico is also the displacement of agricultural workers—due to environmental ruin—into urban communities already under the siege of poverty. Often these areas are also industrial toxic dumping zones for the metropolises. In both India and Greater Mexico, a complex set of social disenfranchisement and displacement issues has affected both the rural, often immigrant, poor and indigenous peoples. These issues establish continuities and discontinuities with older colonial histories of relations between other (often immigrant) groups and the indigenous peoples whose interests were disregarded in the civic structures imposed by the new arrivals. While Spain's colonization initially dominated indigenous peoples in what would become the future sites of Chicano homelands, U.S. people of Mexican descent have developed a community/cultural identity that proactively responds to the later appropriation of Mexican land by Anglo-American domination and the accompanying settler colonialism. Likewise, while the British predominated in the colonizing of India beginning in the 19th Century, previous immigrants had, over the course of India's history, encroached upon the lands and cultures of indigenous peoples who, today, are among the most marginalized groups in the country. Indian Indigenous or Tribal history has clear parallels with the experience of Native American peoples, and to the extent they identify with their indigenous ancestries and connections, with Chicana/os in the US. Mahasweta Devi discusses these parallels telling American readers "see what has been done to [Native Americans], you will understand what has been done to the Indian tribals" (*IM* xi).

---

12 México included areas that later became the states of Arizona, California, New Mexico, and Texas, and parts of Colorado, Kansas, Nevada, Oklahoma, Utah, and Wyoming (Gómez-Quiñones) and Oregon (José Angel Gutierrez papers https://digital.utsa.edu/digital/collection/p15125coll9/id/3657/).

Geo-cultural naming is complex in both contexts. At first glance, it may appear that "Greater Mexico" does not describe a category that can be compared with a nation state, but deeper reflection reveals both placenames denote varying degrees of *appropriate* and *appropriated* meaning. Américo Paredes coined the geopolitical delineation "Greater Mexico" to identify historical boundaries that primarily coincide with territory that once belonged to Mexico but is currently under the rule of the United States. The term has been extended to include all communities of people of Mexican descent within the United States. César Augusto Martínez explains that Paredes's concept acknowledges that "there are indeed two Mexicos: one a recognized republic, and the 'other' a 'lived reality' in the United States (also referred to as the 'Greater Mexico North') 'constructed' by people of Mexican descent...negotiating geopolitical borders, or *fronteras*" (28). In the 21st Century scholarship, Mexican America gained currency as a name for the community of people of Mexican descent in the United States.

Aztlán is another term that covers similar political geography to Greater México but has the added significance of being the signifier of mythical origins reframed by Chicano Nationalist discourse. As a mythical homeland, Aztlán may seem to have no equivalent juxtaposition in recent Indian history. However, India itself may be seen as a more tenuous term than either Aztlán or Greater Mexico. India, the source of Columbus's misnaming of the peoples of North America was itself misnamed by Alexander the Great. Centuries later, even in Independence, the British role in the partitioning of India, Pakistan and other parts of South Asia was colossal. Its geographical boundaries have been conscribed primarily by foreign hegemons (Spivak 1990). In comparison, Aztlán is a cultural community's self-referential definition, and is thus relatively more appropriate terminology.

India might be better served by a geopolitical term such as "South Asia" that affirms the geo-cultural connections of an entire region that has been partitioned, or "Bharat," the Hindi name most used in the country, might be appropriate. However, I have retained India as the primary referent term for the area in this study, since the sites I study fall within the nation-state's boundaries and are affected by the nation-state's internal politics, as well as regional and international politics, and since it is the term by which the country is known, internationally.

While vast differences—particularly in territorial relationships to the "mainland"—exist for Indians and Chicana/os, there are some striking parallels (both major and minor) in their cultural influences on the dominating country: witness merely the role of the culinary "contributions"—or co-optations—of India and México in Britain and the US, respectively. While denigrating the cultures at large, the dominating countries have co-opted culinary traditions, distinctively improving the flavor of their own spectrum of national foods and adding to their

GNP through commodification of a dominated culture. Historically, several rough parallels exist in the frames of experience of the peoples of India and Greater Mexico. As India was considered the "jewel in the crown" of the British Empire, so Greater Mexico, though never a formal colony, occupies a similar, though less celebrated, geopolitically subordinate role relative to the US. The popular representations of both relationships obfuscate the structural violence perpetrated by the dominant country even as they celebrate the "favorite colony" or the best southern neighbor.

Language and literature are particularly productive fields of comparison. English, as the language of the most recent imperial power in both regions, has been adopted and transformed by both Indians and Chicana/os. One of the most interesting things about writing in English is the variety of multilingual aspects the language adopts. Both Indian English writing and Chicano/a writing are examples of this. Salman Rushdie has argued that Indian writing in English is the most interesting literature in India in the twentieth century.[13] While I have not found such a claim regarding Chicana/o writing in English in the U.S.—such a claim could be at least as justifiable as Rushdie's claim. Decades of major studies have established Chicana/o/x Literature's multi-faceted significance in the (U.S.) American literary context.[14]

Within these socially engaged, cultural traditions, environmental justice is being established as a foundational necessity for the creation of local, and ultimately global, equity and enfranchisement. In both contexts, but particularly in India, there are many more flourishing sites of late 20th Century environmental justice activity than I cover in this study. Beyond the scope of this study, such work develops and expands in the 21st Century.

Because I am interested in representations and their reception, examining those social movement activities that have been most publicized, both within and outside of the movement during a comparative period, is particularly rele-

---

13 Rushdie makes the claim in *The New Yorker*, Summer 97; it is questionable in that it effaces the rich diversity of writing occurring in the many Indian languages. Though he concedes that he's not read much Indian writing in translation, Salman Rushdie might do well to further clarify the perspective from which he makes his claim. As Ralph Nazareth points out "Rushdie's claim without proper contextualizing will feed an inadmissible homogenization of the so-called non-English Indian literatures" (Nazareth, Email correspondence 7-6-97) Nonetheless, in the context of literary writing in English, it is an important acknowledgment of the significance of Indian writing.

14 Louis Mendoza's *Historia: The Literary Making of Chicana and Chicano History*, Sonia Saldivar's *Feminism on the Border: Chicana Gender Politics and Literature*, Ramón Saldívar's *Chicano Narrative: The Dialect of Difference*, and José E. Limón's *Mexican Ballads, Chicano Poems: History and Influence in Mexican-American Social Poetry* are a few late 20th Century examples.

vant. From these sites of production, women and men depict global capitalism's trespassing of community borders. Combat zones created by business and government extend from pesticide spraying in L.A. barrios to the corporate theft of genetic material taken from within the cell walls of crop seeds developed communally by Indian villagers over several centuries. These images trace a dialogue of international networking and alliance-building, especially among peoples from the "Third World," "Third World" within the "first world," and indigenous communities.

1.2 Environmentalism that Attacks Racism: Describing the Terms

"Environmental racism," the antithesis of "environmental justice," foregrounds environmentally related discrimination based on race, but not divorced from class and gender. The term "environmental racism" was coined in 1982 during demonstrations against a PCB landfill slotted for Warren County, North Carolina, a rural, economically disenfranchized, predominantly African American county. Benjamin F. Chavis. Jr. explains that: "For the more than 500 protesters who were arrested, the behavior of county officials was seen as an extension of the institutional racism many of them had encountered in the past" (Chavis in Bullard 3). Chavis's subsequent definition of "environmental racism" is similar to other definitions that circulate:

> Environmental racism is a racial discrimination in environmental policy making. It is racial discrimination in the enforcement of regulations and laws. It is racial discrimination in the deliberate targeting of communities of color for toxic waste disposal and the siting of polluting industries. It is racial discrimination in the official sanctioning of the life-threatening presence of poisons and pollutants in communities of color. And it is racial discrimination in the history of excluding people of color from the mainstream environmental groups, decision making boards, commissions, and regulatory bodies. (Chavis in Bullard 1993, 3)

As is demonstrated in Chavis's explication, environmental racism pervades institutions on all sides of the environmental question; it enters interpersonal interactions and individual attitudes about environmental responsibility as well. Historically, it has shaped world development. From environmental justice movement perspectives, mainstream environmentalists, ecofeminists, and deep ecologists, along with government institutions and globalizing corporations, must come to terms with the environmental racism in their own ranks and in the policies they make. Chavis's lengthy list of sites of environmental racism is continually updated.

As the environmental justice movement expands its base, long-standing issues are redefined as "environmental" and new environmental issues arise. For instance, a constantly changing source of trouble is the workplace. It is a major site of environmental racism, defined as such by workers' protests such as the farm workers' struggle against the agricultural industry's misuse of pesticides that directly harm farm worker families. Nearly worldwide, manufacturing industries largely owned by US-affiliated multinational corporations, function through the labor of workers who are exposed to dangerous work environs and have little or no means of recourse. As new technologies are developed, industrial workers face dangers of exposure to inadequately tested toxic materials. Environmental racism in these instances includes withholding and deemphasizing knowledge about the potentially harmful results of exposure, levels of safety, and related issues.

How have activists responded to these inequities? In the US, the new focus of environmental justice activism initiated in the early 1980s is reflected in mission statements, manifestos, and lists of principles that primarily organizations of color set forth based on their experience with both environmental degradation and racism. The First National People of Color Environmental Leadership Summit, held October 24–27, 1991 in Washington D. C. developed seventeen "Principles of Environmental Justice" that illustrate the multiple ramifications of the term.[15] In brief, the Principles affirm ecological protection and the "sacredness of Mother Earth;" "the fundamental right to ... self-determination of all peoples;" worker rights' to a safe work environment (including an environmental hazard-free habitat for those who work at home); and the need for ecological policies "to clean up and rebuild our cities and rural areas in balance with nature, [while] honoring the cultural integrity of all our communities and providing fair access" to resources. The Principles demand that "public policy be based on mutual respect" and be free from discrimination; they also call for the "cessation of the production of all toxins, hazardous wastes, and radioactive materials," the accountability of past producers of such products, and the right to participate as equal partners in decision-making. They mandate "the right to responsible resource use" and protect the compensation and reparation rights of victims of environmental injustice. They call for "universal protection from nuclear testing;" strict enforcement of informed consent principles; and education on environmental issues based on "diverse cultural perspectives." They oppose military occupation and "the destructive operations of multi-national corporations" and they require that individuals reprioritize lifestyles to reduce waste of resources and insure a healthy and sustainable future. All these

15 For a copy of the Principles, see https://www.ejnet.org/ej/principles.pdf.

demands are made in the name of environmental justice. However, it is important to acknowledge not only the breadth of the Summit's definitions of environmental justice that expand on Chavis's definition of environmental racism, but also the Summit Statement's omissions—such as an in-depth concern for gender-specific discrimination. While the "Principles of Environmental Justice" remains a foundational, unifying document for the U.S. environmental justice movement led by people of color, definitions and areas of emphasis vary from group to group.

Grassroots activist poetics often stress the efficacy of prioritizing what one is working for—thus attaining justice becomes a common goal. In league with this, I have chosen to center on "justice" rather than "racism" at most points, because I wish to focus primarily on the poetics of active *resistance* involved in fighting for justice, rather than foregrounding *victimization* through racism. Because environmental racism is a term that has been politicized more precisely in the contexts I am writing about, and because it is less ambiguous, I use "environmental racism" rather than "environmental injustice" in most instances. Promoting environmental justice means fighting against environmental racism. Just as a discussion of feminism that does not address the racial implications in sexism is lacking, so a thorough discussion of justice cannot take place without articulating all the bigotries involved in the situation that need redressing.

My study replaces both universalizing and provincial representations by linking local, national, and international concerns. While this has been a longstanding base of my comparative interests, this imperative was crystalized for me in Texas-Northeast México borderlands research in which daily existence, as well as long term environmental health degradation, is irrevocably both local and international. In South Texas, we would be well-advised to look to the U.S.-México borderlands before we articulate US domestic issues as solely involving one nation.

A landmark study, "Toxic Waste and Race in the United States: A National Report on Racial and Socio-Economic Characteristics of Communities With Hazardous Waste Sites" was led by Dr. Benjamin Chavis, and commissioned by the United Church of Christ Commission for Racial Justice in 1987. The most significant data demonstrates that "regarding the demographic characteristics of communities with **commercial hazardous waste facilities**, race proved to be the most significant among variables tested in association with the location of commercial hazardous waste facilities. This represented a consistent national pattern" (Panos 6). Specifically, the study found that more than 50% of Blacks and more than 40% of Latinos and approximately half of all Asian/Pacific Islanders and American Indians in the U.S. live in communities with at least one uncontrolled toxic waste site (Panos 6). That the most severe environmental racism was found in commercial facilities is additionally troubling in the wake of the privatization, in conjunction with "free trade" agreements and economic globalization in the Americas and South Asia.

In 1990, Robert D. Bullard published *Dumping in Dixie*, arguably the first book focusing on environmental justice in "African American and poor communities" (*xiii*), which, as Bullard planned, is "a readable book that might reach a general audience while at the same time covering uncharted areas of interest to environmentalists, civil rights advocates, political leaders, and policy makers" (*xiii*). Several collections of essays came out in the next few years that addressed grassroots environmental justice activism, including *Toxic Struggles: The Theory and Practice of Environmental Justice*, edited by Richard Hofrichter (1993), and Robert Bullard's *Confronting Environmental Racism: Voices from the Grassroots* (1993). Early books focusing on Chicano environmental justice struggles are Laura Pulido's *Environmentalism and Economic Justice: Two Chicano Struggles in the Southwest* (1996) and Devon G. Peña's *The Terror of the Machine: Technology, Work, Gender, & Ecology on the U.S.-Mexico Border* (1997). Devon G. Peña edited the superb collection focusing on New Mexico, *Chicano Culture, Ecology, Politics: Subversive Kin* (1998).

"Environmental racism" is what Kimberlé Crenshaw terms "intersectional;" it includes not only racial discrimination but also the corollary discriminations that are often intractable from racism. Thus, much of the activist poetics represents race, class, nation, gender, and sexuality issues as interlinked, and social environmentalists find it crucial to identify these links. For example, on an environmental justice radio show that PODER produced on Austin's Community Radio Station, members of the Austin Latino/a Lesbian and Gay Organization (ALLGO), and Informa Sida, a Latina/o AIDS information and services organization, discussed the connections in communities of color between the impact of AIDS and environmental racism. They drew links between the lack of recognition of and the devaluation of the community's specific needs by mainstream AIDS service providers and the lack of mainstream environmental organizations' response to environmental racism issues such as the poisoning of borderland communities and the prominence of toxic industry and waste in people of color communities.[16] They also pointed out barriers in facilitating education

16 The January 24, 1995 environmental justice show sponsored by PODER, which aired on Austin's (TX) co-op radio station featured speakers from the ALLGO who identified the links between the high incidence of AIDS and HIV in communities of color with a high occurrence of other social problems, such as environmental racism, that these same communities face. In another example, ALLGO included with a Summer 96 newsletter the mailing for an Honor the Earth '95 Golden Circle Party and Indigo Girls Concert to benefit The Indigenous Women's Network-Alma de Mujer Center. Such a support system between organizations builds mutual support and, in this context, the flyer implicitly

when the organizations working on alleviating social problems do not know the predominant language in the communities in which they are working and are not sensitive to the communities' differing social norms.

A term often used for activists who focus on environmental justice is "social environmentalist." Gilberto Rivera's usage of the term "social environmentalist," as quoted in the Introduction epigraph, initiated my understanding of it. When I interviewed him for *The Polemicist*, during his campaign for Austin City Council Place 2, he defined the self-identifier: "To be a social environmentalist is to be a person who is concerned about humanity and also about all living things in our world. You cannot do one without being the other." Rivera connects environmental issues and social justice issues in an irrevocable and reciprocal manner; such connections facilitate women's empowerment and increased participation at leadership levels. He explains how the connections between issues work in Austin, Texas:

> Many times, in the poorer sections of town where the majority of people of color live many of our struggles are related to social justice issues; but at the same time if you do an accurate analysis of the struggle, they are also environmental issues. For example—I live in East Austin—we have many toxics stored in East Austin that need to be cleaned up. We have many warehouses that store toxic chemicals. Very few people know what is inside of those warehouses. We have factories that emit toxic fumes on a continuous basis. All of those are environmental issues but looking at it from a working class/people of color perspective those are also social justice issues. We have gotten the most destructive elements placed in our backyards.[17]

Environmental justice organizations, overall, have determined inclusive interests and leadership and have revised the historical tendency of mainstream feminist movements, including ecofeminism, to subordinate or ignore women of color/working class women.[18] Additionally, as noted by Laura Pulido, environmental

---

links issues without specific reference to AIDS activism. The slogan on the flyer "Protect Endangered Peoples, Protect Endangered Species" brings together environmental justice and environmental concerns. A graphic of an indigenous woman supersedes a small silhouette photo of "Amy and Emily," the *Indigo Girls*. For those unfamiliar with the *Indigo Girls* repertoire, the indigenous woman is merely an often-repeated trope, an image meant to solicit concern, perhaps respect, and often guilt to liberal environmentalists and social justice workers alike. Those who know the music, however, will more likely see the image as Anna Mae Aquash, the Micmac woman from Canada an organizer for indigenous people, involved with AIM, and in anti-uranium activities, killed by political assassination. The specificity moves the viewer beyond abstract emotions and historicizes the struggle that the music commemorates and that the ticket price supports, financially.

17 Gilberto Rivera. Interview for the *Polemicist*, Spring, 1991.

18 Sonia Saldívar Hull in her book *Feminism in the Borderlands: From Gender Politics to Geopolitics* (2000), and Jenny Sharpe in *Allegories of Empire* (1993) as well as articles in *Third World Women and*

geographer and urban planning and Chicana/o studies scholar, the environmental justice movement has the prerogative to develop itself by redressing the weaknesses to which other organizations have succumbed. "Unlike traditional trade unionism, [the environmental justice movement] should both combat racism and discrimination and attend to the environmental impact of development. Unlike the mainstream environmental movement, it should both emphasize economic equity and community empowerment" (in Bullard, 1993, 125). Through environmental justice activism and poetics, Chicanas and Indian women who are both "victims" and leaders, often achieve these ideals, and, in doing so, they achieve oppositional consciousness, self-empowerment, and alliance-building.

1.2.1 Cultural Poetics, Social Analysis

Basic to my decision to investigate and subsequently incorporate interdisciplinary theorizing in this study is my belief that Cultural Studies is implicitly interdisciplinary. I realize that I am engaging some fields of inquiry beyond my conventional academic training, however, I believe it is the onus of the practitioner to support her disciplinary borrowings with appropriate background understandings and try to do so by various means. The interdisciplinary nature of this project is a practical result of acting on these beliefs.

My examination of texts from women whose poetics express their lived experience has led me to consider a spectrum of social and cultural issues linked to environmental justice. Consequently, my study melds interdisciplinary, theoretical methodologies—a combination of cultural studies, postcolonial literary theory, theory by feminists of color and new social movement sociological theories to best meet the demands of diverse cultural poetics reflecting multiple lived experiences.

Based in the struggles for environmental protection, women cultivate both traditional and nontraditional cultural production. Within the contexts of Chicana and Indian women's cultural poetics "tradition" itself becomes multivalent. The texts simultaneously contest and contextualize the hegemonic rendering of the term "tradition" by provoking questions such as "In which context is fiction more 'traditional' than grassroots theater?" In general, the texts encourage a theoretical

the Politics of Feminism (1991) edited by Chandra Talpade Mohanty, Ann Russo and Lourdes Torres, and many of the writers in *Making Face Making Soul Hacienda Caras* (1990) and *This Bridge Called My Back* (1983) edited by Gloria Anzaldúa and Anzaldúa and Cherríe Moraga, respectively, and bell hooks in numerous books, are among the many who have addressed the issue of mainstream feminism's exclusion of women of color.

approach that is informed by experience, and they promote diacritical interpretations that break down boundaries and encourage alliances between educational institutions and marginalized communities and between academically empowered and societally disenfranchised women. However, women's various vantage points via-a-vis these social boundaries point to the uneasiness of these alliances, especially in broader social contexts. This may be partially due to media representations, which erroneously suggest that those under the siege of environmental racism are a threat, even, ironically, an environmental threat. These popular, often gendered misrepresentations have not been adequately uncovered by "mainstream" feminists. In examining oppositional consciousness in India and "Greater Mexico," I draw out conversations between the articulation of environmental justice as a goal and socialist strategies for the most efficacious means to attain "justice," because both approaches view economic systems as a foundation where a restructuring of society must begin. Vandana Shiva and Gail Omvedt, sociologist and Women's Studies scholar participating in and studying Indian grassroots organizing, contribute to the juncture.

Unlike many European and North American social movement scholars, Omvedt does not omit groups that adhere to a strong Marxist or Maoist analysis when she identifies new social movement (NSM) groups. The fact that Marxian ideology may exist within organizations that otherwise fit the definition of new social movements may well be an attribute of new social movements in the "Third World" that has not been thoroughly examined. Except for Omvedt's work and a few others such as Eduardo Canel's work on Latin American social movements, "Third World" groups have rarely been the subject of study for the new social movement scholars whose theoretical methodologies I've found particularly influential to my study. Since the 1970s, NSM sociologists have honed the methodologies with which they approach social, cultural, and political organizing. Many of the essays in *Frontiers in Social Movement Theory* (1992) call for reassessments based on the recognition that previous study has often been distorted by gender, race, class and nation bias and viable and important foci, concepts, and narratives have been ignored in these distortions.[19] Similar assessment in literary studies led to the development of new "area studies": American, Chicano, African American, third world, women's, gender, gay and lesbian studies, Diaspora studies and various other ethnic studies. This reorientation guided other literary scholars to cultural studies or postcolonial and subsequently decolonial approaches.

Because my study ventures into many of the areas I have just mentioned, it is best described, in a broad sense, as a cultural studies project; it falls under T. V.

---

19 Both Paul Gilroy and Angela McRobbie critique cultural studies for making similar oversights.

Reed's category of Environmental Justice Cultural Studies and shares ground with Environmental Humanities and Ecocriticism. My use of cultural studies identifies an origin in a series of related methodologies beginning at the Centre for Contemporary Cultural Studies founded at Birmingham University in 1964 by Richard Hoggart. Stuart Hall was director of the Centre during the 1970s and, according to Ann Gray and Jim McGuigan, his writing has made the largest contribution toward "establishing [cultural studies] as a curriculum subject;" they also cite Raymond Williams as "the single most important figure in the original formation of cultural studies" (viii).[20] Though cultural studies has been viewed as an offshoot of literary theory shaped by historicist philosophies, it has frequent and sometimes conflicted intersections with sociology, anthropology, and geography.

My study builds on the class-foregrounding British school and incorporates subsequent cultural studies practitioners whose work expands the previous studies geographically—in particular, to North America, the Caribbean and South Asia—and with diverse and interdisciplinary agendas.[21] This synthesis balances a specific vertical history of the field with the horizontal expanse of interests that enriches cultural studies. For instance, Raymond Williams' 1982 essay "Socialism and Ecology" has been invaluable in extending the history of ecological and civil rights issues in theoretical writing; the essay lays groundwork that resonates with environmental justice political theory.[22] At the same time, select articles in the more recent collections of both U.S. and Black British cultural studies have been indispensable in my understanding of other aspects of cultural poetics, and are conversant with the interests of Third World Feminisms, in particular.

As we traverse unfamiliar paths, as scholars, we must hold ourselves accountable to learn the comprehensive "natural history" of the terrain. This next section lays out geopolitical and natural histories of environmental justice and salient concepts borrowed from social theory.

---

20 For the novice in cultural studies, the collection, *Studying Culture: an introductory reader*, edited by Gray and McGuigan (1993), "foregrounds the social" (x) in cultural studies while offering brief introductions to more than three decades of writing that has impacted the field; they focus on predominantly British work. For more in-depth deliberation, at least three other collections deserve mention. *Marxism and the Interpretation of Culture* (1988) marks cultural studies' juncture with contemporary Marxisms. Lawrence Grossberg and Cary Nelson who edited this collection were joined by Paula Treichler in editing the 1992 anthology entitled *Cultural Studies* and subsequent collections; their work demonstrates substantial further expansion in the field. These anthologies have been followed by a plethora of writing on various aspects of Cultural Studies.

21 Edward Thompson (*The Making of the English Working Class*, 1963) was a forerunner.

22 See the essay in *Resources of Hope*, 1989, 210–226.

2 Environmental Justice: Coining a New Social Movement

> ...the very act of representation urges a distinctive kind of political consciousness upon us through a deliberately constructed set of imaginary and symbolic productions.... these imaginary and symbolic productions serve both a unifying communal function as well as an oppositional and differentiating end....
>
> Ramón Saldívar (89, 4)

> In the past twenty years emerging social conflicts in advanced societies have not expressed themselves through political action, but rather have raised cultural challenges to the dominant language, to the codes that organize information and shape social practices. The crucial dimensions of daily life (time, space, interpersonal relations, individual and group identity) have been involved in these conflicts, and new actors have laid claim to their autonomy in making sense of their lives.
>
> Alberto Melucci (in SM&C 95, 41)

> The central argument here is that class consciousness, race consciousness, gender consciousness, and the like cannot be understood comprehensively or properly assessed as independent entities. In this view it is the interrelated system of political consciousness and the systems of human domination that gave rise to them in the first place that should become the focus of analytical inquiry.
>
> Aldon Morris (92, 359–360)

My interest in environmental justice cultural poetics was initiated by hearing about PODER's (People Organized in Defense of the Earth and her Resources) activities from Austin friends who were members at the same time my graduate comparative literature courses required I interpret texts within their social contexts and encouraged my long-standing inclination to broaden the conventional definitions of "literary texts." My interest in New Social Movement (NSM) theory was spurred by fellow graduate students who, having witnessed my struggle with how to approach movement narratives that begged for deeper cross-disciplinary interpretations, suggested I read Alberto Melucci, the Italian NSM scholar, whose *Nomads of the Past* was an early and influential text for other NSM theorists. Hearing of my interests, my uncle, a sociology professor at UT, Austin, offered his copy of Zald and McCarthy's edited volume (1979) *The Dynamics of Social Movements: Resource Mobilization, Social Control, and Tactics.* Resource Mobilization was the birthplace to NSM theories in the U.S. and John D. McCarthy is my uncle's long-standing family friend, as well as previous colleague. The emergence of the environmental justice movement, when compared to the beginnings of new social movement theories, shows several parallel developments. In the U.S., both the grassroots activism of the environmental jus-

https://doi.org/10.1515/9783111041575-003

tice movement and the sociological scholarship concerned with New Social Movement theories have partial origins in the 1960's Civil Rights Movement that received inspiration from the Gandhian Satyagraha Movement—a primary force behind the Indian Independence Movement and the direct predecessor of the Chipko Andolan.

In examining the "act[s] of representation" in the poetics of women active in environmental justice organizations in conjunction with interdisciplinary thought in new social movement, cultural studies, and postcolonial theories, Part One juxtaposes the stories and analysis of community and college and it evokes an exchange of ideas produced in the promotion and study of environmental justice. It uses sociological theory to elucidate narrative texts—primarily educational, promotional, journalistic, and philosophical treatments of environmental racism and resistance. Taking this distinctive, interdisciplinary route into a study of poetics that links fields whose interrelations previously have been inadequately studied or articulated, exposes useful connections which otherwise go unheeded.

Of primary interest for this study is the new social movement theory (NSM) work described in the epigraph from Aldon Morris that explicitly focuses on the interrelations of the "political consciousness systems" (such as class, race, and gender) that groups develop in response to "human domination systems"—white supremacy, global capitalism, and patriarchy. In particular, I draw upon articles in *Frontiers in Social Movement Theory* (1992) edited by Aldon D. Morris, and Carol M. Mueller. Such studies examine "theoretical perspectives on culture as a factor in ... social movements" to find "movement culture as manifested in phenomena such as collective identity, symbols, public discourse, narratives, and rhetoric" (Johnston and Klandermans vii).[23] Representations of environmental justice evoke both the communal and the differentiating aspects of representation noted in the epigraph from Ramón Saldívar and demonstrate the complex importance of Aldon Morris's interrelated systems.

In the U.S., both academic study and activism often share a weakness in their absence of information about the "Third World" outside, as well as within, the U.S. and Europe; social movement scholars and social environmentalists are no exception. While social environmentalists are keenly aware of the "Third World" communities within the "first world," analysis of the relations with international "Third World" oppression and resistance is often lacking. Despite these weak-

---

23 Some of the best examples of late 20th Century NSM studies with an emphasis on cultural poetics appear in *Social Movements and Culture* (1995) edited by Hank Johnston and Bert Klandermans.

nesses, both social environmentalists and NSM scholars have evolved through a process of refining their perspectives on the interrelationships of social, economic and environmental factors at work in human group interactions. Both have been concerned with the implications of cultural activists' representations and their effects on social movements and on society at large. Both fields include educators who acquire, create, and disperse knowledge as a primary aspect of their work. Both fields of work are decentralized despite the common approaches of the groups involved. They are made up of smaller groups of individuals who are pursuing specific "local" interests in their research, educating, theorizing, and/or activism. While much environmental justice scholarship has come from sociologists with social movement interests such as Robert Bullard, Devon Peña, Laura Pulido and Mary Pardo, I found little attention in general paid to the work outside of these fields at the time of my study.

These parallels between fields are notable, if only because, despite their common interest in grassroots activism, the fields initially appear to be disparate in their approaches and their goals. Generally, activist and academic worksites are often represented as being at odds, even sometimes by those who occupy both arenas; such casting desensitizes both groups to the substantial common ground they share. An analysis of the common interests between the divergencies allows for mutual translations that enunciate potential solidarity. Environmental justice advocacy is practiced primarily in activist worksites whereas NSM theory has developed mainly in the "Western" academy; "east/west," "North/South," and class divisions further the perceived separation of interests in common. However, given that many of these reasons have more to do with representation than experience, communication about—as well as across—these barriers may be beneficial to the production of knowledge and progressive struggle in both areas. My aim is not to conform one side to the other or to appropriate knowledge. Rather, I wish to probe perceived representations on both sides to describe the complex cultural poetics of environmental justice as it is informed by activism and scholarship.

The categories "academic" and "activist" are not absolute divisions but only "working terms," which prove fallible in several respects. They are in no way mutually exclusive. For instance, activists like Vandana Shiva and Sylvia Herrera ground academics in activism and back up their grassroots political positions with their academic training. Furthermore, in some current academic practice, scholars in disciplines such as anthropology, sociology, comparative literature, and cultural studies may advocate—to varying degrees—on behalf of and/or in conjunction with—the groups their research describes. These categories must be taken in their broadest sense to include all the people whose work is discussed in the following chapters. Progressive journalists like Elizabeth Martínez, winner of the National Association for Chicana and Chicano Studies (NACCS) 2000 Scholar Award, lawyers like Indira Jaising, visual and performing artists, novelists, poets, playwrights and essayists who produce the poetics do not fit neatly or exclusively into academic or activist (or artist) categories. However, I retain the terms to articulate differences in the producers' identities, goals, and cultural production through loose categorization, despite the false polarizations potentially created in the process. In cautioning the reader against seeing these categories as binary oppositions, this approach reenforces a main feature of the juncture of the combined terms "environmental" and "justice:" inherent to the conceptualization of "environmental justice" is the deconstruction, complexification, implications and historicization of the nexus of the terms.[24]

While recognizing the historical tensions and hierarchies present between university research and resistance activism, I have seen dialectical paths allow for "post"-hierarchical discussions; in other words, they get people interested in talking and listening to each other across conventional boundaries. Such dialogue occurs between some activist groups under study and academics with related concerns. For instance, MELA (Mothers of East Los Angeles) has undertaken such "post"-hierarchical relationships with academics by supporting UCLA student campaigns to increase Chicano Studies curriculum. Meanwhile, students (albeit not necessarily the same students) have provided research support for MELA's social environmentalist work. In India, Vandana Shiva turned from an academic career in nuclear physics to search out an environmental education with the women of Chipko and other activists whose knowledge she deemed more appropriate to her redefined goals as a social environmentalist. The semantics of "post" in "post-hierarchical" are analogous to a primary usage of "post" in the term "post-colonial" in that "post" calls attention to the history of hierarchy/colonialism and the continued influence of previously dominant/colonialist power; engagement in the process of de-hierarchizing is implied by my use of the term, as decolonial replaces postcolonial among activists and in many ethnic studies departments. By turning to activism for its internal, initial theorizing, and then testing academic theorizing in light of activist analysis, I hope to assist in this process of breaking down hierarchies that is part of environmental justice

24 I use the coined term "complexification" to refer to the phenomenon of "complicating" without reverting to the term "complicate." "Complicating" acquired a popular stance in theory, but nonetheless causes confusion because the term has multiple and sometimes euphemistic meanings in common parlance as well as theoretical jargon that often cannot be precisely determined by context.

work. In doing so, we do well to remember Jenny Sharpe's epigraph beginning Chapter One that evokes Gramsci's observation that the academic follows behind the activist in creating and understanding social change.

Hank Johnston and Bert Klandermans in the chapter "The Cultural Analysis of Social Movements" (in SMC 1995) place one strain of sociological theory in relation to culture, pointing both to theoretical accomplishments and to necessary future directions.[25]

> The analysis of culture has been embraced as the answer to many unresolved questions in social movement literature. The shortcomings of resource mobilization, the salutary nature of new social movement literature, and the "identity boom" in new social movement literature have been seized upon as an argument in favor of cultural analysis. Often culture has been a neglected aspect of the study of social movements. This is the more surprising because it is so obvious that social movements are shaped by culture and at the same time form and transform culture. Symbols, rituals, patterns of affective orientation, values, discourse, and language—to mention only a few often-neglected key elements of culture—have been steadfast elements of social movements. (20)

Cultural poetics, artifacts of cultural practices, reveal what Melucci describes in the epigraph to this section as an expression of autonomy that is a "cultural challenge to the dominant language."

To begin a study of social movement culture, a culture shaped by and shaping concepts of environmental justice, word derivation study articulates connections. An extended study of related terms such as "ecology" and "economics" (words that for some may not appear to have much in common) demonstrates a common linguistic ancestry which, in close readings of poetics and scholarship, bears out their more-than-merely-symbolic relationship. John B. Cobb, in his paper "Oikos, Ecology and Economics"[26] pointed out the common Greek derivation of these terms which, he argues have become false oppositions in contemporary dominant society. As noted in *Hunger TeachNet*, "[t]o better understand the troubling silence that resides in the interstices of academic disciplines, Cobb reconstructs an ancient dialogue between the economic and

---

25 Hank Johnston and Bert Klandermans' (editors) volume *Social Movements and Culture.* Social Movements, Protest, and Contention Series Vol. 4 Minneapolis, MN: University of Minnesota, 1995) builds on the work of *Frontiers in Social Movement Theory.*

26 The paper was delivered at the "Environment, Development and Peace: Exploring Connections in Undergraduate Education Conference, Bethel College, North Newton Ks., February 18–20, 1994. This chapter offers an extended study of the symbiotic relationship of economic and ecological/environmental justice in the work of MELA and PODER that further illustrates the connections.

the ecological. The two disciplines, whose traditionally intimate conceptual link is often overlooked, share a common linguistic root: *oikos*—the household" (2). Women's activist groups, such as the Mothers of East L.A. (MELA), demonstrate this ancient and continuing link in their activism that extends the mothers' responsibility for the well-being of the kinship family to their local communities (Pardo). Thereby, such women activists extend the home economists' duties—a responsibility for the wellbeing of their families and the housekeeping in their family dwellings—to preserving the "ecology" of their communities by protecting the ecological integrity of their neighborhoods; in the process they have become responsible for improving sustainable economic opportunities for their families and their neighbors. Using motherhood as a symbol for "community connectedness" does not correlate with biological motherhood, but the iconography seems more prevalent in groups that identify as women's groups per se (such as MELA) than among women in mixed-gender groups (such as PODER or the United Farm Workers (UFW)). This observation may give us pause to ask about representations of men's parenting abilities, or to alleviate gender entirely—is it not possible to transfer "good parenting" to conceptualize environmental justice concerns? And if not, does this reflect society's sexist assumptions about men's "natural" good parenting abilities? Queer and Trans studies weighing in on these nexus of representation questions in the 21st Century continue to extend our understanding of gender, identity, vulnerability, justice, and nature.

Representing children as an icon for the idea that we need to save and protect the environment is widespread. Martha McMohan in her sociological study *Engendering Motherhood* finds in her symbolic interaction analysis of interviews of young mothers that "[c]ultural meanings of motherhood...provide guiding metaphors not simply for the construction of identity but for the representation of idealized social bonds" (276). These representations do not biologize motherhood but construct it *socially* in opposition to "dominant masculinist myths of the abstract, separate, autonomous individual of liberal political thought and market economic theory" (276). In other words, McMohan argues that motherhood (adopted as a frame for social relations) moves us beyond Modernity and in opposition to the "negative consequences of privatizing and biologizing caring relations" simultaneously (277). Both the women's and the mixed environmental justice groups carry forth such an agenda. However, the gendered concepts of group identity and demands vary with contexts. Members of environmental justice groups in the U.S. (such as People Organized in Defense of the Earth and her Resources (PODER (of Austin, TX)), Southwest Organizing Project (SWOP), and Southwest Network for Economic and Environmental Justice (SNEEJ)) emphasize the relationships vis-á-vis dominant societal power structures as well as to the "natural" environments, which the groups hold in common—based upon their status as working-class people of color. Yet they also differentiate subgroups or individual identities according to gender, ethnicity, sexuality, religion and/or other factors.

Images of children communicate the importance of environmental concern. Collective identities based on "the value of family" run against the grain of contemporary right-wing definitions of "family values." Rather, they are theoretically involved in recognizing the interconnections of deleterious social factors such as racism, sexism, and economic domination and their environmentally threatening results as they play out against different members of nuclear, extended, and non-traditional families.

To my knowledge, the cultural production of environmental justice—the Narmada Dam opposition, PODER, the United Farm Workers (UFW), the Chipko Movement, The Mothers of East Los Angeles (MELA and Las Madres), and Bhopal survivors rights groups—has not been examined as poetics of "new social movements" in a collective study, per se.[27] Through the following overview of NSM theories and organizationally-generated texts, I hope to deepen my cultural study of textual representations that define and promote the actualization of environmental justice. Having briefly established the conceptual junctures between the theoretical field of environmental justice and that of new social movements it seems germane to expand on Johnston's and Klandermans' observations about culture and ask what "creative" narratives contribute to sociology. And equally, if not more important, what does sociology, specifically, new social movement theoretical approaches, have to offer cultural studies in the humanities? Both are methodologies by which scholars approach the semantics of culture, of the social, and of the political. Yet even qualitative sociology retains an empirical and statistically based bent, compared to literary and cultural studies' figurative, narrative, and philosophical terrain. As social sci-

---

27 Early sociological studies of women's environmental justice organizing include Mary Pardo's study of the mothers of East L.A. in her dissertation entitled, *Identity and Resistance: Mexican American Women and Grassroots Activism in Two Los Angeles Communities,* Teresa Córdova's "Grassroots mobilization by Chicanas in the environmental and economic justice movement" (*Voces: A Journal of Chicana/Latina* Studies MALCS, 1997, 31–55) and Andrea Simpson, "Who Hears Their Cry? African American Women and the Fight for Environmental Justice" in *The Environmental Justice Reader* (Eds. Joni Adamson et al, 2002). Environmental groups are often mentioned in general discussions of new social movements. An example that resonates with my study is T.V. Reed's chapter "Dramatic Ecofeminism: The Women's Pentagon Action as Theater and Theory" in *Fifteen Jugglers, Five Believers: Literary Politic and the Poetics of American Social Movements.*

ence scholars disposed of the myth of "objective" methodologies, and literary practitioners moved beyond the New Critical and other "text-in-a-vacuum" approaches to culture to historicize and anthropologically and sociologically theorize their objects of study, and as social theory has solidified its place in advanced study, we of different disciplines find our paths crossing (and occasionally double-crossing) more often.

2.1 New Social Movement Theories, Cultural Poetics and Environmental Justice: Developing Continental Cartographies and Historiographies

> The resource mobilization approach emphasizes both societal support and constraint of social movement phenomena. It examines the variety of resources that must be mobilized, the linkages of social movements to other groups, the dependence of movements upon third parties for success, and the tactics used by authorities to control or incorporate movements.
>
> Mayer N. Zald and John D. McCarthy (1977)

> In contrast with the economistic rational actor of early resource mobilization theory, the new social movement actor both actively constructs and is constrained by a world of social meanings rooted in specific historic contexts and based in the experiences and identities of race, gender, class, and nationality. Within these contexts, the new actor identifies and constructs the meanings that designate the relevance for mobilization of grievances, resources, and opportunities.
>
> Carol McClurg Mueller (1992, 21–22)

This section maps historical and theoretical trajectories and junctures of sociological and social environmental movements. By putting into conversation, the work of NSM scholars and environmental justice practitioners, I show how environmental justice organization could help meet NSM mandates (Mueller, Ferree, Morris) for a diversification of the grounds of social movement study. The conversations between NSM and environmental justice illustrate and build on the contention that activism can teach academia, as well as vice versa.

First, an initial inquiry: Do environmental justice organizations meet the developed definition of new social movements? Eduardo Canel explains the attributes that European NSM scholars found in "new social movements" that prevented them from being adequately understood by Marxism.

> [N]ew collective actors had moved to the centre of contemporary conflicts a
> nd displaced traditional working-class struggles. These new actors were not class actors, because their identity was not constituted by their place at the level of production. Their prima-

> ry concern was not with economic issues, but with collective control of the process of symbolic production and the redefinition of social roles. They raised non-class issues related to gender, ethnicity, age, neighbourhood, the environment, and peace. Their identity was defined in relation to these issues and not by class position. Thus the identities of contemporary social movements could not be a mechanical reflection of economic interests. They were themselves the product of ideological and political processes. NSM theorists made it clear that economic and class reductionism had prevented Marxism from explaining the mediated nature of the passage from condition to action. In the new framework this transition was said to be mediated by ideological, political, and cultural processes. (23–24)

Mayer N. Zald and John D. McCarthy initiated new social movement thought in North America, where sociologists had been influenced by European thinkers who preceded the North American academicians in charting initial agendas for analysis of new social movements. Zald and McCarthy had published a groundbreaking article, "Resource Mobilization and Social Movements: A Partial Theory" in the *American Journal of Sociology* in 1977 and followed that up with an edited volume, *The Dynamics of Social Movements: Resource Mobilization, Social Control, and Tactics* in 1979. Despite the scores of years since this early resource mobilization work was published, several of the essays in *The Dynamics* offer concepts that can be applied to environmental justice contexts and may point to areas of study that should prove productive for justice scholars. These include discussion of relationships between social movements and media, government and NGOs. In my first example, Charles Perrow's "The Sixties Observed" examines 1960s social mobilization with an interest in the domino effect of one movement's success on others. The domino effect he discusses is made apparent in the environmental justice movement as well, when one successful campaign has triggered others in close geographical proximity. For instance, in East Austin (Texas) campaigns against disregard for adjacent communities by an oil tank farm, Sematech, and the massive Holly Power Plant, all situated by corporate design in el corazón del barrio, have been successful to varying degrees, and community activists have mobilized people from one battle site to the next. Similar phenomena can be witnessed between groups with alliances to other environmental and social justice groups, like the Mothers of East L.A. or in an umbrella organization like SNEEJ, who can ally communities to create movement poetics surrounding a particular issue. The Chipko Movement spread from community to community in Uttarkhand, in the Himalayan foothills, following the advances of lumber companies in a similar domino effect which eventually spanned out to other states, challenging threats to forest survival in its wake. Perrow's later concept of a "normal accident," developed in analyzing industrial accidents like Three Mile Island has been used in understanding various levels of representation of the Bhopal gas leak (Jones 223).

Harvey Molotch's assessment of social movements' relations with the media is especially salient to cultural poetics analysis as it delineates the fine line between self-representation and media representation. This is apparent in Molotch's discussion of the "politics of masturbation," the politics of those who are accused—unjustly, Molotch believes—of merely wanting "to see their names in the newspaper" (73). Molotch sees the gratification and legitimization of media coverage—regardless of whether it is complimentary or critical—as an essential part of organizing. His concept of "doing news" (73) is basic for several of the groups that I examine; furthermore, media exposure is sometimes a primary impetus for cultural production. While the preference of most groups may be for control of the representation presented to the public, often funds do not allow for extensive publicity to be generated for a particular environmental justice event by its planners; in such a situation, a sympathetic media is crucial. Additionally, media reports are often used afterward to construct a narration of events: Thomas Weber in *Hugging the Trees* mentions utilizing newspapers in his story of the Chipko Movement. *Bhopal: a People's View...* is a collection of primarily newspaper reports from the first days after the gas leak. Both MELA and UFW Latina organizers pulled out files of media reports for me to peruse and copy when I visited their offices, and several of my investigations of organizing in India originated with newspaper clippings brought to me by family or friends who were aware of my study and had been travelling to or living in India.

In the last decade of the 20th Century, an increasingly unreceptive, corporate-owned media in the U.S. has been supplemented by digital media—internet listservs, info-emails and organizational websites. The Zapatistas in Chiapas whose activities were made public January 1, 1994, in a carefully timed response to the initiation of NAFTA broke ground through a digital, technology-based alternative media campaign. Since that time, Narmada Dam activists, Texas-based environmental justice activists and many others have developed websites and social media presence.

As the scholarship of activists and academics makes clear, damage from government or other infiltration of social movements can be even more direct and deadly than "bad press." In "External Efforts to Damage or Facilitate Social Movements: Some Patterns, Explanations, Outcomes, and Complications," Gary T. Marx investigates another segment of the social movement habitat that pertains to environmental justice organizing when he analyzes government responses to 1960s social organizing. He discusses both sabotaging and facilitating by government forces with vested interests in the outcome of various social issues. While no covert action on the scale of the FBI's Cointelpro, carried out against civil rights and other left groups in the 1960s and 1970s, has been reported in environmental justice organizing in the U.S. or India, lessons learned from experiences in the 1960s might serve these movements. In many countries, governments collude with cover-up or inadequate investigation of assassinations of activists involved in environmental justice as part of their work. Some of the names in the latter 20th Century are familiar: Karen Silkwood, Ana Mae Pictou Aquash, Chico Mendes, Ken Saro-Wiwa and other Ogoni activists. The lessons learned from such violence show the need for cohesion of different organizations and individuals in the movement to provide a buffer against infiltration. The political finesse that many environmental justice activists have cultivated protects them from developing false alliances that offer short-term support, but in the long run damage the larger movement. Furthermore, the reality of outside infiltration in social movements raises the question of what attributes offer protection from sabotage. The Gandhian inheritance in Chipko that does not keep things hidden from "the enemy" may seem an unlikely proposal, but its useful application might be studied. Most scholarship on Gandhian strategy has looked at ethics but overlooked the efficacy of following the movement's principals for facilitating contemporary social change and resisting contemporary forms of oppression. Yet a broad study of environmental justice activism could do both. My work only points toward such scholarship. A critical analysis of the efficacy of such a strategy that engages both spiritual philosophy and political strategizing would be a vital contribution in future study of environmental justice organizing.

As the first U.S. collection of NSM scholarship offers avenues of analysis by which to address some basic aspects of environmental justice praxis, so more current work offers insightful resonance with a maturing environmental justice movement. Carol McClurg Mueller opens the 1992 *Frontiers* collection with a chapter that briefly maps the development of the field at large and then examines the direction and interconnections of the essays. She summarizes three crucial points that the essayists of the collection reiterate: the actor is embedded in social networks, social locations intersect, and a new model based on shared fate is necessary (7). The significance of these points is reached in their intersection: "[t]he authors cited here continue the task of identifying key social locations in constructing meanings and securing loyalties that challenge dominant assumptions and create or transform communities" (13). Since the task of "identifying key social locations [and their intersections] in constructing meanings" is precisely one that I undertake in my study, the *Frontiers* collection is particularly valuable. Furthermore, the model of shared fate (and shared identities) is utilized widely by environmental justice groups and is indeed basic to the definitions of environmental justice and racism discussed here.

The limitations and consequent restrictions of past directions in new social movement theory are also articulated by several essayists (17); traditional lines of thought are challenged by the overlays of race, gender, class and nationality issues that are at the heart of much environmental justice organizing and were beginning to be considered in depth by new social movement theory, particularly through the examination of collective identity. Increased attention is paid to the structural relationships and power differentials that are at the basis of analysis made by many social environmentalists. Mueller explains that,

> [m]any of the writers here argue that further theorizing requires the reintroduction of those elements that will connect social movements more closely to social structure and to the associated disparities in resources and opportunities that lead differentially to the use of violence and conflict in the choice of tactics. That is, social location helps determine the nature of grievances, resources, and levels of organization. (18)

Mueller's argument about social location provides substantial evidence of the importance of examining more diverse communities' struggles than previously have been investigated in new social movement approaches. NSM scholars recognize this need, at least peripherally.

Myra Marx Ferree demonstrates how the rigorous study that social movement scholars have undertaken can be recycled to be used more appropriately by exactly the groups that it has effaced.[28] A "post-RM" vantage point would offer grounds for the recognition of multiple rationalities as well as the means for both scholars and activists to digest theory and experiential data to establish the limitations and advantages any given perspective might offer. Whether one works with metaphors of recycling or cannibalism, Ferree envisions just such a view. Her work thus presents a frame of analysis that is useful for considering the transformative social praxis of environmental justice poetics.

---

28 The cannibalistic concept behind the "Manifesto Antropófago" (1928) written by the Brazilian modernist, Oswaldo de Andrade, seems appropriate here: de Andrade proposed that Brazilian modernism cannibalize European Modernism, utilizing the influence with which it could nourish itself and expunging what it could not use. Likewise, feminists, social environmentalists, social movement activists, and scholars, along with others who find resource mobilization and subsequent theories useful, but flawed, might digest the theory along with their own experiential data in order to create a more balanced and informed sociology/cultural studies.

K. David Jackson suggests the importance of "Manifesto antropófago" for postcolonial cultural analysis when he observes that,"[T]he ultimate consequences of its scandalous and deceptively playful attack on society create a spirit of complete and permanent rebellion, a transformation of ideas into a cultural point-counterpoint between colonized and colonizer, the particular and the universal: an ex-centric appropriation and expropriation of imported models, altered for local consumption in a rebellion of the periphery against the center. Shakespeare is tropicalized." (8).

In Chapter Four, I discuss how MELA activists demonstrate the viability of the social actor whose rationality is based in an alternative value system such as Myra Marx Ferree distinguishes. Ferree evokes "Michael Schwartz's postulate that 'social movement participants are at least as rational as those who study them'"(30) and she suggests that the research that adhered to this ironic proposition remedied an earlier assumption that social actors are irrational. She demonstrates how it is again time for scholars to take stock of this satirical observation as an admonition, and she shows what it would mean to then current condition of new social movement thought. Studies of environmental justice actors like the women in MELA, the Chipko Movement, farmworkers' rights organizations, or the movement to stop the Narmada Dams all offer the strengths Ferree asks for. Simultaneously, Ferree's essay is crucial to my study in that it precisely identifies and explains assumptions in sociological thought that, in certain social locations, distort NSM analysis. Ferree's analysis applies to locations—such as those in which environmental justice mobilization is most likely to be found—in which the actor's experiences do not adhere to the traditional researchers perceived universal condition.

The evolution of new social movement thought is evident in the argument Myra Marx Ferree makes in her essay, "Political Contact of Rationality." Because she finds Mancur Olson's model of rationality and the resulting rational choice theory to be based on tautology and dehumanizing assumptions, she argues that, "the model of rationality thus imported into the RM approach, the microeconomic theory of rational choice, is a Trojan horse" (30–33). The dehumanizing aspects she finds particularly dangerous to social movement studies. "In particular, [rational choice theory] has led to first, a neglect of value differences and conflicts, second, a misplaced emphasis on the free-rider problem, and third, a presupposition of a pseudo-universal human actor without either a personal history or a gender, race, or class position within a societal history." (Ferree 31)

Ferree uses feminism to critique the rationality model and provide an alternative with an "expanded vision of rationality, [in which] both self- and other-regarding behaviors are seen as structurally situated" (31). Rational Choice theory effaces the effects of "ambivalence, altruism, and emotional experience" (32) and privileges individualism and self-interest over community concerns. Using the work of both feminists (especially Nancy Hartsock) and social identity theorists (especially Craig Calhoun), to support her argument, Ferree shows the gender, class, and racial/ethnic biases of a perspective based on "the assumption of independent adults as the basic social actors, rather than acknowledging infant dependency and the human community as our universal history" (36). Gender bias is demonstrated when she illustrates that rational choice theory privileges the male independent adult as a natural state or norm of universal human experience. Class bias (and I would argue, ethnocentrism and nationalism) is evident in the concept of individualism as the 'natural state'; this reflects "the perspective of the modern bourgeoisie" when in fact "evidence about pre-industrial societies suggests that most forms of social organization are based in group needs to manage given interdependencies to ensure collective survival rather than in some perception of individual advantage" (36). To further illustrate, Ferree points out that,

> even in modern American cities, poor and working-class households rely on extended networks of diffuse obligation that rapidly absorb individual windfalls and block individual mobility... Women, working-class people, and disadvantaged racial-ethnic groups may be especially likely to reject competitive individualism as a feasible value and put considerable emphasis instead on maintaining viable networks of relationships. (37)

Environmental Justice organizing itself has depended on just such networks to enable mobilization against toxic intrusion. Myra Marx Ferree's ideas are crucial to the juxtaposition of theories I've undertaken. The "Feminist Justice, Environmental Justice" section that begins the next chapter returns to several of the gender issues Ferree raises. The cultural poetics, subsequently discussed, possesses public elements of creative communication that promote collective survival through fostering "collective action" and "collective identities." Thus, they illustrate Ferree's points.

To conclude this survey of NSM theory interests in conjunction with those of social environmentalists, I turn to the work of William A. Gamson in conjunction with Alberto Melucci. Gamson draws heavily on Melucci when he centralizes the establishment of "collective identities" by new social movements (56). For Melucci, "[t]he creation of an ongoing collective identity that maintains the loyalty and commitment of participants is a cultural achievement in its own right" (in Gamson 1992, 57). He shows that such identities are "political" because they "challenge the logic of complex systems on *cultural* grounds.... Linking personal change with external action, collective action functions as a new medium which illuminates the silent and arbitrary elements of the dominant codes as well as publicizes new alternatives" (italics, mine) (Melucci, 1989, 23 & 63 in Gamson, 1992, 57). The *political* expressed through culture identifies the precise nexus of environmental justice poetics and NSM theory that incorporates social identity with political transformation and expressive culture; this is the crux of the relationship that proves productive to this study. Similar linkages and results occur in Literary Studies in the composition and study of late 20th Century testimonio texts, illustrated in discussion of María Elena Lucas's work. Gamson stresses the self-reflexivity of new social movements, making the following subpoints: collective identity is a goal requiring the rethinking of success in collective action; "any strategic paradigm necessarily presupposes a theory of identity" (57). One of the problematic blind spots of new social movement theory is that it renders invisible, movements that don't immediately fit the conventional paradigms of scholarly examination. Environmental justice groups could be investigated in each of the areas I've proposed, although they have not been—to my knowledge. Were such studies to be undertaken they would almost by definition need to address the blind spots Gamson mentions. They often do not fit the typical paradigm of white middle class organizations, yet their concerns parallel many of the issues evoked in the study of new social movements. Hence blind spots might be made apparent and overcome by considering this predominantly people of color movement. Additionally, the environmental justice movement in India could be examined as a "Third World" South site that breaks down the "first world" emphasis that has thus far prevailed in new social movement theories. The lack of fit as a "traditional" new social movement is a strength that environmental justice mobilization might bring to the NSM body of theory.

Gamson discusses framing extensively, contending that "[f]rames like metaphors are ways of organizing thinking about political issues. One should ask not whether they are true or false—that is, their empirical validity—but about their usefulness in increasing understanding and their economy and inclusiveness in providing a coherent explanation of a diverse set of facts" (71). New social movements, he claims, institute collective action frames which, alternately, could be called injustice frames. Mass media discourse presents a different set of influential frames to each situation. In the rest of this chapter as well as in my studies of Bhopal, MELA and Chipko, Gamson's concept of framing, as metaphor, will be loosely applied to representations of environmental justice produced both internally and external to the movement—by media, corporations and the like. First, however, a brief focus on the recent work of one scholar who succinctly marks the juncture of theory and cultural poetics that my study pursues.

2.2 Activism Expanding "Political Consciousness" in the Realms of Theory

The *Frontiers* collection (1992) concludes with Aldon Morris's chapter "Political Consciousness and Collective Action," in which he re-charts the current field by pinpointing drawbacks that still exist. By tracing "political consciousness," as it has been perceived in new social movement theory, Morris suggests a neglect of the complexity of political consciousness in social movements; in particular, he raises the issue of the influence of race and gender consciousnesses. His concept is briefly explicated in the epigraph from him at the beginning of this chapter—"it is the interrelated system of political consciousness and the systems of human domination that gave rise to them in the first place that should become the focus of analytical inquiry." Furthermore, he calls for "research that addresses the institutional and organizational conditions under which oppositional consciousness matures and becomes combatready" (371). I believe a study of environmental justice organizational poetics can respond to Morris's call. Thus, my decision to elaborate on an examination of social movement theory—as applied to environmental justice organizing—by referring to his work. Morris's article marks a crucial juncture for NSM theory that may also serve my project as a useful link to the concurrent body of NSM thought. It is significant that Morris's article concludes this collection of NSM articles because, as is demonstrated in his observations, above, it primarily points to work *to be done*, rather than work that has been done.[29]

Morris's mandate implicitly suggests that NSM theory and environmental justice might enjoy symbiotic relations. (The present interstice between sociological study and broader environmental activism is an active, but limited, space.) The complexification of "political consciousness" occurring in environmental justice/ racism thought is recognized by sociologists, but the synthesis of these concepts has largely escaped permeation into new social movement theorizing. This point requires elucidation. The Environmental Justice Movement is particularly indebted to Robert Bullard, who undertook early toxic waste and race studies, and has continued to produce his own and others' research anthologies (and has spread and expanded the work decades into the 21st Century.) Environmental racism became a prevalent topic of study for sociologists in the late 20th Century. In addition to previously mentioned books on Chicano environmental justice organizing by Peña, Pulido and Pardo, African American sociologists such as Cynthia Hamilton, Andrea Simpson, and Dorceta Taylor joined Bullard and Ben Chavis in research. At American Sociological Association meetings, a focus on environmental justice increased. Among the offerings on environmental justice issues, Robert Bullard organized roundtables including "Environmental Issues and Race, Gender, and Class" which included

29 While Morris establishes the most extensive agenda in terms of race and class, many other articles contribute to this project as well and bring additional vital issues to light. For example, Verta Taylor and Nancy E. Whittier in "Collective Identity in Social Movement Communities: Lesbian Feminist Mobilization" explore the concept of "collective identity" in expressive culture and political consciousness as it relates to women's lesbian political and sexual orientation.

activists as well as sociologists (1996) and panels focusing on both African American and Chicana/o environmental justice activism (1999). While within the broader discipline, environmental sociology was also increasing, theoretical work on environmental justice was minimal in that field. Social movement theory, social constructionist theoretical areas such as collective action, political opportunity, and cultural theory work rarely overlapped with, or conversed with, research on environmental justice mobilization.[30] Groups that focus exclusively on the nonhuman natural environment have been studied as NSM theories, particularly in Europe. It is understandable that the warranting of empirical evidence of environmental racism provides quantitative research, but this should not relegate environmental justice organizing to only these realms of research. It is precisely because environmental racism is *not* an unknown in sociological study that it is imperative—considering Morris's mandate—that environmental justice organizations be considered potential new social movement terrain.

While "environmental justice actors" fit Canel's description, that is, theirs is not *primarily* a class struggle, their relationship to struggle is very different than many of the organizations that have been studied by New Social Movement and Resource Mobilization scholars. To understand the implications of those differences one must, with Morris, bring "consciousness back into social movement analysis" (351). Morris believes the means to do this dwell at the "intersection of culture and structure" where culture and structure "function as both constraints and promoters of social change" (351). He identifies class consciousness—in particular E.P. Thompson's description of the rise of class consciousness in Britain between 1790 and 1830—as a historical beginning point for social movement theory's unveiling of the relationship between consciousness, structure, and collective action. Raymond Williams describes a precursor to environmental justice in his discussion of "ecological socialism."[31] However, Morris is dissatisfied with work that considers class to be the exclusive entity shaping political consciousness. He observes that "the real possibility that class consciousness is only one kind of political consciousness and cannot be understood or properly assessed apart from a larger interactive system of political con-

30 For an explication of concurrent theoretical areas within the broad range of European and U.S. American new social movement thought, see "Social Construction of Protest" by Bert Klandermans, especially pages 78–82. For a concurrent collection from the Canadian perspective, see *Organizing Dissent: Contemporary Social Movements in Theory and Practice*, edited by William K. Carroll. Hamilton, Ont.: Garamond Press, 1992.

31 See the section entitled "Socialism and Ecology" in the chapter "The Challenge of the New Social Movements" in *Resources of Hope* London & NY: Verso, 1989.

sciousness has received scant attention in the literature" (358). Morris explains the weakness of the "ahistorical approach" that is commonly practiced in that it "is not likely to unravel the complex historical interactions among various forms of consciousness and how such interacting streams of consciousness affect the overall volume and nature of collective action" (359).

Morris's discussion identifies a version of a problem in U.S.[32] scholarship on class consciousness that coincides with the problems in literary studies, mentioned in the introduction, to which contemporary feminist and ethnically conscious literary theorists repeatedly have called attention: in both fields, the complex interacting properties of class, race, and gender oppression are often not recognized as bound together, but are instead separated, siloed, and hierarchized. Morris finds that such views, which procedurally efface the particularities of race and gender issues, make this scholarship "ahistorical and divorced from real group struggle" (356). As illustrated in the epigraph from Morris, he identifies a "conceptual narrowness" (356), which "sidesteps the possibility that class consciousness, race consciousness, gender consciousness, and ethnic consciousness may all be part of the same phenomenon" (359).

Similarly, Jenny Sharpe is concerned with the linkages of social identity categories. However, she calls for a delineation of the linked consciousnesses—a differentiation of factors rather than a unification of concerns, which, she finds, risks a conflation of the issues.

> Inasmuch as feminism calls attention to gender as a category that cuts across the discursive field of colonialism, it can be a force in displacing the binarism's of colonizer/colonized, Self/Other, oppressor/oppressed, and East/West. Yet unless we see that gender itself is overdetermined by other relations, we risk reducing colonialism to a narrative of sexual difference. To read social contradictions as overdetermined involves seeing how the axes of race, class, and gender are "linked through their differences, through the dislocations between them, rather than through their similarity, correspondence or identity." An analysis that begins with difference and dislocations between them, rather than identity and correspondence is crucial if we are to perform the race, class, and gender analysis that continues to elide feminist studies.[33]

At first blush, Sharpe's argument for "analysis that begins with difference..." might appear to stand at odds with Morris's suspicion that different political consciousnesses "may all be part of the same phenomenon," but given the call

32 Despite his identification of the problem as specifically "American" Morris's discussion of the problem suggests that it is not confined to the U.S. See, for example, his discussion of Eric Wright's *Classes*.

33 Jenny Sharpe, *Allegories of Empire*, 1993, 11.

for historicized recognition of difference on the part of both theorists, I suggest Sharpe's mandate nuances and builds on Morris's and may expand our vision of a solution to the problem he poses.

As Sharpe calls for a recognition of "difference and dislocations" to precede any unifying concept, she protects difference from being effaced by a focus on commonalities. Morris, in calling attention to the parallel impulses of class, race, and gender consciousnesses does not suggest that they are "the same," but rather that they are of equivalent importance; no such consciousness should be relegated solely to an emotional response, for instance. Nor should a single individual have to choose between one consciousness and another. Morris's argument, like the environmental justice production, demands the recognition of the complex relations between group identity and community environmental status. Thus it intervenes in the debilitating "divide, [hierarchize] and conquer" tendencies of sociological thought, multiculturalism, environmentalism and other ideologies that risk deteriorating into sameness. Jenny Sharpe's words of caution protect this productive theoretical shift from encountering another pitfall.

Morris points to shortcomings in previous studies of race in order to revise the concept as he expands on the idea of "conceptual narrowness." "Conceptual narrowness" either ignores other forms of consciousness or employs an analysis that has been labeled as "either/or" thinking about consciousness. Given that race is such a persistent reality in the U.S. context, researchers in this tradition have investigated whether Blacks identify with their class *or* their race; class consciousness, they presume is "of a different objective order"—race and other forms of consciousness are perceived to be "driven by personal attributes" (359). Morris points out the racially skewed problematic in the attitude that he characterizes as the scholarly norm; racial consciousness is seen as an "emotional preoccupation with race" (360). He explains, as follows.

> The assumption usually underlying such studies is the view that there exists an uncluttered class consciousness in the mental and cultural worlds of human beings that operates according to a unique class logic....In this approach the boundaries of class consciousness are not treated as analytically problematic....[T]he real possibility that class consciousness is only one kind of political consciousness and cannot be understood or properly assessed apart from a larger interactive system of political consciousness has received scant attention in the literature. (358)

Morris cites, as an example, one scholar whose assumptions are particularly transparent. In *Classes* (1985), Eric Wright identifies class-consciousness as "based in what he calls the objective properties of the class structure" while he considers "race, gender, ethnicity, and age" to be "personal attributes" that do not shape consciousness (360). Another scholar claims that Blacks are "increasingly likely to be emotionally preoccupied with race" (in Morris 360); this assumption suggests that race consciousness is not rational, while class-consciousness is. Environmental justice organizing refutes such bias and discriminatory visions. The thematic nature of environmental justice crosses over race, class, and gender boundaries, creating a concern in which multi-faceted identities are bound together by social difference (as advocated by Sharpe) as well as by mutual concern.

Morris demonstrates through two examples—one from the United Mine Workers' history and one from a Suffragists' struggle—that "white supremacist race consciousness has affected collective action in both the labor movement and the women's movement." He explains that "in situations where choices had to be made, white workers and white feminists usually followed the dictates of the hegemonic white consciousness rather than develop an oppositional consciousness that would simultaneously promote worker, women, and nonwhite interests" (366). Morris concludes that these incidents "attest to the strength of the system of racial domination in America and to the durability of the hegemonic consciousness from which it draws support" (366). Environmental justice activists call attention to precisely these issues as well. In U.S. environmental organizing, it has been primarily the environmental justice groups who have linked issues of race and class—and to a more limited extent, gender—to environmental degradation of human habitats.[34] That other environmental groups often have not recognized these issues supports Morris's recognition of the strength, durability and pervasiveness of racism in the hegemonic consciousness. Jenny Sharpe's differentiating of issues is necessitated when, as suggested in Chavis' definition of environmental racism, racism pervades in environmental organizing. Representations from the environmental justice movement with-

34 As mentioned in the Introduction, ecofeminists have been the primary group in the U.S. who have linked gender and environmental issues, but most have overlooked the relationship that race plays in both gender and environmental issues. Exceptions grow as both ecofeminism and the mainstream environmental movement became more receptive to environmental justice issues. For instance, the periodical *The Ecologist* has initiated and maintained a significant focus on linked issues of environment, race and gender. *Toxic Struggles: The Theory and Practice of Environmental Justice* edited by Richard Hofrichter contains several essays which simultaneously address ecofeminism and environmental justice. Other groups in the environmental mainstream such as *Sierra Club* promoted concern about environmental justice issues while being proponents of environmental racism in other situations. Indigenous environmental justice groups have a longstanding holistic view of eco-cultural relations, which in some cases benefit from a matrilineal worldview.

in the U.S. tell us that—using Morris's terminology—"white Supremacist race consciousness" plays into environmental decision-making at many levels in U.S society. Thus, social activists seek many venues of resistance.

While my area of focus is on resistance within Chicana/o and Mexican American[35] communities, environmental racism exists in most, if not all, communities of color in the U.S. The concept has developed and has been refined and addressed within and among communities of color and in coalitions of people of color. Environmental justice issues often provide common agenda by connecting ethnic groups who may feel alienated from each other's ethnic nationalism agenda, but who nonetheless support each other's struggles. For an example of such an alliance, we might look back to the quotation from PODER at the beginning of the introduction that asserts that people of color must "collectively set our own agenda." Such agenda in common initiates a "womanist" or a "border feminist" as opposed to a more single-issue oriented, gender-separatist feminist position.[36] In this way, an environmental justice agenda can intervene in a negative aspect of nationalist agendas that may preclude the identification of common interests across groups; this process intervenes in Morris's three "major interlocking systems" of domination in the American context: "white supremacy, a procapitalist stance, and male chauvinism" (364).[37] In addition to the ways in which these "interlocking systems" provoke environmental injustices, I explore three other systems of domination that affect environmental decision-making, namely national, indigenous, and caste identities, as I investigate political consciousness as it developed around the concept of environmental justice outside the U.S. context through comparative work on class, gender and race consciousness in environmental justice sites in India.

---

35 I use both "Chicana/o" and "Mexican American" here to pay heed to the diversity of self-identifications among people of Mexican descent within the U.S.; Chicane (used in México) and Chicanx or Chicanaox combine, rather than divide gender identities in 21st Century transformation. While people of Mexican descent often identify themselves by other terms such as Latina/o and Hispanic, Mexican American and Chicana/o, and in the 21st Century, Chicanx, etc., I use concurrent terms that retain the specificity of identity in their link with Mexico. Mexicano/a is preferred by some U.S. citizens of Mexican descent, but it is also used by some to distinguish those of Mexican citizenship; thus, to avoid confusion I don't use Mexicano/a without specifying my usage unless I use mexicana/o without capitalizing the first letter, as is the Spanish-language custom, to indicate I'm referring to Mexican citizens.

36 See Pardo 1995; see also Saldívar-Hull 1991 for derivation of "border feminist."

37 While I do not believe our understanding of the phenomenon being named differs substantially, I prefer the term "patriarchy" to Morris's "male chauvinism," which also has the meaning of discrimination against and stereotyping of women on a predominately personal level; the term "patriarchy" marks the structural element of the pervasive phenomenon.

Morris lays out a blueprint for the researching scholar: "When a researcher is investigating political consciousness in any specific society, the first task is to identify, describe, and analyze the existing systems of domination and the ways in which they converge and diverge" (364). I utilize Morris's model, turning specifically to narratives that name and describe systems of domination that are, among other things, environmentally racist. Thus, each subsequent chapter of Part One "Narratives of Social Environmentalism: An Oppositional Consciousness on Two Continents" investigates strategies of opposition to environmental injustice that raise the political consciousness of systems of domination, establish self-defined social identities as a means of empowerment, and theoretically mark the links between different kinds of environmental and social degradation. These strategies range from urban marches to rural padyatras, from boycotts to fasts, from embracing trees slotted for "slaughter" to withstanding arrest and harassment by police.

3 Narratives of Social Environmentalism: Environmental Justice, Transformative Culture, Narmada Bachao Andolan and People Organized in Defense of the Earth and her Resources (PODER)

3.1 Feminist Justice, Environmental Justice

Chapter Three considers environmental justice concerns in conjunction with social identity issues, namely women's and immigrants' issues by discussing the nexus of environmental justice and feminism, environmental racism, and immigrant rights. The chapter concludes by discussing two narratives of environmental justice struggles.

Myra Marx Ferree has illuminated how gender asymmetry has negatively impacted the scholarship of new social movement scholars, and a similar phenomenon is at work within environmental racism. One example of gender asymmetry is the way that many toxins disrupt healthy reproduction. Another instance occurs, particularly in the "Third World," when occupational division of labor create differing gendered effects when "development" strikes. Women are less likely to profit from the introduction of a cash economy and more likely to face increased manual labor because of such intrusions. Furthermore, in the move from rural to urban environments when land, livelihood, and community are lost due to environmentally destructive development, women are more likely to have to turn to prostitution as the only viable employment open to them. This presents another set of economic, legal, health, and patriarchal issues with which they must contend. Such a set of issues demonstrates the ways in which many environmental issues are intrinsically linked to other issues of structural violence (Shiva, 1987; Omvedt, 1993; Usher, 1994).

In short, to describe the relationship, one might borrow a slogan that links AIDS with other social justice issues: "Diseases don't discriminate; people do." Transposed to environmental racism, it would proclaim: "Toxins don't discriminate; people do." In other words, women do not give birth to *unwhole* or *unhealthy* children because of biological differences—their more complex reproductive systems. Women give birth to children who have been poisoned because few of the chemicals used by industry have been tested for toxic effects to workers and consumers of either gender, and because "Western" medical

https://doi.org/10.1515/9783111041575-004

study has not yet adequately prioritized research on women's—particularly women of color's—health issues. The toxins may impact women's biological makeup more harshly, but the *repercussions* of that impact are essentially sociological. Therefore, I am primarily interested in the *gender* differences—as opposed to biological or *sex* differences—that feed environmental racism in the societies that I study. Generally, I find a major similarity across cultures that both allows for environmental inequities to take place and facilitates combating them in very direct ways through the production of cultural poetics: knowledge is missing—often intentionally obfuscated. Furthermore, accumulated knowledge is not being dispersed to those whose lives could be directly affected by it. These are both environmental and feminist issues; I use "feminist" here in a broad redefinition of the historical usages by the mainstream women's movement that aligns with renaming—using terms such as womanist and "mujerista" by women of color—and correlates with inclusive usage of the term "environmental racism." In both cases, while the whole spectrum of related issues is being addressed as interconnected, specific issues—race and gender—are foregrounded by the terms "environmental racism" and "feminism," respectively. Linguistically, this corrective move is important to retain. These feminist, environmentalist issues are the grounds for structural interrogation of the double societal discrimination against women of color.

In turning to the "Principles of Environmental Justice," put forth by "The First National People of Color Environmental Leadership Summit," as a source of definitions of environmental justice, I alluded to omissions in the principles that need close consider, here. As a unifying statement from people of color, both the preamble and the principles of environmental justice mark the problem primarily according to race/ ethnicity. Despite the pledge "to respect and celebrate each of our cultures, languages and beliefs about the natural world and our roles in healing ourselves" (in Hofrichter 237) the *differences* in the ways in which environmental injustice[38] is perpetrated against different groups of people of color—especially gendered differences—are largely ignored or subsumed into a broad category.[39] For instance, no aspect of the particular effects of environmental injustice on women's reproductive systems or gender-related illness-

---

38 I use the term "injustice" here because it, rather than "racism," is used throughout the Summit document. The Principles are reprinted widely, but the easiest digital access is at https://www.ejnet.org/ej/principles.html.

39 Reproduction rights are mentioned in relationship to experimentation and "signed consent" only; the workers' rights principle mentions the right to a safe home atmosphere "for those who work at home" which addresses some women's vocational vulnerability to environmental injustice.

es such as breast cancer is mentioned.[40] So while the document underscores the disproportionate risk of environmental injustice according to race and ethnicity, it fails to document risks according to gender. Thus, it also fails to note the double risk factors for women of color. Additionally, environmental justice issues relating specifically to class, nationality, LGBTQ+ identity, culture, and age remain understated. The "Principles of Environmental Justice" statement is not alone in neglecting to delineate particular effects of environmental toxins on women. Few studies in the 20th Century focus on how gender issues exacerbate environmental racism and affect environmental justice organizing in communities in the United States.[41] In my focus on women's work, and specific ways that environmental racism affects women, I attempt to begin to ameliorate this gap in scholarship. Through a critical reading of Vandana Shiva's work, I find aspects of her study of gender issues and environmental justice in India an invaluable source of information as well as a standard for our work in the U.S. context. That said, Vandana Shiva, though most prolific, is one of many researchers engaged with gender and environmental justice in India.

An Indian statement of principles entitled "An Assertion of the Right to Life"[42] authored by the National Alliance, a coalition of social movement organizations is in some ways comparable to The First National People of Color Environmental Leadership Summit's Principles. Included in the coalition are the Narmada Bachao Andolan, the Bhopal Gas Peedit Mahila Udyog and the Himalaya Bachao Andolan; (Andolan translates as social movement). These organizations were initiated in three of the sites of social environmentalist struggle in India that I researched, and each organization has many, if not a majority, women members. It is not surprising then that their statement on gender is a prominent plank that lists several of the concerns raised in the poetics under consideration.

---

40 Because gender issues never affect women exclusively, it is important to acknowledge in discussing breast cancer that male electrical workers also experience high rates of breast cancer. This break with the normal gender division of susceptibility to the disease only illustrates the prevalence of its environmental cause.

41 Sylvia Herrera's work on women's environmental health, especially on the Texas-México border is an importation exception.

42 In India, the phrase "the Right to Life" does not carry with it the anti-abortion currency that it has in the U.S. and the document does not address such issues. A 21st Century National Alliance of People's Movements website is at https://napm-india.org/. However, a "People's Resolve" here (https://napm-india.org/about-us/) does not include the many references to women from the earlier document. Medha Patkar of Narmada Bachao Andolan was a founding member in 1992.

> While some change in the status of women is achieved through the opening of opportunities in education, employment and other sectors of life, the disparity between men and women continues to appear in newer and more subtle forms of discrimination and exploitation. Women are to suffer the most through a package of economic reforms sweeping our country today, whether it is industrial retrenchment or reduction in social security measures. On the other hand, a feminine perspective that necessarily favours fulfillment of basic needs and human approach to change has a great potential to straighten our distorted development priorities and inhuman processes of change. Women, therefore, deserve not just protection against social and political injustice, economic exploitation, or abuse, as a 'sexual commodity' but a rightful place in every sector and social movements [sic], leading to a liberation and not a blind equalization. (5)

The National Alliance priorities acknowledge gender injustice—past, present, and future—in very specific terms and so-called economic reforms are foregrounded as most harmful to women; the meaning and direction of reform is brought into question (reform for whom?) by this passage. However, the gendered victim is also presented as the proactive force that offers an alternative to the structural distortions of justice. It is based upon this offering to society that women are seen as deserving "liberation." Thus, this statement suggests that the "feminization" of the social structure is necessarily not a separatist proposition, but an acknowledgment and support of women's involvement and leadership in progressive social movement organizing.

The National Alliance's statement of principles also includes an "environmental sustainability" plank that is especially salient to environmental justice worldwide.

> [The] unsustainable exploitation that destroys the [natural] capital should be stopped for it affects the socio-economically downtrodden, benefiting the higher echelons of our society....[The] results of our environmentally blind policies and development projects...have brought in an irreversible degradation and destruction of our land, water, forests and air. Peoples who face the impact are necessarily the rural and tribal and hill communities along with the urban poor. (4)

This "environmental sustainability" plank notes that in India, in both rural and urban contexts, the poor are most impacted by environmentally unsustainable development. This phenomenon is paralleled in the U. S. context and, on another level, internationally, as the poorer countries suffer most from the destructive development imported from the richer countries.

A plank addressing "fascist and communal tendencies" specific to the Indian context suggests that "[a]n all out and concerted campaign against these fascist and fundamentalist forces, by mass-based, secular movements addressing the basic socio-economic issues of life" could be an answer (5). But while terms such as "communal" specify fundamentalist Hindu ideologies, an increasingly significant parallel exists between the communal Hindu supremacy movement in India and the White Supremacist and Christian Far Right forces in the late 20th Century U.S.A.

These National Alliance planks identify many of the concerns prevalent among the Indian movements that work in environmental justice. This does not mean that these groups always agree on procedures, ideologies, methodologies or means of mobilization. Within given contexts different groups have often developed radically different, and often conflicting, agendas. My overviews for the most part do not explore the complexities of such disagreements except when the areas of focus of my study are central to organizational disagreements. The critique that addresses these environmental justice issues comes in verbal testimonies and community organizing campaigns that challenge corporate, environmentalist, and other institutions practicing social discrimination to recognize the crucial need to redress environmental issues that directly impact human communities.

Through study of the gender dynamics within environmental activism and poetics, the significance of many women who have laid groundwork in environmental justice groups and in cultural poetics creation is established. My research interrogates the essentializing of the female subject and provokes the opening up of traditionally male-dominated theoretical territories in order to examine the work of those who have been socio-historically marginalized. The issues inscribed in the primary cultural texts I study inform a broad discussion of gender, race, and class dynamics as they are played out in current grassroots political arenas. There is a diversity of women's strategies of self and community representation within the arena of environmental justice work in the north and south hemispheres; in each site, gender plays a different, but—to varying degrees—definitive role. Proponents of environmental justice and ecofeminists share the contention that analysis articulates lived experience; however, their stances on shared arguments differ. Ariel Salleh observes that, "[s]ome ecofeminism, then, is contiguous with radical or socialist paradigms, but by going back to women's lived experiences in a time of global crisis, it brings fresh understandings to these movement ideologies" (1992, 202). The environmental justice movement extends this predominantly "first world" ecofeminist argument with the additional recognition that gendered experience is *racially-defined*—and defined by class and nation.

In the past, race issues often have been neglected in ecofeminism, like in other environmental activism and philosophy. For example, despite a title—"Class, Race, and Gender Discourse in the Ecofeminism/Deep Ecology Debate"—that suggests a focus on social identity issues, Ariel Salleh's essay does not extensively address racism as an environmental issue in the "first world." Although she recognizes both the environmental oppression in the "Third World" and the "model" contributions of "third world peasant women," she creates a false dichotomy between "first" and "Third worlds" that, among other things, fails to recognize the women and men who reside in *both*. For instance, she tells us that "in supposedly advanced industrial nations, women's maintenance work as housewives or imported guest workers is made dependent on and largely mystified by 'labor-saving devices,' such as dishwashing machines, blenders, and the like" (225). However, she fails to recognize that the "imported guest workers" that she describes are doing maintenance for their own families as well, without the infamous "labor saving devices." Thereby, she ignores the interwoven complexity of environmental and economic justice issues in the "first world" and their links to race, class, *and* gender oppression: specifically, that in the situations she describes, "first world" money buys both technological and human labor power, contributing to environmental demise, and to the economic gap between "haves" and "have-nots" based on "first world/ Third World" status.[43]

In a related inattentive moment, Salleh also does not expand upon the *gendered* nature of what she calls "women's maintenance work" done by working class women. Unfortunately, Salleh's negligence is, the norm rather than the exception among ecofeminists. Such oversights suggest a lack of awareness of the activism that addresses the many manifestations of environmental racism in the U. S. Such activism is substantially represented in a body of cultural poetics and should be recognized both as a political (environmental) force and as a cultural force. The histories, pedagogies, and strategies I examine, serve to inform and critique eco-feminism and eco-criticism from perspectives that have historically often been silenced by progressives as well as conservatives in the academy and in the nonacademic corporation.

Social environmentalist images of self-representation often describe being situated in multiple, sometimes inimical communities and within multiple sites

43 A generalized abstraction of the phenomenon shows that the same money that buys the polluting and resource-consuming, "labor-saving devices" comes from the interstices of the international (and national) discrepancy between "first" and "Third Worlds." For instance, economically disenfranchised people pay for their countries' "Third World" debt. And because of the imperialist hierarchy between North and South, life in their home country becomes economically unsustainable for many in the South, and they migrate to worksites where, because of their "Third World" status, they are vulnerable to further exploitation in communities that are environmentally degraded.

of often conflicting struggles. Lourdes Torres expresses these crucial corrective perspectives:

> It is not enough to speak of double or triple oppression; rather, women of color are themselves theorizing their experience in radical and innovative terms. Their condition as women, as people of color, as working-class members, and in some cases as lesbians, has led them to reject...theories...which have failed to develop an integrated analysis sensitive to the simultaneous oppression that women of color experience. Rather, third world women are making connections between the forces of domination which affect their lives daily and are actively participating in the creation of a movement committed to radical social and political transformation at all levels. (275)

Such "feminist thought," produced in analysis of environmental justice issues, defines itself differently in relation to other feminisms, in particular, ecofeminism. Despite emphasizing environmentalism that includes human experience with injustice, ecofeminism has rarely recognized their common ground with the U.S. environmental justice movement or that environmental injustice is racially determined as well as gendered. However, an important shift is underway. Some ecofeminists such as Greta Gaard and Catriona Sandilands recognize that environmental justice activists in the U.S. and ecofeminists do have projects in common and activists are attempting nonhierarchical discussions between the two groups.[44] Such North American intracontinental connections have been more slowly realized than inter-global connections with activist-intellectuals, such as Vandana Shiva who claims the title of "Ecofeminist" as well as Environmental Justice cultural worker. Shiva strategically situates herself vis-á-vis many ecological movements. She has worked with often inimical groups—Deep Ecologists as well as Ecofeminists, for instance. Though she applied the terminology of "environmental justice" to the Indian context quite early (IPAG 1992), it was several years later that her writing has supported environmental justice groups in the U.S. Her Foreword to *Chicano Culture, Ecology, Politics: Subversive Kin*, edited by Devon G. Peña, is an example of such an alliance.

---

44 See, for instance, Gaard's collection *Ecofeminism: Women, Animals, Nature*, especially "Questioning Sour Grapes: Ecofeminism and the United Farm Workers Grape Boycott" by Ellen O'Loughlin. Ellen O'Loughlin examines UFW activities as furthering ecofeminist agenda; in an innovative conclusion she switches perspectives and suggests that the reader re-view ecofeminism given the UFW realities she has discussed. Also, Sandilands' *The Good-Natured Feminist: Ecofeminism and the Quest for Democracy* recognizes environmental justice practitioners' work in her discussion of ecofeminism.

One of the incongruencies between much mainstream U.S. feminism and the world's majority of women is that for most women, in most situations, extensive gender separatism (whether theoretical or literal) doesn't work. Dialogue may at least bring women from different camps to a tolerant understanding of each other's positions. This dynamic problem, which I discuss more extensively later, offers insightful issues that bear mention here. One, while my focus is on women, many of these women are working in coalition with men, and some environmental justice work is being done—often in occupationally related contexts—in which men are the primary leaders. Two, the efforts of the men who support the social environmentalism in which the women are involved, and/or when women's interests are at stake, are important to this study. Rather than dismiss some cultural poetics, based on constraining identity politics alone, I have chosen to examine such work that men have executed and to mark the gendered absences as well as the women's voices that are present in these texts. (Gilberto Rivera's description of a social environmentalist, quoted above, is an example.) With this strategy, I hope to better understand the complexities of the role that gender plays in situations in which women are affected by and effecting change. (In the 21st Century, Queer and Trans thought/ theories have opened up gender binaries such that these approaches are being refined.)

In many instances the work that men contribute, in coalition with women, is integral to the environmental justice community. For example, I would not have heard the poetry and narrative analysis of West Dallas community women, whose families had been poisoned by years of exposure to the byproducts of a lead smelter, or the concerned anger of East Austin women, whose land was affected by erosion and oil tank farms, if René Rentería had not been at these sites with his video camera and community-supportive film-making skills in order to hear and disperse community issues as represented by individuals from the communities that were involved.[45] My focus on women allows their presentation of issues to be foregrounded; it does not aim to silence men or those who identify nonbinarily who are contributing constructively to the women's work. Likewise, while my focus is on the work of people of color, my study includes the supportive contributions to the issues at stake from non "Third World," white people/(s).[46]

45 Several of Rentería's videos were sponsored by PODER and East Austin Strategy Team (EAST). His current website and the Facebook page linked there show subsequent collaborative work, particularly with indigenous groups: https://renerenteria.wordpress.com/about-me/.

46 I am not using the terms, "of color" and "Third World" interchangeably, though they describe overlapping groups; "of color" I use mostly when speaking of communities within the

3.2 Immigration and Environmental Racism

A cursory view of the contemporary landscape might suggest that environmental justice and immigrant rights have little in common; however, investigation into the alternative press and immigrant rights organizations shows otherwise. In the United States, in a move that has particular effect upon Latina/o communities, some mainstream environmentalists—alongside mostly right-wing politicians—have represented population increases due to immigration as the source of environmental, as well as economic and political problems, thus transferring blame from economically and politically privileged elites in the dominant culture to its most disenfranchised.[47] The numerous state and federal anti-immigrant legislative initiatives that continued in the wake of the passage of

---

US where the term is most salient in contexts where "Third World" conditions may or may not prevail. Norma Alarcón traces the origins of the term, "women of color," to a feminist conference in 1981 at which U.S. women of color were categorically marginalized and came up with the term to replace the term "third world women" which had been appropriated for them and which they felt, conflated their experiences in the U.S. with those of structurally disenfranchized women, internationally. Chela Sandoval reports on the discussion of the complexities and problematics of the two terms in "Feminism and Racism: A Report on the 1981 National Women's Studies Association Conference" in *Hacienda Caras*.

47 The term "dominant culture" is a catch-all label that needs dismantling. In the context of Greater Mexico, the term is used in U. S. theorizing to identify a dominant culture that is predominately white, specifically Anglo (as in, of British descent) and is male and middle to upper class. The power differentials between individuals of different ethnicities, genders, and classes, within the dominant culture, are due to the systematic empowerment of individuals with dominant "socio-biodata" at the expense of individuals with other backgrounds; and additional corresponding disempowerment results for the nondominant classes. Generally speaking, to the degree they are excluded, individuals are systematically denied empowerment. The "real" specificities of this systematic skewing of power have changed over the country's history and vary regionally as well, however the relational model has remained largely consistent. Those privileged may lose status due to ideological variance with dominant culture, particularly if they are outspoken, act upon their beliefs, politically, and/or ally themselves with excluded parties. This national (U.S.) model, through acts of imperialism, in alliance with other (post)colonizing bodies, and in some places, the national elite of "third world" countries, can be transposed into an international model, especially in terms of the globalization of capitalism. This international model however is not synonymous with the national model. This model renders a monolithic "American" culture wherein outsiders are marginalized unless they assimilate. The international model is a phase of the monolithic "New World Order" in which others are forced into compliance through military and economic force. Dominant control of multinational corporations and global capitalism overlies both international and national arenas. How this increasingly dominating force manifests itself through dominant cultures and/or splits up and thus obtains more intimate entrance into already dominated cultures is an important and repeated narrative in the discourse I studied.

California's Proposition 187 in 1994 give cultural critics at the cusp of the new millennia responsibility for understanding the intersection of environmental justice issues and immigration rights issues. This site of conjunction for racist assumptions gives further credence to the importance of viewing the cultural poetics of environmental, economic, social, and civil justice in a landscape that includes icons and images from those doubly disenfranchised (by eco-material conditions and by false blame for those conditions).

Vandana Shiva identifies and contextualizes a faulty division between environmental concern and inaccurate blame for environmental degradation internationally. She cites environmental racism within the U.S., as she observes that "[e]nvironmentalists of the North...need to learn that the poor of the world should not be made the scapegoats for ecological degradation" (IPAG, 3). Shiva raises issues of scapegoating in relationship to "first world" environmentalists who blame the higher population growth rates in much of the "Third World" for environmental problems without acknowledging that the much higher rates of extraction and consumption in the "first world" contribute most profoundly to environmental problems.

In both North and South, the intersection of race and the environment is particularly salient in its juncture with immigration discourse. Not long after arriving at University of Oregon for a research fellowship with the Women, Science, and the Sacred program at the Center for the Study of Women in Society in Spring, 2000, I was given a Network for Immigrant Justice publication that describes (through testimonios, letters, interviews...) several large and horrific INS raids that took place in Lane County, Oregon in Spring, 1998. The inhumane brutality of the raids described in an effective multi-genre, cross-communities presentation, along with my own sense of displacement, affected me as profoundly as any narratives of La Migra/INS violence closer to the U.S. borders that I had heard previously. I called the phone number on the front of the booklet, unsure of who would be at the other end, but quite sure I would like to speak to them. That is how I met Guadalupe Quinn, who generously provided twenty some years of contacts and stories of Latina/os working in social justice issues in central Oregon.

When I asked her about environmental racism, Guadalupe first suggested contacting farm worker advocacy groups; clearly the pesticide issue is a primary concern for the many predominantly immigrant, Latino farm workers in the Northwest and is central to Oregon's environmental justice struggles. I questioned further, interested in whether the urban environmental justice issues so prevalent in many Latino communities in Texas were part of Oregon Latinas' lived reality. While I learned subsequently about many members of the Whiteaker community (home to many Latina/os and a predominantly progressive area of Eugene) experiencing Guadalupe's answer to my probe evokes concerns the larger body of environmental racism literature raises: the largest environmental justice issue that the organization she works for, the Network for Immigrant Justice, has had to face is at University of Oregon in the form of speakers at environmentalist conferences who scapegoat immigrants in their uncritical discussion of population issues. Guadalupe said that when they hear an environmental conference is coming up, the Network tries to send someone to offer a critical perspective—to point out that immigrant families, whether large or small, are living lifestyles that have much less negative impact on the environment than most of the country, including the middle-class environmentalists who point fingers at immigrants. She pointed out that the immigrants are an environmental model for all of us, including Latina/os, like herself, who have settled into a more economically privileged lifestyle, and lost environmentally concerned values in their acculturation to consumer-mainstream lifestyle. The new immigrants waste much less, eat lower on the food chain, hand down or recycle clothing for their children, use far less space for living quarters, and use the bus or walk rather than having fancy cars or SUV's. "Who uses the most resources?" she asked. Yet environmental racism blinds the environmentalists in question from seeing the Latinas/os as contributing to solutions rather than problems, and they also do not historicize the context in which Latina/os are immigrating to the U.S., a context in which the exploitation of land and community that is driving people from their homes is an environmental issue, most often with roots in the U.S.

This issue was expanded upon by Carmen Bauer, director of El Centro Latino Americano, in the Whiteaker neighborhood of Eugene Oregon, who also described health problems related to migrant labor conditions, including skin problems from pesticide use, and a suspected relationship to corporate-generated toxins causing an inordinate number of cancer cases among recent Mexican immigrants. She mentioned five recent cases of thyroid cancer among immigrants under 30 years old coming from Nayarit in Northwest México. In these discussions, it became clear that in Oregon the immigration-environmental racism matrix comes sharply into focus in ways that provide examples for struggles elsewhere. For the most part, a strong environmental consciousness means that industry does not position itself or its workers in environmental harm's way to the extent that it does in other parts of the country. However, the progressive accountability that keeps out environmental toxins is lacking in other arenas, namely, in issues involving race and ethnicity. Because the Latino and Black communities in most of Oregon are small, and many white Oregonians buy into, or do not notice, the pervasive structural racism that triggers incidents of police and INS violence, these problems are intensified for many people of color, at least in Lane

County. A description of environmental justice's relation to immigration issues, as spelled out in the journalistic press, replicates the social concerns over immigrant bashing expressed in environmental justice and immigrant rights organizing. The passage of Proposition 187 in California solidified both an attack by white supremacists and a solid defense represented in the large coalitions of Latina/os and others working for immigrant rights. As Elizabeth Martínez has observed, youth played a strong role in this resistance to hatred. Both Proposition 187 and the demonstrations of resistance to, and indictment of, 187 operated on a figurative level. This figurative depiction also occurs in fiction such as Ana Castillo's novel, *Sapogonia*[48] and in the U.S. alternative press that has exposed the connections between prejudicial constructions of race, perpetuation of environmental racism, and immigrant bashing.

Progressive media reports reflect a troubling relationship between the issues of environmental justice and immigrant rights. Arnoldo García and Nancy Stein report that almost "the entire spectrum, ranging from right-wingers to liberals (who have been encouraged by the participation of environmental organizations...) have converged on the idea of dramatically curbing or fully halting immigration, both documented and undocumented"(6). In an article entitled "Environmental Justice Needs No Green Card," Cathi Tactaquin explains the history of the phenomenon of blaming environmental problems on immigration,

> The "immigration/population" issue began to percolate some years ago when ads in California newspapers blamed immigration for pollution, overcrowding, traffic congestion and even the state's drought. More recently, groups such as Californians for Population Stabilization initiated direct mail campaigns urging stricter controls on immigration to protect the environment.... (13)

The double meaning of "green" in Tactaquin's title puts forth a figurative relationship of immigration and ecojustice: too often the green card that allows one to

---

48 Aside from the prominent critique that exposes the ramifications of deleterious heterosexual relationships, the predominant social issue presented in Ana Castillo's second novel, *Sapogonia* (1990) is immigrant rights. Castillo identifies concerns about disenfranchised Latina/os that intervene in the borders marked on paper. Using a postmodern historiographic narrative form, Castillo remaps an imaginary country into Latin America. This country, called Sapogonia, and placed south of the United States, is charged with concrete historical and geopolitical implications that mirror north-south relations in the western hemisphere. In the relationship between the fantastic and the historical, *Sapogonia* critiques U.S.-Latin American relations that have deleterious effects on immigrant rights, as well as, on the environment. Castillo's texts, *Sapogonia* and *So Far From God* offer their own parallels between immigration and environmental issues and might be examined comparatively for the ways they represent these social justice issues.

pass as a legal resident in the U.S. does not allow one to pass into a "green" clean environmental zone. Rather Latina/os—recent immigrants, as well as families whose presence in the region preceded the moving of the border—are likely to have their neighborhoods and job sites turned into toxic dumping zones.

Luke Cole, in *Race, Poverty and the Environment* identifies a coalition that preceded the coalescing of right wing and predominantly white and Republican support for the racist Proposition 187 that dehumanizes immigrants. It is the racialized dehumanizing of immigrants, that is the phenomenon-in-common that allows environmental racism and immigrant bashing to be seen as "acceptable" behavior. Cole marks this current juncture of issues. Cathi Tactaquin quotes Luke Cole's useful analysis in the following passage that illustrates how environmental racism has contributed to the racial hatred perpetrated against recent immigrants:

> This new anti-immigration 'environmental' alliance is a frightening sign of our times. It takes the familiar population control argument a step further, including in its anti-immigration pitch the very arguments that opponents of population control have long made. And it threatens the necessary and growing dialogue between the environmental movement and communities of color, at a time when we must reach across a growing divide rather than exacerbate tensions among these groups. The new anti-immigration alliance, based on flawed logic, is strategically and morally a mistake. (13)

Several trajectories of "flawed logic" that Cole and Tactaquin describe are ripe for investigation, but the most blatant flaw disputes mainstream environmentalist rhetoric itself. I am thinking here about the transference of nation state "borders" upon an "environmental" map to create "pure" green zones. In these racist, nationalist, environmental impulses, the nation-state border keeps outlawed toxins from being used most places within the U.S. but allows for the export of toxic waste and toxic products. Not only does this policy transgress the long-standing environmental concept of global, ecological, and especially bioregional interrelationships, it dehumanizes "third world" peoples in the same way that toxic dump sites placed in economically disenfranchised communities of color disrespect the neighborhoods' human rights to a healthy environment in which to live and work.[49]

---

49 Malcolm X advocated the use of the term "human rights" rather than "civil rights" in order to counter the construction of people of color as subhuman, and such usage seems particularly appropriate for immigration discussions in order to stand against the revoking of civil (and human) rights.

Likewise, to surmise that immigrants cause population problems is not only what Vandana Shiva terms "green imperialism," but the logic behind the assumption is simplistic and flawed. Those environmentalists who advocate bioregionalism must apply their ecological framework to human as well as nonhuman communities: if, *rhetorically*, they advocate fluid borders based on ecological communities, then, *in practice*, they should work against nation-state containment that allows money, but not people, to pass freely across national borders, particularly when they cut across bioregions.[50] But the environmental justice movement, unlike many mainstream environmental groups, does not adhere to such political borders: the undocumented community in the U.S. as well as toxin-threatened communities on "el otra lado" are among the protectorates of environmental justice organizers. They align themselves with Tau Lee's social analysis that details environmental racism in the context of anti-immigration rhetoric:

> Many good organizations and honest people are buying into the myth that immigrants are ruining the environment and people's lives in this country. Excuse me, but I don't recall immigrants poisoning rivers and people's drinking water. I don't recall immigrants controlling and operating chemical and petroleum factories. I don't recall any of us siting landfills, dumps and incinerators in our communities. (4)

Tau Lee extends her critique of immigrant scapegoating, which demonstrates the relations between corporate, political, and economic powers and the perpetration of environmental degradation, by developing a Marxian analysis. She shows how immigrants are used to promote capitalist growth, often at the cost of humane or safe living conditions for migrant families:

> I do recall that the same system which produces those problems also produces capital's need for cheap labor. That means immigrants. Then immigrants are blamed for problems like environmental damage. At the same time, they are forced to live in communities where the housing stock is old and saturated with lead. In areas designated for mixed use, where schools, parks and housing are located next to toxic-using facilities like auto-body shops and dry cleaners. In communities cut through by freeways that bring smog and chemical spills....[C]alling for limits on immigration doesn't address the real reason why the environment is being destroyed. Today we have a system that allows industry to poison and destroy the environment, denies people the right to a stable, decent livelihood, and perpetuates fear and hatred. We need to change that system! (4)

---

50 Numerous analysts have condemned the capitalist impulse behind (nearly) open borders for money and (nearly) closed barriers for people illustrated in the U.S.-México relationship developed under NAFTA. See also Spivak's assessment quoted in this chapter and Vandana Shiva's discussion of the environmental racism in which Northern environmentalists engage.

Tau Lee exposes another angle on the same indictment of imperialism in relation to North-South relations made by environmental justice practitioners, Chicana journalist Elizabeth Martínez and Indian activist/scholar Vandana Shiva, among others. The progressive journalism examined above proposes constructive change in our understanding of the lives of immigrants and brings to bear many of the issues involved in conjoining social and environmental issues to frame the concept of "environmental justice." Such re-evaluation of the dominant culture's representations of immigration and environmental issues becomes crucial for the reader who is moved by the encounter with the "reality" of lived experience as portrayed in ecojustice literature. The remainder of this chapter examines environmental critiques from sites—where dam building in India, and agricultural practices and oil company's storage and dispersal of fuel in the U.S. threaten both human and other "natural" habitats.

3.3 Narratives of Social Environmentalism: Environmental Justice, Transformative Culture: Narmada Resistance

This chapter's applied juxtaposition of environmental justice poetics and new social movement theories begins at the Narmada River, one of the largest, most sacred, and mythologically important rivers on the Indian subcontinent. Modern plans for an interstate series of large hydroelectric dams on the Narmada have been under protest and contention for three decades already by the end of the 20th Century. The first recorded plans for dams on the Narmada River, initially proposed to divert water for crop irrigation in the state of Gujarat, were issued by a "British entrepreneur" in 1863, almost a hundred years before construction on any such project was started (McCully 93). Hence, as happens repeatedly in India, environmental injustice was built upon the direct foundation of colonial domination of land and peoples. After India gained independence as a modern nation state, the dam project was again considered seriously, and in 1961, construction began when Jawaharlal Nehru, who called dams, "temples of modernity," laid the corner stone. However, the dam-building was halted shortly thereafter because of disagreement between the states through which the Narmada flows. Negotiations were eventually resumed, resulting in a Narmada Water Disputes Tribunal (NWDT) in 1969, which came up with an "Award," or agreement, in 1979; construction on the Sardar Sarovar dam began in 1987 (Omvedt 267; McCully; Mies and Shiva 306). The project became a proposal for the largest dam system in the world and acquired World Bank and other international funding (Mies and Shiva 306).

Activists charged that the project did not seriously consider the detrimental impact of the project on the land and on the people in the area, many of whom are Adavasis, indigenous Indians. International Groups such as Third World Network and The Asia-Pacific People's Environmental Network (APPEN) called it "India's greatest planned environmental disaster."[51] Such national projects often acquire what Maria Mies and Vandana Shiva consider to be "a new colonialism based on development financing and debt burdens" in the relatively new, independent nations of the South (10). As the "environmental movement revealed the environmental and social costs generated by maldevelopment, conceived of and financed by these institutions the international lending institutions appropriated environmental rhetoric furthering their false legitimacy in their projects in the South" (Mies & Shiva 10). In addition, global and national concerns were considered more valid than local ones, by both national and international bureaucratic institutions. The Narmada Dam Project was no exception. Mies and Shiva find that, in the 1980s, as groups that had sprung up in resistance to such projects began to talk to each other they "realized that what was being presented as the 'national interest' were the electoral and economic interests of a handful of politicians financed by a handful of contractors and industrialists who benefit from the construction of all dams such as Tehri and the Narmada Valley project" (10). Thus, as networks of resistance work spread so did "the collective struggle of communities" that revealed itself as "the real though subjugated common interest" (10). These informative networks developed the alternative collective communication that Myra Marx Ferree discusses. The collective interest here stands in contrast to the "naturalized" individual interest of the elite dam planners, thus illustrating the importance of Ferree's corrective. In this case the collective interest slowly gained influence.

Over the course of the project, many groups have formed in opposition or partial opposition to the dam project and even the World Bank pulled its support (formally at the request of the Indian government) when its feasibility and advisability came under continued questioning. *The Times of India* account by McCully notes that an independent review board for the World Bank reported in June 1992 that "the Sardar Sarovar Projects as they stand are flawed, that resettlement and rehabilitation of all those displaced by the Projects is not possible under prevailing circumstances, and that the environmental impacts of the Projects have not been properly considered or adequately addressed" (McCully in *The Times of India* 8-7-93). Perhaps most significantly, the review board,

---

51 See *Damming the Narmada: India's Greatest Planned Environmental Disaster* by Claude Alvares and Ramesh Billorey (1988).

headed by a former UN Development Programme chair, Bradford Morse, found that "the Bank shares responsibility with the borrower for the situation that has developed" (McCully). About half the money that had been spent had come from the World Bank.

Though the problems with the project have been internationally recognized, the Narmada activists, like the activists in support of the gas-affected people in Bhopal, suffered police violence and undue arrests. The foremost "grassroots" group, the Narmada Bachao Andolan, led by Medha Patkar, maintains an office in the village of Manibeli Maharastra, a focal point of the group and a village that would be submerged by proposed dam extensions (McCully). They have used Sarvodaya techniques such as dharnas (fasts), yatras (marches) and they have threatened jal samarpan (suicide by water, the pledge to remain even as the land is submerged by dammed water) as well as mass demonstrations and letter writing to further their cause. Despite harassment and attempts at discrediting, the Narmada Bachao Andolan has gained respect in environmental movements worldwide and among progressive groups in India. Their actions have received consistent press coverage in India. This marks a relationship between Indian activists and Indian media in which (though sometimes at odds,) the media remains generally more (and differently) supportive than in most U.S. activist media relationships observed in my studies. Additionally, the NBA have benefited greatly from the unprecedented leadership of Medha Patkar, "the first woman to head a mass movement in India" (Omvedt 259).

Medha Patkar began organizing at the village level in 1986, when she was employed by Achyut Yagnik, a Gujarati working for Tribal and Dalit advocacy; they traveled about the areas to be submerged by the Sardar Sarovar dam, mobilizing village level committees, and alerting other social activists. Medha Patkar soon broke with Achyut Yagnik, formed the Narmada Bachao Andolan, a group that spanned three affected states—Gujarat, Madhya Pradesh and Maharastra—and brought together villagers and urban-based environmental organizations. In the strongest mobilization, (in Madhya Pradesh) "rural women were mobilized for the first time and dalits, tribals, and caste Hindus [were] brought together in a movement" (Omvedt 267). During 1987–88 the movement radicalized from a group seeking justice for evictees and workers to an opposition to the dam as such, "a full-scale, total radical environmentalist opposition to the Narmada project" (Ibid). Gandhian social worker Baba Amte was instrumental in initiating this change; his style was charismatic, "an appeal to sentiment" (Omvedt 271). As the movement developed, a difference in style of leadership and affinity-development was revealed between Medha Patkar and Baba Amte.

As support for Baba Amte's style of organizing waned, "themes of struggle symbolized by Patkar ... began to take predominance" (Omvedt 271).

Early in 1991, Patkar and six other activists, including two tribal women, began a "fast to death," which was called off after 22 days; an NBA statement linked environmental abuse with social disenfranchisement:

> Behind our exploitation of nature often lies our exploitation of each other. By taking away the traditional rights of millions of tribals and small and marginal farmers from subsistence use of natural resources...the benefits are derived at the cost of enormous suffering to the affected population and massive overuse and degradation of the surrounding resources. (Omvedt 272)

NBA activists felt that a break with elected officials and party politics was necessary since the government was not addressing the roots of disenfranchisement, as identified by the movement. They called for a boycott of elections and of all government officials and declared political decentralized self-sufficiency in the Gandhian slogan "our village, our rule." Gail Omvedt observes that environmental activists, in particular the NBA, raised the rhetorical "'Marxist' question of property rights—but in contrast to the traditional left, they were giving the 'Green' answer: decentralization" (272). Their persistent militancy forced "a dialogue in which more concrete formulations of the nature of exploitation and environmental destruction, as well as the assertion of popular power from below (as opposed to enlightened state intervention from above,) began to replace the originally vague and romantic slogans" (272).

In 1991, the Narmada Bachao Andolan—that was increasingly emphasizing decentralized village decision-making and ownership—won the Right Livelihood Award, the alternative Nobel Prize, thus attaining high international respect. While insider politics might suggest differently, in many ways the NBA might be seen as a model of social environmentalist organizing, and Medha Patkar, a mentor for social environmentalists. Here, Omvedt points to a common phenomenon recognized by environmental justice activists in many parts of the world: degradation of natural resources and surroundings is inevitably accompanied by degradation and disenfranchisement of human communities. A photo in *The Times of India* (8-7-93 11) pictures "Ms Medha Patkar" being detained and driven away. She sits contemplative and calm while to her right in the street below supporters and activists, mostly women, gaze toward her in concern, or smile at one another as if proud to be protesting. A policeman pushes his way through the crowd, ruffling an otherwise consistently stolid and confident force. Medha Patkar's composure might be compared to that witnessed in Burmese leader Aung San Suu Kyi, when she gave rare statements during her house arrest during this period.

Medha Patkar, along with Vandana Shiva and Maneka Gandhi, then state minister for the environment, have been leading voices on the environment, both nationally in India, and internationally, representing grassroots NGOs and, in Gandhi's case, central government. In the same decades in the U.S., neither environmentalists nor, more specifically, social environmentalists, neither women nor men have attained the degree and particular quality of international respect that these Indian women have achieved. Medha Patkar has helped shape that representation in India by bringing Tribal and Dalit village women before international and national audiences with an agenda that demands local enfranchisement and global negotiations. Patkar's leadership and the NBA's socio-political stances raise many of the questions under consideration by NSM scholars during this time.

Poetry from the antidam movements raises questions that are similar to those raised in movement poetry that will be discussed in Chapter Nine. Like the United Farm Worker (UFW) and PODER and Chipko, Bhopal and MELA mobilizations and poetics, they show that collective identity questions arise repeatedly within movements as they negotiate their own self-representation and attempt to influence how they, as organizations, are viewed, and how their issues are represented in the world. For example, in *Staying Alive* Shiva presents Daya Pawar's song, sung by Maharastra's Dalit women which "captures the anti-life force of the dammed river which irrigates commodity crops like sugarcane, while women and children thirst for drinking water" (Shiva SA 195).

As I build this dam
I bury my life.
The dawn breaks
There is no flour in the grinding stone.

I collect yesterday's husk for today's meal
The sun rises
And my spirit sinks.
Hiding my baby under a basket
And hiding my tears
I go to build the dam

The dam is ready
It feeds their sugarcane fields
Making the crop lush and juicy.
But I walk miles through forests
In search of a drop of drinking water
I water the vegetation with drops of my sweat
As dry leaves fall and fill my parched yard. (Shiva SA 195)

The song suggests that the personal life of the poet is sacrificed for the dam-building not out of dedication to the cause, but rather from necessity. The poet knows that the dam will only further the chasm between those who own the sugarcane fields (those who have money, land and water) and Daya Pawar and her neighbors. The poem is built upon juxtapositions and many of the juxtapositions surround the building of the dam—the "lush and juicy" (irrigated) sugarcane as opposed to the miles of forests she walks through, for water. Collecting "yesterday's husk for today's meal" suggests a desperation at a most basic level—she turns to the part she cast off the day before when no new food materializes in the new day. She "water[s] the vegetation with drops of [her] sweat" in the fields where she works and yet when she returns to her home, there is not even moisture to sustain life—"dry leaves fall and fill [her] parched yard."

The poem makes clear that she suffers from, rather than benefits from, the dam she helps build and her suffering raises questions: when does the two steps back for one step forward of the "progress" march to the "Green Revolution" leave the poet and others like her without the stamina to even move? Is it, literally, when calories spent outweigh calories available? In thinking through such parallels, Pawar establishes an identity and value system that counters the one brought in by the dam builders. Her "driving change" is what Verta Taylor and Nancy Whittier (borrowing from Giddens (1991)) term "life politics." Dawar's song represents a politics that differs from earlier class-based "emancipatory politics" and speaks out of the context of postmodernity that Taylor and Whittier describe [52] (181). The poet challenges the "contested terrain" that her "domain of life" has become. She challenges "civil society" specifically [an] institution specializing in the transmission of cultural codes, in this case the development of industry (181). The proclamation of implied protest "I bury my life" that begins the poem is representative of a larger resistance project though the specific concerns are basic to those of Narmada Bachao Andolan and related groups.

Such "life politics" describes Medha Patkar's mission as a leader, as well. However, many of those working the Narmada Resistance do not fit the prototype that Taylor and Whittier note, in that they are not "drawn from the ranks of the middle class and are [not] well-educated" (181). Taylor and Whittier imply that middle class and high education status are prerequisites for the "struggles for the right to choose their own kind of life and identity, the production of

---

52 They describe postmodernity as "characterized by an explosion in communication, information, and new technologies associated with what Thompson (1990) terms the "mediazation of modern culture"; the rise of increasingly rationalized and abstract professional discourses of medicine, science, education, and therapy industry" (181).

knowledge and new normative guidelines, or enunciation of new discursive frameworks that confront dominant cultural codes" 181. Not only in Narmada, but also in the other sites of environmental justice activism, the struggle characterized above has developed and few of the participants fit the middle class and high education status. Perhaps this suggests that the class analysis that Taylor and Whittier make applies more because of the types of groups—LGBTQ, in much of their work—(and their class levels) that Taylor and Whittier (like many other NSM theorists) set out to write about, rather than reflecting the norm of organizations with new social movement characteristics. International comparisons may complicate easy analysis.

The Tehri dam project, though smaller than the Narmada Valley Project raised similar issues. Women activists, who have protested daily for almost twenty years have a slogan that voices their feelings against the project quite bluntly and in absolute terms: "Tehri Dam is a symbol of total destruction. (Tehri dam *sampurna vinash ka pratik hai*)" (in Shiva 1989 189).

In the following Santhal song, from Bengal, a dam and the destruction it causes are treated in detail, creating a major indictment, both poetic and empirical, against the DVC:

> Which company came to my land to open a karkhana?
> It awakened its name in the rivers and the ponds
> calling itself the DVC?
> It throws earth, dug by a machine, into the river.
> The water runs beneath.
> Roads are coming, they are giving us electricity,
> having opened the karkhana.
> The praja all question them.
> Then ask what this name belongs to.
> When evening falls they give paper notes as pay.
> Where will I keep these paper notes?
> They dissolve in the water.
> In every house there is a well which gives water
> for brinjal and cabbage.
> Every house is bounded by walls which make it look
> like a palace
> This Santhal tongue of ours has been destroyed in the district.
> You came and made this a bloody burning ghat,
> calling yourself the DVC. (in Shiva SA 190)

The poet exposes the contradictions and the lack of respect for the self-determination of the local people on the part of the DVC. Perhaps the juxtaposition is most clear when s/he observes that she is given paper notes for her land but has no place to keep the notes once the water comes, and in the water the notes will dissolve. Hence the payment is worthless to her. The obvious and accountable solution—providing her with an alternative living situation—has not even been offered to her. She understates the problem (addressing only what will happen to the money when the water comes) leaving the reader to realize the surrounding issues—what will happen to her and her neighbors, their families, livelihood, homes, and belongings when the water comes.

Vandana Shiva uses these poetics as grounds for her assertion that

> The damming of two of India's most sacred rivers, the Ganga and the Narmada, have been seriously resisted by women, peasants and tribals whose sacred sites will be destroyed and whose life-support systems are being disrupted. But the people of Narmada Valley resisting dislocation and displacement from the Sardar Sarovar and Narmada Sagar dams, or the people of Tehri, resisting the Tehri dam do not merely struggle to preserve their homeland. Their resistance is against the destruction of entire civilizations and ways of life in the very process of dam building which involves the large-scale dislocation of peoples and river systems (Shiva 189).

In other words, as Shiva, Omvedt, and others demonstrate in scholarship [and] as the people of the andolans show through poetry, song, slogan, politically active practice and storytelling, cultural tactics are used to preserve culture and the right of communities to self-define lifestyle and their relationship to the natural world. Vandana Shiva sets up the active resistance in a philosophical binary opposition to what she terms "The reductionist mind which sees 'environment' as passive and fragmented has viewed the 'recovery' of ecological balance merely as a matter of creating plantations in the command...." She makes clear, however that the resistance forces are not anti-technology but for appropriate and natural technological establishment within the historical context of a community's relationships with its natural habitat in part, its water systems.

Over the centuries, most rivers in India have been used for irrigation. Irrigation systems were created like the 'round river', taking off from the river to nurture agriculture, and going back to the river to recharge it. Modern irrigation, overpowered by the 'masculinist' trend of the large and spectacular and by the principle of overpowering the river, has created systems that work against nature's own drainage. On the one hand, this leads to a destruction of irrigated agriculture in the river valley and turns skilled farmers into 'unskilled refugees' (Shiva 189). Shiva's dichotomy is gendered, and in her masculinist—feminist delineation she slips into what might itself be critiqued for its reductionism. That said, she has used these dichotomies to illustrate why women are often most heavily impacted by environmental injustices

To avoid this problematic in Shiva's work, and more broadly, I suggest a different model of engagement: I propose that Shiva's strength does not lie in a reading as linear argument so much as a document that is "open for discussion."[53] Using the Jewish tradition that the Talmud follows, the model counters the linear track that Shiva finds in the 'masculinist opposition.' It would be valuable to see the responses of various communities to Shiva's woman/forest-centered philosophy. Indeed, a text like *Staying Alive* creates such a chorus itself. It is often the addition of poetics that keeps her own work from narrow linearities, that textures her argument. In a sense the fact that Shiva pulls information and poetics from such diverse sources is one of her greatest strengths.

In the following passage, she uses a quote from Donald Worster to recognize the familiar Western spectre distinctively and memorably, the river as beast. "The natural river has been regarded by a succession of planners as an unruly dangerous beast that must be tamed and disciplined by modern science and its commodities" (184). Shiva finds the same faulty metaphor operative in an advertisement for cement: "The river is furious, but the dam will hold. The cement is Vikram" (193). The image of the river as adversity set in stone by the cement commercial encourages the development of what Shiva terms the "crisis mind," and it creates short-term solutions that further degrade river–community relations. That cement production and its embodied energy are hefty contributors to GHGs in a time of climate change only heightens the politicized irony. Shiva notes "Taking water in large canals to arid regions to 'make the desert bloom' has been a particularly favourite masculinist project" (SA 192). This often causes the earth to leach salts. Shiva finds the

> cure to the problem of water scarcity as created by the crisis mind demands more water and more energy—a cure that at some point becomes even worse than the illness.
> The reductionist mind-set treats the river as a linear, not a circular flow, and is indifferent to the diversity of soils and topography. Its engineering feats continue to be ecological failures because it thinks against the logic of the river. (Shiva SA 192)

53 I am thinking here of the journal by this name that was produced at Nassau Community College by Hedda Marcus, Richard Newman and Jo-Anne Rondell…which draws its model from the Talmud in which the original text is accompanied by several sets of commentaries on the same page. Each page of *Open for Discussion* presents a section of the article that has been chosen for commentary and alongside it the responses to that portion of the document. A second document may be run parallel to create further "discussion." Unlike the Talmud, the commentary in *Open for Discussion* may revoke the original, at points. Shiva's work could present an invaluable "initial document."

Thus, Shiva finds the reductionist masculinist mentality at work in the cement advertisement like the technological schemes that fail to recognize the "river's logic" and she shows how, in the context of anti-river technology human and environment communities have suffered under what Shiva sees as a patriarchal Western project. "The masculinist mind, by wanting to tame and control every river in ignorance of nature's ways, is in fact sowing the seeds of large-scale desertification and famine."

Shiva provides evidence that a series of dams built in Ethiopia contributed to famine there. Turns of phrase serve her well when she tells us that rivers have become a "source of cash" rather than a "source of life" (194).

> The premium on visibility and dramatic impact, and ecological blindness toward the water cycle have facilitated the commercialisation of land and water use.... Rivers imprisoned in dams and wasted by giant hydraulic systems are prevented from performing the multi-dimensional functions of maintaining the diversity of life throughout the basin. (Shiva 195)

Shiva's technological dichotomies may seem redundant and reductionist, but to some extent this is because the technologically inappropriate development she monitors is redundant in the degradation it causes. But she always examines these projects in detail so that she gives the gendered, and race and ethnic or religious breakdown of the economic /technological divisions. Shiva finds that "the devaluation of the work of the river is associated with the devaluation of the work of women, and both arise from the commoditisation of the economy which forces violence on nature and women" (194).

Medha Patkar builds on this connection using it as a symbol for resistance when she states that "The concept of womanhood, of *mata*, [mother] has automatically got connected with this whole movement, although the concept of Narmada, as *mata* is very much part of [it]. So if the feminine tone is given, both to the leadership and the participants—then [it all] comes together" (Medha Patkar in Mies in Shiva 5).

What are the repercussions of Patkar's "feminine tone?" How does her *feminine* project overlap with various *feminist* projects? What does it mean if one contends that *in her context* Patkar escapes essentializing notions of feminine and masculine? Are these translated in Shiva's work or in the transferal to a different context is the argument rendered reductionist? Parallel questions will be raised in examining poetics from other sites. I raise them here as referent points and leave them unanswered because, as I argue above about Shiva's work, I believe they are most productive to keep issues in circulation, to generate responses, to juxtapose perspectives. Like Shiva's river, their spiraling motion must be recognized and retained.

3.4 Narratives of Social Environmentalism: Environmental Justice, Transformative Culture: PODER

"We seek to empower our communities through education, advocacy and action. Our aim is to increase the participation of communities of color in corporate and governmental decisions related to toxic pollution, economic development and their impact on our neighborhoods." This is from the mission statement of People Organized in Defense of Earth and her Resources (PODER), the community organization in Austin, Texas. In the statement, part of which is quoted on a T-shirt (as described in my preface), the group sets forth the agenda for the organization.

PODER's homebase is in the eastern part of Austin, Texas, which has traditionally been the home of African Americans and Chicano/as. PODER works from the premise of establishing environmental justice to determine the needs of neighborhoods of color and to work with the neighborhoods in activism and education campaigns. Sometimes this has meant establishing good neighbor campaigns targeting area industry (such a tactic was used with Sematech); sometimes it has meant pressuring toxic industry to move from urban, residential neighborhoods, as in the cases of the Govalle Oil Tank Farm and the Holly Power Plant.

Most of PODER's poetics promotes the grassroots organization's presence in the barrios and neighborhoods of East and South Austin, Texas. Thus, the poetics is used for education in environmental hazards in the area and about the affected neighborhoods themselves. When a problem is uncovered, PODER asks "are people experiencing ill health or other impacts of industrial intrusion?" PODER conducts surveys and holds town meetings to find out. The results are publicized to officials, the media, and the neighborhoods. PODER has sponsored toxic tours to show local politicians, media and activists who do not live in an area, the extent of the damage that is going on. As a result, the *Austin American Statesman* coverage of the oil tank farm saga, which followed a three-part exposé on Environmental Justice activism in the area, was consistent. During the height of that campaign the oil tank farm issue was covered relatively extensively by local media. The Mexican American press, both the "arts and business news" weekly *Arriba*, "Austin's oldest [continuous] Mexican-American community newspaper" and the decade old weekly *La Prensa* that "serv[es] the Hispanic community" have provided in-depth and early coverage of PODER's projects as well as national environmental justice news. (Spanish-language media coverage, however, has not been substantial.) *NOKOA: the observer*, an African American community paper, which identifies itself as "Austin's Leading

Progressive Weekly Newspaper" also gave environmental justice issues ample coverage during the mid 1990's. The *Austin Chronicle*, another progressive weekly, produced for a largely westside (predominantly white) audience also covered environmental justice issues somewhat regularly, largely through Chicano/a writers such as Jacob Daniel (Dani) Apodaca. In the mid 1990s, PODER contributed to *(sub)TEX*, an independent newspaper that was published by the (sub)TEX Collective, a group with largely university ties and/or community radio ties. Austin community radio also became a venue for PODER in the mid 1990s and since has maintained a weekly environmental radio program. Thus, media has been an important resource in the environmental justice movement in Austin and certainly a study of its effects would be worthwhile.

Coalition has been important to PODER as well. Most significantly, locally, they have worked in tandem with East Austin Strategy Team (EAST), a (predominantly African American)

> coalition of East Austin community groups and neighborhood associations formed to increase East Austin residents' participation in corporate and governmental decisions that impact on the social, economic and environmental well being of [their] community. To that end, [they] seek to empower the East Austin community and build effective leadership to address issues of environmental, social and economic justice. (EAST brochure)

Environmental justice issues that they have addressed include seeking "modification of Hazardous Materials and Industrial Expansion Zone ordinances to protect the environment and residential issues of East Austin" and "the relocation of facilities, with proper property and health compensation, for the residents adversely affected by the cluster of fuel storage tanks ('Tank Farm') in East Austin." (EAST brochure)

One of the early and most impressive fights against environmental racism that PODER undertook occurred in Govalle, a predominantly Mexican American barrio in East Austin and the site of an oil tank farm with polluting facilities that was closed by community opposition initiated by PODER in cooperation with East Austin Strategy Team (EAST). PODER member Sylvia Herrera lived in the Govalle neighborhood and first brought attention to the Tank Farm issue when she found a tiny public notice of an oil company's proposed expansion in the back of a newspaper. The company was complying with the letter of a law that requires public notice before beginning industrial expansion in a neighborhood. PODER was able to take this notice and develop the kind of notification that might have been more in keeping with the spirit of the law. Once the community consciousness was raised, the mandate was clear: the toxic tanks were not welcome. Herrera put together a slide show that presents a chronology of the events in the Tank Farm story that she narrates. During the Tank Farm struggle, presentations using video were given to the City Council and media and local government tours were held to publicize the situation.

When all oil companies except Exxon had agreed, through negotiation, to relocate, PODER and EAST organized a "Say No to Environmental Racism Boycott Exxon" campaign. Radio, TV, and newspaper programs on the issue were numerous and bumper stickers against Exxon and environmental racism began to appear around town. When all the oil companies agreed to relocate PODER and EAST held a celebrative fund-raiser. Local restaurants provided multicultural fare, young musicians performed, activists spoke, and two film-makers showed their videos of the local environmental justice struggles. In the years since, such fundraisers/ anniversary celebrations and commemorations have become annual affairs.

Soon after the 'Tank Farm' was largely resolved,[54] PODER produced illustrated educational brochures and called neighborhood meetings to discuss the Holly Street Power Plant, which, in addition to constant noise and electromagnetic field pollution, had had dangerous malfunctions in the months preceding; this history further convinced the community that the plant needed to be more environmentally designed and relocated outside of a dense urban community. When activists uncovered evidence that a wealthy westside suburban township had prohibited large-scale electrical development in its region (despite that community's substantial electricity use) it became clear that environmental racism had played a role, both in the original siting of the plant in an already established barrio, and in the continued neglect of safety measures, including failure to warn the community of the plant's substandard and dangerous aspects. When the city agreed that the plant should be shut down but set plans that would have kept the plant functioning for nearly a decade, PODER and the surrounding community launched a campaign to get the plant out more quickly.

Initially, PODER created multi-media presentations for education and information dissemination on the issues in which they've been involved and later built a website. In addition, they have put together longer manuals such as Sylvia Herrera's "Información Sobre Desechos Industriales Peligrosos y los afec-

54 The 'Tank Farm' left in its wake a community with long-term health problems, contaminated land and houses whose property values had plummeted. Its effects on its previous neighbors were not resolved with the oil company's retreat. The oil companies themselves continued to fight the community group via other venues; in the mid 1990s, two of the most prominent leaders of PODER were issued subpoenas.

tos en la Salud" that was compiled with the additional support of Primer Encuentro, Border Justice Campaign, and the Southwest Network for Environmental and Economic Justice (SNEEJ). This manual to dangerous industrial wastes in Mexico charts out dangers such as cancers, and reproductive system problems from miscarriage to abnormal fetal development. The problem toxins from various industries are identified and health effects discussed. PODER has also been concerned with environmental hazards for workers in the expanding Electronics Industry in Austin.

Three women—Susana Almanza, Sylvia Herrera and Sylvia Ledesma were especially active co-founders and leaders in PODER's early struggles. Each brought a particular set of strengths to the struggle, and all had been involved in related activist work prior to PODER's formation. Sylvia Herrera combined her community activism with scholarship in environmental health and has been able to share her studies with communities (in talks as well as documents such as "Información Sobre Desechos...)." Among other studies, she researched the environmental effects of toxic industry for women living along the Texas-Mexico border. Susana Almanza, through her work with the Texas Center for Policy Studies, has also been involved with fighting environmental racism in South Texas. Sylvia Ledesma, an educator outside of her activism, as well, developed several community education programs with innovative approaches rooted in Chicano/Mexicano culture and indigenous heritage. Susana Almanza, a member of the Brown Berets during Chicano Movement activism in Austin has spoken about the continuities of the two struggles. Both the issues around which struggle took place and the gender roles within the organizations have changed; they have shifted in priority with the change in context. Susana Almanza continues leadership in the organization as the group celebrated 30 years in existence in 2021. (https://www.poderaustin.org/celebrating-30-years)

The 1997 book, *Sacred Waters: Life-Blood of Mother Earth: Four Case Studies of High-Tech Water Resource Exploitation and Corporate Welfare in the Southwest,* which PODER authored in conjunction with other groups in SNEEJ and the Campaign for Responsible Technology demonstrates—even in its title—the links between activism and scholarship, and the sacred and the secular that are entailed in PODER's environmental justice work. For these Chicanas, their Chicano counterparts and other people who have joined with them "in defense of the earth and her resources," success leads on to the next struggle. For that is how Las Luchas Continuas.

4 Mothers in the Hood: Latinas Serve and Protect East L.A.

> Yo como madre de familia, y como residente del Este de los Angeles, seguiré luchando sin descanso por que se nos respete. Y yo lo hago con bastante [cariño] hacia mi comunidad, y digo mi comunidad, porque me siento parte de ella, quiero a mi raza como una parte de mi familia, y si Dios me permite seguiré luchando contra todos los gobernadores que quieran abusar de nosotros.
>
> Juana Gutiérrez[55]

> Instead of binary definitions of feminist and nonfeminist organizations determined by whether or not the group addresses issues of sex inequality, a multidimensional definition of feminist groups may provide for a more dynamic and contextual concept that involves class, ethnic, and gender struggles. If we open the borders of feminist frameworks and theories, we may broaden, strengthen, and enrich feminist political agendas and equate women's rights with other human rights.
>
> Mary Pardo 1995, 370

4.1 A Theoretical Framing Through Host Verification

While I found the methodologies and conceptual frames of several new social movement researchers to be beneficial as I conceptualized my approach to cultural poetics, the attentive, self-reflexive consideration of sociologist Mary Pardo, who studied the Mothers of East Los Angeles extensively during the late 1980s, was most useful. Her work on women in social organizing most precisely exemplifies the issues of representation, reproduction, and relationship, which I find central in analytical examination of women's texts. Pardo's dissertation, *Identity and Resistance: Mexican American Women and Grassroots Activism in Two Los Angeles Communities*, related articles and subsequent book, offer insight to my study of the Mothers of East L.A.[56] Furthermore, Pardo's description

---

55 Quoted in "Juana Beatriz Gutiérrez: La incansable lucha de una activista comunitaria" by Raymundo Reynoso in *La Opinión* 6 de Agosto de 1989; file received from Juana Gutiérrez, October, 1993. Approximately the same quotation is given by Mary Pardo (1990, 139); however, the "cariño" that Pardo includes is absent in Reynoso's rendition of the quote. I include it as it seems necessary. Parts of this chapter appear in the article "Chicana Strategies for Success and Survival: Cultural Poetics of Environmental Justice from the Mothers of East Los Angeles" in Frontiers: A Journal of Women Studies, vol. xviii, Number 2, 1997. 48–72.

56 Particularly "Doing it for the Kids" (1990) and book *Mexican American Women: Identity and Resistance in Two Mexican American Communities.*

https://doi.org/10.1515/9783111041575-005

of her relationship to the women who were the subjects of her research, and her relationship to the research itself has proven invaluable in helping me think through my role as producer of academic texts on activist poetics. Pardo's theoretical foundation in new ethnographic and participant-observer frames contributes extensively to discussions of ethnographic narratives, and several concepts are applicable.

Mary Pardo explains how she activated the concept of "host verification" by giving copies of her articles to the activists about whom she had written.[57] In one instance, the critical response that Pardo received expanded her "research experience [with] what before had been an abstract point raised in the review of the literature on methodology. It heightened [her] awareness of the varied experiences and interpretations held by the women and in turn compelled [her] to further 'texture' the experiences and analysis" (I&R 1990, 84). Pardo's procedure underscores the importance of follow-up communication between researcher and social actors that has been procedurally omitted from much social science investigation. Additionally, her work documents empirical evidence for an important tenet in my own study—the importance of identifying the varying perspectives of a diversity of actors and investigating and reporting this spectrum in detail to break down binary generalizations.

One of the reasons that Pardo decided to undertake her study of activism among women of Mexican descent was "that throughout much sociological writing, women, ethnic/racial minority group members, and working-class men and women were often either absent from the discourse or became the victims of social problems rather than active participants in social relations" (I&R 1990 54). Her amplification of the problem correlates with the lack of adequate and appropriate representation, as noted by Aldan Morris, especially in relation to race and ethnicity issues, and by Myra Marx Ferree and Patricia Yancey Martin, predominantly in terms of gender issues.[58] Pardo fully addresses both race and gender issues in the context of Mexican American women's experiences, facilitating the de(con)struction of the activist/academic, researcher/subject dichotomy. Pardo's sociological analysis presents the critical perspectives of activists, seeing the women *as actors*, not merely as research subjects. Thereby, Pardo

---

57 Pardo quotes Schatzman and Strauss in defining the concept of "host verification" which she borrows from their work. As they explain it "host verification" is a means by which to establish whether the "hosts recognize the validity of the events upon which the interpretation rests" (in Pardo 1990, 82).

58 See, for instance Morris in *Frontiers in Social Movement Theory* (1992) and Ferree and Martin in *Feminists Organizations: Harvest of the New Women's Movement* (199).

begins to remedy this exclusionary phenomenon by viewing her subjects as actors resisting victimization. Similarly, my study is designed to include the activists as actors primarily through their cultural poetics.

At the same time, I realize the limitations of subjectivity. Pardo makes the extremely important point that the presentation of information is always partial—both in the sense of incomplete and in the sense that it is shaped by the producer—she states that "[i]n the end, it is the researcher and her selection of informants, editorial decisions, arrangement of quotes, and analysis that mete out significance (Sacks 1989; Mascia-Lees, et al. 1989) and translation is always interpretive and partial" (I&R 1990, 86). Following Pardo's example, researchers must apply this fact, first and foremost to their own work. Only when we own our own polemics vis-à-vis our projects will our work on social representations from others be credible.

Given these parameters, my study of the Mothers of East Los Angeles's poetics analyzes MELA's contribution to conceptions of women's social environmental politics. A synopsis of MELA's origin, purpose and activities leads into consideration of textual materials generated by and/or about their organization. Strong self-representation in their community action graphics, demonstrations, brochures, letters, and interviews, and in the articles that they have generated in a broad range of publications are germane to my study. MELA's ally-building with other grassroots groups, institutions such as the academy, the corporation, and the media, demonstrates the members' poetic and practical strategies for success and survival.

4.2 Philosophical Historiography of The Mothers of East L.A.

> In the Eastside Los Angeles barrio, women refashioned ethnic and gender traditions into strategies for resistance against a state prison and a toxic waste incinerator. Symbols of Mexican culture textured the mobilization efforts of "Mothers of East L.A."[59] The women rooted their theories about grassroots activism in their work as wives and mothers. They used traditional social identities in community action rather than being confined by them. Women's social identities became something new as they entered city-wide political arenas.
>
> Mary Pardo (1990, x)

59 MELA (and occasionally MOELA) is the acronym used initially by the group. When they split into two organizations the second, though seemingly most active group, changed their name to the Spanish and added their parish identity—Madres del Este de Los Angeles, Santa Isabel (Las Madres). Therefore, when I refer to events after the split, and I am not specifying either branch, I use both acronyms.

Despite a history of activism and mobilization, "little has been written on the dynamics of [women's political] participation" (Pardo 1990, 5). While Mary Pardo makes her claim in the context of sociological study of Latina activism, it could be applied in other disciplines. Verta Taylor and Nancy Whittier address an extension of ignored histories in terms of the gaps particular to resource mobilization and political process theory (in Morris and Mueller, FSMT 104). They cite a 1990 study by Steven M. Buechler that analyzes "organizational forms" in U.S. women's movement history. While the study works toward filling the gap in research focusing on women's social histories, "like most work in the resource mobilization tradition, it overlooks the values and symbolic understandings created by discontented groups in the course of struggling to achieve change" (Taylor and Whittier, FSMT 106). In addressing this hiatus in qualitative and symbolic aspects of the mobilization of knowledge, the details of women's activism must be fleshed out, and the contrasts and similarities of their experiences and beliefs described. I utilize such an approach in the following narration about their cultural poetics and activities of the Mothers of East Los Angeles (MELA) and their subsequent branch, Las Madres de Este de Los Angeles, San Isabel.

Grassroots organizing, as undertaken by MELA and similar groups, is often an alternative means of political participation that—compared to electoral politics—is more accessible to marginalized groups (I&R 6). In the U.S. as increasing numbers of people become disenchanted with the inadequate democracy of the two-party system, and as voting is not an option for an increasing number of disenfranchised peoples (including some who have been convicted of a felony, are immigrants without citizenship, and those who are not provided with first language voting facilities), alternative political options become increasingly important. However, the chronology of MELA involvements suggests that as the group became active in the vital nonelectoral juncture, their influence on electoral politics grew along with their influence in other sociopolitical arenas. For instance, years after the initial articles covered MELA's early grassroots activism, several articles on electoral politics in the *L.A. Times* seek opinions from MELA on issues extending beyond their fields of activism. William A. Gamson believes that "American media discourse systematically discourages the idea that ordinary citizens can alter the conditions and terms of their daily lives through their own actions. But this message comes through more equivocally on some issues, and in some special contexts a sense of collective agency is even nurtured" (in SM&C 97). MELA has been able to foster an unusual number of "special contexts" and in so doing has created a credible group persona vis á vis the Chicano community in Los Angeles, and more broadly.

Pardo finds that "the experiences of women as wives and mothers are intimately linked to their community activism. However, [these findings] add that just as community activism is tied to a wom[a]n's traditional role in the family, her community activism has the potential to transform her role in the family. The relationship is not unidirectional" (1990, 24). Thus, grassroots political involvement for women like the Mothers of East Los Angeles offers more than an extension of the domestic role; rather, it *transforms* that role (Pardo I&R, 4). Such a transformed social role has served MELA and their Las Madres branch, as they have successfully utilized university, media, "good neighbor" corporations, and progressive governmental forces. MELA activists illustrate how social environmentalism is a particularly salient issue for promoting such a transformation by linking the symbolic and practical relevance of environmental justice to the protection, nurturance, and caretaking of the family—be it nuclear, extended, "nontraditional," neighborhood, or raza. MELA women "manipulated the boundaries of 'mother' to include social and political community activism and redefined the word to include women who are not biological mothers" (1990, 140). When a young Latina qualified her presence in the group as a resident, not a mother "Erlinda Robles replied, 'When you are fighting for a better life for children and "doing" for them, isn't that what mothers do? So you don't have to have children to be a mother'" (1990, 140). Indeed, Aurora Castillo, an octogenarian in 1995, when she won the Goldman Environmental Award, is MELA's most esteemed, nonbiological mother. In some cases, the relative freedom from birthing and rearing children may facilitate activism as a community mother. Before describing these women's roles, however, a summary of MELA's formation as an environmental justice group and their subsequent projects will demonstrate how MELA's poetics and politics have garnered respect from many quarters.

MELA was formed in 1985 to protest plans for a proposed prison in their East L.A. barrio.[60] While the exact chronology of events that led to the inception of the organization varies somewhat, two separate outside players clearly aided in initiating the group. When City Councilwoman, Gloria Molina found government unresponsive to her concerns about placing a state prison in a neighbor-

60 The term "barrio" is not often used in the grassroots writings I examined. While I might speculate that most popular media, alternative media, and academic reports were considering the possible negative connotations the word might have for the largely non-Latina/o audiences, I use the term in my study to be consistent with its usage in Chican@ literary studies. Furthermore, I believe that the Spanish term, in the context of Chicana/o cultural studies stands "against the grain" of a stereotype and undermines it, much as movement and academic use of the term "Chicano" redefines earlier negative connotations.

hood with 34 schools, she called a meeting with several residents of Boyles Heights to inform them of the plans for yet another detention center nearby. Juana Beatriz Gutiérrez, co-founder and president of MELA's Las Madres Santa Isabel branch marks this meeting as the first she heard about the proposed state prison (Pardo 1990 138).

Meanwhile, Father John Moretta, an Italian American priest for one of the neighborhood parishes called together a group of women in his parish. "Does MELA mean anything bad in Spanish?" he asked. When the Latinas replied in the negative, the name "Mothers of East Los Angeles" was adopted.[61] Moretta proposed the name for the group as an adaptation of "Las Madres de la Plaza de Mayo" the Argentine women's group that demonstrated for the return of their children who (were) *havían desaparecido*, disappeared.

Initially, at Moretta's suggestion the women also wore white scarves at demonstrations to identify their connection to the Argentine women who wore white mantillas. While it achieved a desired effect in encouraging media attention, it did not portray the message that the East L.A. group wanted. Some Latinas felt they looked like "poor homebodies" or "las obligadas" (the submissive ones) (Pardo 1995, 361). One woman expressed her personal dislike for the scarves because she said, "frankly I associate wearing a scarf with doing housecleaning" (Pardo 1995, 362). Another felt that it made the demonstrators look like a religious group. While they chose rhetorical symbols that transferred their influence in the home to the community in terms of providing a safe and clean environment, they express the clear desire not to transfer either the manual drudgery of "housework" or their conventional submissive roles to their public personas. Variations on the scarf tied under the chin were created as both women and men began wearing them as headbands, armbands or around their necks. Thus, the women reshaped, and eventually dropped the symbolic fashion. Their responses to the scarves as evoking a religious sect suggests a link to the traditional head-coverings that Catholic and some Protestant denominations of Christianity require of their orthodox women followers when in church. The quiet rebellion against the head coverings may be one way of establishing boundaries for religious traditions in social movement space. Though part of MELA's group identity stems from Mexican Catholicism, MELA activists transform both domestic roles and the shape religious ideologies take.[62]

---

61 Juana Gutiérrez set the date for the inception of MELA as May 24, 1985 (interview with author, October 1993). & Nexus Lexus article 88/100 MELA search.

62 María Elena Lucas offers parallel transformations of Mexican Catholic religious experience into social justice struggle in the context of farmworker organizing. For instance, she makes

While the scarf imagery transplanted by Father Moretta proved to offer "foreign" and misread associations and was discarded when it had outlived usefulness, the symbology of motherhood—also generated in the perceived connection with the South American women's political group—was expanded to fit the political context in which the women were operating. The Argentinian imagery may have somewhat ironically served the Mothers in establishing credibility among liberal audiences who are often more familiar with and sympathetic toward those suffering from political repression in Latin America than East Los Angeles. That said, long term coalition building is not served by patronizing sympathies; ultimately, MELA's agenda was served by asserting comfortable self-identities that fit them. Thus, the move away from the scarves also may indicate the degree to which MELA became self-defining as a political women's group despite its respect for Father Moretta's initial leadership and continued support. MELA activists' practical flexibility with the manipulation of cultural symbols is also evident in relationships. The women sustained their familial relations and responsibilities while using their more flexible schedules as non-wage-earning homemakers "as a resource in their work as community activists and leaders" (Pardo 1995, 363).[63]

Not long after the group had formed around the prison siting issue, a toxic waste incinerator was slotted for Vernon, an industrial town bordering East L.A. MELA immediately expanded its agenda to tackle the blatant environmental racism at the heart of the decision, and the group became more than a single-issue organization. Other political supporters, like State Assemblywoman Lucille Roybal-Allard, joined forces with MELA to fight the incinerator and subsequent toxic intrusions, thereby creating a network of concern that incorporated a wide range of political bases, including church parishes, environmental groups, university student groups, and state and city legislatures. While the initial concern—the siting of a new prison—is not likely to be perceived as an environmental justice issue and some aspects of the stance might divide community members, environmental justice became the common ground for most of the subsequent issues that MELA took on.

---

picketing more acceptable to the farmworker women when she tells them "it's holy; it is like baptism" See discussion in Chapter Seven.

63 This arrangement also allowed the women in general to avoid conflict in their families and encouraged their husbands to demonstrate support when marches and other mass mobilizations were planned. The women planned their schedules around their children's school schedules, taking the children along to meetings and mobilizations when they were not in school. From similar childhood experiences accompanying both my parents, I can't overemphasize the awareness value of such exposure for their children.

When I visited with cofounder and president, Juana Gutiérrez in October of 1993, the group had been involved in several timely environmental justice issues including the struggle against a proposed oil pipeline that would have curved out from the ocean across East L.A., lengthening the dangerous project in order to avoid the upper class, predominately white neighborhoods of West L.A while running three feet under Hollenbeck Junior High School. MELA had demonstrated against the urban spraying of the pesticide malathion and had been to Kettleman, California, to stand in solidarity with the rural struggle against pesticide use there. The women had made trips to Sacramento to lobby the legislature, and they had developed pro-active solidarity with several other California groups struggling for environmental equity. A flyer, promoting the group, lists their victories in white print on a black background. At the top of the page, large letters proclaim Juana Gutierrez's declaration: "After you experience a community victory, the pursuit for justice is no longer voluntary, it is obligatory." The "victories in... battles in defense of our community" include stopping the 1987 Lanser incinerator project; participation in a citywide coalition to oppose the oil company pipeline; the 1989 abandonment "under pressure" of the Vernon "first of its kind toxic incinerator;" and forcing the 1990 halt to plans for a Chem-Clear hazardous waste treatment plant. Las Madres concluded, "[t]he Mothers have also marched with César Chávez to protest pesticides, lobbied for the Mexican preservation of Olvera Street, assisted in Voter Registration and Citizenship drives and partic[i]pated in numerous grassroot[s] political camp[ai]gns." These activities demonstrate the broad network of mutual support that the organization had developed by the time the flyer was made; they had built alliances with both Chicano groups like the United Farm Workers and environmental groups like Greenpeace.

At the time of my visit, their most recent march had been in support of renaming to Avenida César Chávez a stretch of road that runs west from East L.A. in commemoration of the UFW leader with whom MELA had worked closely. Indeed, one of the newspaper clippings that Juana Gutiérrez copied for me contains a photo of César Chávez walking with Martin Sheen in a grape boycott march; alongside it, the next photo shows the mothers with a banner reading "Madres de East L.A. Santa Isabel Contra Pesticidas." [64] MELA's presence in the

64 The photo appeared in *La Opinion*'s Metropolis section, Sábado 21 de Julio de 1990. An accompanying article by Marcelo M. Zuviría opens as follows: "El Sindicato de Trabajadores Agrícolas (UFW), cuyos líderes dicen que la uva está contaminada con insecticidas, intensificó su compaña contra el consumo de esa fruta, al declarar un boicot total contra la cadena de

streets, originally marked by their white scarves, continues as predominantly middle-aged and older Latinas, accompanied by children, youth, and babies are joined by students, male supporters and an occasional legislator or movie star, all voicing their resistance to toxic invaders.

Banners and signs proclaim their stands in English and in Spanish, for language is MELA's battleground in several senses. One of their most basic demands, a common one among grassroots organizers, is that when a project is slotted for placement in a community, the community be informed in its own language. Hence, meetings in Spanish—and in at least one instance in the area, Chinese—are a prerequisite to any show of good faith by outsiders. A common understanding of language expectations for other-than-English native speakers creates ground for coalition even when languages of those involved differ.

The importance of alliances forged between MELA and other groups is apparent in media representations, and in their own writings, just as the importance of alliances is established in New Social Movement literature. MELA has played an important role in the umbrella environmental justice group, Southwest Network for Economic and Environmental Justice, (SNEEJ). The leaders of MELA/Las Madres offer political clout not only to their own struggles, but also to other struggles with which they choose to ally themselves. This was evident in the large number of media articles that mentioned MELA as a community-based presence in events ranging from elections to proposed cuts in medical facilities to police brutality.

The English-language press has published a substantial number of articles on MELA. Building from two articles on MELA from 1986, which appeared on the computer news collection service Nexus Lexus, to a high of 27 articles in 1992, when the press, most often the *L.A. Times*, ran articles on MELA activities and referred to MELA's position on a wide variety of issues.[65] This indicates the significance of their role in local politics by the early 1990s. MELA's place in the progressive environmental press has expanded with the growing—though sometimes ambivalent—promotion of environmental justice by mainstream

---

mercados Tianguis, tal cual lo hizo el mes pasado con la cadena Vos, se anunció ayer al mediodía en un acto en el City Park de la ciudad de Montebello donde se contó con la participación del dirigente sindical César Chávez y el actor Martin Sheen."

65 The Nexus Lexus (computer news collection service) collected the following number of articles that included reference to MELA in the respective years: 1986-2; 1987-1; 1988-6; 1989-7; 1990-24; 1991-17; 1992-27; 1993-16.

environmentalists, as evidenced in the large number of publications that published articles on environmental justice in the 1990s.[66]

Spanish-language press, especially L.A.'s *La Opinión* covered MELA with an insider's perspective. For instance, an early article entitled "Juana Beatriz Gutiérrez: La incansable lucha de una activista comunitaria" praises MELA's organizing skills as mothers. Raymundo Reynoso, the reporter, remarks on a demonstration that he attended: "lo admirable fue presenciar que los participantes, eran casi en su totalidad madres de familia" (Acceso 1 in *La Opinión*, 6 de Agosto de 1989). Reynoso explains his admiration for MELA as follows: "Con el tiempo, ellas, las iniciadoras de MELA, se convertirían en el alma, vida y corazón de un movimiento popular que ha sido motivo de análisis, que ha aportado experiencias y métodos de lucha a otras organizaciones comunitarias, y cuya existencia y actividades han trascendido las fronteras del barrio de la cuidad, del estado y del país" (Ibid). Reynoso's rave commentary is voiced from his vantage point in the demonstration itself and he centers MELA's activities in the barrio, observing how MELA's significance has grown from local to global; he speaks from familiarity with both worlds. The second half of the article lists names of those mothers and the priests involved with MELA and other community activists who have offered their support. In this passage only men are named. "Pero gracias a Dios el padre John Moretta, de la Iglesia Resurrección, vino a nosotros y él fue quien nos organizó y nos dio el nombre de Madres del Este de Los Angeles. Sumándose al padre Moretta, vino el apoyo de las cámaras de comercio de Lincoln Heights, Boyles Heights, y gente muy importante como Steve Kasten de Lincoln Heights, Frank Villalobos de Barrio Planners, José Luis García y muchos otros que fueron algo muy valioso para las madres en esta lucha, y quienes nos apoyaron económica y moralmente" (*Acceso* 6).[67] Reynoso details how MELA's struggle is the community's struggle. In naming the players, Reynoso establishes accountability with his audience, which presumably also has close ties to the L.A. barrio. His journalism acts as publicity for environmental justice organizing in ways that the English-language media rarely does.

Reynoso's article was written relatively early in MELA's development. Since that time MELA matured, and its focus changed. MELA/Las Madres, like the Chipko Movement and others, has moved from early, almost entirely resistance work—blocking both symbolic and literal toxic intrusions by demonstrating in

66 For an extensive treatment of MELA in a "mainstream" environmental context see Dick Russell, "Environmental Racism," *Amicus Journal* 11:2 (spring 1989): 22–32.

67 Frank Villalobos, an architect, is mentioned repeatedly as a supporter of MELA and other community activism.

response to crisis—to initiating structural change and sustainable, appropriate development projects in the community. (Their brochure announcing the one-year anniversary for the ULFT (Ultra Low Flush Toilet) Water Conservation Project lists educational, health, and community improvement projects that are being supported by the project's profits. An *L.A. Times* article from June 25, 1995, on MELA student scholarships, another means of community improvement, reports that MELA boasted 300 members.[68]

My awareness of the Mothers of East L.A. had begun when I heard interviews with members on National Public Radio in the spring of 1993. In discussing her insider-outsider relationship to MELA, Mary Pardo explains how initial research led to her own participation in their "communication network."

> After I attended more hearings and meetings, I experienced how the communication network functioned. The phone bank now included my name and number. The women informed me about hearings, events, meetings, and demonstrations. In one community, the women saw me as someone who could bring additional attention to their cause. This did occur. After I made a presentation at [a] conference at UCLA, a reporter in the audience asked me for my contacts and followed up with a story for National Public Radio. (1990, 74)

While I have not verified that the program, I heard was the one initiated through the NPR reporter's contact with Mary Pardo, the possibility of that concrete connection points to the success of the very "communication network" that Pardo observes, and it suggests the crucial links for grassroots, barrio-based organizing that may be formed in conjunction with the university and progressive media. Furthermore, the "communication network" that Pardo describes is replicated in my own experience with environmental justice activism. When, during the autumn following my initial radio exposure to the group, I took a research trip to Los Angeles to learn more about MELA and other California groups, UCLA students with connections to Chicano communities, as well as students involved in the environmental movement provided me with the contacts to find previous studies of MELA activities and to visit Las Madres headquarters at the home of Juana Beatriz Gutiérrez. Students have also been contracted to research information needed by the Mothers. For example, a UCLA master's thesis in Architecture and Urban Planning entitled "A Community at Risk: the Environmental Quality of Life in East Los Angeles" was undertaken by Cynthia Pansing, Hali Rederder and David Yale at the request of MELA. MELA is

---

68 in "Community News: East: East Los Angeles; Mothers Group Awards Scholarships" by Erin J. Aubry, *Los Angeles Times* 6-25-1995, 7.

acknowledged as the "client" for this project, which "documents the cumulative effects of an industrial belt on residential areas in East Los Angeles" and the "important elements of the aggregate land use, political and legal patterns that have led to an intense concentration of unwanted projects in and around unincorporated East Los Angeles" (6).

MELA/Las Madres have developed bridges that allow for mutual support networks between grassroots communities and students that make them distinctive. For example, the UCLA environmental newsletter *Shades of Green* presented the Mothers of East Los Angeles in their "Local Heroes" column (April & May 1992). The Mothers were on campus at UCLA to support the Chicano hunger strikers who were calling for the initiation of Chicano Studies. For many MELA members, these relationships have been fostered by the very experience of mothering itself. For instance, Juana Gutiérrez's children boast so many degrees in higher education that an *L.A. Times* article suggests they could "practically start a university among themselves."[69] Education was a priority the Gutiérrezes held for their children, although Juana Gutiérrez did not seek further schooling after finishing eighth grade in México before immigrating to California. Ricardo Gutiérrez, Juana's husband, commented on the stereotypes that the media perpetrate and how the Gutiérrezes attempted to intervene through their responses:

> We were interviewed by a reporter from the *Sacramento Bee*. He was telling us that we were so lucky[,] that there were so few families like us that had children who went to college. I said whenever you want to meet more like us, tell me and I will get a dozen families around here. Because their kids are professional and went to school with my kids. We have educated people in the community, but the press always gives the bad news the coverage. (Pardo 1990, 292)

Juana expanded on the race and class stereotypes that they were correcting for the reporter: "Some people think that east LA is the worst area with nothing but gangs and people with tat[t]oos and that is not true!" (in Pardo 1990, 292).[70]

Media reports that focus on the educational and community justice achievements of the Gutiérrez family reflect a wider media-revision agenda on the part of MELA/Las Madres as a whole. The media, in depicting the agenda and nature of MELA/Las Madres, reform (albeit too often through cultural stere-

---

69 The institutions from which they graduated include UC Santa Barbara (twice) and Princeton (twice).

70 An element of Gutiérrez' response may engage in its own societal stereotype. Like wall art, tattoos are an often-demonized artform, perhaps partially because it is an artform that has been developed and finessed in prisons.

otypes), their usual practices and revise the depiction of East L.A. as dangerous and dirty. An underlying strategy for MELA is to educate outsiders about the barrio by telling potential sympathizers the obvious, but often unacknowledged, facts—that when incinerators and pipelines and prisons are sited in East L.A., they will encroach on healthy family neighborhoods.

MELA's self-identity as a group of *mothers* allows them a symbolic base that demands a wider span of respect. More than perhaps any other institution, motherhood is at least symbolically revered, and this respect allows for the communication that Juana Gutiérrez finds so important. Furthermore, the value system that emphasizes the community caretaking is transferred to the next generation resulting in augmentation: the Mothers have been able to solicit resources from their grown children. For instance, several of Juana and Ricardo Gutiérrez' children work for Las Madres in various professional capacities. One daughter, Beatriz Mojarro is an artist who is designing computer graphics for the group to use in publicity, education, and consciousness-raising.

Las Madres' most prevalent computer graphics, used on handbills, brochures, business cards etc., also foreground the mother-child relationship. The symbol—a circle-shaped image of union between Madonna and child, the silhouette of a mother holding up a child in the sweep of a rebozo that drapes down from the mother's head, across her arms, and around the child—evokes the religious aspects of the union. The swaddling cloth on the baby suggests the holy nature of the child to those familiar with the Christian iconography of the swaddled baby Jesus. For the largely Mexican Catholic barrio as well as the largely Christian society at large the cloth sanctifies the child; likewise, for those of Mexican descent the cloth over the mother's head could represent the indigenous tradition of the rebozo or the Mexican Catholic tradition of the cape worn by the santas. The image implicitly recalls the ineptness with which researchers have addressed the roles of religion in grassroots activism. Such images, which provide both religious and political significance are usually described as conveying either religious meaning or the politicized secular meaning, effacing the more complex combined significance.

In addition to the symbolic weight of motherhood put forth in the poetics, MELA produces the social institution of mothering/homemaking as work that promotes political activism in two ways: 1) by making use of the flexible schedule allows for it, and 2) the commitment to family easily transfers to political commitment, especially when it involves issues like environmental justice that so overtly endanger the health and wellbeing of the family. Mary Pardo tells of one of the Mothers who is a long-time resident "on a street just below a very large arched concrete bridge built in the 1940s. Her block, lined with small, single-story homes, begins at the foot of the bridge. ... This scene, or one similar appears in numerous films that focus on gang violence in East Los Angeles" (1990 292). The Mother narrates the story of her encounter with Hollywood on this site, explaining how the film industry perpetuates the stereotypes of East L.A. by figuratively and literally dirtying the neighborhood. "They did a lot of filming near the bridge where I live. They would come and throw trash and write on the walls to make it look terrible. The films they make are all about gangs and shooting and it is not like that." (in Pardo 1990, 293). The women in the area disrupted the film crews that were disrupting and degrading their neighborhood: "We would come by honking the car horns. And, you could hear them saying, 'Cut, Cut!' I would go out and call real loud, 'ARMANDO! DANNY! EDUARDO' [The names of her three sons]. Some women would yell 'why not put something good about us?'" (in Pardo 1990, 293). Finally, the women protested to their councilman, Art Snyder, and the film crews' visits were less frequent—until after Snyder left office (Pardo 1990, 293). In the informal protests against the film crews' occupation of the community, Robles uses a tactic—calling for her sons—that is part of her role as a mother.

The Latina's performances are important even if they are conducting only antagonistic, low-level warfare because they call attention to the media's "dirtying" of the communities in East L.A., which affects the barrio in detrimental ways. The filmic representation of the barrio as violent and dirty not only reiterates stereotypical misrepresentations, but it also contributes to the communities' vulnerability to the toxic effects of environmental and other racisms. The physical invasion of the barrio becomes the moment in which the women of the barrio challenge the long-standing mainstream symbolic attack, popularized by media and dominant culture. MELA activists understand well how negative imagery can serve the interests of "urban development." The pattern is well worn: allow conditions of disintegration to worsen, label it 'blighted,' condemn property, purchase it with federal urban renewal funds, sell it to developers, and allot mass federal subsidies for its improvement. (Parson 1982; Mollenkopf 1983; Logan and Molotch 1987) (Pardo 1990, 294–295).

Additionally, if a community is perceived of as disintegrating and dirty, a polluting corporation is more likely to see it as an easy and unnoticed victim for toxic, industrial colonization. As Pansing et al observe, the literal dirtying of the neighborhood on any level creates a symbolic invasion: "For [MELA], the California Reception Center and the Vernon Hazardous Waste Incinerator symbolically and physically invade their community, continuing long-term deterioration of the residents' quality of life. These two facilities are only symptoms of racial and economic discrimination with far-reaching political, social and environmental dimensions" (Pansing et al 8). In response, MELA transformed the role of "keeping house" by taking it into the streets. In such sites of resistance, the Mothers demonstrate what the first chair of the community organization UNO, states: "As homemakers we know if you don't do it, it is not going to get done. I guess when we come out into the community, we bring that same feeling.... if we don't get it moving no one else will" (in Pardo, 108). At the same time, lest we forget the extent of the transformation of that domestic role, it is important to remember the comment of the Latina who rejected the scarves because she felt it made her feel like she was housecleaning—something she did not want to be doing on the street.

Aurora Castillo, a founding member of MELA, an octogenarian, and one of the 1995 Goldman award winners, though not a biological mother herself, identifies MELA members' responses to neighborhood invasions as a kind of maternal instinct.[71] While she has not given birth to or raised children herself, she clearly takes on the image of mother as a powerful archetype with which to serve her ethnic community. She has been quoted in numerous publications as telling the press that "The Hispanic mother will fight like a lioness, for her children [who] are at risk. Our children were at risk so we fought like lioness[es]." [72] However, MELA did not stop at protecting their own streets; they have extended the role of the lioness and made her charge in the courtroom and corporate boardroom.

In 1979, Gary T. Marx pointed out that the multinational corporation was a "fascinating and almost completely unstudied source of external mobilization and constraint;" he predicted, correctly, that "increased overt and covert intervention efforts may be expected" (Zald and McCarthy 1979, 108). A cursory survey of new social movement theory suggests that the major studies of local community organization—global corporation relations that Marx proposed did not materialize. However, the corporate—community juncture is a vital point of contention, conflict, and occasionally, cooperation; a study of this juncture is at least as timely, decades later, as it was in 1979. Indeed, the interface between community and corporation can be considered a borderland as defined in some contemporary "borderland studies."[73] Or to borrow Mary Louise Pratt's concep-

71 The prize carries with it a monetary reward of $75,000.

72 This example is from a NEWS byline by Laurie Wolfenschmidt on April 30, 1995.

73 Studies of borderlands in the social sciences and literary studies abound; for one example the 117th Annual Spring Meeting of the American Ethnological Society (Austin, Texas: April 26-29, 1995) was entitled "Border Anthropologies." Thus, the term "borderland studies" seems

tualization, community concerns and corporate concerns intersect in "contact zones."

Gloria Anzaldúa's concept of being a bridge, which evokes connections initiated by members of a historically disempowered community with members of a dominant group as a means of dismantling domination, is activated in the interstices between community and corporation by the Mothers of East LA. [74] The history of that conjunction is narrated in a brochure that commemorates the first anniversary of the ULFT Water Conservation Project, that was developed jointly by Las Madres del Este de Los Angeles, Santa Isabel and the CTSI Corporation.

> In the summer of 1992 at Bakersfield, California, Juana Gutiérrez, President of Las Madres del Este de Los Angeles, was once again re-iterating our communities['] desire for self-determination when her call was answered by Jim Kraft of an Irvine based Corporation, CTSI. Seizing this rarest of opportunities, Las Madres directed their full efforts to the development of a unique public agency-private corporation-community based organization partnership. [75]

The resources from the corporation and the local government provided Las Madres with the opportunity to become a more proactive group. Having proved their ability to effect change through resistance to toxic intrusions into their community, they broadened their agenda of "self- determination" to include community-based development.

In its first year, the UTLF Water Conservation Project provided free ultra-low-flush toilets to East L.A. residents and generated 27 jobs with "medical coverage and salaries well beyond the poverty levels of many inner-city employment projects" ("Si se Puede"). Furthermore, funds raised by the ULFT Water Conservation Program have been contributed to an elementary school, a high school, and an adult education program in Boyles Heights, to undertake an immunization project for children from birth to two years of age, and to initiate

appropriate for the interdisciplinary focal point on political, social, cultural, and other geographic and semantic intersections that range from the analysis of García Canclini "of the border as a laboratory of postmodernity" (Barrera Herrera Abstract 22) to the study of "immigration wars," from the history of land disputes to the edges of cyberspace (Lisa-Justine Hernandez dissertation prospectus, 1995).

74 Anzaldúa developed this concept, implicit in the titles of the collection of essays *This Bridge Called My Back* extensively in a lecture at UT, Austin in the early 1990s.

75 "Si se Puede!" MADRES DEL ESTE DE LOS ANGELES SANTA ISABEL, ULFT Water Conservation Project 1st Anniversary Celebration, July 31, 1993.

a Community Youth Graffiti Abatement Project that hires youth to paint over graffiti for local businesses.[76]

Elsa López, a MELA member illustrates how the water abatement project contributes to environmental wellbeing both locally and on a wider scale in a letter to the *L.A. Times* concerning Mono Lake. Additionally, she refutes the largely erroneous stereotype that environmental justice groups are not interested in preserving the natural world but only in protecting people, illustrating instead the interconnections between wilderness and urban preservation:

> I am writing on behalf of the Mothers of East Los Angeles-Santa Isabel. This is a community-based organization that sponsors programs to help our community by creating jobs, expanding resources and fostering programs such as water conservation.
> Reading your article, it seemed that Southern California is going to lose out if Mono Lake is protected. I believe that we are going to win. Our organization and eight groups in Southern California are doing our part to conserve enough water so that we can protect Mono Lake and still meet our water needs. Through our ultra-low flush toilet exchange program, we have conserved 6.5 billion gallons of water per year and added economic stimulus of $3 million into the inner city.
> This past summer we took 25 inner-city children to camp at Mono Lake. Many of them had never had such an experience and Mono Lake's natural beauty made a big impact on their lives. We all stand to gain if Mono Lake is protected. (Lopez 10-2-1994)

Representing MELA, López intervenes in a long-standing debate and calls the *L.A. Times* on misrepresentations that have a long history. William L. Kahrl's *Water and Power* is a study of Southern California's water controversies that describes the roles of various sectors of the city in the Mono Lake controversy as it played out in the 1970s when earlier concern over the water levels in the lake was voiced. MELA's interest in preserving the lake has precedence in that the campaign to save Mono Lake was initiated by another urban group, "an Audubon Society chapter in far-off Santa Monica which had a greater concern for the future of the lake than local county officials initially exhibited" (431). Furthermore, the *Los Angeles Times* stance—that "Southern California is going to lose if Mono Lake is protected," which Lopez contends is erroneous, is also part of a history of misrepresentation. According to Kahrl, the "*Los Angeles Times* has generally cooperated with the department line, portraying the op-

---

76 Graffiti abatement may again be seen as taking the homemaker role to the streets. My view of the mainstream "demonization" of graffiti creates misgivings for me about this project. However, I understand that the graffiti clean-ups for MELA and the barrio are differently nuanced than those perpetrated by national/ mainstream campaigns against graffiti; thus, within the setting it may be entirely appropriate.

position of the Owens Valley as the reflection of little more than a misguided concern for plants over the needs of the people of Los Angeles" (434). [77] López's letter defines the barrio's willingness to do their part in water conservation, a declaration which, at least symbolically, gives the onus of accountability to corporate water users to do the same. Additionally, Kahrl's following assertion is important to our understanding of MELA's water conservation project as a whole:

> More than the discovery of gold and oil, the construction of the railroad and freeway systems, and the rise of film and aerospace industries, the development of water has shaped the patterns of settlement within California and laid the basis for the modern prosperity of the nation's richest and most populous state. No problems for the future hold so great a potential for changing the quality of life in California as the current controversies over water policy.... In the story of the aqueduct, therefore, we confront not only the foundation of the modern metropolis of Los Angeles but the origins as well of California as we know it today. (viii)

While low flush toilets suggest the everyday mundane, the project represents MELA's intervention in one of the most vital and precedent setting controversies in the state and by extension, the nation.

The "rarest of opportunities" in which Las Madres is engaged with CTSI marks a dynamic union that must be studied and lauded, for such bridge-building is tantamount to both the danger and the accomplishment of the technological feats of engineering. The danger lies in the immense threat that exists a priori in the current global economic structure for a grassroots community in cooperation with a capitalist corporation. The accomplishment lies in the rupturing of that threat—albeit along one small border.[78] The question that must be

---

77 Kahrl constructs his story of Southern California water usage primarily from "published documents and other materials available to the general public" (xi) to bring up to date and reassess the legends, fictions and other histories surrounding the Owens County/Los Angeles controversy in and prior to the 1930s. He less than adequately acknowledges what I would contend is an important polemic in the controversy—that the real issue in legislating water rights is often "a misguided concern for plants"—as in industrial plants and agri-business—"over the needs of the people." However, Kahrl's text is important in that he presents the controversy as a "story" that has "been shaped in a large part by the controversy itself" (viii).

78 To an extent, the omnipresent threat could be likened to the ever-present structural power differential between partners in a heterosexual relationship. However, the corporation-community dynamic is more absolute. While the power differentials between differently-gendered individuals may fluctuate according to other criteria—race, age, class, socialization—the community organization is almost always at an economic, social, and legal disadvantage to the corporations.

asked here is whether this one constructive union, while overtly in support of community struggles, is simultaneously furthering the corporate power-hold on disenfranchised communities. Such a dichotomy may exist if a corporation receives appreciatively larger economic or representational benefits in the relationship.

For instance, if tax breaks or loopholes received in exchange for corporate contributions to community work are of greater benefit to the corporation than the benefit that the community receives from the corporation, then the corporation's economic political power grows while the community continues its struggle, subsidized by small corporate handouts. Or, if the corporation uses advertising campaigns announcing grants for environmental justice interests to keep a clean corporate image even while polluting other communities, even the grant-winner loses in the bigger picture. The structure of the relationship thus ensures continuous community dependence on the corporation while obstructing the possibility that the community might become an equal player. If further corrective measures to reorient the dynamics are not undertaken, such a relationship does not ultimately dismantle the structure of economic domination, but rather acts as a steam valve to keep the community sedate. Questioning such relationships poses a variation on a revolutionary dilemma. Here it asks, "Can a community organization committed to the sustenance and wellbeing of its group ever work hand in hand with a corporation whose very existence is necessarily built on capitalist success that will always undermine the non-dominant community's creative development?"

MELA's experience illustrates that within the given boundaries, such coalitions can be constructive at the community level. While at the turn of the century, some may argue that anti-WTO demonstrations restored dormant faith in a people's revolt against corporate take-over, there were still bleak prospects for a global revolution that might issue in a post-capitalist era. MELA's decisions may not represent compromise so much as a new version of revolution. This discussion will be picked up in later sections that examine South Asian sites.

In a more overt and often intentional contradiction, a corporation may use a publicity campaign of community support to cover up the fact that in another arena it is desecrating the same or adjacent communities. Green corporate advertising by polluting and environmentally racist industry is a case in point. In a more complex but similar situation, Levi Strauss & Co. is partial funders of the Goldman Environmental Award, which was given to Aurora Castillo in spring of 1995. Five years earlier, Levi Strauss & Co. had closed their Zarzamora Street garment industry plant in San Antonio, shipping their business to

Costa Rica and failing to honor even their limited agreements with workers for pensions, benefits and severance pay. Thus, while one Latina was applauded for the environmental justice community struggles in which she participated, which did not directly confront Levi Strauss & Co.'s unjust actions, approximately 1,000 Latinas in San Antonio who were "devastated after years of hard work and dedication... feel that [Levi Strauss & Co.] must be held accountable for the devastation [they] have caused to families, communities, and the environment."[79] The San Antonio plant closing at a time of record profits was part of a long trend. As Fuerza Unida, (the Latina organization formed to fight Levi Strauss & Co's unjust labor practices and support Latina workers) explains: "[u]nder the ownership of the Haas family, between 1985 and 1990 Levi's shut down twenty-six (26) plants, laid off over 10,000 workers (mostly women of color), and moved production to Third World Countries where workers are paid $4 per day."[80]

Fuerza Unida's economic analysis of the Zarzamora Street plant closing gives insight into Levi Strauss & Co.'s involvement with Latina communities that is glossed over with the Goldman prizes. In a February 20, 1992 letter addressed to fellow activists Fuerza Unida proclaims: "WE ARE THE EARLY VICTIMS OF THE FREE TRADE CLIMATE IN THIS COUNTRY AND OF CORPORATE GREED. Levi Co., for example, posted record profits in 1989, in 1990, and again in 1991, but they sought to obtain a **SUPER PROFIT** by paying $3.00 a day to Costa Rican women without paying for any benefits or being responsible for the severe carpal tunnel nerve injuries."

So far as I could uncover, Aurora Castillo has not advocated for Fuerza Unida or pointed out the blatant inconsistency in the Levi Strauss & Co's relationship with Latina communities; however, in contemplating the possibility of such an event, one is faced with the difficult complexity of such power relations. Does Aurora Castillo's award represent a real window of opportunity through which the community organization can break into the corporate struggle with a new set of values to structure future relationships and mend past ones? Does her reward represent political power or merely a monetary handout meant to encourage progressive groups to turn their heads on the same corporation's ignoble dealings with its Chicana workers? Levi Strauss & Co. have also contributed to Latino cultural centers such as The Guadalupe Cultural Arts Cen-

79 Fuerza Unida form letter to Bob Haas, CEO for Levi Strauss & Co. protesting the closure, summer 1995; the exact nature of the "devastation to the environment" is not specified.

80 Fuerza Unida flyer "Boycott Levi's: Latina Garment Workers Fight Corporate Greed Youth Leaders Speak Out in Support" (summer 1995).98 ASZ.

ter in San Antonio, even as they have continued their shutdowns, and failed to provide just compensations to San Antonio's laid off workers. Such behavior suggests that they do want to buy off Latino groups who have expressed concern or even outrage but are also looking for funding.

In a letter to President Clinton on the occasion of his inauguration,[81] Juana Beatriz Gutiérrez, President, Mothers of East Los Angeles examines the fragile balance to be kept in corporate-community relationships.

> Our communities can no longer be viewed as guinea pigs on the path to corporate profits. By the same token, corporate America must be viewed as a source of jobs, innovation and advancement, not as a source of despair, demagoguery and regression. There is one piece of advice we would like to offer in tackling these problems, please give community-based organizations equal standing with corporations when it is time to come to the table. We may not be able to bankroll any political campaigns, but we as people of color are America's primary investment.

Gutierrez' "motherly" advice to the new president is a revolutionary proposition. What would it mean for Fuerza Unida and the Mothers of East LA to have an equal place at the oval office table with Levi Strauss & Co. and California Thermal Treatment Systems, the monetary support of the proposed Vernon incinerator?[82] For the Eklavya of the Arera Colony of Bhopal to sit down on equal terms with Union Carbide? For the UFW to meet on equal grounds with agribusiness? For Exxon to break bread (or tortillas) with PODER? Gutiérrez acknowledges fatalism in treating the dichotomy between community and corporation as a good—bad dualism, and the alternative option she proposes dismantles the domination system that holds the rest of the world in the iron clinches of transnational corporate capitalism. Furthermore, the corporation—community relationship envisioned by Gutiérrez provides a model to answer the questions on power relationships that I posed earlier. While the details are not in hand, the descriptions of the project issued by the MELA tracts and Gutierrez' description of an ideal corporation—community power relationship suggest that CTSI—Las Madres union is a productive one for the East L.A. community and for larger global—local encounters. The significance of MELA's work is paralleled by other Chicana environmental justice organizers, artists, and academics; these activists provide a range of feasible answers to some of the most crucial social and environmental dilemmas.

81 published in *Environmental Action* 25:1 (spring 1993), 35.
82 "Incinerator is challenged in court by locals" November 8, 1984, 1.

In the following chapter, a discussion of Indian women involved in the Chipko Movement that began in Northern India allows for examination of community–corporation interactions with the added dimension of national "first world/Third World" country politics that Fuerza Unida alludes to in terms of workers' rights, and that MELA touches on in its work with "immigrant" communities and rural agricultural workers.

5 Chipko: Human(e) Arms to Defend Lifestyle and Environment

> ... for Chipko women, forests provide food, and the movement to protect them is a movement to provide food to their families, their cattle... and their soils.
>
> Vandana Shiva (SA 97)

5.1 Theorizing the Chipko Andolan

The name "Chipko" comes from a North Indian word meaning "to embrace;" during demonstrations to stave off lumbering, local participants hugged the trees and tied sacred threads around them as protection. Since these demonstrations to bar detrimental outside development during the 1970's, Chipko has become a coalition of villages working on a wide range of forestry issues including cooperative replanting and tree nurturance, forestalling major corporate development, and beginning reforestation projects.[83]

The current Chipko Movement, which began in the Garhwal region of Uttar Pradesh arose in a nation and a region with a long and rich heritage of activism for land/forest protection and women's rights. It has evolved into a coalition of villages working on a wide span of forestry issues including cooperative replanting and tree nurturance that has forestalled major corporate development in the area. Chipko is only one example of the sophistication of women's activism in India that has not been given adequate attention in the Western academy, even among feminists and "Third World" Studies scholars. My examination of the ideologies and poetics of environmental politics in this context samples only a small segment of these important Indian women's (and their allies') work. After a cursory ecohistory of Indian forest homelands, I will offer a quick synopsis and discussion of the implications of women's Chipko activism. Thus, this chapter provides a framework for subsequent focus on the Chipko movement's poetics, primarily a collection of songs, poems, murals, poster art, and performance/demonstration strategies addressed in Chapter Nine.

Within the rubric of postcolonial studies, little attention has been paid to the ecological repercussions of the colonizers' attacks on the environments of

83 Parts of this chapter were published in an article for the *San Jose Studies Special Issue in Tribute to César Chávez.* entitled "Cultural Poetics in the United Farm Workers, the Chipko Movement, and the Seringueiros" and in "Two Centuries of Indian Writing" *The Literature of Nature: An International Sourcebook.* Patrick Murphy. Editor. Chicago: Fitzroy Dearborn, 1998. 315–324.

https://doi.org/10.1515/9783111041575-006

the colonized. In cultural texts that promote environmental justice, the late twentieth century produced a rich body of socially engaged poetics that summons a re-evaluation of colonial links to race, class, ecology, and gender issues in light of the ecological degradation of the habitats of human and nonhuman communities. These texts historically link environmental injustice with structural prejudice, patriarchy, colonialism, and imperialist capitalism. They demonstrate that an understanding of the socio-ecological results of colonial policies and actions is essential to adequately theorize India's cultural presence in a postcolonial and de-colonial present. As Vandana Shiva, Gail Omvedt, Ramachandra Guha, Madhav Gadgil and others have demonstrated in the Indian context, the history of environmental racism is one legacy of European colonialism that has not diminished in the postcolonial independent state.[84] In order to contextualize discussions of the Chipko movement, I will turn briefly to the nexus of post/coloniality and environmental racism in India.

In This *Fissured Land: An Ecological History of India* (1992), Madhav Gadgil and Ramachandra Guha argue that "British colonial rule marks a crucial watershed in the ecological history of India"(5); they repeatedly emphasize the interconnectedness of politics, culture and nature, an empirical relationship that meets the definition of environmental justice: "[w]hile there is limited research on the specific changes in different geographical regions, clearly the century and a half of colonial rule had introduced manifold social and ecological changes whose interdependence has rarely been appreciated" (145). However, Ramachandra Guha, a *Green* Gandhian worker and "left-environmentalist theorist" (Omvedt 1993, 12) and Madhav Gadgil find that "[w]hile sharply critical of colonialism, Indian historians have, in the main, been indifferent to the ecological consequences of British intervention" (Gadgil and Guha 5).[85] The indifference of Indian historians to ecological history appears to be shared by postcolonial researchers across the globe, creating a hiatus in study that Gadgil, Guha, Shiva and others took the lead in redressing.

Theoretically, as well as historically, the effects of environmental demise have been ignored. Gadgil and Guha point out that, within Marxism, ecological contexts for analyses have been ignored: an "economic 'infrastructure'—the so-

84 Gadgil and Guha address this in *This Fissured Land* ... and in other writings; Vandana Shiva treats the issue in *Staying Alive* and in her 1996 book, *Biopiracy: the Second Coming of Columbus* and Gail Omvedt discusses it in *Reinventing Revolution*.

85 As examples of Green Gandhian workers, Gail Omvedt refers to Ramachandra Guha the "left-environmentalist theorist" and Kumarappas—Gandhian socialists—who promoted "villagism" (1993 12).

called relations of production and productive forces"—does not investigate "the ecological context...in which the infrastructure is embedded" (12). In recent geo-historical scholarship "the most major lacuna...is an inadequate appreciation of the *ecological* infrastructure of human society." Furthermore, "an ecological approach to such questions suggests that the mode of production concept is not adequately materialistic in the first place" (12–13). Thus, for Gadgil and Guha, the question is not only the absence of ecological subject matter, but misanalysis based on that hiatus in subject and frame; they remedy this problem by supplementing Marxism's "modes of production with the concept of modes of resource use" (13).[86] Thus, they introduce ecological concerns into Marxist, as well as postcolonial theory.

Vandana Shiva links these eco-colonial issues and material analysis to gender issues, suggesting an irrevocable bond of mutual sustenance between women (and often all native forest peoples) and the forests. Her classic text *Staying Alive* (1989), like *This Fissured Land*, draws from the Indian context to contrast the ecological conditions and ideologies at work in pre-British India with the subsequent colonial and postcolonial Indian conditions, narrative representations, and ideologies. Shiva demonstrates early examples of a loosely defined "feminine principle" Aranyani, goddess of the forest, whom Mackenzie in "*India: Myths and Legends* identifies with a hymn in the Rig Veda (Mackenzie 74); in the Aranyakas or forest texts that speak of Earth mother as a tree mother (Shiva 56); and in Amrita Devi, the legendary leader of the first Chipko movement in the eighteenth century.

Shiva shows through her examination of written and oral tradition that Indians have had a long-standing reverence for their forests, and that that reverence has often been integrally related to the "feminine principle." Recent research affirms Shiva's observations by demonstrating that for centuries, religion and its narrative mythologies—especially the region's major religions, and to a less-publicized extent, its tribal religions—have been important aspects of a generalized Indian view of nature in life and literature. For instance, the Upanishads are possibly the first extensive environmental writings in India. An early example of early environmental thinking comes from Sanskritic linguistic evidence in the lexicon, the *Namalinganusasana* (colloquially known as *Amarakosa*), which shows the many viewpoints from which a tree is viewed (Shiva 58). "Pre-British ecological principles, often spread through oral tradition, sustained a symbiotic relationship between people and forests through 'local production for local use'"

86 The hiatus in research that they mark in India is beginning to be researched and theorized worldwide.

(Gadgil and Guha 39). The preservation of sacred groves and ancestral sites of forest peoples in India (for example, the *aurans* in Rajasthan and *Devaranyas* of the western ghats) has been a mechanism for continual and sustainable forest maintenance (Shiva 68; Gadgil and Guha 23, 29). Familial relationships with nature objects encouraged respect, and the forest helped people meet spiritual needs (Gadgil and Guha 20), while taboos and prescriptions often promoted resource conservation and helped avoid environmental collapse (Gadgil and Guha, 22 & 24). For instance, harvesting would often be curtailed when resource densities fell. Pastures were held in common, though herds were private property; this arrangement encouraged group care for the land (Gadgil and Guha 228). This refutes the (Western, and implicitly, Capitalist) environmentalist assumptions, put forth in Garrett Hardin's classic environmental essay "The Tragedy of the Commons," in which Hardin maintains that resources are always degraded when held in common. However, Gadgil and Guha's observation of the positive environmental effects of communal land holdings in India are supported by many subsequent studies that have indicated that in cultures where the public good is an important motivating factor, and where effective management systems are in place, commonly owned resources can be managed sustainably.

Vandana Shiva substantiates the continuation of the bond to the forests by pointing to a wide range of twentieth century, (male) Indian writers who created literature about the relations between humans and nature in the national context even during the British occupation; for example, J.C. Bose, the scientist, M.K. Gandhi, the political activist, and Rabindranath Tagore, the poet, each wrote extensively on the forest homescape. Tagore wrote of the forest "as the language of liberation" and in creating a contrast between the West and India, and between urban and rural, he argues that the "culture that has arisen from the forest has been influenced by the diverse processes from species to species, from season to season, in sight and sound and smell. The unifying principle of life in diversity, of democratic pluralism, thus became the principle of the Indian civilization" (Bandyopadhyay and Shiva, 67).

Rabindranath Tagore, like Shiva, Gadgil, and Guha, describes what might be called an "ecocracy" in the Indian pre-British and pre-Portuguese world. Shiva's ecofeminist forest philosophy—which stresses the necessity of diversity, renewability, and sustainability—is deeply influenced by Tagore. This ecohistory is not, however, as seamless as Shiva, Tagore or other advocates might have us believe. As mentioned previously, Vandana Shiva's work does at times exhibit theoretical weaknesses especially vis-á-vis ungrounded generalizations. To more clearly view the vital and distinctive arguments that Shiva presents, acknowledgement of these shortcomings in *Staying Alive* is important. In most cases, the crucial arguments regarding international environmental justice relations stand, despite the critical weaknesses of Shiva's underexamined, sweeping statements. However, in the paradigm of a single, homogenous Indian culture, the non-Hindu tribal forest people—whose lifestyles in many ways most closely resemble the "Indian" side of the dichotomy—are left on the margins. Such a binary vision also ignores distinctive Islamic and other religion's ecological respect, pro-diversity impulses in the West and the environmentally detrimental impulses inherent in Nehru's industrial socialism that came to fruition with Indian Independence and industrial development.

Another of Shiva's weaknesses affects an otherwise strong point in her work—her portrayals of gender. Shiva does not always clarify where the women she writes about fit in the local (or national) social hierarchy, nor does she explain the local complexities of social relating. In this sense, she is quite different from Mahasweta Devi whose writing is discussed in Chapters Twelve and Thirteen. Though most of Mahasweta Devi's translated work is fiction, the reader receives a more clear and explicitly articulated description of social relations from her writing than from Shiva's. Since, particularly in *Staying Alive*, Shiva reads almost everything in terms of binary dichotomies between men and women and between Asia and Europe/North America, Indianized forms of Modernization are subsumed as mere Western derivatives and she minimizes the influences of Western thought on Gandhian practitioners. It seems fair to say that *Staying Alive* is a polemical and vitally important, but not always self-critically astute, text. Shiva does not extensively describe ideological splits in the Chipko movement. Nor does she discuss in depth the multivalent and sometimes contradictory impulses that contribute to the *diversity* of, and conversely the *colonization* of nature. This homogenizing of Indian culture into one monolithic experience of gender inequity is troublesome. Given these considerations, Shiva's work is most useful when she discusses specific groups or individuals and their contributions.

Despite her generalizations about "Indian civilization" that disregard Islamic, indigenous or "tribal," Christian, Jewish, and other traditions for the dominant Hindu-inspired culture, Shiva's argument is especially compelling and convincing in terms of the multiplicity of ecologies functioning in India that were pre- and extra-British Colonial.[87] Colonialism's role in environmental racism becomes clear in the particularities of how the British forestry system was created for the needs

87 Critiques of Vandana Shiva's writing apply to work focusing primarily on Indian women that was produced up to and circa turn of the century. She is among the most prolific writers on the world's environmental justice crises and her work continues to evolve. Her immense 21st Century body of work is beyond my study's purview save to say its importance is incalculable.

of colonialism (Shiva 11). Most rural communities who lived a subsistence lifestyle had had free access to the forest as a provider of their needs until the British assumed control of forest areas (Jain 166). While a forest-based subsistence lifestyle does not indicate equitable distribution of rights and power across communities, Jain's assertion does suggest a major social and environmental shift that came with British colonization and the installation of a British forestry management system based on a German model (Gadgil and Guha 6). In many places, the curtailment of a sustainable lifestyle grounded in the local environment inevitably resulted. The erosion of this basic right weakens the foundation of both human communities and surrounding ecosystems. Contemporaneous scholarship offers examples that span centuries to dispel the commonly held mischaracterization that the British brought 'scientific' forest management to India as a misrepresentation of history (Shiva 58). Rather, researchers show that the British brought environmental injustice enacted through a charade of so-called positive preservation that was essentially a cynical and prejudiced landgrab:

> When the British colonised India, they first colonised her forests. Ignorant of the wealth of knowledge of local people to sustainably manage the forests, they displaced local rights, local needs and local knowledge and reduced this primary source of life into a timber mine. Women's subsistence economy based on the forest was replaced by the commercial economy of British colonialism. (Shiva 61)

The names and techniques have changed in the years since the colonial project Shiva describes, but as environmental justice poetics such as narratives from the Chipko Movement show, many of the detrimental effects of domination, especially those affecting women, remain. Though there is disagreement on the role gender plays in defining the divisions initially created by British colonialism in the forests of the Indian subcontinent, I found no disagreement on the broad historical phenomenon of deforestation. The colonial divisions of power and resource access have, in most cases, remained intact and in many cases have been magnified by the forces of imperialism, corporate capitalism, and subsequently, privatization and globalization.

The management and utilization of forest resources became "possibly the most important aspect of the ecological encounter between Britain & India, largely because Britain needed teak, sal and deodars for its railroads and for building navy ships" (Gadgil and Guha 118). Colonization followed "an industrial factory model." In the eighteenth century, British military needs for teak initiated a proclamation that switched the right to teak trees from the local government to the East India Company. The shift in models created a shift in normative structures in forest communities from a forest-centered normalcy toward "normalcy dictated by market values" (Shiva 69–71). This ecohistory remains crucial in understanding environmental justice activism today for many reasons. If only the continuous channel of abusive relations that link colonialism to environmental racism is made clear, the comparison serves well.

5.2 A History of Ecocolonialism and Ec(h)oing Resistance/Response

Its own forests already devastated by 1860, Britain became the world leader in deforestation; the destruction of forests was used by Britain to symbolize political victory not unlike the smokestack that marked progress for industrialists in the United States (Gadgil and Guha 119). After five decades of largely uncontrolled destruction of the forests by British commercial interests, the first Indian Forest Act was passed in 1865 (Shiva 62); the Forest Acts of 1878 and 1927 merely legitimized and further encroached on local peoples' rights. The shift of control to state property rights centralized property control and increased deforestation. Not only had practical local control previously discouraged destructive use of forests (Gadgil and Guha 124), but under British management, the oak forest, needed for local use, was particularly reduced; thus, the consequent increase of unmet local needs led to further forest exploitation (Gadgil and Guha 3).

Not surprisingly, the critical role of women in Indian forests went unrecognized by the British colonizers (Shiva 64). "Indigenous forest management, as largely a women's domain for producing sustenance, was...in an evolved state when the British arrived. Since the British interest in forests was exclusively for commercial timber, indigenous expertise became redundant for their interest and was replaced by a one-dimensional, masculinist science of forestry" (Shiva 61). Fodder collection and food gathering from the forest are primarily women's work; thus "women as foragers were critical in managing and renewing the diversity of the forest" (Shiva 60). Shiva states that the public domain of the forest was open to women, and she suggests that the public/private gendered spheres that have held sway throughout modernization in the West were less stratified in India prior to the 18th century wave of European colonialism. In Shiva's representation, women's work is complementary to men's; she downplays gender inequities in native (Indian) systems while demonstrating the balanced, sustainable treatment of nature.

Indians involved in different modes of production were impacted in different ways as village common lands became government lands (Gadgil and Guha 55). Restrictions were placed on hunter gatherers who practiced a mode of production that is "simultaneously" a mode of resource use, and jhum (shifting land) cultivators became landless. The changes were "accompanied by an ideological debate legitimizing the claims of the British modes" through the claim of scientific superiority (Gadgil and Guha 56); stratification and inequality in access and control of resources increased. Finally, domination, itself, granted further penetration into Indian resources: "The right of conquest," thundered one forest official, "is the strongest of all rights—it is a right against which there is no appeal" (Amery 1875, 27 in Gadgil and Guha 126). While in many cases, local communities lost access to land they had utilized for centuries, the face of the land also changed, often irreparably, in the wake of British forest control. Deforestation affected the land and the social and economic relations of the residents indirectly as well as directly; flood and drought began to plague many of the areas where the polycultural ecologies had been upset, causing further environmental socio-economic havoc.

Such devastation did not go without response. The history of forest struggle against the British dates back to at least the 19th century when land grants went exclusively to the British, and a consequent timber monopoly established the British as "conservator" of forests. The conservatorship was misrun and abolished in 1823. Deleterious forest policy met with the forest satyagraha (an early form of the resistance techniques based on "Truth Force," which Mohandas K. Gandhi later popularized), which spread across India as protest against British commercial reservations of forests. Villagers removed what they needed from the forests in civil disobedience; the resistance was especially successful in the "Himalaya, the Western Ghats, and the Central Indian hills" (Shiva 66). Although villagers demonstrated using nonviolent civil disobedience, they were "systematically crushed" by the British. In the most extreme cases in the 20th century, the Gond tribals in Central India were "gunned down" (Shiva 66). While the British were not always the direct perpetrators of violence against disenfranchised forest dwelling communities who rose in protest to protect their forest homelands, they had imposed the system of hierarchical, power-based forest policies that devastated local lifeways. In 1930, unarmed villagers were killed and injured "in Tilari village in Tehri Garhwal, [later a central area to the Chipko Movement] when they gathered to protest against Forest Laws" instated, there, by the local rulers (Shiva 66). These acts of resistance are seen as precursors to later forest resistance and to, most famously, the Chipko movement.

Since the late 19th century, despite the local resistance struggles, the forestry department created by the British has been India's largest landlord; the "edifice of colonial forestry has been taken over by the government of independent India" (Gadgil and Guha 6). The destruction of the forest ecosystem, begun by the British colonialists and carried on most extensively by the imperialist interests of corporate development, continues to hurt the economic interests of those dependent on the *natural diversity* of the forest (Shiva 62). The history of forest struggle, thus explicated, underscores that the battle is not—as is sometimes simplistically portrayed—a struggle between ecological and economic interests but, rather, it is a fight to determine *whose* economic *and* ecological interests will be respected. Community-based systems continue to be delegitimized by commercial and corporate interests, and the ideology of the market, not of nature is venerated (Gadgil and Guha 44–45). The end of colonialism merely meant a shift in the items exported; the flows of export remained "highly asymmetrical, with industrial societies receiving large volumes of unprocessed resources at low prices and exporting small volumes of processed resources at much higher prices" (Gadgil and Guha 43); moreover, historically incomparable, and often toxic, waste is now being created by this system. Environmental racism has extended from colonial India connecting into the very structure of Independent India. The forest continues to be a site of skirmish over Indian economic independence many decades after political independence was won.[88]

5.3 Satyagraha Workers—Precursors to the Chipko Movement

> ...there was a Gandhian heritage in the organization of women in the area, provided by the ashrams established by the various women pioneers.
>
> Gail Omvedt (1994, 133)

Decades of poetics and praxis has enabled the Chipko movement to establish itself as a new social movement with successful resistance strategies. In the mid-1990s, the movement's success was heralded in the popular, flashy, consumer-oriented *India Magazine*: "Chipko, the unique ecological movement, led by the women of Garhwal to save trees, has assumed folkloric status" (Jawahara Saidullah 30). The contemporary "folkloric status" has a historical precedent: "[t]hree hundred years ago more than 300 members of the Bishnoi community in Rajasthan, led by a woman called Amrita Devi, sacrificed their lives to save their sacred *khejri* trees by clinging to them. With that event begins the recorded

---

88 India's long forestalling of multinational corporate takeover and its subsequent move toward privatization after the breakup of the USSR is not unrelated to the poetics of environmental struggles. As Fredrik Jameson predicted at the 1993 MLA, privatization affects Indian culture as well as its economic dependency. On the national and local levels Shiva's "feminine" paradigm offers a radical alternative that better serves the interests of the environment and marginalized communities.

history of Chipko" (Shiva SA, 67).[89] With Amrita Devi—legendary predecessor, both figuratively and literally, to the Chipko movement—as a point of departure, other precursors to Chipko deserve discussion.

A mimeo by Mira Behn describes how she discovered that environmental destruction due to forestry was destroying local people's homes. Mira Behn writes:

> Within a year or two, I witnessed a shocking flood: as the swirling waters increased, (there) came first bushes and boughs and great logs of wood, then in the turmoil of more and more water came whole trees, cattle of all sizes and from time to time a human being clinging to the remnants of his hut… The sight of these disastrous floods led me each summer to investigate the area north of Pashulok whence they came. Merciless deforestation as well as cultivation of profitable pines in place of broad-leaf trees was clearly the cause. This in turn led me to hand over charge of Pashulok to the government staff and to undertake a community project in the valley of the Bhilangana. Here I built a little centre, Gopal Ashram, and concentrated on the forest problem. (69)

Mira Behn, a European who had been closely involved with Gandhian theory during and following the Independence Movement, had moved to the Garhwal hills in the 1940s to continue village "reconstruction" on the Gandhian model. Her description of her concern for the local forest shows why Vandana Shiva and Gail Omvedt and others discuss Mira Behn's role as a precursor/ originator of the contemporary Chipko Movement.[90] Mira Behn's legacy brings up a crucial

---

89 The Rajasthani folktale about Amrita Devi leading 300 people to save khejri trees has been depicted outside of India as well. For instance, see "The People Who Hugged the Trees" a children's book by Deborah Lee Rose, a science writer at UC Berkeley, and Swedish artist, Birgitta Saflund; this book demonstrates how the poetics of social environmental activism can inspire cross-cultural and cross-centurial retellings for intergenerational audiences. See also Nina Sibal's representation of the folk story in *Yatra* as discussed in Chapter Nine. I have not researched the extent of knowledge of the Rajhastani legend in the "west," but it has been suggested to me that that is where the term "tree huggers" for "earth firster types" originated; however, few "tree huggers" in the Northwest with whom I spoke knew about the Chipko Movement. And there are inherent, fundamental differences in the approach to nature of the majority of U.S. forest activist compared to the movement in India, in which activists are protecting what is integral to their daily lives as opposed to a "wilderness" area to visit occasionally.

90 'Behn' is an honorific term meaning sister. Gandhian workers who were women often adopted "Behn" and were sometimes, as in the case of Mira Behn, given a first name by Gandhi, as well. Gandhi named her "after one of India's great legendary mystics who was a dedicated devotee of Krishna despite ridicule and torture by her husband" (Weber 5). Mira Behn's birth name was Madeleine Slade (Nehru, *Toward Freedom*, 220). Born into a family of country esquires who were descendants from the Plantagenets, Mira Behn's ancestors, especially on her mother's side, "boasted many senior army officers, even a general or two, who had joined

observation: as is discussed earlier, vis-à-vis men, it is important not to write off the work of women working outside of their native-dominant culture, in support of, or in alliance with, a local resistance group. At the same time, it is important to recognize that while westerners such as Mira Behn may have become, by experience, insiders in the Gandhian Movement surrounding Indian Independence, they had neither the same limitations nor insider knowledge as the local resident women involved later in the Chipko Andolan. The dynamics in such situations, never easy, may often be contradictory, but these contradictions—if understood—may serve as toeholds toward reaching transcultural changes. We will understand the diversely chaotic influences of gender and race on human interaction only when we consider the multiple identity representations that change agents hold.

Mira Behn embarked on eco-sociological research in order to determine the reasons for the environmental degeneration that was becoming prevalent: "Mira studied the environment intimately and derived knowledge about it from the local people. From the older ones she learnt that, earlier, Tehri Garhwal forests consisted largely of oak;" she also learned that Garhwali folktales and folksongs repeatedly described two species—*banj*, an oak and *kharik*, a hackberry (*Quercus incana* and *Celtis australis*)—that had largely disappeared from the region. Mira Behn felt that a primary reason for environmental problems might be that the *banj* and mixed species forests were being replaced with the more exportable pine tree. She wrote about her ideas in mimeos and passed them directly to her younger co-worker Sunderlal Bahuguna, who would become one of the main Chipko activists, and the primary activist who has also written about the movement in English (Shiva 1989, 69–70). Through the *combination* of the extensive experiential knowledge of local natural history provided by residents of the foothills and Mira Behn's writing, environmental demise was documented and diagnosed, probably at an earlier stage than most deforestation has been. Mira Behn's concern for the Indian forest was comprehensive, passionate, and

---

the lists for the glory of the British Empire" (Gupta v). Her father was a British Admiral who had earlier served time in India; "it is an interesting twist of events then that Gandhi welcomed Slade to India with the words 'You shall be my daughter'"(Weber 5). In many senses, Mira Behn lived out the progression from British Admiral's daughter by birth to Indian spiritual and political leader's daughter by spiritual adoption; her life—like Marjorie Sykes and other British (particularly women) who worked for Indian Independence and subsequently served Indian interests—illustrates the heterogeneity in individual British-Indian relations, especially where women were involved. However, from a feminist perspective one might question the relationship endorsed by naming a grown woman "daughter" and ask whether Mira Behn was able—as a woman—to grow beyond the role of (very proficient) follower.

long lasting. She wrote articles with titles such as "Something Wrong in the Himalayas," "Deforestation, Waterlogging and Soil Erosion" and "Vanishing Oaks." Her articles were most often published in *Harijan*, but also appeared in the *Hindustan Times*, *Sunday Statesman* and, early on, in *Young India*. A list of her articles addressing issues of "Livestock, Forest and Environment" begins with "Our brethren the trees" published in 1929; the last article was published 50 years later. Her diagnosis of the causes of flooding and other secondary environmental problems has been repeatedly born out.

In 1981 when Sunderlal Bahuguna visited Mira Behn in Austria—where she had moved in her elder years—with news of the Chipko Movement's progress, she "was overjoyed," having herself written to "Indira Gandhi requesting an end to the commercial exploitation of the Himalayan forests and protection for the remaining stands of oak" (Weber 28–29). Bahuguna was her final visitor the day she died in July 1982. When he assured her, "one of the movement's chief inspirations, that her work in the Himalaya was to continue... she allegedly managed a smile" (Weber 29).

Mira Behn was not the only woman in the area writing about the threats of environmental demise to forest community wellbeing. Another foremother of the Chipko movement was Sarala Behn, also a Gandhian, and a European relocated in India, who had started the Laxmi ashram in Kausani that was dedicated to education and empowerment of hill women (Jain 172). In 1978, in *Blueprint for Survival*, Sarala "reiterated the Chipko women's demand,"

> the main role of the hill forests should be not to yield revenue, but to maintain a balance in the climatic conditions of the whole of northern India and the fertility of the Gangetic Plain. If we ignore their ecological importance in favour of their short term economic utility, it will be prejudicial to the climate of northern India and will dangerously enhance the cycle of recurring and alternating floods and droughts. (in *Ecologist* in Shiva 1989, 72)

Sarala clarifies that the forests play a nature-oriented role in sustaining society, and that society must thus sustain the forest. Short term economic interests should therefore be considered secondary.

Sarala's philosophy reflects a Gandhian humanistic communalism; she blames the split between private and public spheres for oppression and injustice. On her 75th birthday (and the 1975 International Women's Day celebration) Uttarakhand activists named her "daughter of the Himalaya" and the region's "mother of social activism." That year, Sarala wrote in her autobiography about her development of a social justice philosophy/praxis:

> From my childhood experience I have known that law is not just... that a centralised government, indifferent to its peoples, is a cruel joke in governance; that the split between the

> private and public ethic is the source of misery, injustice and exploitation in society. Each child in India understands that bread (*roti*) is not just a right to the one who has money in his pocket. It is a more fundamental right of the one whose stomach is hungry. This concept of right works within the family, but is shed at the societal level. Then the ethics of the market reigns [sic], and men get trapped in it. (Shiva 1989, 71–72)

Like the women of the Mothers of East Los Angeles (MELA), Sarala Behn upturns the public and private spheres; however, neither Sarala Behn nor MELA merely follow the conventional "Women's Movement" demand that women be given a place in the public space. Rather, both radicalize that demand by articulating their summons for change, *from* the standpoint of the private sphere, but *to* the audience of the public sphere. No longer are the spheres separate, no longer are women operating submissively in either sphere and no longer are the ethical aspects of the justice system of the private sphere limited by the foundation of the private home: rights that hold in private should also hold in public. In their proposals, the walls between the spheres, so long defined by gendered territorialization, crumble. This is not to suggest that women have equal rights in the private sphere, in either situation, but that they are creatively extending the rights they do have in one sphere to empower themselves, elsewhere.

Bimla (sometimes spelled Vimla) Behn, who worked in Sarala's ashram and subsequently married the Satyagraha and Chipko activist Sunderlal Bahuguna bridges the work of the precursors and the Chipko Movement activists. After working with Sarala for eight years, Bimla began the Silyara-based Navjivan ashram which became an organizing center for Chipko activism. While the Gandhian precursors are mentioned by the majority of Chipko chroniclers, Bimla's ashram is ignored by many of the chroniclers who refuse to recognise women's leadership. There is little consistency of opinion on the continuous participation and roles of women in Himalayan ecological justice work (Omvedt 132) as the Chipko movement emerged and began to flourish (Jain 60).[91] This controversy

---

91 According to Shobita Jain, "the women's more intense and immediate interests in a forest economy were based partially on their continual presence in an area where men often left to become migrant laborers to the plains;" Jain conducted a two month study (9-10-1982) to the Chamoli area during which she conducted "open-ended interviews" and found that most people in the area owned a small amount of land, most families less than a half hectare. Crops—wheat, paddy (rice), pulses and oilseeds—were grown; subsistence farming was possible three to six months a year; during the remaining season men became migrant laborers (few migrant labor jobs were available for women). She also suggests that it may be due partially to the men's absence that the women have led and defined Chipko organizing. Thus, the interweaving of traditional structures and commercial structures together creates the complex system of occupational gender divisions that influence peoples' attitudes toward the forest in which they live.

will be discussed in more depth in the section that follows the brief chronology of the movement offered immediately below. However, it is crucial here to acknowledge that the telling of the story itself also reflects one's investment in the gender issue.

5.4 The Chipko Andolan

According to participants quoted in texts written in English that describe the Chipko Andolan, the movement has been led by women, but some chronicler's overlook or deny this; Vandana Shiva, however, was one of the earliest writers in English to extensively document women's participation. The back cover of the Zed Books Ltd. edition of her 1987 book *Staying Alive* lists the book's and author's accomplishments as follows:

> Vandana Shiva is one of the world's most prominent radical scientists... in *Staying Alive* she defines the links between ecological crises, colonialism, and the oppression of women. It is a scholarly and polemical plea for the rediscovery of the "feminine principle" in human interaction with the natural world, not as a gender-based quality, rather an organizing principle, a way of seeing the world. (*Guardian* blurb on cover of *Staying Alive*)

While this description and the other blurbs on the back cover foreground the important, and often controversial, theoretical links that Shiva explicates, they efface the main players in *Staying Alive*. It is from observing and working with the women in the Chipko Movement that Shiva grounds her philosophical eco-feminism and offers empirical evidence of the links between the oppression of "women, nature, tribals and peasants." She discusses at length the resistance movements led by women to preserve their lifestyles and land from development based on what she calls patriarchal capitalism. I mention women's participation in events to the extent that I find it narrated and I address the negation of their presence or importance in these events on the part of some critics when I discuss the role of gender at length in the following section.

The "significant catalysers" of the transformations who made Chipko resistance possible and acted as leaders in their communities, as Chipko activists and organizers are listed by several chroniclers; they repeatedly name women such as Mira Behn, Sarala Behn, Bimla Behn, Hima Devi, Gauri Devi, Gunga Devi, Bechni Devi, Itwari Devi, Chamun Devi and "many others." The men of the movement like Sunderlal Bahuguna, Chandi Prasad Bhatt, Ghanshyam Shailani and Dhoom Singh Negi "have been their [the women's] students and followers" (also Jain 174 and Shiva). Bahuguna himself claims that the women are the leaders in the Chipko movement: "We are the runners and the messengers–the real leaders are the women." Antje Linkenbach, a cultural critic and anthropologist who has addressed the theoretical make-up and reception of the Chipko Andolan in a thorough study of documents, misquotes Bahuguna from Thomas Weber's *Hugging the Trees: The Story of the Chipko Movement* as saying that women functioned "only as the limbs of the movement, not as its brain" (Linkenbach 77); Weber attributes the quote to G. Joshi and uses it in opposition to Bahuguna's position—which he finds romanticizing that Bahuguna is only "the messenger of Chipko women" (in Weber 96).

In an article, co-written with Jeremy Seabrook, published in *Earth Ethics* (Winter 1996), the "romanticization" in Bahuguna's writing may be detected, but it is, nonetheless, a powerful corrective that demands we pay heed to a worldview of a nature—human relationship that may be ecologically more appropriate than those we encounter within many environmental movements. In the following passage, Sunderlal Bahuguna establishes Indian village women as having the quintessential ecological relationship with nature.

> People in the West imagine the ecological movement was born in the West. It was not university professors nor political leaders who gave birth to it, but village women, because this message is inbred in their hearts. They had no formal education, but they worshipped the tulsi plant, the sacred symbol of the flora. My mother was illiterate, but after taking her bath, she always watered the tulsi plant. (9)

For Bahuguna, knowledge and understanding (wisdom) are based in longstanding interaction of the spiritual and the material, the traditional and the contemporary combined; the rural women with whom he works perform these interactive tasks most readily. In relating the events of Chipko activism he tells us that "[i]n 1977, the women turned axemen away with their demonstrations. Then they tied sacred threads around trees marked for felling; they tied raki ribbons around them (that is the ribbon sisters tie around the wrists of their brothers) as symbols that they would protect them with their lives" (10). This important symbolic act—which will be expanded upon in the Poetics section—is a marking of trees that directly confronts the lumber companies marking of trees for felling.

According to some chroniclers, and like for MELA in California, the crystalizing moment for the Chipko Movement begins prior to establishing the contemporary movement's direct environmental justice concerns. In the 1960s, Gandhian workers—including C. P. Bhatt—in the Chamoli District established cooperative schemes to increase employment for local people, predominantly men (Jain 169). The group formed a "workers' co-operative and entered the market by buying forest rights through auctions to supply its small workshop making farm tools for local use. After initial success, however, the group was outmanoeuvred by other, richer contractors" (Jain 169) and the group continually faced problems with government policies such as the following example illustrates.

A major dispute arose over ash trees that the villagers wanted to use for making their agricultural implements in Mandal, a local village; they were not given permission to cut trees for this purpose. On October 22, 1971, the people protested at the forestry department in Gopeshwar. Soon after, the Simon Company, a sporting goods manufacturer, was granted permission to use the ash to manufacture tennis rackets. A struggle over ash trees ensued: on March 27, 1973, at a Gopeshwar town meeting, the people decided not to let the Simon Company fell a single tree. A rally of three hundred people was formed; they sang traditional songs, marched and drummed; the lumbermen retreated, and no trees were cut (Jain 169–170). The Simon Company moved to the nearby forest of Phata (Rampur Fata); on June 20, 1973, local people in alliance with Sarvodaya workers began a Chipko demonstration which became a five-month vigil to protect their forest. Thus, the Chipko Andolan began to spread across the Himalayan foothills.

Thomas Weber relates two versions of the birth of the idea of hugging the trees. In one version, Chandi Prasad Bhatt adds his idea for preventing the Simon Company from felling trees to others produced by the group of activists: "Let them know that we will not allow the felling of ash trees. When they aim their axes upon them, we will embrace the trees" (in Weber 40). In the second version, a village elder produces a maternal, protective metaphor that, like Aurora Castillo's often-quoted line about the MELA mothers acting as lionesses in protection of their children, includes a feline image—in this case as the perpetrator of danger. The villager stood up to suggest that "When a leopard attacks a child the mother takes his onslaughts on her own body." "This observation inspired another villager to propose" "Yes that is it, we'll hug the trees when Simon's agent comes to axe them" (in Weber 40).

The movement, at first confined to "problems of local unemployment" and local control of the use of forest products was, at its foundation, a fight to retain "*cultural self-determination*" (Linkenbach 73). Linkenbach suggests that outside analysis has established a false dichotomy, which divides Chipko activists themselves, between economic interests and the subsequent ecological emphasis. The mischaracterization is based on "a very narrow understanding which identifies economy with only market economy and suggests an interpretation of ecology that (in the modern sense) identifies it with conservation and natural aesthetics, thus neglecting nature's life-supporting role in the hill economy" (73). Analysis from the U.S. environmental justice movement that sees environmental and economic issues as inseparable is important here. The broader view necessary to get beyond the mischaracterization also evokes the derivation of both words in the Greek "oikos," as described by John Cobb. It is not surprising that environmentalists have picked up on models from groups like the Chipko Andolan more readily than economic theorists have. Yet an equitable and sustainable lifestyle necessary—some would argue—even for ultimate survival of the planet, will depend upon the widespread reconsideration of such value systems, as offered by Chipko, by economists as well.

Vandana Shiva downplays the Gopeshwar events, presenting a different "false dichotomy" as a gender split with the women on the side of the forest, and the men on the side of "masculinist forestry." Shiva suggests a later date for the conception of chipko in the movement, when she claims that it was in Mandal that the tree hugging itself began (73). It was 72-year-old Shyama Devi who "mobilized the local women" after a group from Mandal had walked to the Rampur Fata forest area in Kedar Ghati (73). Shiva also tells us that it was during the period following a June 1977 activist meeting held in Sarala Behn's ashram that the methodology of hugging was used on trees for the first time by Dhoom Singh Negi in Salet forest near Pipleth in Henwal (Shiva 77). The discrepancies noted above illustrate the extent to which even a chronological narrative of Chipko events and dates is colored by one's perspective on this gender issue. This is not surprising given the recent, critical analysis—addressing testimonios–of the interviewer's role in interpreting and presenting information, but it demonstrates the futility of determining precise roles at specific times enacted as Chipko evolved as a social movement. Nonetheless, it is important to recognize that all representations of these cultural events, including my own, are shaped by sequencial interpretation of events in a time frame, and by the reporting, or lack thereof—of events and actors' presence. Despite discrepancies, however, almost all chroniclers agree that the following episode at Reni, is one in which women emerged on the forefront as concerned social actors.

In 1974, when an auction of 2500 trees was announced in Reni, an area where floods on the Alaknanda River and landslides on the hill slopes had alerted people to environmental demise, C.P. Bhatt found residents—especially the women—receptive to the need to challenge forestry policy. Again, resembling MELA: A male organizer (a priest in MELA's case, a Gandhian in Chipko's) facilitates some of the original impetus for the organization, largely though sharing information, which is particularly relevant to the community who become involved. Such a phenomenon evokes neither the fetishization of subaltern women's involvement, nor its erasure. Rather, it shows a workable model in which those with more privilege offer support and knowledge in the service of a disenfranchised community seeking to transform its position in society, and in the process, society itself. In this way, at least in the large picture, the men involved work toward gender equity.

A woman named Gaura Devi organized Lata village to go meet the workers for the company which had won the auction. Gaura pushed herself in front of the guns of one of the workers and "challenged the men to shoot her instead of cutting down the trees, comparing the forest with her mother's home (maika)." Eventually the men retreated; the Uttar Pradeshi government decided to appoint a committee to make a forestry policy decision and the company withdrew until the decision was made. After two years the committee reported that Reni was ecologically sensitive and that trees should not be cut there; they placed a ten-year ban on tree-felling in a 150 square kilometre area. (Jain, Omvedt 132). According to Shiva,

> ... when the women of Reni protected their forest, they told the contractors' men: "This forest is our mother's home. When we have food scarcity, we come here to collect fruits for our children. We collect herbs and ferns and mushrooms. Do not cut this forest, otherwise we will embrace the trees and protect them with our lives." (Shiva 97–98).

The women's words intervene in the common dichotomy between ecological sensitivity and human habitation because the women depend on respect being paid to ecological sensitivity to sustain their homes and lifestyles. Their chant also illustrates that by this point, the women's activism was developing a consistent ideology based on the forest as the primary source of sustenance for their villages. The relationship of humans to forest was portrayed as one of familial, filial concern for the continuation of mutual wellbeing. This presents a stark contrast to most of the forest activists in the U.S. Northwest at the turn of the millennium.

In January 1975, women started a 75-day trek from Uttarkashi to Kausani and a 50-day trek from Devprayag to Naugaon to "mobilize public opinion on women's increasing workload due to deforestation." Long-standing activists Bimla Behn and Radha Bhatt took part in these padyatras (foot marches) (Shiva 75).[92] As women such as Gauri Devi, Gunga Devi, Hima Devi and Shyama Devi took the lead in Chipko demonstrations, they began to become involved in village meetings, an arena in which previously they had participated very little (Jain 174).

---

92 For a description of the activist role of the padyatra in fiction see Chapter Nine on Nina Sibal's novel, *Yatra*; Sibal commits these events to fiction, thus preserving the Chipko history in a novel.

Women in Reni acted because the men were away (mainly, in migrant labor), and Reni demonstrated that once they took charge, they succeeded. However, at Dongri Paintoli, a major site for earlier, anti-liquor campaigns, they stood up against the men's decisions (Jain 175). At Dongri Paintoli, Horticulture Department officials and village council members (all male) met, and the department promised "a cement road, a secondary school, a new hospital and electricity for their village" in exchange for felling trees. The women decided that if the trees were to be felled, they would chipko and they asked for C.P. Bhatt's help. The men of the city council told the women to go back to the kitchens and fields and threatened Bhatt's life if he came back to the village; on the ninth of February 1980, activists held a Chipko and prevented the tree cutting. Nine days later, the government ordered felling in the area to stop and within a month cutting was stopped. However, women leaders were "defamed and asked not to attend further meetings" (Jain 175). This successful protest was another turning point for the movement. Following this, local women intent on saving their environmental lifeways in the Himalayan foothills repeatedly stood against development ideology-prone men as the movement progressed. The women continued fighting to save the forests even when the perpetrators of destruction were the local men interested in obtaining commercial gain from the market economy by cashing in the forests.

The Chipko Movement in the Himalayan foothills has transformed as it has matured. A loose network of groups promoting local protests were successful in forestalling forest destruction, and they began to develop longer term strategies for educational activism and forestry training that went beyond crisis intervention. In this sense, the Chipko Andolan is like MELA, which turned to job-producing, preventative measures such as the installation of water saving toilets throughout the community once the major toxic intrusions were put at bay. Women—always at the forefront of agriculture and food gathering—organized educational and protective projects to sustain forest health and productivity.

In Gopeshwar, women have formed Mahila Mandal—a women's cooperative to protect the forest. They pay watchwomen to stand guard over the forest—extraction of forest produce is conducted under their guidance and violators of their policies are fined and their tools may be confiscated. BGSM's educational camps are attended by more and more women; "informal forestry colleges of women" have been initiated more widely (Shiva 66). The Chipko performative tactics have spread and are being used against other industries besides forestry that threaten the forest-based lifestyles of rural villagers. For instance, beginning on September 16, 1986, Doon Valley (which had a history of forest struggle dating back to the 19th century and Britain's exclusive land grants, was the site of a Chipko blockade against forest-threatening mining operations. Itwari Devi, a "village elder" and one of the demonstrators, reported on their unswerving determination and the strength of the movement which grew in proportion to their opposition: "Each attempt to violate us has strengthened our integrity. They stoned us on March 20 when they returned from the mine. They stoned our children and hit them with iron rods, but they could not destroy our shakti" (Shiva 208). That the women's sense of inner peace is not destroyed is central to the ideologies of activism that they hold. Its role in new social movement organizing is an issue of vital importance that has largely been ignored.

The Chipko Movement has spread across India "to Himachal Pradesh in the north, to Karnataka in the south, to Rajasthan in the west, to Orissa in the east, [witness the Chipko inspired by the Kalahandi District mural on this book's cover] and the Central Indian highlands" (Shiva 67). Consistent themes can be traced from village to village through a cartography of Chipko activism and poetics. Women, hill people, tribals and peasants are demonstrating why they must be the managers of their own lives and natural surroundings; their lived experience is the most direct base on which to build a theoretical understanding of a sustainable lifestyle that benefits the local ecosystem: "[s]ince it is women's work that protects and conserves nature's life in forestry and in agriculture, and through such conservation work, sustains human life through ensuring the provision of food and water, the destruction of the integrity of forest ecosystems is most vividly and concretely experienced by peasant women" (Shiva 65). Chipko offers good evidence of how "forestry is married to food production," how lived experience is affected by destructive forestry (Shiva 65); using Chipko as an example, Shiva shows how lived experience is the most direct base of a theoretical understanding of oppression based in extraction that is countered by reciprocity set forth by indigenous environmentalist groups in North America. This ideology of sustainable, local "cultural self-determination" is evident in the Chipko poetics described more extensively in Chapter Nine.

5.5 Debates: Competing Ideologies and Genders

Gandhiji had called women out of their homes to work for the cause of independence. In the Chipko movement women were more able to define the direction of the struggle in which they were taking part. Chipko workers such as Sunderlal Bahuguna and Chandi Prasad Bhatt spoke with the victims of environmental disasters in the hill areas of Garhwal. They were mostly women who, as the agriculturalists and caretakers for livestock and children, lost everything in reoccurring landslides and floods. Chipko was a "direct appeal" to them.

"They were able to perceive the link between their victimization and the denuding of mountain slopes by commercial interests;" they supported the Gandhians' work out of their own survival interests (Jain 165).

Gandhian strategies not only led to the Chipko Andolan, but as Thomas Weber illustrates, they have helped shape its controversial success. Chroniclers have questioned each other's perceptions of the movement's ecological ideology, the extent to which women play leadership roles, the theoretical impact of women on the movement and of the shifts on gender issues, the impacts of "outsiders" on the movement, and other aspects. These ideological debates within the contemporary movements have taken on their own characteristics and continue to influence the perceptions of racism, patriarchy and colonialism in villages, universities, and other public venues. Specifically, they can be followed in the pages of the Indian intelligentsia's and Left's journals such as *Economic and Political Weekly*, *Frontier*, and *Lokayan Bulletin*, and in the Women's press such as *Manushi*, *The COSAW Bulletin*, and *Sangarsh*.

In *Reinventing Revolution: New Social Movements and the Socialist Tradition in India*, Gail Omvedt is concerned with debates surrounding social movements that have "taken place largely within the context of Marxism" (xiii). She finds that "as people have begun to struggle in new ways and formulate new theories and ideologies, they have done so, quite often, in confrontation with what [she] describe[s] as 'traditional Marxism'" (xiii). Academics as well as activists are included in Omvedt's observations—the academics are often confronted by the activists. Omvedt explains that,

> [f]or this reason [she] ha[s] treated the studies and theoretical positions of intellectuals regarding the social movements as part of the ongoing ideological debate in and about movements, conditioned by their own social position and related to the hegemonic ideological structures of the society—not as theories that should be used to analyze the movements or which are to be tested with reference to the movements. (xiii)

Given Omvedt's interest in the mutual influences between academics and activists and given that I concur with her very apt description of the subjectivity of academics, I find it important to investigate the various ideological stances taken by academics, activists and others who have studied the Chipko movement. In controversies over the role women have played in the Chipko Movement, women academics' roles have been nearly ignored although individual woman scholars have been maligned by some and celebrated by others. The academic work of Indian women concerning environmental justice is central to the poetics I discuss and included in my definition of poetics. Women writers have many perspectives on the importance of the Chipko Movement as well as the role of gender within it. While I discuss several of these in the following pages, extensive analysis categorized by the gender of the academic is not productive to my work. Rather, what follows is my summarized assessment of the breakdown of actors and of who and what motivated Chipko activism and poetics, with what results.

My interpretation of the claims and counter claims on women's involvement in the Chipko Andolan suggests that, considering the different positions of the women involved and the different contexts in which they were operative, assertions on both sides of the question hold some truth. However, both sides may have elided details to produce more homogenous pictures than exists empirically: Mira Behn was a proto leader for the Chipko Movement, and she was a mentor for Sunderlal Bahuguna, but she was out of the country by the time the activism was full-fledged. Certainly, Sarala Behn and Bahuguna's own wife Bimla played leadership roles as Sarvodaya activists, developing a new aspect to an old praxis and ideology; (one wonders how much Bimla is responsible for stances chronicled as Sunderlal's—we might tentatively insert her name beside his at each mention of Sunderlal Bahuguna in the following discussion.) Some of the other women who were most heavily involved had already become change agents through anti-liquor campaigns in which they stood up against many male villagers, including at times their own spouses. It is hardly likely that these women only followed the men's lead or only participated when the men were away, as some chroniclers claim. [93] On the other hand, the structure of village society in the area did not publicly endorse local female leadership. Initially the village women may not have had the opportunity to assert themselves in a struggle that already sanctioned male leaders/activists, were promoting. However, as is repeatedly verified in narratives, women were the most experientially familiar with the problems of deforestation that activists discussed with the villagers. This fact, coupled with other factors, such as women's continual presence in the area, their lack of access to cash economy jobs, their creative and organizational skills, and their religious roles as purveyors of certain

93 Shiva (72), Bahuguna (9) and others report that many of the women who subsequently became involved in the Chipko Movement had, in the 1960s, been involved in a liquor prohibition movement; this activity was gender-defined and indicates that some women did have previous activist history. The local men were spending their cash earnings on liquor rather than making an adequate contribution to the upkeep of their families. While this campaign presumably did not give the women the political voice that the Chipko mobilization engendered, it did give precedence to their Chipko stands against the local men. This occurred primarily at Dongri Paintoli.

sacred traditions, allowed them to assert themselves as "leaders" at many crucial points in the struggle for environmental justice.

This said, the village women's stance on education, reported in the Himalayan foothills disrupts a gender dichotomy that puts women always on the side of easily defined progressive insight. Like more obviously detrimental development, education was not welcomed by everyone. Because education encouraged the village's educated young men to go away, leaving women alone to face the foothills' harsh circumstances, women were particularly adamant about seeing it as a bad thing. A general parallel between the arguments that commercially interested technology destroys native forest functions and that education disrupts traditional cultural knowledge cannot be drawn, though a comparison of both stances' refusal to accept outside manipulation of village lifestyles might prove useful.

In both cases, one might argue that it is not education or technology so much as how they are used that is the problem. Some chroniclers have used essentially the same argument to promote developing appropriate technology (Jain 168). From the outside, it seems more progressive to fight the skewed social structure that sends primarily boys to school and encourages them to leave rather than work for and within their villages. The village women's dislike of education helps illustrate the complexity of the situation regarding outside influences on village life. As villages face increased interfacing with various aspects of the outside world, scholars need to come to terms with our own place in our projects and face our manipulation of situations to match our view of what is "progressive." Such a stance that harks back to Pardo's cautioning in Chapter Four partially parallels the position that Linkenbach takes. Glimpsing even a portion of this immense complexity, it is less easy to simply accept Vandana Shiva's almost essentialist "feminine principle" that sanctifies women's relationships to the forest.

Other movement issues and stances may also be less rigid than is often presented in academic debates. At different stages in the movement, leading groups have advocated different relationships to the forest, based on differing local needs. The relationship of natural ecology and human economy continues to fluctuate. What is often not taken into consideration when the critics say that certain interests (usually male) do not respect the forest, or that it is only later that the movement becomes an ecological one is that the local people are likely to treat their own forests better than outsiders would. For them, sustainability cannot be negotiated away, yet some people simultaneously believe that negotiations with government—though not with outside corporate interests—need to happen. Gandhian co-ops developed resin and other forest products to support the local cash economy. In India the purist wilderness stance that forest produce should be kept separate from a cash economy has a direct, ideological disconnect to Gandhian village development models. With an ecopolitical grounding that is very different from most U.S. wilderness purist stances it may be most radical among localist stands. Nonetheless, all local stances, are best understood as part of a shifting spectrum of interests and perspectives that speak to a variety of concerns.

Shobita Jain tells us that the history of Chipko is the "history of the visions and actions of exceptionally courageous women" and she places the Chipko Movement as part of international women's history: "Environmental movements like Chipko have become historical landmarks because they have been fueled by the ecological insights and political and moral strengths of women." She addresses a specific universal women's audience: "the experience of these powerful women also needs to be shared to remind us that we are not alone...others have walked before us" (172–173). According to Jain: "[t]he Chipko process as a resurgence of woman power and ecological concern in the Garhwal Himalaya is a similar mosaic of many events and multiple actors" (172–173). Jain's description marks one end of the spectrum of academic attitudes regarding the role of gender, and the predominant gender of those involved in the Chipko Movement.

Academics debate to what extent Chipko is a women's movement and how opposed the women's service clubs or mahila mandals interests are to male-dominated gram panchayats, which had interest in commercial development. A second related debate is over differing ideological trends. Shiva associated with Bahuguna's "deep ecology." Guha sided with Bhatt's "appropriate technology" stance. Then in "Will the Real Chipko Please Stand Up?" Guha favored a third option "represented by the Uttarkhand Sangarsh Vahini (USV) working in the Kumaon area on issues that included an anti-alcohol campaign and a demand for a separate state of 'Uttarkhand.'" The USV believes the "human-nature relationship must not be viewed in isolation from existing relationships within humans.... USV sees social and economic redistribution as logically prior to ecological harmony." USV became part of Indian People's Front; and in the Indian left press, ecology was posed in opposition to economic development (Omvedt 134).

Omvedt's description, like others, returns to the ecology-economy divide showing that it is tied in with gender identities, but also it is at its most strident and polarized among the intelligentsia's discussion of the Chipko movement. At the local level it appears to have differing and more complex implications. The divisions most often noted in narratives about Chipko narratives involve divisions in political, ideological, and practical strategies.

Chandi Prasad Bhatt and Sunderlal Bahuguna, the two Sarvodaya workers who became key figures in the Chipko movement, split ideologically in their conflicting feelings toward the ban that curtailed all forest cutting, including that being done for local needs (Linkenbach 75). Bhatt and Bahuguna "heard long stories of suffering by women. This experience gave them both an insight into women's problems and an unprecedented direct contact with them" (Jain 171). While Jain's description and Bhatt's described role in the Reni demonstration suggests that he is working in sync with the women's desires, he is seen as philosophically parting company with Bahuguna (and presumably with most women) in his readiness to create local forest production for export. Bahuguna rejects Bhatt's alternative plans for local technology because he felt it would destroy the earth when he acknowledges that "[t]oday I see clearly that establishing sawmills in the hills is to join the project to destroy Mother Earth" (in Omvedt 1993, 133).

Bahuguna's group became involved with politically active coalitions. Meanwhile, Bahuguna expanded his audiences with "his prophetic style, padyatras, and theorizing in radical Gandhian fashion on the relation between human and forest" and he promoted the Chipko movement nationally and internationally as an ecological issue; he often also expressed the ecological concerns as "women's concerns" (Omvedt 1993, 132–133). Thus, while both Bahuguna and Bhatt challenge "prevailing projects of development" and both claim Gandhian roots, their spheres of influence have shifted in almost ironical ways. Antje Linkenbach suggests that the debate that emerged between these two leaders emulates a preceding debate—over two visions for independence—that evoked the deep ideological differences between M.K. Gandhi (and others) and J. Nehru (and others) during and following the Independence Movement. However, Linkenbach's comparison elides feminist-provoked ideological cultural shifts reflected in Bahuguna's more progressive view, relative to Gandhi's, towards more equal partnering with women. Also, Linkenbach overlooks changes in the context of ecological understanding and devastation, both of which have increased greatly in the intervening years.

5.6 The Gandhi Nehru Divide on Nature

Gandhi's project is a precursor to the ideal model developed by Sunderlal Bahuguna and the Chipko women in that Gandhi wanted to limit desires, and decentralize economically, creating an essential role for the political structures of villages. Economic and political control would thus be localized, and skills and talents locally expanded. Gandhi pressed for reconstruction of villages as a universalist moral utopia not unlike the real communities elsewhere that offer ecological models, such as the Ganados de Valle community in New Mexico on which Ana Castillo models her fictional town's community governance in *So Far From God*. Linkenbach argues that Nehru's project, on the other hand, can be seen as a precursor to contemporary development of global corporate capitalism in India (Linkenbach 65–66); this seems ironical, if not dubious, given Nehru's socialist ideals and the ultra-capitalist nature of current development models. In a section entitled "The Crossroads of Modernity—Development or Reconstruction," Linkenbach traces Gandhi's gram raj (village rule), which has continued to be used by leftists and militants versus Nehru's socialist industrial model of modernization that was to end "all exploitation of nation by nation and class by class" (64). For Nehru, political freedom would be followed by economic freedom; for Gandhi economic freedom was a precursor to political freedom. For Nehru, villages were backward, village life was irrelevant to modernization and nature was a resource for industry. For Gandhi, independence was a condition for allowing a revival of morals, and the character of "Indian tradition and civilization" that critiques the West and claims universal relevance (Partha Chatterjee in Linkenbach).

In a subsequent section entitled "Progress or Plunder?—Disenchantment of Development" Linkenbach states that environmental degradation in India illustrates that "the conflict between industrialization and life-supporting systems has reached its climax and calls development itself into question" (Linkenbach 67). To warrant this geopolitically, she paraphrases Daryll D'Monte: "Nehru's 'temples of today' have turned into tombs for millions. Due primarily to so-called *ecological movements* these consequences surfaced in the public arena" giving a previously academic discussion a "practical impact" (Linkenbach 68).

Gail Omvedt voices a similar, but less polemic view compared to Linkenbach's when she finds that Gandhi, like other nationalists and leftists, "is critical of industrial capitalism and, indeed, much of today's Indian environmentalism refers back to Gandhi" (Omvedt 1993, 12). He is more distinctive in his goal for Indian independence "in terms of the regeneration of Indian village society, a small-scale, labor-focused society" (Omvedt 11). This led to his current image as "a kind of early 'Green'," a forerunner of the ecological movement, the root of an alternative socialism in India. However, Gandhi's critique of industrialism is based on a religious outlook which is "founded on Hindu *advaita*, that stressed the limitation of human needs and was in the final analysis opposed to both technology and sexuality..." (Omvedt 1993, 12). Gandhi's was not finally a materialist analysis, and his vision of reform of the system for women and Dalits was still based on a framework of paternalistic kingdoms and caste-categories, according to Omvedt (1993, 12–13). In comparison, the subsequent, new social movements, including ecological movements and the women's movements, (which Omvedt addresses in separate chapters) and Dalit rights movements, have moved away from such discriminating limitations and restraints.

Nonetheless, numerous chroniclers suggest that the Gandhian legacy and philosophy influenced the Chipko Andolan both directly and implicitly, as, for example, Weber notes:

> Political oppression, economic oppression and exploitation rest to a large degree on the acquiescence of the exploited. With this in mind, Gandhi noted that the 'exploitation of the poor can be extinguished not by effecting the destruction of a few millionaires, but by removing the ignorance of the poor and teaching them to non-cooperate with the exploiters.' And this was the job that the *sarvodaya* activists and constructive workers set out to do when they began their active work in the Uttarkhand hills in the 1950s and 1960s. The results were the Chipko andolans. (86)

While Linkenbach's assessment of the current ecological crisis and its relationship to development is sound and she is justified in attributing the divisions in Chipko to Nehru's versus Gandhi's ideologies, she is not justified in dismissing gender from the constellation that affects the debates. Linkenbach's focus is in studying the "academic discussion" and understanding the "practical impact" is shortchanged. I find her work useful in thinking through ideological stances from a somewhat traditional modernist approach, but less applicable to the theoretical apparatus generated from within the Chipko activism and poetics.

While, on one level, Linkenbach favors the Gandhian model, she has a strong critique of how groups that follow this model have been *perceived*, nationally and internationally. She sees representations of ecological movements as panacea that are creating new economic values for global survival, yet she believes that "[e]specially in the West, ecological movements have various additional significances for people criticizing development;" they ease first world guilt and develop a lazy romanticism: "Glorification of movements...[provides a] useful excuse for resting (while others are fighting)" and, at the same time, "ecological movements seem to succeed in reinforcing one's own struggle for environmental conservation, women's empowerment" (69). In this context, "non-hierarchical structures of social interaction...[and] certain features of the movement like women's participation, spontaneity and equality are easily exaggerated" and interpretations of ecological movements engage in "mystification, heroization and oversimplification; movements are functionalized and 'used' according to the interest of the interpreters". Middle class Indians, Indians in the West, including academics, social activists, journalists and the "leaders and activists of ecology movements" all come under Linkenbach's critique. "Far from being the 'authentic' voice of 'the' movement they often are expressing their own ideas and targets—which are at best more or less influenced by the ideas of 'common' participants. They are speaking *for* the others, articulating what they call 'their' (the others') ideas and concepts." (70)[94]

Linkenbach's sketch of the Indian social context does not address all the issues that new social movements for environmental equity and justice in India are facing today. Often theirs are the issues that theories of economic nationalism didn't confront, such as the "drain from the villages upward to the capitalist or bureaucratic elite" (Omvedt 8) or issues of indigenous rights, women's rights and forest rights that post-colonial theories have not adequately addressed. Gail Omvedt cites Jotirao Phule as a forerunner to new social movements, including the women's movement, for in the 19th Century, he had already written on women's enslavement, as well as caste and class exploitation. In Maharashtra, in the mid 19th century, Phule espoused the "liberatory reversal of the 'Aryan theory'" rejecting the popular belief that upper castes were descended from Indo-Europeans, but emphasizing, rather, that "their conquest had imposed an exploitative caste hierarchy over an indigenous population that had lived in a state of prosperity and equality" (Omvedt 15). He founded Satyashodhak Samaj the "truth-seekers society" dedicated to rationalism...and... education for boys and girls, and he started the first school for girls in 1848 and for untouchables (girls as well as boys?) in 1851; late in life, he also attacked the double standard of sexual behavior applied between men and women (Omvedt 15).

In Omvedt's view, Communist tradition in India "derived from the radical nationalism symbolized by Tilak, defined itself against the 'anti-industrial peasantism' of Gandhi and ignored Phule and similar low-caste traditions" (Omvedt 15). Omvedt looks at women's environmental justice organizing, examining, and critiquing the sociological complexity of the Indian communist tradi-

94 Linkenbach asserts that she is not "devaluing the movements themselves"—but saying that the "'indigenous' voices and especially the voices of 'common' participants are judged by others, transformed and translated" (70). The shortcomings to this phenomenon that she lists are 1) "Movements as monolithic phenomena;" 2) "One-sided classification, a priori definition of targets" (she suggests movements are labeled with inherent implicit meanings and they are then used for different purposes); 3) "Movements as spontaneous indigenous expression of uneasiness" (she claims that outside initiation is not given its adequate due; again she asks whose "voices" are being heard);. 4) The "[m]ovements as conservators of traditional lifestyles" stance on the fight against development overemphasizes the effort to "conserve or restore 'traditional' ways of life" (70). She says we are "putting them [villagers] into prehistory, we are denying them co-presence and the right to live in modernity." She says we do this because then they are no longer "competing to get an equal share of the cake;" rather, academics can find that "[t]he burden of preserving nature should be their task, the benefit of exploiting nature ours" (5). For Linkenbach, this means that "[m]ovements as authentic forms of agency" are foregrounded, while other forms of resistance are devalued.

tion thus moving beyond more narrowly defined agendas of some NSM and even socialist scholars to show that the definition of poverty, itself, is an ideological formation with empirical results for those to whom it is applied. Vandana Shiva sums up a similar observation: the "cultural perception of prudent subsistence living as poverty has provided the legitimisation for the development process as a poverty removal project. As a culturally biased project it destroys wholesome and sustainable lifestyles and creates real material poverty, or misery, by the denial of survival needs themselves..." (Two Kinds of Poverty" in *Staying Alive)*. Both strains of Chipko are rejecting such bias, replacing it with their own forest-respecting strategies for reform.

5.7 Conclusions

Despite questions raised about Vandana Shiva's descriptions of the nature of the Chipko Andolan, the *model* she utilizes—perhaps, at times, imperfectly—is sound, and bears our examination. Her practice of conceiving theory from praxis sets an important precedent for cultural theory. While the concept of basing theory in activism is now banal, it is rarely carried out in the radical sense that, at her best moments, Shiva executes.[95] Such a practice may be crucial to understanding and organizing social movements because it can fine-tune our conceptions to the contextual specificities of the given social situation.

An example of this from my mother's research is illustrated in her post-project analysis of The Barpali Project, an American Friends Service Committee (AFSC) development program in Barpali thana in Orissa in the 1950s that marks some of the differences between foreign co-workers, Indian personnel, and Indian villagers (not entirely mutually exclusive categories):

> Probably the most troublesome difference was one of timing or pacing. Western personnel, coming from a cultural background in which the emphasis was on action and achievement rather than on reflection, had difficulty in adjusting to the pace of villagers *who spent much time in discussion and reflective thought before arriving at the point of action*. This was particularly frustrating to Western staff who were eager to accomplish as much as possible during their two-year assignments. (E.L. Platt 1990) (emphasis, mine)

---

95 Others such as Shobita Jain and Gail Omvedt, whose work I have drawn on in this chapter, replicate theory from activism models without articulating their intent to do so as thoroughly as Shiva.

The observation of extensive, albeit unwritten, theorizing undertaken on the part of Indian villagers, in distinction from outsiders—in this case, development workers with benevolent intention—suggests the necessity for scholars to reconsider where the most astute analysis of local, and by logical extension, global, situations, is occurring. That we often ignore the extensive process of "theorizing" when it is not written down is an academic bias that scholars have yet to remedy. Re-conceiving of villagers as people in consistent negotiation over the acceptance, rejection, resisting, reworking, or repurposing of outside forces who wish to impose impacts on their village communities, one uncovers pictures that contrast with the description from many outside chroniclers. In both theory and story, discussions that remain unwritten may retain better, unaltered local perspectives. The implicit suggestion that villagers are passive objects of victimization to be acted upon and spoken for is dispelled. Likewise, urban-dwelling activists, such as the women in MELA offer models of resistance in ways that counter the stereotypical "victims." When such local poetics—in whatever form it is generated—is examined comparatively it, at times challenges, and at times substantiates, the theories of postcolonial and decolonial scholars, cultural critics, and sociologists; in these cases, the comparison is immensely valuable.

This chapter has examined the poetic and philosophical means by which one of the most successful and famous environmental justice groups in the world have carried out their purposes; their work offers models of empirical success and theoretical quests. Ultimately, my discussion does not so much draw conclusions, as pose new windows of opportunity for alliance-building, scholarship, and activism. It raises questions about the frameworks upon which much scholarship on activist poetics has been conducted.

The following chapter will focus on another site of desecration of environments and human beings that has resulted from the increasing chemicalization of the planet. Groups seeking restitution and a new start in the aftermath of the Bhopal gas leak in India, like the farmworkers seeking curtailment of the agricultural pesticides that cause health problems in their communities, continue their struggle into the 21st Century. I examine the first decade of their poetics that demands a halt to environmentally racist policies and reparations for those who continue to suffer the results of past grievances.

6 Bhopal: Writing Tragedy as Ultimatum for Change

> Bhopal ... revealed for the whole world the murderous nature of the multinational companies and of the capitalist "development" that was the major ideological base of postindependence third world regimes.
>
> Gail Omvedt (1993, 149)

> It was the year of the Ogre, Union Carbide, the multinational which showed the ugly face of Capitalism. Hell's fire and sulphur would have been preferable to the gas that enveloped Bhopal ....This may be how the world will end—not with a bang but with a whimper.
>
> Abu Abraham[96]

In the decade afterward, a variety of poetics exposed the massacre—and legal, medical, and environmental aftermaths—that resulted from a gas leak in the Union Carbide Corporation (UCC) pesticide plant in Bhopal, Madhya Pradesh, India on the night of December 2–3, 1984.[97] On the streets of Bhopal, sculpture and graffiti commemorate the gas leak. Bhopal survivors, residents, and workers played instrumental roles in challenging the injustices wrought by Union Carbide Corporation and the governments of India and Madhya Pradesh in the wake of the initial tragedy. They demonstrated with banners, posters, effigies, and street theater and consequently have been harassed by police and arrested. They set up clinics and work rehabilitation centers only to have them dismantled. Survivors toured the world to publicize their cause, leading meetings and demonstrations and facing arrest on foreign soil, in places like Houston, Texas. They spoke at International Tribunals on Industrial and Environmental Hazards and Human Rights. At crucial junctures they produced collections of testimonials and anthologies that approach the disaster from journalistic, legal, medical, and other perspectives. One could develop a complete chronology of the events following and implications of Bhopal from these anthologies.[98] Each year on the anniversary of Bhopal's UCC plant gas-leak, demonstrations are held in Bhopal

---

96 In *Sunday Observer* 23/12 quoted in *Bhopal: a people's view of death, their right to know and live...* (6).

97 Here I use the term that Larry Everest has chosen to describe the events in Bhopal. As Everest observes, "massacre" "certainly isn't the word Union Carbide Corporation or the U.S. media are using" (8).

98 The Delhi Science Forum reportedly produced a Dec 12, 1984, account but the earliest work I was able to locate is *a peoples view...* which Eklavya produced on Dec 25, 1984. One of the most comprehensive reports from those affected is *Bhopal The Inside Story: Carbide Workers Speak Out on the World's Worst Industrial Disaster.* compiled by T.R. Chouhan, who had been an MIC Plant Operator at UCC's Bhopal plant.

https://doi.org/10.1515/9783111041575-007

and among other events an effigy of Warren Anderson, UCC's top executive at the time of the leak, is burned.[99] Activists vow that until the time when just compensation for victims is granted, and the survivors' health and other basic needs are provided for, such demonstrations and other cultural forms of protest will continue.[100] The ten-year anniversary in 1994 was commemorated with renewed attention to the situation by organizations worldwide. In subsequent years, as internet access increased globally, the struggles of the survivors' organizations became increasingly widespread. The effects of the internet on activist cultural poetics and the movements associated with them can be thoroughly studied only when we have a baseline sense of what came before—that time is covered here.

July 27, 2006, Sunil Kumar died in his Bhopal apartment by his own hand. A 13-year-old in 1984, who lost seven members of his immediate family in the explosion, Sunil, one of the most politically active of the survivors, traveled internationally to seek justice, was arrested in Houston at the UCC meetings, and founded Children Against Carbide; he also developed mental illness, a common malady among survivors. Sunil's story is readily accessible now on the internet, but what is the significance of this poetics to the survivors?[101] There is little evidence it is bringing them closer to justice or to meeting their needs. A calendar note at the top of the International Campaign for Justice in Bhopal website notes the days (currently over 8000) and the average compensation survivors have received—6,2 cents per day. While the Bhopal cultural poetics may have less than desired effects in bringing justice overall, the longstanding record of survivors' organizations is, by contrast, extraordinary—exemplary in social movement longevity and efficacy.[102] Like many social movements' groups that start with a single issue, they have expanded to address the many embedded issues of global corporate domination. In January of 2007, they made the news internationally with a call for a boycott of Tata tea and salt as the company was supporting Dow Chemical (then, 100 % owner of Union Carbide) against the survivors groups who claim Dow is responsible for the compensation and clean up that never came from Union Carbide; a similar campaign continues in 2021 with the disabled children of Bhopal

99 "Bhopal" has acquired metonymical status and, to facilitate brevity, I use it thus.

100 In "Bhopal Ten Years After" (in Chouhan 113–180) Claude Alvares reports a chronology of each years' events which culminate in a description of that year's anniversary demonstration.

101 See, for example: https://www.bhopal.net/?s=Sunil.

102 At the end of 2022, in *The Indian Express* article "Four decades on, fresh hope for victims of the Bhopal gas tragedy" Upendra Baxi writes: "Babasaheb Ambedkar constantly reminded us that past injustices carry no expiry date. Revival of a curative petition in the Supreme Court marks a new commitment to justice for the Bhopal victims."

survivors.[103] Thirty-seven years after the event, Bhopal.net homepage reported anniversary commemorations, noting groundwater contamination, high rates of Covid suffering, continuing corporate and government discrimination and continued action by survivors' groups. What then lies behind the active longevity of the Bhopal survivors? The poetics of the past may help us understand.

The Bhopal victim's organizations include Bhopal Gas Peedit Mahila Udyog Sangathan (Bhopal Gas-Affected Women Workers Association), Bhopal Gas Peedit Mahila Stationary Karmachari Sangh (Bhopal Gas-Affected Women Stationery Workers Union), Zahreeli Gas Kand Sangarsh Samiti Morcha, (Poisonous Gas Disaster Struggle Front (ZGKSM)) and Bhopal Nirashrit Pension Bhogi Sangharsh Morcha (Bhopal Gas-Affected Destitute Pensioners Struggle Front (NPBSM)). National and International support organizations such as Self-Employed Women's Association (SEWA), ECLAVYA, Delhi Science Forum, Medico Friends Circle, Delhi Committee on Bhopal Gas Tragedy, The International Coalition for Justice in Bhopal, The Permanent People's Tribunal (PPT), the International Organization of Consumer Unions (IOCU), No More Bhopals Network, the Consumer Council of Zimbabwe, The Bhopal Action Resource Center, Communities Concerned About Corporations and the Council of International and Public Affairs are only a few of the NGOs that have promoted the struggle for survivors' rights in Bhopal.[104]

Photographers, journalists, scholars, artists, filmmakers, cartoonists, social activists, medical doctors, foreign correspondents, lawyers, and environmentalists from India and around the world–in particular, the US, Canada, Japan, Malaysia, Netherlands, Ireland and Germany–have also educated the public internationally and rallied support for the survivors. Award-winning films have been produced.[105] Fiction, drama, poetry and children's books have commemorated Bhopal in literature.[106] Articles and books have been produced, many with

---

103 See https://www.bhopal.net/disabled-children-born-to-gas-exposed-parents-urge-pm-cm-to-ensure-their-legal-rights-from-ucc-dow-chemical/.

104 Morehouse and Subramaniam list organizations (as of 1986) in *The Bhopal Tragedy* (148–161) and Morehouse lists a few groups that continued to be active in "Unfinished Business ..." (1994). *Bhopal Lives!...* lists the Hindi and English names of groups that remained active in 1994.

105 For example, *Bhopal–Beyond Genocide* a film by Suhasini Mulay, Salim Shaikh and Tapan Bose won the best non-feature film in India's national film awards in 1988 (*Lokayan Bulletin* 186). Granada television produced *The Betrayal of Bhopal* in June of 1985, an acclaimed documentary that established that it was UCC's cost-cutting measures that led to the gas leak. The media was put up to making slanderous reports about the filmmaking which were proved to be completely unfounded. The attacks on the film illustrate the perceived threats as well as the effectiveness of investigative filmmaking.

106 "Dastan-e-Gaskhand" a dramatic play "on the Bhopal Tragedy" was written by Rajesh Lochan et al. (Rajan 30); Kasmiri Lala Zakira has written a Hindi novel *lasakara ka akhiri*

the purpose of presenting what the mainstream media in the US, India, and elsewhere often does not divulge—a continuing "holocaust" that left some survivors feeling that the ones who had died were the lucky ones. (Vivek 4, Morehouse 1994 UB, 165, "The International Medical Appeal for Bhopal" poster).

As the aftermath of what at the time was considered—apart from Chernobyl—the world's worst industrial accident continues, mainstream media coverage trickled off, except as anniversaries are noted.[107] Bhopal has, however, become a subject of study for medical researchers, sociologists, law scholars, environmentalists, and UCC's financial recovery has become a model for business students. By the mid 1990's Bhopal was also appearing on internet websites. Bhopal Action Resource Center in NYC and other groups have homepages, however, Bhopal groups did not initially appear to be using the internet with the intensity of some groups from the South, like the Zapatistas used emailing. Poetics in the 1990s reveal that little improvement in meeting the basic needs or honoring the rights of the survivors had been made: in most cases, gas leak victims have not received remuneration that in any way equals the cost of what they have undergone and continue to endure. Attempts to comprehend the MIC gas-induced afflictions that hundreds of thousands of people experience continued to be stymied by misinformation, withheld information and lack of both funds and sufficient organized study.[108] Meanwhile, like on the Texas-Mexico border, multinational corporate rights—usurping the rights of survivors—expanded through international agreements in the intervening years, especially through India's privatization in the early 1990's. An inverse correlation expanded between honoring corporate rights and dishonoring human and environmental wellbeing.

When released at Bhopal, MIC-generated gases spread and quickly diffused, but the toxins' effects remain in the atmosphere and in the bodies of those who

---

sipahi: Bhopala gaisa trasadi para adharita (1993) which is "based on the Bhopal Union Carbide Plant Disaster ... its social, economic effects, and physical disability faced by the people effected by it." (Columbia University Library Catalogue, 7-19-96). A children's book on Bhopal with illustrations that are both explicit and exquisite was published in Japan in 1985. *The Bhopal Chemical Leak* by Arthur Diamond with illustrations by Bryan McGovern is part of the "World Disaster Series" for youth. Indra Sinha's *Animal's People* (2007), a novel about the Bhopal gas tragedy offering a critique of a loss inside neoliberalism is discussed in Chapter Seven's treatment of cultural poetic discourse generated in support of Bhopal's survivor communities.

107 For a study of the first two months of mainstream U.S. media coverage, see Lee Wilkins' *Shared Vulnerability*.

108 Methyl isocyanate (MIC) was used at Bhopal for pesticide production; when the runaway reaction occurred it created gases, the complete contents of which have not been uncovered.

were exposed. Irreversible damage may continue to produce cancers in years to come and genetic mutations in future generations. However, "official" representations of Bhopal were created by an industry concerned with retaining stockholder interests and renouncing culpability and by national and state governments that were more interested in protecting potential corporate investment than providing for the needs of their people. Like the long-term effects of the gas exposure, their images of what happened and who was responsible continue to affect relations between local communities and industrial corporations.[109] However, the poetics of environmental justice strive to expose and reverse the demise of victim's rights, health, and environment. Ward Morehouse, president of the Council on International and Public Affairs in NYC, stated that "[t]he resistance shown by the thousands of Bhopal survivors is the only redeeming aspect of an unmitigated tale of abuse and exploitation" [110] (UF 1994, 168).

Bhopal's most consistent and continuous—though often overlooked—voices are those of its survivors and those, like Morehouse, working in support of their rights. They have chosen activism and analysis as means to expose false representations of the "accident" and "worker sabotage" (as the gas leak has been defined by government and corporation, respectively).[111] For instance, 'Tara Jones,' an Irish environmentalist involved in struggles against toxic hazards and the author of *Corporate Killing: Bhopals Will Happen*, points out that removing "worker control over the work process" makes accidents more likely (3).[112] This assertion directly counters Union Carbide's strategy of scapegoating workers for its mishaps, and is consistent with U.S. environmental justice's worker advocacy in regard to

---

109 While Bhopal may have forced the chemical industry to make some changes toward promoting human safety, publications within the corporate arena seem more interested in stockholder interests and preventing anything that might interfere with the maximization of profits, be it accident or remunerations. However, the *Chemical and Engineering News* has given relatively consistent and fair-minded, if not progressive coverage to the situation over the years. See: Wil Lepkowski reporting on the 1984 Bhopal disaster for Chemical & Engineering News in Wil Lepkowski Papers (1934–2019) https://archives.sciencehistory.org/subjects/991.

110 Ward Morehouse, president of the Council on International and Public Affairs in NYC, was a founder of the International Coalition for Justice in Bhopal and is considered a "UCC gadfly" by many. Attending the UCC annual stockholders' meetings, he reminds them of the continuing suffering due to their unmet responsibilities in Bhopal (in discussion 7-17-96).

111 UCC created an extensive public relations campaign to suggest that sabotage by a "disgruntled worker" caused the leak. In so doing, UCC attempts to move beyond the definition of "accident" (potentially "no blame") to accuse an Indian worker, thus creating a scapegoat. See discussion of the video *Union Carbide: Disaster at Bhopal* for further amplification of this.

112 Jones further develops her analysis of the scapegoating of workers when she analyzes the common terminology of "human error" and negligence. See pages 212–236.

the crucial importance of "the workers' right to know."[113] Survivors and their allies represent very different *decades since* than those who, despite the massacre, ultimately benefited from UCC and its profit-making carelessness.[114] Activist poetics promote environmental justice in the wake of a monumental industrial tragedy and map the disaster onto territories of environmental and gender justice. They demonstrate that women (economically disenfranchised women in specific) and other societally disenfranchised groups were distinctively impacted, directly and indirectly, by the environmental effects of the malfunction and its aftermath. Women have been substantially represented among the leaders in confronting the medical, legal, social, and political issues that the gas leak raised, and they have often suffered harassment and arrest.[115]

An exhaustive study of the many sobering accounts that offer comparative summaries of events and ramifications would be an immense task—hence, my choice of a focus on the iconography of a few survivors' groups, along with journalistic, environmentalist, and social activists' narratives in comparison with UCC's own narratives. Two texts bear mention at this point, as they roughly mark the perimeters of my study. Indira Jaising, a lawyer, and C. Sathyamala, a doctor, are among the Indian women whose own *writing* about Bhopal, in the

113 "Workers right to know" legislation in the United States was passed following the Bhopal gas leak. It is politically ironic and an indication of the continuing double standard in safety concerns between "first" and "third worlds" that the Bhopal runaway gas reaction may have had more positive effect on such social environmentalist legislation in the U.S. than in India.

114 UCC CEOs and stockholders turned around financial losses that resulted from the disaster. For instance, in a brief public statement on February 14, 1989, Union Carbide Corporation indicated that the settlement reached at that point would result in no more than a 50 cents charge per share against the 1988 profit. Thereby, profit per share fell to about $1.09 from $1.59. Carbide was the most active issue on the New York Stock Exchange that Valentine's Day. About 6.4 million shares changed hands, and the stock price shot up by two dollars. (UCC had reserves of $250 million for potential liability insurance coverage) (Gupta 32). That the economic impact of the accident sidestepped administrators as well is repeatedly illustrated. For example, consider the implications of the title of a March 13, 1995, Inter Press Service story by Pratap Chatterjee: "Bhopal Chief Retires to Beach Resort in Florida;" when compared to accounts of contemporaneous situations for the gas leak survivors, the circumstances of those in charge become particularly audacious. Business students have shown me textbooks using UCC's handling of Bhopal as a case study in economic recovery of a disaster.

115 For examples of feminist summaries that address women's activism in Bhopal, see Joni Seager's *Earth Follies: Feminism, Politics and the Environment* 1993, 96–101 and Radha Kumar's India feminism history *The History of Doing: An Illustrated Account of Movements for Women's Rights and Feminism in India 1800-1990*. Almost all the extensive, later accounts of events mention women's primary roles in struggle; some of the earlier accounts do not.

decade following, is available in English.[116] Their article "Legal Rights...and Wrongs: Internationalising Bhopal," in *Close to Home* (1994) documents the global and local ramifications when justice is dispensed with, rather than dispensed. Their legal and theoretical contextualization helps me frame my understanding of the physical, societal, and political implications for the women involved. Another resource insightful to my study is *Bhopal: a people's view of death, their right to Know and Live: A reconstruction of the gas tragedy, its background and aftermath, from press reports and local information*, produced by a collective of unnamed individuals within days of the gas leak. *A people's view...* provides the source for a close reading of figurative language that contextualizes more specific concerns.[117] In addition to these sources, a plethora of materials have aided me in producing the following gendered history of Bhopal's environmental injustices and the subsequent iconography of resistance.[118]

In its broadest sense, my comparative study of activist-aligned poetics demonstrates a new version of a well-worn adage: discrimination against people of any class, gender, race, religion, national status, sexual orientation, etc. based on prejudice ultimately threatens the civil, environmental, and human rights of a large majority of humankind. More specifically, these poetics demonstrate how such discrimination and prejudice gain power for their perpetrators through unmitigated representation. Moreover, I show how historicized counter-representations from multiple relevant perspectives may be used to further what Gayatri Spivak calls the "ethical singularity" in intergroup interactions that may counter the prejudice-based power that is pervasive in a corporatized world.

Transnational communication, language barriers, and in particular, the very elements of containment discussed here, have contributed to severe, pre-internet limitations on the availability of work on Bhopal. Despite the international concern and the numerous chronicles, Bhopal groups have not received the widespread publicity that, for example, their sister Indian environmental justice movement against lumbering, the Chipko movement (discussed in the preceding chapter), has attained. This may be due to a phenomenon like the one (mentioned in Chapter

---

116 My research suggests that women have produced few book length texts; reasons for this may include cultural and societal limitations against such work in India and elsewhere.

117 I am grateful to Barbara Harlow's Third World Literature courses where I realized the value of the practice of close readings (the greatest contribution of the literary New Critics) for reading texts for cultural study and historicization. Possibly this practical method is also a useful academic contribution to activist analysis. It is one good way I can gather the literary equivalent of "empirical data" in examining environmental justice organizing as a new social movement.

118 The Bhopal Action Resource Center in NYC generously provided me with an abundance of resources.

Three) when one Latina activist, Aurora Castillo, is celebrated by an elite power behind the very corporation that is denying rights to their previous Latina employees—the activists in Fuerza Unida. Bhopal survivors, perhaps more emphatically than most other groups, bring the rest of the world face to face with the empirical results of corporate-sponsored chemicalization of the planet. Yet, they struggle against what was, at the time, one of the three largest chemical corporations, and they also often struggle against their own federal governments. Their continuing strength despite corporate power establishes their vital importance to those promoting environmental justice but may also be one very basic reason they are vilified by multinational corporate and governmental interests.

6.1 Manifestations of a Massacre: A Chronology: Language in the Service of Deceit

> Writing about Bhopal interrogates authorial integrity. Bhopal epitomizes the dichotomy between 'suffering' and 'thinking' humanity, a dichotomy that Karl Marx tried to resolve when he spoke of the existence of "a suffering human being who think[s] and of thinking human beings who are oppressed" ... Put another way, the possibility of a new world respecting [the] humanity of those who suffer lies in the capacity of thinking humanity to suffer and suffering humanity to think: Bhopal victims, in their articulate silence, invite us to a fellowship of suffering, a fellowship which has the potential of turning the catastrophe back on its makers. Bhopal summons us to a struggle, at all levels, to recover the common humanity of humankind from its expropriators.
>
> Upendra Baxi

Many narratives report UCC and government cover-ups of the nature, extent, and effects of the mishap.[119] This misinformation has a history that preceded the gas-

119 UCC would not disclose the chemical composition of the mixture of gases that leaked. When asked to divulge this information, "they pleaded trade secrecy and took shelter behind patent laws" (Jaising 95). The Indian Council of Medical Research (ICMR), after double-blind control trial on the gas victims, reported that "the toxicological studies carried out so far have ruled out the possibility of carbon monoxide poisoning" and have "clearly shown that at least in the survivors there is evidence of chronic cyanide poisoning operating as a result of either inhalation of hydrocyanic acid or more probably subsequent generation of cyanide radical from the cyanogen pool in gas afflicted victims ..." (Brojendra Nath Banerjee 122). The pesticide plant in Bhopal was partially owned by Union Carbide India Limited (UCIL) however, I identify UCIL only when speaking specifically about UCIL. At several points before the leak UCIL and UCC did not see eye to eye. UCC has tried to shift blame for the massacre onto UCIL and the Indian government. While considered unjustifiable on UCC's part, the fact of India's ownership impacted legal settlements. See Jamie Casels' "The Uncertain Promise of Law: Lessons from

leak: the cover-up extends back to a negation of the pre-existing hazardous conditions. The post-disaster cover-up has only continued a dismissal of safety concerns that initially produced the climate in which an "accident" was likely to happen.

Numerous chroniclers report a famous journalistic prediction of the UCC Bhopal runaway reaction. Raj Kumar Keswani's warning is so often alluded to in the aftermath literature that it could almost be discussed as the prologue to these writings.[120] For three years before December 1984, Keswani, a Bhopal-based journalist, had warned repeatedly that the UCC plant was a disaster waiting to happen. In a series of articles printed by *Satahik Report* (The Weekly Report), a local Hindi newspaper, he pleaded, "Save! Please Save the City," "Bhopal on the Mouth of a Volcano," and "if you don't understand you will be wiped out."[121] In June 1984, barely five months before the disaster, he repeated his warning in an article published in the Hindi daily, *Jansatta*. As Jaising and C. Sathyamala observe, "[t]oday, the corpses of the dead and the suffering of millions stand in mute testimony to the prophetic nature of his warning" (88). While recognizing the importance of critiquing media misrepresentations that obscure environmental racism, media reports—such as Keswani's—may also prefigure and contribute to activist analysis. Indeed, Keswani in his diligent concern for Bhopal's people demonstrates the accountability in journalism that media critics such as Lee Wilkins have called for.

A worker had first alerted Keswani to the dangers of the plant and other workers had mobilized to demand safer conditions prior to the gas-leak. T. R. Chouhan, a former UCC operator relates the story of a previous "accident" that made famous a UCC Bhopal workers' adage that "anything can happen in this factory."

> In 1978, there was a big fire in the factory. I was working in the Sevin plant on the first shift. As we were leaving at the end of the shift, I saw that all the four rear wheels of the factory fire truck had been taken off, with the vehicle resting on a jack. I commented to my coworkers about the possibility of a fire breaking out with the only fire truck out of commission. My friends thought the management was much too stingy to invest in another fire truck so that there would be at least one fire truck always in readiness, and our discussion ended with an ominous chant of "anything can happen in this factory."
>
> When we reached Peer Gate about 3 km away from the factory, we saw fire trucks rushing in that direction. When we looked back, we saw smoke billowing out .... (27)

Bhopal" for a thorough study of the legal implications of Bhopal. See also "The Jurisprudence of Remedial Justice" by Chhatrapati Singh and "Accountability, Justice and Prevention: From Victim Exploitation and Victim Blackmail to Victim Empowerment" by Clarence J. Dias.

120 For instance, see de Grazia page 44–45.

121 The series appeared in September/October 1982. (Jaising and C Sathyamala 88).

While many believed that this fire was started by management for political reasons, reducing the likelihood that the fire's bad timing was a coincidence, Chouhan documents the many reasons that workers felt their plant was not safe and tells how union organizing for a safer workplace was quashed when key organizers lost their jobs (35). Having been forced to take risks during their work, sometimes suffering ill-health as a result, most of the workers felt strongly about the need for safer working conditions and were committed to action. It was more difficult to mobilize the surrounding communities to attend the public meetings that the union held at the factory gates in 1982; many feared losing their homes because they didn't have *pattas* or paper land deeds (35).[122]

The workers and their friends and allies were not the only people who realized the potential danger of plant conditions, nor were they the only ones who afterward realized the underlying cause and severity of the gas-leak. However, corporate and government responses to the Bhopal gas leak almost immediately rallied control of the legal and medical implications removing all say from survivors and workers. UCC claimed "moral responsibility" thus maintaining a representation of humanitarianism, (mainly for the U.S. public) that served as a cover-up of its lies and calculated economic concerns.

Through tactics such as the paternalistic concern based on a 'limited responsibility' stance taken by UCC, and later, and in a different manner by the Indian government, the disaster was "appropriated" or "managed" at various levels. "The catastrophe demanded from the Union Carbide Corporation...a response that was humane and in keeping with the image that industry wishes to project[—]that of a concerned partner" (Jaising and C. Sathyamala 89). While the true "concerned partner" or, in PODER's terminology, the "good neighbor" is precisely the relationship some environmental justice groups would like to have with industry, UCC's motives were anything but true. Factory management claimed that the gas wasn't poisonous, but an irritant 'just like tear gas' and that its effect on the eyes could be relieved by washing with water. The audacity of issuing such claims in the face of thousands of violent deaths indicates a lack of respect for the victims, not to mention, for the honest practice of medicine. UCC medical experts assured recovery was nearly certain and declared that there

122 These "undocumented" people, who later became gas victims were in a situation of enforced powerlessness that has parallels with the "undocumented" immigrants' situation in the U.S. Foremost among the parallels is the mistreatment and injustices committed against them by their employers and corporate neighbors. See this aspect of the farmworkers struggle in Chapter 10. For an early, extensive study of agri-business industries' unjust and sometimes inhumane vocational treatment of immigrants, see Carol Andreas' *Meatpackers and Beef Barons*. Niwot CO: Univ. of Colorado, 1994.

would be "no long-term effects from the exposure" (Jaising and C. Sathyamala 89).There was immediate recognition, if not complete understanding, of the severity of the poisoning: the fact that cyanide was present was verified by Dr Hiresh Chandra, director of the department of forensic medicine at Bhopal's Gandhi Medical College who had done autopsies of victims the first day after the leak and had found cyanide in hundreds of corpses (43). The government and corporate interests, working with the dean of the Gandhi Medical College, Dr. N. P. Misra, (who was on the UCC payroll,) suppressed this knowledge to protect themselves, thereby causing further damage to the victims' health (Sathyamala 43; Dakin 70). Jaising and Sathyamala explain that,

> [g]overnment research units ... were given an exclusive right to conduct epidemiological surveys and toxicological research and to suggest ... treatment .... Because of the monopoly on medical information, it was virtually impossible to keep vested interests in check, and the consequences of this appropriation were a minimizing of the nature and extent of injury and a failure to come up with the required line of treatment for the victims. (91)

Here, as elsewhere, environmental racism is based in the withholding of knowledge—in this case, medical knowledge of an antidote. Jaising and Sathyamala's description demonstrates that the legal, medical, and political factors are inextricably interconnected: "[t]he logical consequence of the legal appropriation of the disaster was its medical appropriation as well" (91). The following passage indicates the unprecedented gravity of and the reason for the cover-up: to hide the fact that people had been exposed to cyanide, the antidote was withheld.

> NATS [sodium thiosulfate] is a specific antidote in cyanide poisoning and had been suggested by Dr Bipin Awasi, the Medical Director of UCC in the period immediately following the disaster. It was opposed by UCC and a section of the medical community of Bhopal .... Although this debate was posed as a medical controversy ... it was in fact political .... Accepting NATS as a treatment would have meant acknowledging that the toxic gases had indeed crossed the lung-blood barrier to cause systemic damage. (Jaising and C. Sathyamala 91)

Other sources further defined this as a class conflict: the elite Bhopal medical community in collusion with the elite corporate community acted against the best interests of the poor. The controversy left concerned doctors to improvise in attempting to remedy severe symptoms: to use a frequent metaphor, What should be done with eyes that felt as if they had been rubbed with hot chilis?[123] Extensive detoxification never took place.

---

123 In researching library holdings, and Bhopal bibliographies I found only a few articles that focus on the health implications of Bhopal. My own research did not depend on finding such

The process of naming has been used to depoliticize, as well as cover-up the facts surrounding the event. Corporation, media, and government sources have continuously misrepresented the event as an "accident" or downplayed its impact, calling it an "incident." [124] The term "accident" hides the intentional neglect of environmental safety practices in certain cases—a double-standard that followed a hierarchy according to race, class, gender, and, most significantly here, metropolitan-peripheral or "first world"–"third world" nation status.[125] However, in describing the factors that made predictable the malfunction at the Bhopal pesticide plant, Jaising and Sathyamala focus their analysis on the complexity of metropolitan-peripheral environmental relationships, noting terrain that is similar to representations of environmental inequity patterns identified by U.S. "third world" social environmentalists:

> In the late 1960s, a decision was taken at the Union Carbide Corporation (UCC) headquarters in the U.S. to set up a factory for the manufacture of pesticides in a populous section of the city of Bhopal, capital of the state of Madhya Pradesh in India. The nature of the product, the process of manufacturing, the secrecy surrounding all procedures, the double standards in safety maintained by the transnational company, the measures taken by management to cut costs, the run-down condition of the plant all added up to create the right mix for a massive environmental disaster. (89)

Toxins released in densely populated areas have created familiar scenarios in communities of color and low income in the US—albeit not in the intensity of the UCC India situation. Decisions that disregard human and planetary health

---

articles, and I did not search in Medical Data Banks per se. Since the lack of knowledge about treatment for gas victims was a serious problem in Bhopal, more attention might have been paid to Bhopal by the medical community globally. However, both supplies and personnel were turned down or sent away by the government and Bhopal's medical elite. Any "complete" medical story, were it ever to be revealed, would probably indict UCC and the Madhya Pradesh and Indian governments, with repression as one main reason for the hiatus of studies. For an extensive understanding of how corporation and government forces affected the medical service that was provided, see 'Tara Jones', *Corporate Killing: Bhopals Will Happen*, Chapter Three; Sathyamala "The Medical Profession and The Bhopal Tragedy;" and Arvind Rajagopal, "And the Poor Get Gassed: Multinational-Aided Development and the State—the Case of Bhopal."

124 A similar misrepresentation is identified by the Centre of Indian Trade Union (CITU) who "pointed out that though many deaths in the chemical factories were caused by the work conditions and occupational hazards, doctors certify these as natural deaths. Hazardous work in most cases was given to temporary or contract workers .... The multi-national Madhya Pradesh corporations were the biggest culprits in this regard" (de Grazia 30).

125 'Tara Jones' uses the terms "metropolitan" and "peripheral" frequently. I use them at points where they do not seem to "naturalize" the hierarchy as much as other terms do in the context.

made in the money districts almost always impact most negatively on societally disenfranchised communities both nationally and globally, as happened at Bhopal.

Jaising and Sathyamala complicate the parallel as they point to "double standards in safety maintained by the transnational company," a phenomenon in which the "third world" that is geographically outside of the "first world" is considered less "human" than any segment of the geographical "first world." This U.S. impulse toward considering those of "third world" citizenship as "less human" is found within the geographical boundaries of the U.S., as well: witness the intense environmental—as well as other kinds of—racism against migrant workers.

Cross-cultural comparisons can expose such racism. For instance, similar symptoms, long-term effects, and maltreatment were experienced by the victims of Agent Orange in Vietnam. As the combined work of several authors demonstrate, the chemical makeup and effects of the poison were only the beginning of the similarities between poisonings in Bhopal and Vietnam. Jaising and C. Sathyamala map subsequent legal battles as long-drawn-out affairs in which the victims' interests were sacrificed at the added cost of distorted justice: "Bhopal was not an isolated incident .... The Vietnam veterans who were exposed to Agent Orange, an herbicide used in the Vietnam war, had to accept a settlement very unfavourable to them, against their will and through a legal process" (95). However, the Bhopal chronicler, Alfred De Grazia evokes the "First World–Third World" structural disparity in terms of human life value. He reports that in the climate of "widespread suspicion of American motives and conduct in international affairs" there was immediate doubt expressed about compensation for victims because they were Indian and not U.S. citizens. He cites a weekly tabloid *Blitz* which criticized "American law that gives compensation to U.S. servicemen who have suffered from their exposure while employing the defoliant 'Agent Orange' in Vietnam but offers nothing to the Vietnamese civilians who suffered from the same poison in much greater numbers" (35). His observation, which underscores Jaising and C. Sathyamala's comment on a "safety double standard" does not diminish, but rather broadens their subsequent argument about Vietnam Vets and Agent Orange. Victims of the U.S. military (and the increasing economic) aggression in "Third World" countries are rarely, if ever, given the opportunity to demand justice and seek judgement against the parties perpetuating injustice. It behooves those working for justice within relatively privileged communities in the U.S. to mark the even greater manifestations of injustice existing for the disempowered in transnational contexts where often there are not the civil laws between nations that offer even a charade of justice.[126] Given this scenario, it is likely that industrially related environmental concerns become a major battleground between North and South, with human and environmental casualties in the South devalued by the North's economically powerful elite.

In a 1994 assessment of costs of climate warming in *The Ecologist*, Daphne Wysham, coordinator of the Women's Power Project and research fellow at the Institute for Policy Studies (Washington D.C.), warns of the growing trend of an economic "global cost–benefit analysis" that has been adopted by the fossil fuel industries and is "gaining influence at the UN level" (204). Wysham refers to Samuel Fankhauser's economic value scale in which "richer people in the North, together with their land, their wetlands, and their endangered plant and animal species, [are assigned] a value ten times that allocated to the poor in the South;" she notes the "bitter irony that while the U.S. and other Northern countries top the list of leading greenhouse gas emitters, it is the southern countries—whose citizens contribute less than 30 percent of all greenhouse gases—which are predicted to suffer [and in the 21st Century are suffering] the most serious consequences" (205). Aubrey Meyer, coordinator of the Global Commons Institute (London) calls this economic response to the problem of global warming "the economics of genocide" and Wysham explicates that definition: while the economists admit that people will die because of global warming in the South, some, such as William Nordhaus, from Yale, believe that "the richer countries could profitably adapt" (in Wysham 204). Economists suggest that only 229,545 deaths will occur in response to climate change in the next 25 to 50 years, a number they consider insignificant in relation to the 10 million people presently dying annually from starvation (some of whom they smugly claim they will save with the "savings" from not cutting back on fossil fuel use.) (Wysham 204). Economists underestimate the number of deaths and engage logical fallacies when they ignore the fact that scientists anticipate that most deaths from climate changes in the "Third World" will be from crop failure and resulting starvation. Extrapolations from current scientific data suggest that if carbon dioxide levels double as expected by 2030, 135 million to 900 million (some suggest figures in the billions) people will die as a result (Wysham 204).

Whatever the exact statistics, the economist's model works against humans and the environment on two levels. By using economic scales that create a hierarchy of value for different subject positions by nation, they are advocating an attack on the South and dismissing human death in the South as an inconse-

126 For a good example of such international concerns included in the US, see "The Principles of Environmental Justice," discussed in the introduction.

quential result of "progress" in the North, as exemplified in the dismissal of Bhopal deaths as the price of progress. Graciela Chichillnisky, an Argentinean economist contends that "any 'rights by income', such as that implied in the Fankhauser document, should be moderated by concurrent responsibilities for the impacts associated with the generation of that income" (in Wysham 206). One might also factor in the increased impact associated with the spending of that income. In addition to being an attack on the South per se, on another level, the devaluing of life in Southern countries means that the total global costs—both environmental and human—are being grossly underestimated. Bhopal, among other events, has laid the groundwork for the model generated by the economic and industrial elite who represent the situation as a North-South battle in which blame is often transferred to the victim and the victims' suffering is naturalized or dismissed. (They would have died of starvation; their sickness is a result of poverty.) As many of the following (South and North) thinkers suggest, only if people in the North join with people of the South in a "fellowship of suffering" and "of thinking" (in the words of Upendra Baxi) will this trend be reversed as people in Bhopal and around the globe begin "to recover the common humanity of humankind from its expropriators."

6.2 Manifestations of a Massacre: A Chronology: Effects on Women, Children and Reproduction Systems

> The children in the shantytowns of Bhopal have a new game. One plays the "mother," another the "father." Just as they have settled down for the night with their "children" around them, one shrieks, "Gas aagayi hai" (the gas has come!). Then they all leap up, thrash around, choke, and fall dead.
>
> Vasanta Surya, journalist who visited Bhopal[127]

Brief accounts of the health effects of the gas on women and children occurred in most narratives, and several studies address reproductive health issues for women extensively. However, the medical cover-up that prevailed over victim treatment necessarily affected the state of research as well. Studies such as "Effects of the Bhopal Disaster on Women's Health: An Epidemic of Gynaecological Disease" completed in 1985 by Mira Sadgoval and Rani Bang, (women doctors associated with the Medico Friends Circle, a Delhi-based medical activist group) verify the gynecological problems that result from gas exposure; Sadgoval also establishes that there was a cover-up of those effects. Their study

127 In Alvares in Weir 89.

and others that indicate severe results from the gas exposure were ignored, dismissed, or repressed by much of the medical profession. For example, Sathyamala provides chronologies of governmental debauchery in the medical service and research, especially in that pertaining to women's health. While activists focused work to confront women's issues, government constraints extended the difficult effects that women suffered. Sathyamala summarizes her study "The Medical Profession and the Bhopal Tragedy" as follows:

> the medical establishment's response to the Bhopal disaster has been to constantly underplay the extent of damage to the gas victims, suppress all information, and never to challenge constituted authority. The challenge before voluntary groups is not only how to provide a measure of counter-expertise, but also provide the ethical texture and the moral tension that medicine as a noble profession boasts of. (54)

While many of the activists' attempts to render medical aid were quashed, and activists beaten and arrested, Sathyamala recognizes their work was pivotal in establishing what the future will hold in terms of medical care for those who continue to suffer gas-affected ill health, and for policymaking and treatment in the cases of future mini and major Bhopals.[128] Despite the few excellent sources available, my account is sketchy and anecdotal because a comprehensive picture of the numbers of women affected and the conditions under which they were suffering was not determined. That such medical accounts are not available does not bode well; without them, experts have little basis upon which to predict the medical and psychological effects of future "accidents" or chronic toxic exposure. However, in a 2023 Century follow-up search of Bhopal women'digital resources, I found many studies and references have surfaced through publication in woman's health and environmental justice studies and interdisciplinary research.

Before the first substantial study of the epidemic of gynecological diseases, released in February 1985 by Dr. Rani Bang and Dr. Mira Sadgopal, silence was maintained concerning women's health issues; those who tried to address them were hampered and harassed. Bang and Sadgoval gave health activists much reason to be concerned when they observed that a large percentage of women from the affected areas had begun to suffer from acute pelvis inflammatory disease (P.I.D.) leucorrhoea (white vaginal discharge) cervical erosion/endocervitis, menorrhoria, lactation suppression and excessive and irregular menstrual bleeding (Banerjee 168, Sathyamala, Jaising and Sathyamala 36).

---

128 Evidence that these challenges continued to be addressed, at least in small ways, comes from clinic-building proposals by The International Medical Appeal for Bhopal.

Spontaneous abortions in gas-affected cattle in the weeks following the disaster proved to be a harbinger of reproductive problems in the human population (Vivek 6). Evidence suggests that women too were experiencing spontaneous abortions already, also, however their complaints were being dismissed.[129] As early as January 1985, scientists from the Industrial Toxicology and Research Centre had suggested the possibility of brain damage to the embryos of women early in their pregnancies at the time of the leak (Vivek 6). Banerjee suggests that this was based on knowledge of the effects of inhaling some kinds of isocyanides (Banerjee 41). The cover-up of fetal affects may have then been connected to the cover-up of cyanide poisoning. The records of births and deaths of infants in Bhopal proved expectations that the negative effects of the MIC-generated gases would be most apparent in children beginning May–June 1985, since a fetus exposed in its first trimester of growth would be most vulnerable to the gas (Banerjee 42).

The Director-General of the Indian Council for Medical Research (ICMR) had stated that birth defects might become evident as pregnancies progressed (Vivek 6–7). A study to follow the progeny of pregnant women was announced by the Gandhi Medical School but there was no acknowledgment of the problems women were facing (Sathyamala 50). Despite the reports and the demand for abortion and test facilities to be provided to the gas-affected women, the authorities did not initiate any action. The demand was termed 'unjustified' by a section of the medical community with UCC connections who claimed it caused an unnecessary scare among women.

Women's groups were trying to confront the situation despite government harassment. Zahreeli Gas Kand Morcha (MORCHA), with the help of Saheli, a women activists' group from Delhi, created a traveling exhibit to educate women and men in the *bastis* (translated with resonance for this study as "barrios") about how to deal with the reproductive problems that were being ignored. The Morcha poster exhibit also mobilized support for NaTs, the cyanide antidote that had been effectively banned by the dean of the Gandhi Medical College (Sathyamala 37; Dakin 67). Women from the *basti*s demonstrated the effectiveness of the exhibit while simultaneously defying stereotypes of themselves as ignorant. When a health official, hoping to dispel the push for sodium thiosulfate, said the victims could not be taught to do the urine sampling necessary to begin NaTs treatments,

129 My comparison here should not be taken as a *sacred cow* argument, an essentialist criticism of Hindu value systems; rather, it is a gendered version of the same socio-economic line of reasoning that is repeated throughout the poetics: for many, monetary worth determines value, and therewith is the *concern*.

women from the *bastis* heard about it and showed up at the clinic "waving bottles of urine at the officials asking for them to be tested" (Dakin 67). This performative act transforms the health officials' representation of women as ignorant victims into self-identification as pro-active survivors, agents of change exposing the officers' attempts at coverup. By the end of the 1980s, the Madhya Pradesh government revealed "a terrible situation which could have been easily avoided. A total of 2,698 pregnancies were recorded at the time of the disaster. There had been 402 'abortions,' 158 in the first trimester, and 220 in the second.[130] Of the 2,210 live births, 150 were dead within months" (Vivek 7).

According to another source, premature, underweight, and physically deformed babies were delivered to half of the women coming into the hospital (Banerjee 44). What is not acknowledged due to the secrecy and ineptitude of the studies "managed" by the governmental medical establishment is made clear in narrative descriptions. An early case of deformity likely due to MIC exposure is described in a child born in Bilaspur's Sardar Vallabh Bhai Patel Hospital. The mother of the child had been exposed to MIC near the Union Carbide factory at the time of leakage. "The child born to her ... had two gaping holes instead of eyes. The baby had no fingers and toes and skin [sic] looked [s]corched." (Banerjee 44). This child was followed by many others with shared symptoms: Indeed, at one point, 20–30 babies with deformities were born each day in the Sultania Janana Hospital, (a large women's hospital) alone (Banerjee 44).

Junior gynaecologists and midwives at the Sultania Janana Hospital reported that the cases of premature or retarded birth among children were also abnormally high (as many as 50 percent) after the gas tragedy (Banerjee 44, Vivek 7), yet a spokesperson at Sultania Women's Hospital denied increases in abortions (Jones 100). It seems highly unlikely that the same hospital would be experiencing the extremely different results indicated by these reports from various levels of hospital staff. While logic would suggest that an obvious site for gathering information about the effects on pre and post-natal reproductive systems and children's health would be the hospitals, the hospital studies that were released were not reliable. Few records were taken and when they were, they were often contradictory or were considered government secrets.[131]

---

130 Miscarriage or spontaneous abortions are referred to simply as abortion in several narratives.

131 Perhaps in a situation where death warrants were not being issued and people were being cremated or buried (according to the requirements of their religious faith) as quickly as such services could be rendered and some were simply being lowered into the river, the religious backgrounds of the dead might have been best figured by consulting the mortuaries. Indeed, more than one chronicler gauges the deaths by the crores of wood ordered by crematoriums. "The

Sexism was a problem that touched even the progressive activist organizations but was rampant and had untold ramifications in the broader relief effort (Sathyamala 50–51).[132] Sathyamala blames the sexist attitudes of the doctors for "the loss of valuable information regarding the specific toxic effects [of] which women complained" that "resulted in the failure to record such crucial information from the medico-legal point of view as well" (51). She also notes a "reluctance" to advise gas-exposed pregnant women about abortion (51) and tells how gynaecologists in field clinics "explained away the large number of women complaining of gynaeocological symptoms as 'usual', 'psychological', or 'fake' and the gynaeocological diseases in these women as 'usual', 'tuburculour' or 'due to poverty and poor hygiene', refusing to accept any special situation" (50).

Several chroniclers tell of discussions with survivors that explicate that women's suffering was often not taken seriously. Often, they replicate the activist-doctors' recounting of inconsistent medical treatment. For instance, Brojendra Nath Banerjee tells of a conversation with Sushila, a 20-year-old who gave birth to a still-born and deformed child. "The back of the child's head was an extended cyst-like formation and part of the skull was missing. This child too had scars and burn marks all over its body. 'The baby died the day it was born,' said Sushila: 'It is the gas that had killed my child. Ever since the time I inhaled the gas, the progress of the child was not normal. But the doctors told me nothing. They simply gave me medicines and injections'" (44). Sushila was aware of and monitoring the abnormality of her post-exposure pregnancy, but the doctor would not validate her observations with information; this is a major indictment of the medical response, which protected the industry at the expense of the survivors. That women were not even taken seriously when they inquired about problem pregnancies is repeated in Mira Sagdoval's report as follows.

> A number of [women] said: 'We wondered whether there was a risk. We tried to get ourselves examined but the doctors just threw us out with some tablets and said everything was all right.' The irony is that these doctors, or others who are part of the same system, are doing research to measure expected foetal defects. I should say they are expecting defects. On the one hand, they say there is no proof of damage, and on the other, they are getting ready to measure it for their research papers. (in Jones 99)

---

moment came when serious estimators were trying to arrive at the figures of the dead by guessing the amount of wood that was used in the fires that the Hindus used as funeral pyres. (The State Government later announced with macabre pride that its Forest Department had provided 20,000 quintals of wood, two million pounds, for the crematory holocaust)" (de Grazia 35–37).

132 Sathyamala reports that "even within a progressive group like MFC, a certain amount of discomfort was expressed ... at the use of the word sexism" (51).

In real life, the doctors' discrepancy is alarming. If it were in fiction, it would be considered social satire. However, in a personal interview with 'Tara Jones', Mira Sadgopal reported what is even more appalling:

> These very same doctors, government doctors, in particular in government service, in public they were not saying, but in private when you talk to them said that they did feel there was a risk and when I specifically asked them what they would do if they were in the position of one of the women, they said that they would not even go in for amniocentesis or ultrasonography, because what would that tell you? It wouldn't tell you so many things, mental retardation or whatever, we would go straight for MIP (medical interruption of pregnancy) because it's a relatively safe thing, and temporary psychological trauma weighted against the possibility of raising a child which might be deformed, we just don't know. (APPEN, 1985, 46 in Jones 99–100)[133]

The withholding of knowledge from victims of environmental health degradation is tied here to the fight for women's reproductive rights. Yet the lack of knowledge extends beyond the survivors themselves. How many proponents of reproductive rights in the U.S. would suspect they shared battle grounds with Bhopal survivors? Long term gas effects that impacted women distinctly were not only based on reproductive system problems; the social repercussions of the reproductive and other problems were immense. Due to their historically determined social position, women had suffered in different ways: a significantly high proportion of gas-exposed women in Bhopal had lost all or most of their children; therefore, ironically, there was increased pressure on them to bear other children (Vivek 7). This situation raised several portentous issues. There was the grave possibility that genetic damage would continue to occur in their offspring. The burden of pregnancy could severely affect the already deteriorated health of the women. The overall situation would give rise to many psychosocial problems for both genders, especially given the fact that several studies have reported a significantly high incidence of impotency among men in the affected population, and the likelihood of sterility cannot be ruled out (Vivek 8). In discussing the social repercussions of "environmental trauma," Canadian feminist geographer, Joni Seager refers to Indian feminist Padma Prakash's report of increased rates of domestic violence, divorce, and abandonment "suffered by poor women who were maimed by the chemical explosion, a side effect

133 Further evidence of the doublespeak emanating from the medical establishment appears in Bang and Sadgopal 1985 study: "We had an opportunity to talk with three gynaecologists in the field clinics and one professor of Ob-Gyn in the hospital, all of whom stated that there are no gynaenocological problems attributable to the disaster" (Bang and Sadgopal, 1985, 7 in Jones 100).

of the mounting frustrations of increasing poverty and ill health"[134] (Seager in Hofrichter 64). Tara Jones points out that ultimately reproductive issues raise concerns for both genders but the impact on women remains distinctive.

Some reports suggest that most children were not considered eligible for payment of remunerations they suffered, and their suffering added to the burden of gas-affected women. Banerjee reports that among the surveyed children, living within a distance of .5 to 2 km from the Union Carbide factory, 50% had suffered damage to the respiratory system; the X-ray findings indicated various abnormal conditions in 67% of those who were tested, and the "mental apprehensiveness of the children" was outstanding (Banerjee 74). Little rehabilitation existed and many who lost family were forced to assume adult responsibilities, even when they, themselves were decapacitated.

Most chroniclers agree that the gas victims suffered needlessly simply because they were poor. A study conducted by the Centre for Social Medicine and Community Health, the JNU survey showed that the socio-economic profile for the dead showed them to have been even more "disadvantaged" than the general population of gas victims.[135] Writers mention the fact that many of the Hindus in the area were low caste and a majority of the victims were of minority religions; Bhopal has a large Adavasi community and also a sizable Muslim community. The religio-ethnic backgrounds of these communities had affected their chances of exposure according to their place in Bhopal's class structure as it affected their choice of neighborhoods in the *bastis* near the Union Carbide plant. Given this, the role of religio-ethnicity in the further victimization of gas-affected survivors has yet to be investigated in sufficient depth. Several years after the gas leak, communal violence in Bhopal turned victims of different religions against each other.[136] Claude Alvares raises a point that is echoed in idioms concerning other issues of environmental racism, AIDS and other crises: "Union

---

134 see also Padma Prakash, "Neglect of Women's Health Issues," *Delhi Economic and Political Weekly*, 14 December 1985.

135 This is not surprising as most of them did not have adequate daily nourishment and their health was worse due to their vulnerable status created by the negative impacts of poverty. Furthermore, those who fled on foot as opposed to motorized vehicles were less likely to survive. Not only did the poor not have vehicles, but they were also less likely to know people who did.

136 In 1993, communal violence occurred in some gas-affected neighborhoods "as a result of the demolition of the mosque at Ayodhya" (Alvares 1994, 171). 140 people died as a result. As Alvares explains, "[s]ince a large number of the gas victims were from the minority community and the BJP was the ruling party in the state, they had to bear the brunt of the state terror" (Ibid).

Carbide's gas had not discriminated between Hindus and Muslims, but the events [including a mosque demolition] at Ayodhya succeeded in creating a wedge between what had hitherto been a single community of victims" (1994 171).

In a country that has tolerated the fomenting hatred of extreme communalists and separatists, it is not unusual that such sentiments should break out among disenfranchised tension-ridden survivors of Bhopal. However, it is my untested assertion that discrimination stemming from communalist sentiments, country-wide may have affected the survivors' situation from the beginning. Surely not only class, but ethnic and religious background played into the degree of Indian dominant culture's ambivalence toward the UCC and Indian and Madhya Pradesh governments' disenfranchisement of the Bhopal survivors. Public ambivalence based on the social alienation of most of the survivors may have made the cover-up work most efficiently, perhaps more effortlessly than other aspects of the Bhopal story.

Despite the lack of scientific documentation of medical effects, most narratives offer expressive attempts to deal with symptoms that, for many involved, transcended the previous perimeters of possibility. While Cherríe Moraga, in "Heroes and Saints" represents the horrors of toxin-induced deformities and diseases in literary drama—that has some empirical basis but employs the fictional tool "the suspension of disbelief"—Bhopal narratives come at the facts from another angle.[137] They intervene in the reader's expectations of reality, suspending disbelief in order to present an experiential empiricist state previously not encountered. In the following cases, the most direct description, when void of euphemisms, may read as heightened language; formal analysis of such narratives must be adjusted by considering the relation of the verbal rendering to the experiential reality of the author. A case in point are the words of Bano Bi:

> The children's father had just returned from a poetry concert. He came in and asked me, "what are you burning that makes me choke?" And then it became quite unbearable. The children sleeping inside began to cough. I spread a mat outside and made the children sit on it. Outside we started coughing even more violently and became breathless. Then our landlord and my husband went out to see what was happening. They found out that some gas had leaked. Outside there were people shouting "Run, run, run for your lives." (in Morehouse 1994, 164; in *Voices From Bhopal*)

Bano Bi's description of the night of the massacre is effective partially because it does not paint the scene in heightened language, so much as describe an interruption to the everyday life of the family. The fact that Bano Bi's husband had

---

137 See Chapter Ten for a discussion of *Heroes and Saints*.

spent the evening at a "poetry concert" interrupts the common middle class and western perception of the Indian worker as "without culture." The fact that her husband and the landlord go out together to discover what is happening suggests that the landlord lives on the premises of his rental property and fraternizes with his tenants; this too, complicates the picture of shanty dwellers readers will garner from most of the journalistic accounts. While Bano Bi is obviously the primary caregiver to their children and indeed talks of her husband in relationship to their offspring as the "children's father" her words suggest that she is a self-defined and assertive person. Bano Bi continues her story, narrating her family's situation following her husband's death, several weeks after the leak, until the time she speaks for the *Voices From Bhopal* interview.

> [My husband] was always treated for gas related problems. He was never treated for tuberculosis. And yet, in his *postmortem* report, they mentioned that he died due to tuberculosis. He was medically examined for compensation but they never told us in which category he was put. And now they tell me that his death was not due to gas exposure, that I can not get the relief of 10,000 rupees [US $330] which is given to the relatives of the dead.
> "I have pain in my chest and I get breathless when I walk. The doctors told me that I need to be operated on for ulcers in my stomach. They told me it would cost 10,000 rupees .... All the jewelry that I had has been sold... How can I go for the operation? ... [I]f I die during the operation, there would be no one to look after my children." (in Morehouse 1994, 164 & *Voices of Bhopal*)

Bano Bi's financial predicament and the related moral dilemma are foregrounded in her matter-of-fact style: the exact amount that she should have received for her husband's death had the postmortem report not lied about his condition would—if she had received it—only just cover the operation she needs. She wonders rhetorically whether it is worse to provide inadequately for her children due to ill health or to risk "abandoning" her children in the case of own death during the operation? Bano Bi's story shows both how insufficient the monetary compensation for survivors is, and how easily survivors can be cheated out of even this small remuneration. The fact that Bano Bi had jewelry to sell suggests that her family was not destitute prior to the gas leak; however, the events of the aftermath have used up the savings that she kept in her jewelry.

Throughout the Bhopal poetics the emphasis on storytelling and narratives, such as Bano Bi's, is consistent. New social movement theory proves useful in thinking about these narratives; not only is their importance clear in terms of their socio-political iconography and form, but they can be examined in terms of their sociological roles in relationship to social movement mobilization. Gary Alan Fine tells us that "a social movement is not only a set of beliefs, actions, and actors, but also a *bundle of stories*. Movement allegiance depends on personal accounts, which concretely clarify that extended effort is worthwhile and that others have similar experiences and feelings" (134). Fine suggests that there are three broad and inclusive categories within which movement stories might fit: "horror stories" or "affronts to the movement actor," "war stories" or "collective experiences within the movement," and "happy endings"—"stories that reaffirm the value of the movement in achieving material or personal ends" (135). Although all three categories exist in Bhopal narratives, the horror stories and war stories are the most common.

Fine suggests that "more narratives are performed in social movements in which attacks on participants' identity and behaviours are a source of complaint than in movements in which alterations in social policy are the primary goal" (137). Environmental justice movements, in comparison to conventional environmentalism are based in a struggle against attacks that have to do with the participating communities' identities. While environmental justice organizing creates movements that set out to change social policy, they do so by proceeding from an experiential base. Hence, according to Fine's analysis, environmental justice groups would produce many narratives. The environmental justice-based organizations that were generated in the aftermath of the Bhopal gas-leak are based in fighting against continuous attacks on survivors, both physically and representationally. The changes in policy demanded by these groups, while sometimes a primary concern, are based in concern for the survivors and others who might be at risk from similar attacks. Thus, numerous Bhopal narratives give weight to Fine's suggestion. In specific, many Bhopal narratives could be placed into the narrative approach that Fine describes as "stigma-deflecting" (138). "Stigma-deflecting" movements "attempt to justify or valorize participants or those for whom the participants stand" and use "narrative to deflect the stigma that would otherwise adhere." In such narratives, "the main figure, typically the narrator, is shown to have been mistreated by a source of power or authority, and has in terms of the story, an *unblemished* self. In movements that contend with injustices, heroic narratives are common" (138).

Fine believes that "narrative structure aids in the process of mobilization" (141). As is demonstrated later in this chapter, the Bhopal narratives set out to mobilize people globally; the extent to which they are successful may depend partially upon the distribution of the narratives, as well as the audience's ability to identify. Identification, too, is aided by story-telling as Fine's analysis explains: "Narrative creates social spaces in which audiences are encouraged to identify with the situations, problems, and concerns of others" (141). Stories, then, play several essential roles in the Bhopal poetics. In the following section, "war stories" are presented that uncover the extent of foul play generated during the Bhopal aftermath.

6.3 Manifestations of a Massacre: A Chronology: Attacks on Social Service Providers and Activists

> Government officials claim they are men in a hurry, and that nothing should be permitted to discourage the welcome aid of progress. Suffering can be managed and normality assured, at least on the surface, for all the world to see. Disasters are a nuisance; Bhopals occur every day in a thousand different ways. Nobody makes a fuss. It is accepted, whether we like it or not, that suffering and death are a permanent feature of all modern progress.
>
> David Weir (BS 1989, 101–102)

> Bhopal's major voluntary organizations worked heroically, defying constant vilification at the hands of the government and a vicious police force. These volunteers and other activists have been branded as Carbide spies, CIA operatives, and elements interested only in fomenting trouble in Bhopal. They have been threatened, arrested, assaulted, and their houses raided.
>
> Ashis Gupta (1991, 22)

The number of women who responded to the tragedy in globally visible ways was severely limited by the government repression of social service providers and activists after the disaster. Police attacks and harassment were especially brutal against women (Morehouse 167). Many demonstrations resulted in mass arrest. This harassment against those trying to ameliorate the situation also extended internationally to allies of Bhopal survivors: a group from Arizona State University that was setting up a vocational and technical training center in Bhopal had its assets frozen and members had their visas denied. Sentinelles, a Swiss organization was denied work permits in Bhopal even when AGAPE (Action for Gas Affected People) an Indian Catholic-church backed organization had agreed to distribute the resources being provided. A medical doctor from the Netherlands who had brought an initial large batch of NaTs treatments was sent away along with his antidotes.[138]

One of the most extensive government attacks occurred June 25, 1985, in the early morning hours, just weeks after medical activists had established a clinic for treating victims whose needs were being neglected. On June 3, 1985, the Jana Swasthya Kendra (JSK; People's Health Clinic) had begun administering NaTs to ambulatory gas-affected survivors in a tent-clinic that was established on the

138 In some of these cases the government feared that UCC might have contributed to the relief efforts, but in other cases, it did not question direct Carbide ties to the relief distribution. A case in point was the $5 million interim relief shipment to be distributed through the Red Cross, even though UCC's head administrator, Warren Anderson was on the board of the Red Cross in the U.S. and the Bhopal Red Cross chairperson was on the UCC payroll as well (Gupta 22–23).

tennis courts in the UC factory compound. Careful examination and record-keeping accompanied the treatment of over 1000 people over the following three weeks.[139] However, the work was suspended by the June 25 police attack ordered by the MP Government in which doctors and paramedics were arrested and JSK records seized (Sathyamala 38; Jones 116). The offensive was broad; not only the clinic but members of most of the activist groups were attacked. Gupta explains that the timing of the "pre-dawn swoop on residential houses ... [in which] the police arrested 31 activists including doctors, [was planned] to prevent them from participating in an agitation protesting government insensitivity towards the gas victims" (Gupta 22). Jones believes that harassment was the "main aim" of the government in this case and that the repression indicated the success of the activists' work. He substantiates this by quoting from the Bombay *Daily*, 21 July 1985: arrests were made "on blatantly false and trumped-up charges like 307 [attempt to murder], rioting and inciting people to riot, etc. ...When bails were obtained by sympathizers for the existing charges, the bail-amount was increased by the new ones, which were equally false .... Some *basti* people, including women with infants, were in gaol more than ten days after the arrests" (Jones 116). These government tactics were successful in diverting activist energies from support work for survivors. On 6 August 1985, MORCHA noted that "[a]ll of our energies were absorbed in legal and civil liberty type work for the past five or six weeks. It is only after having spent a great deal of energy and money of the country that we are able to function again and look beyond our immediate problems" (in Jones 116).

A second series of attacks was directed at social workers and at a "renewed effort" to "document the misery of the gas victims and to disseminate information on the gas disaster and related issues," initiated with the formation of the Bhopal Group for Information and Action (BGIA) (Sathyamala 39). Two BGIA members had attended a meeting of medical practitioners that had been announced in a local newspaper. Since the meeting was being conducted in Hindi and neither of the two men were fluent in Hindi, they decided to record the meeting (Sathyamala 39).

Gautam Banerjee was later arrested "as a spy" for this tape recording; during the meeting two prominent doctors had had a serious disagreement that the government may have not wanted on tape. Another arrest was made in the same neighborhood against another social worker. As Gupta reports a "young Eng-

139 Several organizations had set up the clinic: Zahreeli Gas Kand Morcha, Nagrik Rahat aur Punarwas Committee (NRPC), Union Carbide Karmachari Sangh, Trade Union Relief Fund (TURF), and the Drug Action Forum (Sathyamala 38; Jones 115–116).

lishman, David Bergman, who had cycled all the way from Birmingham to Bhopal and had stayed on to involve gas-affected children in artistic activities as a form of therapy in an abandoned potato warehouse was arrested under the Official Secrets Act for allegedly being in possession of incriminating documents and tapes. Some of the seized tapes contained jazz recordings." (Gupta 23) Bergman and Banerjee later were called CIA agents and even Mira Sadgoval, an Indian citizen, doctor, and American-born wife of Anil Sadgopal, the prominent social worker, came under suspicion as someone with supposed "direct relations" to Carbide's Warren Anderson (Gupta 23).

It is a cynical and repressive move on the part of the government that it would allege that the activists were loyal to the very forces which they were fighting. Examining the government's representation of Mira Sadgoval as a spy for Union Carbide alongside the accounts of her medical work on behalf of the women gas victims, one is reminded of slanderous representations generated by those in alliance with toxins and money. Perhaps the most resonant attack in the US, because of the source of the slander, was UCC's red baiting of the Citizen's Clearinghouse for Hazardous Waste (started by Lois Gibbs to accommodate and expand the battle over toxins at Love Canal) in an internal memo dated November 14,1989, signed by Clyde Greenert. However, false claims of ties to an unnamed "communist party" and "all manner of folk with private/single agenda [sic]," (in *Rachel's Hazardous Waste News #170*) while potentially damaging in the public eye, hardly seem as offensive to those being maligned as accusations by UCC sympathizers against those helping in dire situations being accused of spying for the corporation or the CIA.

6.4 Manifestations of a Massacre: A Chronology: Legal Remnants of Rights to Survival

> Nearly 11 years after, the century's worst industrial crimes remain underinvestigated, unjudged and the culprits unpunished. Again this failure of criminal law is not unique to Bhopal. The tiny number of convictions in cases of industrial homicide and grievous bodily harm, when posited against the frequency and toll of these crimes, speaks of the injustices committed against victims of such crimes worldwide.
>
> Satinath Sarangi[140]

140 Since the catastrophe occurred, Satinath Sarangi has been an activist in Bhopal serving the survivors and founding Sabhavna, a free medical center. See https://www.facebook.com/watch/?v=441138587555931.

Indira Jaising and C. Sathyamala, Jamie Cassels and others theorize the roles of Union Carbide Corporation (UCC) and the Madhya Pradesh (MP), Indian and U.S. governments in the sequence of legal events which followed the disaster by showing that—especially when faced with a choice between corporate and community rights—current legal systems are incapable of dealing adequately or fairly with environmental justice issues.[141] Such Bhopal chroniclers suggest that the equation governing capital's rights in relation to victim's rights needs re-evaluation.

Despite their inadequacy, legal systems have played an important public role in managing the disaster and its aftermath. In what repeatedly has been termed the greatest ambulance chase in history (Everest) U.S. lawyers descended upon Bhopal, to almost everyone's chagrin. They obtained thumbprints or signatures from victims, (often without addressing issues of language difference and limited literacy that hindered adequate communication between counsel and survivor) and thus authorized the lawyers to file suits in U.S. courts on the victim's behalf: "suits were filed in different states in the US, and all were subsequently transferred to the Southern District of New York to be judged by Judge John F. Keenan" (Jaising and C. Sathyamala 89).

It is important to understand all sides on this issue rather than simply writing off the lawyers as opportunists who were successfully ousted from the picture. Although each lawyer came with their own strategies, they hoped for various reasons to represent the rights of survivors against the multinational; in some instances, thousands of survivors were signed up and combined into a single case against Union Carbide. While many of the U.S. lawyers were motivated more by the chance for fame and fortune than humanitarian or social justice interests, they knew their success was based in part in obtaining a just settlement for the victims; this was more so than was the case for the corporation or the governments. While they might have profited grandly, they could not have done so without obtaining substantial remunerations for the victims. This relationship between victim and lawyer stood in contrast to both the corporation-victim relationship and the government-victim relationship.[142] Furthermore, Cassels argues that the lawyers helped clarify victims' rights, both for the victims and for the debate at large: "[t]he presence of U.S. lawyers in India con-

141 For further analysis of legal systems' relationship to environmental justice, see Chapter 12 and 13's discussions from Vandana Shiva and Mahasweta Devi.

142 For an in-depth discussion of this issue, see Jones, 122–133 and Cassels 115–118). In historicizing the lawyers' role, Jones asserts that "[w]hile the US lawyers have been justly criticized for their greed, their intervention was crucial in beginning legal cases against UCC."

firmed the victims' view that the Bhopal disaster was an international incident and further focused their anger on the multinational corporation" (115). Had the lawyers been successful in suits against UCC, the history of the corporate toxins industry's relations with communities throughout the world might have taken a different direction. One should not underestimate the undeveloped potential of the law here.

To briefly explore that potential relationship, consider what could happen in the situation where the legal counsel arriving in Bhopal were all peoples' lawyers, practitioners of poverty law, working pro-bono or sponsored by non-profits.[143] The primary difference would have been in the lawyers' relationship to his/her clients—the survivor communities. The potential power of Spivak's concept of "ethical singularity" might have defined the different quality of relationship.[144] Furthermore, poverty law's stance regarding toxic industry is clear and consistent in that poverty law is rooted in defending the civil rights of those disenfranchised by corporate and other types of dominant structures. For poverty law practitioners, much more would have been at stake than any individual class action suit; the structural racism and class and nation bias, at work in Bhopal both before and following the gas leak, would have been exposed rather than used to the advantage of the "first world" corporation. Possibly, in such a situation, the lawyers could have inserted the concern for the survivors that was missing in the major decision-making. As it was, the lawyers and the survivors lost out when the case was transferred to India, and subsequently, when the Indian government responded to the chaos by enacting a law that gave the country the sole authority to litigate for the victims. The chronology in a brief narration follows.

After it initially proposed a settlement of 350 million U.S. dollars that was not accepted by India, UCC argued that the case should be tried in India. Most sources concur that "[t]he hidden agenda was, quite clearly, UCC's wish to avoid paying the levels of compensation ordinarily awarded by U.S. courts in tort litigation; secure in their assumption that life in India was cheap they were confident that an Indian court would make much lower awards" (Jaising and C.

---

143 Upon his death in 1996, the U.S. media attributed some charitable liberal qualities to Melvin Belli, one of the primary attorneys negotiating in Bhopal. With ironical insight, in defending himself against the press' criticism of lawyers' "enthusiasm for profiting from a disaster caused by a multinational company" Belli had replied that "capitalist lawyers were 'needed in a capitalist system' and that 'I am a good capitalist" (Cassels 115).

144 In *Imaginary Maps* 200–201; see also, explication of "ethical singularity" in relation to Mahasweta Devi and the women writes about in the section "Mapping the Pterodactyl: Impossible Mandates and Indigenous Spaces" in Chapter 13.

Sathyamala 90). Here in the legal decision-making, like in the medical controversy over the extent of the injury, the dichotomy between the value of human life of "First World" and "third world" victims is foregrounded. Class as well as nationality comes into consideration in a complex formula as is shown by the remuneration program of the Air India crash near Ireland in June 1984 in which "the relatives of these victims were handed 1 million rupees ($85,000) for each death almost without delay"[145] (Kurzman 223).

Judge Keenan's acceptance of UCC arguments for transferal to the jurisdiction of the Indian courts "reflects the political reluctance of the American legal system to deliver justice to people of Third World countries who have been the victims of American transnational corporations" (Jaising and Sathyamala 90). He concluded his judgement by stating that "to retain the litigation in this forum ... would be yet another example of imperialism, another situation in which an established sovereign inflicted its rules, its standards and values on a developing nation" (in Cassels 34). Judge Keenan's concern for forgoing imperialism may have been genuine, but misguided, however the concern not to spread "imperialism" can thinly veil more imperialistic acts; "imperialism," in such contexts must be thoroughly interrogated. For example, the UN-proposed project to publish "an international registry of pesticides listing where they're restricted and why" that came to a vote only a week after the Bhopal gas leak—was passed with only one dissenting vote, from Jeanne Kirkpatrick, who declared that the measure would be "an instance of 'regulatory imperialism'" (Schaeffer in Kolpe 38). Keenan's brand of "political reluctance" set a precedent that grants transnational corporations the security that they will not be held fully accountable for the environmental messes they create in the "Third World." It foreshadowed rights granted to corporations by NAFTA, GATT, and subsequent world trade agreements, including intellectual property rights for the patenting of life forms. Such legislation has contributed greatly to the climate of "tolerance" for industrial "friendly fires," especially when "Third World" people are those most often adversely affected. The Bhopal poetics, like much of the cultural production investigated in this book, illustrates that in profound new ways the grassroots' response to ramifications of such decisions built upon previous systems of inequity. The currently developing system of

145 Further complexities of religious, cultural, and linguistic misunderstanding in the payment of such remuneration are described in Bharati Mukherjee's story "The Management of Grief" which tells a fictional story of Toronto-based Hindus and Sikhs who lose family in the plane crash.

global capital violates both ancient and recently articulated standards of human rights to which most cultures adhere.

Under the Bhopal Gas Leak Disaster (Processing of Claims) Act, 1985, India sued Union Carbide; negotiations began before there were any concrete estimates on statistics of the dead and injured or the nature or extent of the long-term consequences. Furthermore, earlier suits were still pending (Jaising and C. Sathyamala 89). Jaising and C. Sathyamala recount that "[t]here was a clear conflict of interest between the demands for justice for the victims, and the need of the Indian government for foreign capital" (91). Complicit in the negligence of the gas-affected people's needs, its motives were not those set forth by the needs of the victims. The Indian government capitalized on the disaster, and in so doing reinforced the altogether too common role of native oppressor taken on by many post-colonized countries. Such a role only contributes to an international neocolonialism. The next major event furthered this process and impacted the "Third World" even more profoundly.

In the west, or perhaps more precisely, in the Hallmark-influenced world, one might find a cynical poetic significance in the date of the "Valentine's Day" settlement made between Union Carbide and the Union of India: "For five years no monetary relief from any source was made over to the victims. Then, on February 14, 1989, they were told that a settlement had been reached: the Union of India and Union Carbide had agreed on a figure of USD 470 million in settlement of all claims past, present and future, and to quash all criminal charges against UCC"[146] (Jaising and Sathyamala 92). The union between country and corporation was obviously a marriage of convenience. The effrontery of the decision, which was eventually repealed, shocked much of the world, creating "national and international outrage at the blatancy of its disregard for the injury caused to the victims, and at the Indian government's sell-out to a transnational corporation" (Jaising and Sathyamala 92). Even greater outrage might have been expressed throughout the world had critics of the decision realized the ramifications of the precedent being set as a prominent corporation was exonerated at the expense of an eminent—if "third world"—nation. As Ashis Gupta explains in *Ecological Nightmares and the Management Dilemma: The Case of Bhopal*, "[t]he February 1989 settlement of ... litigation has proved to be a major windfall for multinationals and other corporations in the Third World .... [T]he

146 The decision to terminate all criminal proceedings was later overturned and criminal proceedings reinstated against Warren Anderson and other UCC and UCIL officials.

Supreme Court of India virtually absolved Union Carbide Corporation of all liability in the leakage ... from the company's pesticides plant"[147] (Gupta 32).

For "Third World" people however, a very different picture was at stake: the case was making clear that decision-making within the legal system, such as it is, may severely limit civil rights in the periphery.

> The locating of a hazardous industry in a densely-populated community, simply because it owns the land and has the right to exploit it, has a direct bearing on the lives of members of that community .... They have no right to decide where hazardous industry should be located, only to claim compensation for the destruction of their right to life as a consequence .... This makes for a significant difference: while the rights to manage capital are determined and defined at the stage of production, the compensatory rights of victims are defined only at the point of destruction of life. Conceptually, the legal system has traditionally been incapable of anticipating rights. (Jaising and Sathyamala 97)

This limitation of the legal systems has powerful implications: withholding people's rights to prevention means that disasters are managed rather than avoided; their repercussions may chronically manifest themselves in people's lives.[148] Jamie Cassels has asserted that "[j]ust as it is necessary to adopt a model of public responsibility towards the individual victims of a disaster, so is it necessary for the world community to develop a model of public responsibility towards its less-developed members and towards the global environment more generally" (Cassels 283). Such an onus would be a monumental development for environmental justice law, one necessary and invaluable as societies face increasing climate inequities, worldwide.

In her article, "A Very Bad Way to Enter the Next Century" Petra Kelly, the German environmental activist, advocates an idea, initially raised by Manikka Gandhi, one time minister of forestry and nature in India that might meet Cas-

---

147 Gupta explains further long-term significance of the settlement in that it "proved to be face-saving device for the major protagonists in the legal case. The Indian government could claim that Carbide had, in essence, accepted the blame .... [Carbide] could rationalize the payment on humanitarian grounds, and legitimately claim that they had never acknowledged any liability on the company's part" (Gupta 32).

148 An analogy lies in the current U.S. health system in which preventative medicine is inaccessible to many people because it is beyond the means of most and often not covered by insurance. Meanwhile, the toxic industry creates many health problems for unknowing individuals that could be identified early on by preventative medicine. Thus, preventable exposure is allowed, early treatment is discouraged, and the consequent disease must be "managed" with expensive drugs or other treatments. In some cases, the same corporation that produces the toxins that cause diseases produce the very drugs used to treat them. See, for instance, my discussion of the political poetics of breast cancer in Chapter Eight.

sels' mandate. At a preparatory meeting for the Rio Earth Summit, Gandhi proposed an "International Environmental Court," a concept that if enacted could facilitate the called-for shift in the perception of true international equal rights (Kelly 142). Others have suggested that the problem of multinationals operating with environmental malice in the "Third World" could be solved in "home-country" regulations that required a corporation to operate in line with the standard regulations of the country where it is based. Yet any kind of international regulation has been seen by some as "a form of environmental and legal imperialism and a new form of legal colonialism" (Cassels 49). In a postcolonial world where neocolonialism is perpetrated by native leaders in league with multinational corporate money, such leaders often unjustly deny the rights of their country's citizens and "contradictory" forms of domination consistently impact poor communities. Social environmental issues show that national barriers are political constructions whose boundaries are enforced against neither toxins nor forces of nature. Such issues nuance the consideration of rights on several levels. The sobering legal implications of Bhopal clarify this.

By foregrounding property rights over individual rights and corporation rights over community rights—by, in fact, eliding community rights altogether, it became clear to fellow Indians that local people had lost their right to collective self-determination.[149] Individual rights as well as community rights were infringed upon. As Jaising and C. Sathyamala track the process, the corporate strategy seems simply a divide and conquer routine that placates those with more power and ignores the property-less. In Bhopal,

> the origin of rights continues to spring from ownership of property rather than from a recognition of the needs of individuals. When the law looks at individuals it does so only in their capacity as political beings; hence, it confers political rights such as the right to freedom of speech, the right to vote, the right to form associations and so on. These rights

---

149 This can be illustrated by looking at public culture. As Ashis Gupta explains, "The amount of actual relief, the quality of services provided, as well as the true beneficiaries [led] many in Bhopal to joke about what [lay] ahead. While the government [claimed to have] spent $32 million by way of free cereals and foodgrains [distribution] … others maintain that the ruling Congress (I) bosses and their strong-armed followers have used free rations to line their pockets, to buy allegiance, or simply to intimidate" (Gupta 34). The November 1989, election was approaching, Rajiv Gandhi's party was in trouble and many Indians "openly lamented the fate of the victims. If they managed to have their claims processed before election day they might have received some crumbs after paying off the powers-that-be. Following the elections, there was likely to be much left for them." (34). Such cynical humor demonstrates the degree to which the victims became political pawns, and the degree to which this was tolerated in the country.

> [adhere] in individuals rather than in communities. It follows that there is no recognition of the right to protection of the environment, for such a right would by definition recognize collective control over common resources and a common heritage. (95–96)

The issue of a collective definition and control of a common heritage, resources and rights within the contemporary nation-state links the struggles of Bhopal victims with groups such as Palestinians, Chicanos, the Romani, and some indigenous groups. The neglect of rights based on issues of a common heritage often seem to go hand in hand with environmental harm in these contexts.

Relatedly, the loss of common properties is an issue that crosses over many national borders and even ties the history of oppression in the colonizing country itself to the history of oppression of the colony. That the British working class often has had more in common with Britain's colonies, than with its bourgeoisie is a crucial fact that is often overlooked in postcolonial studies. One important characteristic of investigating a *thematic geography*—here, marked by environmental injustice—is that it approaches such links based on like experiences marked by difference, rather than creating often essentializing categories based on a singular definition of subject position alone.

Jaising and C. Sathyamala demonstrate that capitalist economics are at the basis of neocolonialism that dismantled systems of common inheritance and resource distribution when they foreground the issue of the monetization of rights that disenfranchises the poor in the colonized and the colonizing countries alike.

> A significant function of the fact that ownership of property alone gives birth to rights, is that all rights are then capable of, and liable to, being monetised. ... The value of life is reduced to the value of its productive capacity measured in economic terms alone. Hence in the Bhopal case there is a total absence of a recognition of the violation of the right to dignity, the right to live in a healthy environment and the right to access to community resources. There is a corresponding absence of a recognition of the need to nurture and restore human life and ecosystems. (96)

This portrayal of the monetization of human rights parallels Daphne Wysham's discussion of the economic analysis of global warming. Based on the Bhopal aftermath, Jaising and C. Sathyamala lay out a new legal agenda for analysis, an effective one that they demonstrate to be unique to their moment in international relationships; they show how and when legal grounds are the base for the disenfranchisement of community rights through their subordination to corporate interests. They demonstrate that "the demand for the international protection of property rights" arose in the Bhopal disaster under the guise of "the protection of trade secrecy" (98). Since this trend is leading to "more and more transnational, rather than national, disasters" they suggest a categorical shift to international legal and activist arenas: "The practice of seeking remedies in national forums based on a plurality of laws is thus losing its relevance, and needs to be replaced by recourse to international forums with an international environmental and legal agenda, defined by a commonly binding set of standards and subject to an international regime of obligations towards people" (98).

Trade agreements which supersede all participating countries' rules make the Jaising and C Sathyamala mandate even more crucial. Furthermore, their proposed shift might accommodate intervention in a concern voiced by many U.S. environmental justice groups—the transferal of cheap labor and environmental toxins to "Third World" countries in order that multinationals, based in the "first world," might maximize profit. Jaising and C. Sathyamala see protection against such violations as basic to the "very nature and structure of democracy" and stress the need for "the inalienability of natural and human resources, rather than their mobility and convertibility" (98). They call for a shift so that rights would "revolve around the relationship between people and their life-support systems, and the right of the community to decide on whether or not a hazardous industry should be allowed and where it should be located, whether or not a mine is dug or a river is dammed" (98). Theirs is an echo of the calls by MELA and PODER for community self-determination over community intrusions by toxic industry.

While Jaising and C. Sathyamala use the legal vocabulary of "democracy" and "inalienability" in defining the ideal direction India must move to avoid future confiscation of "natural and human resources" they acknowledge the country is proceeding in a counter direction. Writing in 1993, they historicize the dangers of privatization by juxtaposing them to a tradition of "strongly held beliefs."

> All the strongly held beliefs regarding the responsibilities of a socialist welfare State—transforming social relations, ensuring distribution of economic and social power, restricting monopolistic trade practices, etc.—have been called into question by the increasing privatization of economies across the world and the yoking of all developing countries to a global market. This has resulted in a systematic dismantling of legislative control over economic activity. (Jaising and C. Sathyamala 98)

In that Jaising and Sathyamala suggest a transnational theoretical agenda to pursue their mandates, they can be compared to activists' agendas and to the texts of fiction writers such as Mahasweta Devi who presents similar issues in the same national setting. Jaising and Sathyamala narrativize the legal systems' acceptance of the corporate "accident" in Bhopal to identify an ominous transnational trend that has been noted by María Elena Lucas (in Chapter 11), Vandana Shiva, and others. And like most of the creative works examined in subsequent chapters, Jaising and C. Sathyamala, among other chroniclers of the Bhopal disaster, focus attention on the effects that the gas played in the lives of the women who were affected by it. In the following chapter, narrations of the most common effects document the degree to which gender and biological sex play a role in lived experiences with toxins and the ways in which women's organizations have responded.

7 Representing Bhopal

7.1 Representations of Attack: Bhopal Poetics: Press and Activism

> The trick for activists is to bridge public discourse and people's experiential knowledge, integrating them in a coherent frame that supports and sustains collective action .... Only general-audience media provide a potentially shared public discourse.
>
> William A. Gamson (SM&C, 85)

> "Bhopal" consists of many tragedies—health, environmental, legal and also media. The press quickly tired of the Bhopal issue .... Journalists saw the disaster as an isolated event, separate from the ongoing social and political conditions that caused it and now inhibit all rehabilitation efforts .... Journalists can help assure that citizens have sufficient information to evaluate thoroughly whether or not hazardous technologies are worth the risk they bring.
>
> T.R. Chouhan (1994, 84)

One of the politicized ironies of Bhopal is apparent in Alfred de Grazia's assertion in 1985 that "the *New York Times* will ultimately have spent half a million dollars" to cover the disaster in Bhopal (de Grazia 42). Given the continuing nature of the tragedy during the time since de Grazia's estimate, it is likely that his figure is low. Despite all the money spent, however, most chroniclers, including de Grazia were critical of most of the U.S. press coverage. In contrast, de Grazia praises the Indian press coverage overall, noting that the Indian press had a symbiotic relationship with the volunteer sector. As the above epigraphs demonstrate, both activists and workers in Bhopal and new social movement scholars recognize the importance and the conflicted nature of movement-media relationships. The following section takes a cursory view of media-movement issues that relate most directly to the international exchange that took place through Bhopal negotiations. Following media representations—in English-language media—this chapter will investigate a spectrum of representations for their sociopolitical, and cultural/literary ramifications.

Despite the critique in Chouhan's epigraph, many chroniclers consider the Indian media–social movement relationship crucial. De Grazia describes the interactive support that existed: "Manifestations of a public opinion that would not have been heard, if left to the victims alone to voice, or to the governments or the corporations, were publicized in advance and afterwards in the newspapers. Authorities made light of the agitation, but with the press writing about it and about the governmental response, some help came fast" (de Grazia 43–44). In de Grazia's opinion, the Indian press generated response to the victim's

https://doi.org/10.1515/9783111041575-008

needs and solidarity with the survivors' call for justice that contrasted sharply with the part the media played in the U.S. context: "[t]he US groups were totally caught off guard; the charities ... responded, but much response was of the 'Just think if it happened here' kind, and much of the Bhopal coverage in the U.S. news was actually coverage of the non-news that nothing was happening, and why a disaster was or was not going to happen at the Union Carbide plant in West Virginia" (de Grazia 43). (This is not to mention the slower but similar poisoning happening in places like Mission, TX where after pesticide plants had been closed but not cleaned up, Bhopal activists would meet Mission activists struggling for health care and justice in their communities' similar horrific exposure-induced health issues in a neighborhood with Union Carbide, Monsanto and other companies' pesticide manufacturing.)[150]

Useful assessment of early press coverage is also available in *Behind the Poison Cloud: Union Carbide's Bhopal Massacre* (1985) by Larry Everest. Everest draws much of his information from both U.S. and Indian newspapers; he addresses the issues the newspapers raise (or neglect) and critiques their perspectives. He too is particularly critical of the U.S. Press citing it as one of the "powerful forces" "who have tried, and will continue to try, to relegate this crime to obscurity" (157).

The press, to some extent, reflected forces of both machination and prejudice. Tara Jones reports that in addition to spreading the medical cover-up of gas-affects to women's reproduction systems, class bias without explication of conditions was present in news reports that did occur.

> It was expected that many deformed full-term babies, first trimester foetuses on 3 December, would be born starting in June 1985. An uncounted number of horrifying births have already taken place among poor women, attended only by midwives, but the only one which I saw in the papers was born in a hospital in Bilaspur, to a woman who had fled Bhopal the day of the disaster. (Dakin, 1985, 7 in Jones 100)

Lee Wilkins in *Shared Vulnerabilities* argues that the common threat that toxic corporate industry poses to people globally was not publicized in the U.S. mainstream media that she observed (for two months following the gas leak). Her argument would be stronger had she recognized that while, as she argues, vulnerability to toxic industry is "shared" between North and South, it is not equal-

150 See https://www.texasobserver.org/2534-slow-death-slower-justice-how-pesticides-poisoned-south-mission-but-no-one-is-responsible/. For mention of XICA MEDIA's digital archive of The Mission Texas Files, see https://deceleration.news/2017/01/13/agent-orange-major-dump-of-toxic-mission-tx-related-docs/.

ly shared. She falls into one of the critical traps she herself describes when she does not recognize the double standards at work in global capitalist media representations.[151] However her researched description of media accounts and the resulting U.S. perceptions is thorough. She finds that Indians were most often portrayed as powerless, even when this meant ignoring a particular aspect of the event, such as the massive immediate medical attention that Indian doctors gave. Some reporting was skewed toward seeing the event predominately as a potential economic disaster for Union Carbide. (She cites a *U.S. News and World Report* article as an extreme example in this.) Women and children were most often portrayed as victims—furthering stereotypical portrayals of "Third World" peoples—women, in particular—as helpless. Furthermore, Wilkins believes that "the debate in which a democratic society needs to engage to decide what technologies, for what purposes, constitute acceptable risks" is not well-served by her sole focus on "portraits of victims" (144). She finds that the event was mythologized rather than nuanced (149); Wilkins puts importance on spreading the awareness that "such catastrophes are not myth; they are man-made and they can be mitigated" (154).

In the "prestige press," Wilkins found that government officials were most often cited, followed by Union Carbide representatives and then other (Indian) news media. It is not surprising then that she finds little mention of the aspects of technological hazards and safety concerns; siting the coverage of Three Mile Island as an example, she observes that in studies of "hazard mitigation" journalists have been found to "error on the side of caution" (141). Thus, she suggests that the media may be ill-prepared to appropriately deal with environmental justice concerns: "[h]umanity's shared vulnerability—regardless of geography—to such technological hazards may somehow demand a different form of reportage, one which emphasizes evaluation and analysis of the value framework underlying scientific and technological discovery" (135). This important observation suggests that the U.S. press needs to be reconceptualized in light of environmental justice concerns; it is further relevant that this opinion comes from a communication scholar, not an environmental or social activist,

---

151 The study is somewhat marred by its own misconceptions of culture in Bhopal. For instance, Wilkins discusses at length conceptions of death in Hindu culture that differ from predominately Christian U.S. traditions. While her concern that "conveying the complete story about the Bhopal disaster, in the abstracted sense of journalists' search for truth, should not take precedence over the dignity of those involved in the process" (139) is well-taken, and she suggests that U.S. journalist's accounts may have been insulting, she does not mention that a majority of Bhopal's gas-affected community is not Hindu and ignores how the journalists' accounts might have misrepresented that majority.

per se. In the following section, journalistic, activist, and corporate languages are examined in the context of Bhopal narratives that represent events from very different perspectives.

7.2 Representations of Attack: Bhopal Poetics: Language in the Poetics of the Bhopal Massacre

> There is a constant tendency, among parties as diverse as the poorest of victims and learned American environmentalists to reduce the Bhopal problem to a particular safety failure for which an assignment of responsibility and quick compensation are the proper resolution. To the contrary, I would say that the meaning of Bhopal needs to be preserved and enlarged. It is a jolting reminder of the gas ovens of Belsen, the radiation cloud of Hiroshima, the burned women shirtmakers of a New York City sweatshop whose death began a new chapter in the history of safety and better working conditions. Bhopal can be a watershed in industrial, even in world, history if the victims receive fair treatment and full justice, and if a new code of conduct comes to govern transnational business operations.
>
> Alfred de Grazia (1985, 47)

In a striking comparison to other texts on Bhopal—that point to the highly political allegiances marked in the likening of one event to a previous one—Bruce Piasecki suggests that "Bhopal was the environmental equivalent of Pearl Harbor, a violent wake-up call that shook many nations and many firms" (24). Certainly, loyalty to the U.S.-centered military industrial complex is reflected in Piasecki's comparison. Extending the analogy, we can only be relieved—if this was the "Pearl Harbor"—that UCC did not respond with a "Hiroshima." Yet for many survivors, and perhaps for anyone conscientiously considering the significance of the aftermath of suffering that continues in Bhopal, it did symbolize a new level of human devastation and cynical acceptance. The world has virtually ignored this fact. Rather, the corporate world follows Piasecki in viewing Bhopal from a narrow "maximization of profits and publicity" angle. He sees the "accident" as ultimately good public relations for the company: "outside the boardroom, Union Carbide was now a name known to every household in America. No advertising campaign, no matter how clever or aggressively circulated, could have achieved the name recognition that the chemical catastrophe had promoted" (23). Yet chroniclers of Bhopal took a very different view.

This section's epigraph engages a comparison—to the Nazi holocaust—that occurs frequently in the discourse on Bhopal. A parallel exists in terms of the nature of the victims' suffering and deaths; while the issue of intent differentiates the situations somewhat, the multitudes of deaths by gas, be it by fire or poisoned air, were similarly horrific. One might even look for the loose parallels between the ruthless and remorseless gendered racism of global corporate imperialism and the Nazi's fascist rise to power.[152] Inhumane treatment of victims and the ranking of political gain above preservation of civilian lives are further similarities.

Furthermore, an analogy could be developed between the socio-economic disenfranchisement of many of the Bhopal victims and the disenfranchising prejudice against the Jews—and others who suffered—in the Nazi context. All were outsiders to the dominant culture, and thus became the victims of a dehumanization process that made their deaths tolerable to the countries at large. Comparisons that contemporize the Nazi experience demand acknowledgment of the common elements of brutality that currently exist, as well as dehumanizing acts and systems. Such comparisons counter an impulse in some popular Nazi holocaust narratives—as in irresponsible examples of postcolonial studies—to exoticize past examples of human exploitation and genocide, treating them as unlinked to our "postmodern" world. Rather, Bhopal narratives resituate what has become conceptualized as a landmark of human inhumanity—Nazi brutality—and thus they demand that readers re-examine current topographies of violence.

De Grazia evokes the twin holocausts of World War II—borne of the German gas chamber and the U.S. nuclear bomb. Mentioned perhaps as often as the Nazi comparison—at least in the early writings—the comparison to Hiroshima is, in several ways, a more resonant one. In terms of the malevolent devaluation of Asian life by those of Euro-American descent, the nuclear attacks on Japanese cities may be even more comparable to the present U.S. environmental racism expressed toward India. Additionally, David Weir contrasts the medical community's organized monitoring of and care for bomb victims in Japan to the Bhopal medical community's collusion that obscured future study of the gas effects and failed in treating survivors' symptoms through withholding of antidotes and information (93).

Susanna Dakin suggests a comparison in that "both Hiroshima and Bhopal are catastrophic events that require us to reexamine and redefine our relationship to technology and our place in the world" (in Kolpe 61). Japan's response to Hiroshima in rebuilding the city and treating the victims is often seen as a model by Bhopal chroniclers. As N. Rajan explains, "The Government and the peo-

152 The descriptive "gendered racism" most adequately recognizes the interconnecting legacies of prejudice. Just as whites are too often implicitly considered "the raceless norm" men are too often the "genderless norm." "Gendered racism" emphasizes (rather than categorically separates) the connections between the legacies of racial and gender discrimination and acknowledges discrimination against as, well as privileges of, white women and men of color. Identifying such links may hold the potential to encourage mutual struggle and discourage the divide and conquer routine that is often the Achilles' heel of progressive politics.

ple of Japan saw to it that Hiroshima was [re]built as a beautiful city. It symbolised the human will to survive the nuclear holocaust. Bhopal is also a warning to humanity against chemical warfare and its consequences" (in Kolpe 16). N. Rajan sees several ways to respond appropriately to Bhopal; these responses address differing concerns. On one hand, he wants to create "a beautiful city;" in this impulse he is like activists who felt Bhopal's bastis could and should be turned into model "Third World" communities. On the other hand, N. Rajan sees Bhopal as a warning that must be heeded by stepping up precautions in our technocratic societies, both "Third" and "first" world.

Hayden White talks about the significance of terms such as "holocaust" when he discusses "tragedy," and the inevitability that it implies in "Historical Texts as Literary Artifact" (67) in *The Tropics of Discourse*. He makes the point that no historical event is intrinsically tragic and that historical events don't naturally constitute stories. His discussion can be usefully applied to much of the descriptive discourse surrounding Bhopal especially that which uses unrestrained or "heightened" language. Despite his Euro-centric New Critical bent, his analysis is significant to the postcolonial Indian context, as we consider why it is the "stories" that seem to be most often used to convey the cruel injustice of Bhopal.

In 1990, an Indian colleague at the University of Texas, whose eyes were damaged by the gas described a "fatalism" among most victims that had grown in the succeeding years.[153] Fatalism among survivors has increased in response to governments' appropriation, management, and institutionalization of the gas tragedy. But the poetics I examine, while they may describe despondency and mental lethargy—perhaps partially because of gas residue in people's bodies that have never been treated to detoxify—do not naturalize these effects as an attribute of the poor. Discussions of "fatalism" could fall into the trap of "naturalizing" a certain socio-political and even toxin-caused response. However, along with a fatalism that is politically redefined comes the means for going beyond it. The path may lie partially in the poetics. The early chronicles I've examined don't express the authors' despair, so much as describe the horror of the gas leak and resulting suffering with a (usually) restrained anger. But from the beginning, many of the texts do use the language of tragedy that White describes. For instance:

> They were asleep and unaware of impending death. But death did visit the people of Bhopal that chill winter night of December 2, 1984. A dense mist spread insidiously through the air turning this city of eight lakh inhabitants into the biggest gas chamber this world

153 Asian Communiqué planning meeting, March 1990.

> has ever known. Maybe, if the lessons of this industrial catastrophe are well learnt, we will never witness such a horrifying spectre ever again. But the memory lingers on, haunting, macabre. (*peoples view* ... introduction 7)

The heightened language does not suggest fatalism; the language *may* reflect Indian society's predominant construction of the event, as opposed to the Indian national and state governments' more calculated and cynical approaches. Such societal constructions are importantly influenced by feudal, caste and other religious hierarchies and (primarily) British colonialism, and contemporary neo-liberalism.[154] The implications of such diverse, often negative influences cannot be adequately investigated in this study but there are lessons to be learned from the poetics generated in response to the harmful manifestations of Bhopal. With this purpose in mind, returning to the first published accounts in book-form offers a useful close reading.

Bhopal: a people's view of death ... was published by Eklavya of the Arera Colony. The preface is not signed but addressed and dated in pen: "Bhopal December 25, 1984." While the date does not have a religious significance for the non-Christian majority of India, Christmas Day is certainly nonetheless a familiar day in the country; the Hindi name for Christmas day translates as "Big Day." Thus, the date suggests intent on the part of the authors.[155] The Preface identifies an audience that underscores this:

154 I use "neo-liberalism" in the sense it has been defined by the Sao Paulo forum and other Latin American intellectual groups, that is, the global corporate capitalist exploitation and disenfranchisement, especially in the South.

155 The debate over the "intentional fallacy" is sometimes invoked in Cultural Studies, as in other fields of literary studies; I contend that it is often grossly inappropriate in this context, however. The question of whether a critic or theorist can determine "authorial intent" is closely related to the question of the authority of the author, as discussed by Michel Foucault in "What is the Author?" and by Roland Barthes in "The Death of the Author." Their undermining of the authority of authorship addressed the issue of biological criticism in which the author contained the limits of the text. The intentional fallacy was invoked against the frame of reinventing an authorial zeitgeist, a "historical" relationship between a (dead) author and the 'spirit of his age.' Politically informed writing by authors in a contemporary context who are experientially engaged in the power dynamics of dominance and oppression overrides any legitimation of the 'intentional fallacy.' Likewise, "intent" cannot be considered a nonissue when discussing fascism, supremacies or manufacturing criminal cover-up, all of which are involved in the contextual milieu in which social environmental texts are being generated in Bhopal. The specific problems that Barthe and Foucault are addressing have been generalized in current usage. The condemnation of identity politics may carry some of the historical baggage of the intentional fallacy, also. However, I contend that the issue of "the intent of the author" is situationally misappropriated in that project as well. To my knowledge, in the 20th Century this

> We address this report to everyone who wishes to act on this information to ensure that the thousands affected in Bhopal get justice and not mere crumbs, and that Bhopal is never never repeated anywhere in the world—not even in the so called developed countries—we don't wish them such horror even though we denounce their power games and economic greed. (5)

Their qualifier—"not even in the so-called developed countries"—marks the complicity of the "so called developed" countries, the origin of the Union Carbide Company, and it questions the value judgement attached to the term "developed." Such a move intervenes in U.S. progressive discourse that often puts "developing" and "third world" in quotation marks but fails to likewise mark doubts about the stance of "developed" or "first world" territory. The quotation demonstrates that its authors have no wish for revenge while it identifies the source of the catastrophe and chastises those responsible. The disastrous impact of "developed" societies is judged, linked to the "horror," and to the culprit gas: "we denounce their power games and economic greed." A parallel sentiment exists in the U.S. "Third World" in the "Not in Anybody's Back Yard"

---

was inadequately theorized, however at least one study proves useful: Gayatri Spivak's discussion of authorial death in relationship to her writing about Rushdie *in Outside the Teaching Machine*. On one hand she is engaging a rather morbid pun when she speaks of the death of an author whose person has been publicly condemned to death for his authorship, however her engagement is, not surprisingly, both dense and useful. Spivak begins by situating what she calls a "metropolitan aphorism"—"The birth of the reader must be at the cost of the death of the Author"—to face "the case of Salmon Rushdie." She asks that we read "the other side" and distinguishes between writer, subject, and agent, as separate from "author" explaining thus: "The author, who is not only taken to be the authority for the meaning of a text, but also, when possessed of authority, possessed *by that fact* of 'moral or legal supremacy, the power to influence the conduct or action of others;' and, when authorizing, 'giving legal force to, making legally valid' (OED). Thus, even on the most 'literal' level of the dictionary, 'the birth ...' takes on a different resonance" (217–218). Barthes, she believes is talking about a reader, not as critic/judge, as above, but as someone "who holds together in a single field all the traces by which the written text is constituted" (218) whose birth is predicated on the death of the author. This is because as Barthes observes, writing has become performative. She explains that "[w]hen the writer and reader are born again and again together, the author(ity)-function is dead, the critic is not mentioned" (218). She ends her discussion with a turn to Derridean deconstruction that shifts authorship from writer/recorder of culture to politician: "Moving with Derrida, I can say, that when Barthes and Foucault are monumentalized as marks for the death and nothingness of the author, everything happens as if the sign 'Author' has no history, no linguistic or cultural limits. I turn back to the dictionary, where I began, and I see that, in the Rushdie affair, it is the late Ayatollah who can be seen as filling the author-function, and Salman Rushdie, himself, caught in the different cultural logic, is no more than the writer-as-performer" (218–219).

(Namby) and BANANA Campaigns initiated by U.S. people of color networks in place of the "Not in My Backyard" (Nimby) campaigns that addressed environmental problems in some predominantly middle-class white neighborhoods without extending their struggle beyond "their own backyards."[156]

The allegorical significance of the Christmas date is extended when its context is considered. The publication coming from Bhopal reverses the conventional logic of Christmas gift-giving. It is after all predominately the "developed" world that gives at Christmas and that gave the "developing" India the disaster at Bhopal.[157] Thus, the date underscores the distance between the two worlds. While the compilers at Bhopal are writing the preface for a series of narrative accounts of an event that killed and maimed thousands of their fellow townspeople, its potential U.S. audience is complacently opening more benign (though perhaps not unlinked) presents. Thereby, the book itself is marked as a sobering gift. The significance of naming—played out above by dating the publication so precisely—arises repeatedly in the language used by those who narrate the disaster and its aftermath. Like other types of figurative language, naming is used to carry out critical analysis, even as it narrates a chronology of events. Thereby, the Bhopal poetics illustrates Jane Jenson's assertion that "[r]outes to representation become available in accordance with the name selected" (in Johnston and Klandermans 118).

The interconnections of transnational and intranational environmental and economic oppression might best be conceptualized through the visual (and experiential) metaphor of the conjoining knots of freeway entrances and exit ramps, overpasses, and underpasses. To return to two texts that I initially introduced for a comparison: Jaising and C. Sathyamala's analysis amounts to an annotated road map with accompanying aerial photo that can lead one through the traffic maze while the Eklavya of the Arera Colony text's superlative-laden summary is tantamount to an expressionistic painting of the maze. *The peoples' view*, like so much writing to follow, documents the immediate scenario of the disaster in a poetic prose that links Bhopal with the violence of Nazi gas chambers. But at Christmas, 1984, no one could visualize the many ways that for those left alive, but injured by the gas, the horror had only begun. Other publi-

156 Discussion with Antonio Diaz, PODER, Austin, 1993. Nimbyism increased LULUs' ("locally unwanted land uses") pressure on poor and people of color communities (Bullard 10).

157 UC itself seems to concur with this figurative analysis—when UC's Jerimiah Kenney spoke on University of Texas at Austin's *Asian Communiqué* radio program in the spring of 1990 he represented the Bhopal plant almost as a kind of gift—not profitable to UC, but built to retain the good graces of the Indian government (Spring, 1990 notes from *Asian Communiqué* tape).

cations would pick up the story, write another chapter at a crucial juncture when support for the victim-survivors was especially important, or when, in some other part of the world, a chemical industry was being fought off or environmental legislation stood a chance of being passed. I will briefly describe important moments in a few of these publications, some produced by groups, others by individuals.

Christmas in Bhopal is described in detail by Anees Chishti, a reporter who had arrived in Bhopal only days before the gas leak to cover the approaching Madhya Pradesh state elections (Sumitra Chishti 17).

> *Burra Din* would come and go on Tuesday but the Yuletide spirit would be absent in Bhopal. Father Christmas may not even visit these parts. There are no Christmas trees anywhere in the city, unless it be the polluted one spreading its branches over one's desolate pavement. The local Christian community has decided not to celebrate Christmas this year as a mark of respect to over 2000 officially reported dead ....
> The imposing St. Francis Church in old city's Jehangirabad had never perhaps seen such gloom in its illustrious 200 year history .... The Holy Redeamers' [sic] Association, patronising the Church near the railway station, situated almost in the eye of the gas chamber of December 2–3 has taken [a] ... decision not to have any celebrations except the morning prayer. (73)

After Christmas, Anees Chishti returned to his own family but would go back to Bhopal in mid-January to report on "The Follow-up Endeavour;" he continues his reports from Bhopal through April 1985. Chishti's collection of articles *Dateline Bhopal: A Newsman's Diary of the Gas Disaster* is a focused study strengthened by its immediacy and depiction of detail. His wife, Sumitra writes a foreword entitled "Bhopal in Our Home" which personalizes their experience with the gas leak in an autobiographical sense that is missing in other texts from allies though autobiography is popular in survivors' texts, especially in testimonials, such as those in *Voices From Bhopal*. *Voices From Bhopal* was produced by the Bhopal Group For Information and Action and contains photos and interviews of victim-survivors. An introduction explains,

> Among gas victims, faith in the legal process is not strong; the courts are seen to be part of the establishment that benefited from Carbide's operations. Victims forcefully argue that they would have been ignored completely had they not carried out sustained public protest, insisting that their lives not be sold in exchange for the glamour of Indian participation in global capitalism.

This text, more than any other series of narratives, gives the victims' unedited (though transcribed and presumably translated) views. *Union Carbide's Bhopal Tragedy: A Time for Solidarity: Special Report to American Workers and Communities at Risk* (1989) was published in April after the February 14th "Settlement or

Sellout" (1). It describes the agreement, gives background on the "Accident Waiting to Happen" (2), describes Union Carbide's response, which only "Compound[ed] Catastrophe" (5), presents the "Victim's Response" (8) how to support their struggle and "Solidarity with U.S. Workers and Communities at Risk" (9). Under the "Victims' Response" the following actions are reported: demanded results of government research on the effects of MIC; asked for resumption of state relief provisions; secured an order to UCC to provide interim relief and have refused to accept unsatisfactory settlement offers (9). The Bhopal victims' international delegation is also announced. *Union Carbide's Bhopal Tragedy* points out that the UCC was spending almost $8 million a year on Bhopal litigation alone, but perhaps its most distinctive aspect is the section on U.S. solidarity. It explains the links between decisions in India over Bhopal and community and worker relations with corporations in the US: "There are hundreds of communities and thousands of workers across the U.S. exposed to reckless corporate behavior who have a major stake in how the Bhopal victims fare in their struggle with Union Carbide. Of special importance is establishing the principle of immediate interim relief for victims of corporate abuse" (9). Based on mutual best interest in a fair decision and immediate interim relief for the gas victims, the section calls for U.S. worker and community support in demanding corporate accountability in the Bhopal case.

Just Cause is also published by a support group in the US: Communities Concerned About Corporations. It was published in November 1994, commemorates a decade of events and contains parts of the interviews from *Voices from Bhopal* as well as several cartoons that have been published repeatedly. The booklet also has reproduced drawings or prints depicting horrible suffering in a style that resembles Kathe Kollwitz' artwork; the design and illustration are credited to Will Hardin and are copyrighted by Will Hardin Studios. These illustrations appear to have been drawn from photographs and while they are well-executed, Bhopal artists' work might have been more effective, if more complicated to attain.

A major section of the booklet is dedicated to reviewing UCC's post-Bhopal environmental risk and accident record, primarily in the Institute plant. A note at the end of the West Virginia section of this history says it is based on "over 1,000 newspaper articles that appeared in two Charleston newspapers from January 1, 1985, to November 1, 1995." The plethora of articles alone suggests a sense of foreboding that counters UCC's attempt at presenting a changed "green" image. The booklet ends with the background, chronology, and the founding declaration of Communities Concerned About Corporations (CCAC). The booklet is condensed from a report commissioned by CCAC on the tenth anniversary of Bhopal. It represents a publication by a group who have in effect taken on Bhopal as a symbol of what happens when what they are fighting for (corporate accountability) is devalued. In this sense their relationship to Bhopal victims is less direct, yet the potential philosophical alliance in terms of demanding corporate responsibility suggests potential symbiotic importance to Bhopal survivor groups.

Perhaps most impressive of such activist publications is a book compiled by a former UCC worker and co-published in the U.S. and India. On the pink cover of *Bhopal: The Inside Story, Carbide Workers Speak Out on the World's Worst Industrial Disaster*, a purple hexagon creates a closed room in which we see a worker with a hard-hat, blue coat, and clip board; the man stands between the fingers of a huge metal clamp. Behind him a fire rages. The cover design by Baiju Parthan suggests the clinches within which workers often find themselves. This book gives the worker on the cover a way out, a way to warn others of the chemical fire raging behind him. Once an MIC Plant Operator at the UC Bhopal plant, T.R. Chouhan has collaborated with other workers, environmental journalist, Claude Alvares, and lawyer, Indira Jaising, to produce a clear record of UCC's record in Bhopal, Madhya Pradesh.

An article reprinted in Chouhan's book declares that "[t]he Bhopal victims have become a mere footnote to a sordid story of transfer of money from one group of vested interests—Carbide or the government—to another: doctors, lawyers, and drug companies, many of them multinationals" (*The Economic Times* (November 29, 1993) in Chouhan 170). While the earlier chronology of the semantic, medical, and legal manifestations of the gas-leak for women and others indicates ways in which mere footnoting the survivors and their environmental rights did occur, the narratives I've just described and the activism and poetics described in following sections fight such dismissive footnoting of victims. They are examples of texts which defy the mainstream narratives of Bhopal. Largely through their use of language, they have done what as a group, international doctors, lawyers, and others have not. They have distributed information, aesthetics, sentiment, and analysis worldwide to facilitate the survivors' struggle for justice and an environmentally sound future.[158]

---

158 In this section, in particular, a few publications are not listed in the Works Cited. In some cases, they are referenced in the text, or in the footnotes, as relevant to broader or tangential study, but not directly used, here. In some cases, their status as poetics is clear but their publication record is less tangible. The internet has allowed me to recover many items from the cultural poetics part of my project that was set aside to complete a literary dissertation, losing some documentation, in the process. Tapping into UT, Austin's Perry Castaneda Graduate Library's catalog has been a godsend since their South Asian collection had offered a wealth of materials, but material that was handed to me, or I was allowed to peruse in community-based collections, is less likely to have been recorded online. Section 7.2's final paragraph lays out why I chose to include them, nonetheless.

7.3 Representations of Attack: Bhopal Poetics: Unraveling the Tragedy at Bhopal: UCC spins its Tale

Alongside figurative identifications that name the horror of environmental devastation of community, the following section looks at government and corporate discourse produced for popular consumption that urges "tolerance" of death and damage for a select few for the (supposed) sake of the rest. For instance, Ashis Gupta states that,

> [i]t is being suggested in certain quarters (that) the Bhopal genocide is the price to be paid for development, for increases in agricultural production, for progress in developing countries. This view was expressed by none other than Dr. S Varadarajan, who headed the team of 'experts' overseeing the post tragedy operations in the plant at a press conference in Bhopal on Dec. 15. He said, 'The whole issue has to be seen in the context of the cost benefit ratio. It has to be looked at in terms of necessity. No technological operation is entirely without risks. (Gupta 1991, 37)

While such attitudes are in no way limited to corporate thinkers and Varadarajan's ideas resonate with those economists who created the hierarchies of human value to judge the cost of global warming, useful analysis on this issue can also be found in Charles Perrow's theory of 'normal accidents' in relation to Bhopal. As Jamie Cassels explains "'Systems,' [Perrow] explains, are complex organizations characterized by their 'interactive complexity,' which makes the entire system incomprehensible to any one individual. Indeed, the increasing specialization and expertise prompted by the technical division of labour may make systems even more unstable by limiting the scope of each person's knowledge [this reiterates the workers' arguments about lack of knowledge being an environmental safety issue.] Any one part of a system can fail in a trivial and unanticipated way and, in conjunction with other components of the system, such failure can lead to catastrophic results" (82). He points out that accidents often follow unpredictable "sneak paths" which delegitimize "risk assessment" processes (Jones 244–245). Perrow deconstructs the representation of absolute scientific knowledge when he observes the history of the chemical industry.

> While experience has helped reduce accidents, accidents continue to plague transformation processes that are fifty years old. These are processes that can be described, but not really understood. They were often discovered through trial and error, and what passes for understanding is really only a description of something that works. Some industrial chemical processing is of this nature. (Perrow 1984, 85 in Jones 244).

Not surprisingly, industry considers Charles Perrow a "doom-monger" who predicts about four "catastrophic accidents" per decade (in Jones 210).[159] His thorough analysis acknowledges what Jones refers to as the "class-blind" nature of "risk analysis" when Perrow concludes that "[t]he signals come from systems, technological and economic.[160] They are systems that élites have constructed, and thus can be changed or abandoned" (Perrow 1984 in Jones, 352). It may be precisely because such systems can be "changed or abandoned," that corporations protect themselves with (mis)representations of events and issues for public consumption.

UCC has generated its own plethora of poetics on Bhopal as part of a public relations campaign geared to neutralize negative feelings toward the corporation. For instance, in January 1985, the *UC World*, an employees' and retirees' magazine gave Bhopal a cover story. (Browning 12); the corporation also produced videos and featured a review of the media's coverage of the Bhopal tragedy in its video series *What's Going On*. Contrasting such a story generated in corporate poetics to the activist poetics, may prove useful. A 17-minute Union Carbide-sponsored "documentary" video entitled *Unraveling the Tragedy at Bhopal,* which was produced by Philip Gittelman in 1988, nuances its "proof" of its "disgruntled worker" theory with racist, xenophobic, and class-biased ideologies.

The narrative plot is relatively unspectacular: a nightshift worker, disgruntled because he had been demoted to a less prestigious job after performing inadequately on a routine examination puts water in tank 610 which contains liquid MIC; he intends to "cause mischief" and is "not fully appreciating consequences" of his act. A reaction is caused; the pressure valve blows, and the gas leak occurs. For unexplained reasons other workers coverup the fact that it was caused by the "deliberate" actions of one of their own.

Before turning to other literary devices used in the film, let us turn to cultural work that illuminates the significance of this plot. Ward Morehouse points out that the story is basically a public relations ploy, a fact agreed to by a UCC representative at a Yale Forum on International Law. His assertion was attacked by Bud Geo Holman (UCC legal representative) in a letter published in a subsequent issue of *The Ecologist*. Holman writes: "Union Carbide, its lawyers and lawyers from the

---

159 See Perrow, C. "The President's Commission and the normal accident" in *Accident at three Mile Island: The Human Dimensions*. Boulder, CO: Westview, 1982. (173–184) and his *Normal Accidents: Living with High-risk Technology*. NY: Basic Books, 1984. Also see Morehouse and Subramanian's description of Perrow's work (1986, 88–90).

160 "Classblind" is used in the sense of the now problematic term "colorblind," before it came to denote a reaction against progressive transformation of structural racism.

'New York-based' firm that assists Carbide on Bhopal Litigation Kelley Drye & Warren continue to be absolutely convinced that the terrible tragedy resulted from the deliberate actions of a disgruntled Indian employee at the plant" (bar frame in Morehouse 1994, 166). Morehouse responds that on 14 December 1989 at Yale University under pressure of questioning, a UCC representative agreed that the disgruntled worker theory "would not have any significant bearing on the legal determination of liability" (166). Morehouse observes that "[i]f the sabotage theory had no legal merit, what was its purpose other than as a public relations ploy to make Carbide appear the victim, not the victimizer, and to divert attention from the real causes of the disaster in the careless design and operation of an extremely hazardous chemical facility" (166). Morehouse clarifies the reasons that UCC holds to "the truth" of its narrative. Examining the film only substantiates his claim that UCC's "disgruntled worker" is a public relations ploy. In analyzing how UCC attempts to convince the public of its solvency (and to the extent to which this video is effective in doing so) we can learn much about the nature of the ideologies of prejudice at work in the US.

The 1988 video does not attempt to offer credible proof that such a disgruntled worker existed. Rather, it reverses the maxim stated by the one South Asian pictured from the UCC research scientist team: "Just because you wish it, cannot make it true." UCC and the film producer seem to believe that if the story is "well-told" it has truth value that translates positively for UCC's image. But what works in the UCC telling? The story does not base credibility on logic. For example, one of the UCC lawyers offers "evidence" that they had identified the disgruntled worker in that he still "bore resentment [against the UCC plant] a year later." Clearly this worker, who lost his job with the plant closing and who had family within a two-mile radius—who were presumably affected by the gas leak—was not alone in his "long-term resentment" of UCC. If resentment proves culpability, the hundreds of thousands who have filed unrequited injury claims would also likely stand convicted. Furthermore, the video bears inconsistencies in its attempt to exonerate UCC for damage: for instance, while it states that the company built the plant on the "outskirts" of town ten years prior to the leak, and, afterward, "makeshift shacks and huts had become home to hundreds of families" near the plant, it later describes a gas cloud that "enveloped most of the *older sections* of Bhopal (emphasis mine)." (While the population near the plant had grown, the plant had been situated originally at a low-cost, high-risk location that was upwind from the city, thus endangering both the most long-standing and more recently expanded neighborhoods in the vicinity.)

To establish "credibility" the video repeatedly indulges in scape-goating and stereotyping that suggests that dark-skinned, lower-class Indian workers are sinister, unintelligent, and not to be trusted. The mostly white, mostly western investigation teams of research scientists and lawyers are compassionate, concerned and completely trustworthy; they are "working around the clock," "find it hard to sleep," and among their first responses upon hearing about the disaster was: "what can we do to help?" When the government discouraged people in Bhopal from talking with them, the investigation team "travelled by train, plain and car to all parts of India." In their naiveté, they are shocked to find "contradictions" in the stories the native workers told and begin to suspect a "cover-up." The Indian government—perhaps with some justification—is blamed for impeding their progress and for "not caring about the victims."

The binary ideology of prejudice that establishes a hierarchy of caliber between imperialist and native, boss and worker, Western and Indian is portrayed in the script, the *mise-en-scène*, the soundtrack and the camerawork. The narration opens with a clipped rendition of Bhopal's grand past: "once described as the gateway to antiquity" the city was built on "a lake created by its founder in the 11th century, but modern Bhopal is more likely to be remembered as the site of one of the most tragic industrial disasters in all of history." There is an unrestrained element of pride—on the part of UCC—in this claim.[161] The disgruntled worker theory itself demonstrates this—as the worker is too ignorant to realize the dangerous consequences of what he does. The grain of truth in this construction of the stupid "Third World" worker is that UCC and UCI did not properly train their workers and punished workers who refused work for which they were not trained. They also withheld knowledge about the substances with which the workers were working.[162]

The video establishes the "world media" as the culprit responsible for "confusing reports" and exaggerated explanations that "range from a careless accident to the sinister act of terrorism" neither of which survive UCC's "intensive examination" which has "revealed the nature and cause of the deadly event in India."[163] The camera focuses on a popularly republished photograph by photographer Raghu Rai of Magnum of a hand wiping dirt from a half buried child's face that

161 While my observation might appear mean-spirited and extreme, it builds on earlier observations of similar sentiments, and I substantiate it with a similar cynical tone established by Bruce Piasecki when he notes that UCC "*earned a place* in the *Guinness Book of World Records.*" In the category of "'Worst Accidents and Disasters in the World,' Union Carbide is *credited* with the worst industrial (chemical) disaster, causing 2352 deaths and over 200,000 injuries." (23 italics, mine).

162 This is substantiated repeatedly by the workers' testimonials in *Bhopal: The Inside Story*.

163 The sabotage theory the narrator is referring to is UCC's own creation involving "Black June," an imaginary group of Sikh terrorists; this theory was based on a single sighting of a poster in an unnamed city that credited "Black June" with causing the gas leak.

has been used repeatedly to symbolize the suffering caused by the horrible gas leak.[164] Then it pans from the barb wire fence surrounding the deserted UCC plant to the graffiti on the pillar below—the image of the skull with dollar signs as pupils and smoke stacks as teeth. As the camera focuses on the words KILLER CARBIDE that are graffitied below the image, the narrator remarks, "those claiming to be affected by the gas number in the hundreds of thousands; but, as with so much about this devastating event, separating fact from fiction has been a torturous journey." This sequence puts the victims' injuries into doubt for the viewer who is willing to accept the narrator's implied message that the graffiti, like the media, and victim's stories is "fiction." For the more critical viewer, this point signals just how ignominious UCC is willing to act. Yet Union Carbide's appropriation of the graffiti skull did transport the icon on film across the world to many who would have never been confronted with it otherwise. In this sense, the filmmaker inadvertently furthers the graffiti artists' intentions.

Unravelling bares more truth about UCC and corporate accountability than it does about the "nature and cause of the tragedy." UCC appears not to believe the viewer will accept as fact the contradictory complexities in the statement that MIC had a role in "preserving life through India's agricultural revolution" before it "became a mass killer." UCC thinks the blurry lens that is used to dramatize the gas will hide the fact that the workers portrayed in the plant in this re-creation are white actors in U.S. work clothes. UCC appears to believe that it has convinced its audience that the cause of the leak was "tawdry not cosmic." It leaves us with a line-up of Indian shantytown dwellers, a sunset, and the eerily prophetic question "how do we protect ourselves and society from the guardian who wittingly or unwittingly turns assassin?"

7.4 Representations of Attack: Bhopal Poetics: Kurzman's Docudrama of Disaster

Like UCC's video, Dan Kurzman's docu-drama is heavily invested in entertaining an uncritical western audience. Though he has acquainted himself with a wealth of texts and rare sources Kurzman frequently misrepresents various aspects of Indian culture and fails to historicize or appropriately critique events. For instance, in describing a tribal couple who have immigrated to Bhopal, Kurzman reports that "Chandabee and her husband, Isaac, thus joined civilization by

164 See Bhopal activist poetics section later in this chapter for extensive treatment of the photograph.

shunning their primitivist animist gods aside and converting to the Moslem religion" (18). Chandabee, nine months pregnant at the time, gives birth on the night of the gas leak, after fleeing with her husband. Kurzman narrates the couple's thoughts, as if writing a fictive account replete with predictable characters out of a wild and exotic Orient: "Though he loved his wife, he could always get another one, but who could be sure of a son? Chandabee, like himself, was a tribal, of course, and was less trained to endure pain than a Moslem woman. Somehow she would have to draw on her new faith to help her survive" (62). He perpetuates a plethora of western constructions of Indian culture that he not only presents unquestioningly, but embellishes with imaginative detail.[165] However, if one reads critically, interrogating Kurzman's suspension of (not only) disbelief, but also of critical analysis, Kurzman's story, more than most, highlights its constructedness, despite, or perhaps because of, his gross gender and ethnicity stereotypes. Close readings of his "dramas" give us a view of the range of public discourse and perspectives which Bhopal supporters face.

While Kurzman's vignettes embellish Indian culture with western prejudice, one of his primary sources outdoes even the journalist/disaster dramatist himself. Kurzman explains that while in Bhopal negotiating with victims, the U.S. lawyer John Coale spun fantastic tales. A figurative comparison between the conflict of Mexicans under Santa Ana and the mostly Anglo colonialists in Texas and the struggle of Indian victims of US-based corporate capitalism represented by a U.S. lawyer like himself is played out in the imaginative writing of one of the lawyers who hastened to Bhopal to recruit clients. Coale incorporates violence from a different hemisphere and a previous century into the setting of the corporate violence that he was witnessing in urban India: [F]lirting with danger only sparked Coale's fantasy, turning the "General MacArther" who had first stormed Bhopal into a heroic defender of the Alamo. "Col. Travis of the Alamo, sitting across from me" he recorded in his diary, "has just thanked me, David Crocket of the Kentucky Brigade, for coming to the Alamo. Santa Anna is outside the gates with 500 Mexicans."

After a few more scares, he wrote, "Our gun bearers have run off into the woods. We are looking for fresh gun bearers. We figure we have a couple more days of sanity before either we go nuts, or they kill us" (Kurzman 219).

---

165 Kurzman not only knows what goes on in his characters' minds; at points he reads the mind of his character, a sadhu, who is reading the mind of his God: "God was listening and had placed a benevolent hand on him to eases his misery. He understood that this simple sadhu loved Him even as he cursed Him, that cursing was natural in an extreme situation like this. That was the beauty of their relationship" (61).

Perhaps their calculations were off by "a couple more days." Suffice it to suggest that neither a sociological analysis nor a psycho-analytical one may be as critically productive here as a close reading of the contexts of Coale's historical comparison. Coale indulges in adventurous trumped-up heroic fictions that compare white male systems of domination on two continents and in two centuries. The "Alamo" he was defending was one in which U.S. lawyers hoped to capitalize on defending Indian victims against UCC; it is a politicized irony that Coale was correct in his summation that survivors would not be compensated properly if the Indian government took over the representation of their welfare. When critically examined, our disbelief at Coale's fantasy is effectively suspended as we recognize the parallels in experience that Coale's crude figurative analogy exposes. The contemporary relations between corporations such as UCC and third world "shanty towns"—like J.P. Nagar—directly downwind from the Bhopal plant, are no less brutal than imperialist conflicts like the Texas–Mexico one was and (through INS/ICE/BP and U.S. policies aggression) continues to be.

Perhaps the Bhopal setting resonates more clearly with contemporary border aggression imposed in the shadow the Alamo casts to the south by La Migra/border patrol/ICE in that the victims are entirely civilians and entirely on one side. If the lawyers are paralleled to those in the Alamo, then is Warren Anderson Santa Ana? UCC employees, the Mexicans? What are the implications of thinking of the Bhopal plant as the Alamo-producing poison for selective protection of life and dealing in death? This rhetorical question raises the necessity to rewrite a fuller version of histories of place, and Mario Salas' 2022 book *The Alamo: a Cradle of Lies, Slavery and White Supremacy* that chronicles, among other hidden atrocities, the Alamo's significance to the African American community as a slave auction ground, comes to mind.

In contrast to Coale's rantings and dubious[166] concern for victims, most of the Bhopal poetics (Kurzman, overall, included) create strong alliance with the survivors themselves.[167] In the following passage, the lack of concern on the part of the plant management might foreshadow our study of Fe's (fictional) deadly experience with corporate apathy in *So Far from God*. Kurzman narrates such stories of the Bhopal community's encounters with environmental toxins as a series of dramas; this was one of the first.

166 He did go out to the *bastis* himself to speak with potential clients. See Kurzman pages 212–222 and for more analytical reading Cassels 116–117 and 123–125.

167 I found few published texts by survivors, but workers at UCC published their story in *Bhopal: The Inside Story* by T.R. Chouhan and other UCC workers (in Morehouse 1994).

> And then began a strange process of disinformation and, often, suppression of information which manifested itself throughout the course of the incident, with telling consequences. In fact it began that very night itself. 'Nothing is wrong.' said a senior factory personnel when contacted by frantic police when things began to go haywire. 'There was a gas leak, but everything is under control now', he was to add later, even as the deadly gas was taking a toll of the hapless people. (Kurzman 9)

Having been lied to initially, most people were not willing to trust the voices of authority. In the following passage Kurzman describes "OPERATION FAITH" the operation in which the remaining MIC was converted and removed. While the operation was successful, the concern of people was not unfounded: it was not the safest, but rather the least expensive option that UCC and UCIL chose to undertake.

> The neutralisation drama only heightened the level of confused information. Was it actually meant to encourage people to flee the city without resorting to the drastic step of an evacuation? How else does one explain the volley of confused and contradictory statements coming from medical, scientific and Government experts regarding the gas and its effects. ... 'Don't panic', said the administration, yet had scores of buses brought in to the city to carry people away. The public did not know what to make of the situation. They disbelieved what was said and fled the city. (Kurzman 10)

Thus, another theatrical event is directed, as well as acted, by people of power who dismiss the onus to be accountable in order to preserve their positions. Like the environmental narratives from Bhopal and elsewhere Kurzman does demonstrate that in the world of global corporate capitalism and its symbiotic relationship with government such corporation-sponsored deadly dramas define environmental holocaust on their own terms and attempt to downstage the victims' informative descriptions of encounters with hell.

Arthur Diamond's *The Bhopal Chemical Leak* is another dramatic Bhopal retelling that has an inconsistent perspective *vis-a-vis* the survivors. Diamond's book, told for youth is dedicated to Raj Kumar Keswani, the journalist who predicted the disaster. It is also part of the Lucent World Disaster Series, sharing the dubious honor of being narrated for Lucent Books alongside events such as *The San Francisco Earthquake, The Titanic, The Challenger, The Black Death, The Crash of 1929, Pompeii,* and *The Irish Potato Famine.* Such a questionable distinction, like Bruce W. Piasecki's assertion that "[t]oday, Bhopal is part of our modern global folklore" (23), reveals the construction of Bhopal in mass culture; the relationship of those public representations and survivors' self-representations may have little in common, but as new social movement scholars, such as William Gamson and Gary Alan Fine suggest, activists must monitor and attempt to shape the public discourse. By examining texts like Diamond's with the concerns of the

Bhopal activists in mind we can determine whether work outside the movement is promoting or deterring the movement goals.

Arthur Diamond, like Dan Kurzman, from whom he has gotten many of his stories, creates a very uneven text. On one hand, he gives rare details of how workers and activists have impacted situations: "Keswani first became interested in the new chemical-production unit after talking to a friend ... [who] used to work at the plant but quit because he felt it was not safe enough" (27). On the other hand, Diamond's accessible narrative does not interrogate the popular misrepresentations that ignore the role of global capitalism and corporate double-standards in India, and more specifically, in Bhopal. For instance, population growth is offered as the sole reason for "desperate poverty" (10).

Moreover, Diamond sometimes accepts his sources uncritically; he references Fergus M. Bordewich who wrote about "The Lessons of Bhopal" in the *Atlantic Monthly* from a "risk acceptance" perspective. Bordewich, quoted Tulsi Ram and Tunda Lal, "severely injured" *basti* residents who agree that they would take "any job" offered by UC, in order to offer proof of Bordewich's perspective that widespread tolerance of multinationals is based on "economic necessity (57). In one sense, Bordewich is right: for individuals or for nations, economic desperation does lead to the tolerance of, but not necessarily the free choice of, corporate control. Bordewich, however, blames the worker's acceptance of risk-in-work over the illogical no-work-and-no-risk situations and Diamond accepts Bordewich, asserting that desperate workers are to be blamed for accepting "hazardous job conditions." Tulsi Ram's final words, which Diamond tells us, "echoed Lal's enthusiasm," are "I'd go too, do or die" (57). Enthusiasm and risk acceptance are the results of certain interpretive strategies here, strategies that don't consider that these men have never been—and therefore do not really know what it would mean to be—UC workers. A postcard created by the Bhopal Group for Information and Action (BGIA) sheds a different light on Tulsi Ram's "enthusiasm." The postcard which lists a few of the (at that time) 4000 people who had died since the gas leak, lists the name of Tulsi Ram. If it is the same person, Tulsi Ram's words had a literal meaning that his interpreters did not grasp.

Diamond has illustrated his text with AP/Wide World photos and drawings by Brian McGovern, a fine artist and commercial illustrator whose "recent clients include AT&T, DuPont, Harvey's Lake Tahoe and Chase Manhattan Bank" (64). There is no indication that either man has extensively researched or spent time in any part of South Asia. Some of the drawings are mechanically well-executed but ridden with details that anyone familiar with Indian cultures would question: saris wrapped strangely and inconsistently, men only in western cloths with a few turbans thrown in, pictures hung on walls in a Western rather than Indian style, no people on top of or hanging from his approaching train, or on his railroad platform. Even when he copied one of Everest's photographs, his rendition left off specific important details—bangles on both mother and child, the mother's hair pulled back in a single braid—and he inserted a white male doctor—an unlikely sight according to the chronicles (Everest 91; Diamond 46).

These details do more than bring up a tired argument about "authenticity;" they may serve as a metaphor for the way that an uncritical scholar imposes him/herself into his/her image of the object of study. They belie a studied perspective, artistic or scholarly in their overlay of Western culture; in doing so they suggest the importance of perspective. Furthermore, the artist's credentials re-introduce the conflicted territory of subject position and alliances. Should an artist freely move from drawing commercially for DuPont and Chase Manhattan to drawing Bhopal victims commercially? How do we as audience interpret this incongruency?

Does it matter that many of the clothes and hairstyles look more like *Vogue*'s "refugee look," popular in the mid-1980s in the US, than like urban India's styles at the time? Would white middle class U.S. children feel more accepting of victims who look like an only slightly darker version of themselves? Should we be teaching them to accept "tolerance" and compassion based on such a model? If readers cannot recognize the cultural misrepresentations, do they matter? If they do not know that this is an interpretative version of India that exists only in a Western mind that is naive about the culture, how will they be negatively impacted? Without evoking any essentializing maneuvers of identity politics, we must feel uneasy with unexamined representations of culture, especially when they are presented as truths in a culture that is alien to their makers.

Artwork would likely be one career that Bhopal gas-affected survivors could accomplish physically. Are there not artists among the survivors? We know that social workers continue to hold art therapy for children in Bhopal; would not those young people's drawings be appropriate for a book for U.S. youth?

7.5 Representations of Attack: Bhopal Poetics: Women and Activism in Bhopal

> Bhopal is symptomatic of the crisis of the major professions in India. In fact, it could be the litmus test of the health of the legal, medical, scientific and journalistic professions. The voluntary groups, despite their pervasive factionalism, may eventually provide the ethical texture and compassion that professionalism in India so desperately requires.
>
> Sathyamala

> Cultural expressions, slogans, and patterns of rhetoric are vital resources—manipulated consciously or emergent spontaneously—that symbolize the causes of discontent for movement actors and serve to energize and justify their actions.
>
> Gary Alan Fine (SM&C 132)

The relative dearth of books by women on Bhopal might suggest that women have not played a substantial number of visible roles in advocating environmental justice in the Bhopal situation. Several sources vehemently refute that conclusion. Radha Kumar in *The History of Doing* sees Bhopal as a landmark for urban Indian women's environmental organizing: "[w]hile there is a long history of rural women's environmental activism, tied to scarcity of fuel, water and fodder, the Bhopal disaster of 1984 saw the rise of a massive movement of women gas victims" (187–188).

Women often responded on local levels that often are not publicized in the journalistic reports or in other published histories of the sagas of Bhopal that have U.S. circulation. Yet the later 20th Century body of literature on Bhopal, especially after 1989, almost always refers—if only briefly—to women's activism. They often note that organizations such as the Bhopal Gas Peedith Mahila Udyog Sanghathan (The Association of Women's Victims of Bhopal) challenged the legal settlement between the Indian government and UCC (Jaising and C. Sathyamala 92). Newspaper reports in India carried the news of protests conscientiously and women were often in the headlines. After the Supreme Court decision in February of 1989 the *Indian Express* in Delhi headlined its article—albeit on page 27—"Women from Bhopal protest outside" (19-2-89). A journalist reporting on a demonstration over "the way in which relief money is being distributed" describes how women were the most outspoken. "There was a demonstration today in front of the chief minister's residence. Many suffering people have complained to the collector Moti Singh at Hamadia hospital about the misappropriation of money for relief" (ND 9/12, 17). One gas affected woman wanted to return the relief money of Rs 200. She had gone blind and said the government was merely trying to palm off Rs 200 on her as compensation. She said she did not want this money (Ibid).

Kumar's research demonstrates that, "[f]rom the very start, it was women gas victims who were most active in campaigns for relief, medical aid and information" (189). While the gender ratio at survivors' demonstrations at first favored women 60:40 the ratio of women grew over the years to 80:20 and even 90:10. After a decade, one women's organization, Bhopal Gas Peedit Mahila Udyog Sangathan—has 14,000 members (Morehouse 1994 167). Activism had not been the norm among Muslim women there and many became politically active for the first time.

Kumar debunks the explanation that circulated that surviving women, "as housewives, had more time—at any rate, their time was more flexible": many of the women were already workers before the disaster and some, afterward, became the sole financial support for their extended families (189). While the time flexibility of housework does play into many women's activism (as the MELA women demonstrate, for instance) it was not a factor for many of the Bhopal survivors. At the same time, employment was yet another problem that they faced after the gas leak. Since the gas hit hardest on the workers' shanty towns near the plant, many who had been employed at the plant, which shut down, were also gas victims and so their families were hit doubly hard. Gas-related health problems and the closing of the plant escalated unemployment problems. Available employment was often demeaning, exhausting, and offered inadequate compensation. One chronicler reports:

> Not long ago, in the world immediately outside the plant, one found several rehabilitation centres for women. In one, fifty women sewed gloves for which they were paid $12 each month—hardly enough to support an individual, let alone a devastated family. In the future they would be paid on a piece-rate basis, about 5 cents for a pair of gloves. The women do not think they can make more than 15 to 20 pairs a day. Many considered the vocational training given to these women as promising no employment potential whatsoever. (Gupta 20).

Parallels exist between women and sometimes youth who are seamstresses throughout most of the "Third World," disenfranchised by (often US) imperialism, and survivors, forced into abusive employment situations; the unfairly paid laborers clothe much of the "first world" and corporation shareholders collect the immense profits made possible by such inscrutable circumstances.

Some sewing centers were started by alternative organizations with good intentions, even though the eye fatigue that comes with sewing made the work inappropriate for many gas-affected women. These centers did sometimes serve as the basis for women's organizing. The Bhopal Gas Peedith Mahila Udyog Sanghathan, which approached the courts for relief and rehabilitation, emerged out of women's protests when government sewing centers, opened in 1985, were to be closed after one year of operation. In 1989 they used a "multi-pronged strategy of demonstrations, litigation, publicity and lobbying" against the government settlement and later in the year with the newly elected government. They won Rs. 360 lakhs as a three-year relief grant, release of medical information, and government support for re-opening the UCC case (Kumar 190). The possibility of getting sewing jobs also brought some individual women into activist groups like Sangathan. For instance, in an interview for *Voices from Bhopal*, Shahazadi Bahar, of Kolipura Barkhedire, recounts her experience:

> I joined the Sangathan in 1988. I was looking for a sewing job. I went to a number of places all around Bhopal. Then one of my friends asked me ... to come for the Sangathan meetings and talk about my problems there .... Now I am so closely attached with the Sangathan that when I do not go for the meetings, I miss it as people miss their dear ones.
> The world is very selfish. I, too, joined the Sangathan with some selfish motive. I thought I could get some sewing job through the Sangathan. But though I have not been benefited, there are others who have. This has brought in a new hope and a new determination. We are certain that we will win this battle.

Shahazadi Bahar points to the community gains accomplished by the organization, along with the relationships fostered within it. It gave her "a new hope and a new determination;" Sangathan changed Shahazadi Bahar's lifestyle and perspective even though she did not find economic work through the organization.

Self-Employed Women's Organization (SEWA) founded by Ela Bhatt has a Bhopal branch where women have set up small-scale income generation through sewing, bookbinding, bidi rolling and file making. The branch publishes the Hindi edition of *Anasuyah*, SEWA Bharat Foundation's monthly newsletter, and have provided rehabilitation for gas-affected women (Rose 259). SEWA has also started a "Gas Victims' Help and Treatment Centre" in Bhopal (Jones 90) and provided some of the very limited medical care for nonambulatory patients as well; because doctors were unwilling to walk through the *basti*s to go to patients who were too decapacitated to get to the clinics, SEWA health workers took on this task.

Strategic use of language is a shared trait of many environmental justice poetics. SEWA illustrates this in its bilingual strategy in naming the organization that, like People Organized in Defense of the Earth and her Resources (PODER) communicates with its two dominate linguistic communities. In each case the acronym for the English name spells a word that, in the predominate language of the region/community, identifies the purpose of the organization: SEWA means service in Hindi; PODER means power in Spanish. Jane Jenson describes four aspects of naming in social movement strategy that are useful in thinking about these naming strategies:

> First, a name generates strategic resources. Drawing boundaries around a community makes the resources of that community available to the movement as well as generating the solidarity necessary for successful action. Second, selecting one name over another sets discursive boundaries such that some claims become meaningful and others are less relevant. Third, any definition of one's own community locates it in relationship to others. Therefore, it presents possibilities for alliances as well as for identifying opponents .... Fourth, any name has consequences for the routing of claims through state institutions. (Jenson 116)

These four aspects apply specifically to the double language strategies in naming that both SEWA and PODER have utilized: first, borders and solidarities are generated in the choice of language and double language use creates more complex relationships. Second, the choice of double language further nuances the name's discursive boundaries. Third, language use defines a community in relationship to like and unlike language communities. Fourth, as non-English language use in the U.S. comes under attack, Spanish or other language naming becomes a more definitive means of routing resistance. In India, the language relationship to the state is even more complex: both Hindi and English have both progressive and regressive impulses that conform to different regional, language, and ethnic communities.

Susanna Dakin describes the Bhopal Zahreeli Gas Kand Sangharsh Morcha (MORCHA) as "an environmentally conscious group of social activists who believe in the 'right to know' and the right to a safe environment" (in Kolpe 64). Dakin lists the many activities of MORCHA including provision for appropriate rehabilitation, adequate health care for the victims, pensions for those who can no longer work, "reliable scientific information" in "understandable language," and the effective use of that knowledge (64). In the long term, MORCHA hoped to establish a "hospital and environmental research institution to serve the needs of the gas victims and to provide a place where the effects of technological production processes and toxic pollution can be investigated, and more beneficial alternatives be developed." Environmental education that is accessible and understandable to economically poor people is an underlying theme of their work (Dakin in Kolpe 65).

MORCHA led some of the earliest survivors' demonstrations. On January 3, 1985, MORCHA brought together 10,000 survivors who led a march to present the Chief Minister of Madhya Pradesh, with a set of demands. The Minister did not show up and asked instead to meet only with MORCHA members; MORCHA believed that he "was trying to deny the legitimacy of the slum residents who were there in force" (Dakin 65). MORCHA immediately began a dharna (relay fast) at the Chief Minister's residence. The next major demonstration on January 12th was met by mass arrests. "[S]everal hundred people, mostly women, staged a 'chakka-jam' in support, lying on the railroad tracks to stop the trains" (Dakin 66). Eight fasters, including Anil Sadgopal, were arrested at the Chief Minister's residence and three hundred people were arrested at the railroad tracks. [168]

---

168 Dakin mentions Anil Sadgopal (Mira Sadgopal's husband) as one of the most effective of the MORCHA members; they came from "Kishor Bharati, a rural education and development organization which puts heavy emphasis on the relationship between access to reliable scientific information, the development of indigenous analytical thinking, and the needs of rural villagers (in Kolpe 65).

MORCHA is arguably one of the first urban environmental justice organizations in India. According to Dakin, "[t]he Morcha represents in India a beginning of the same kind of determined citizen's movement as those which have demanded protective environmental, consumer and workplace legislation in Europe and the United States, forcing industries to exercise greater responsibility for health and safety" (66). Like Jaising and Sathyamala, Dakin sees the organizational necessity of developing allies on an international scale. Dakin believes that an "international communication network with movements like the Morcha is essential if technological development is to develop a 'net world gain';" as she points out "[e]cological destruction and environmental pollution do not respect national borders" (in Kolpe 66). Dakin's observation on the importance of international communication and support of movements of environmental justice was made decades ago. Many of the highly successful organizations with environmental justice agendas have fostered international support; examples would include the Zapatistas in Chiapas who have dispatched worldwide communication, primarily through e-mail, very early on; indigenous peoples' networks, whose membership is a priori transnational; and the Filipino-based network demanding cleanup of toxic waste left in their country by the U.S. military.

7.6 Representations of Attack: Bhopal Poetics: Poetics of Activism

> Our job is to incite responsibility, not pity. If all we did was publish photographs of sick children and desperate women, all we would get is sentimental paralysis. We need to tell a story that counters official attempts to control information and contributes to our understanding not only of the Bhopal disaster, but also to the ways similar abuses of power are so quickly forgotten, and continually repeated.
>
> anonymous activist [169]

> I believe that it is helpful to conceive of a social movement as a bundle of narratives, which when expressed within an interactional arena by participants strengthens the commitment of members to shared organizational goals and status-based identities sometimes in the face of external opposition .... Effective organizations are able to utilize culture to mobilize members both through the appropriation and personalization of established traditions and through the creation of indigenous traditions.
>
> Gary Alan Fine (SM&C, 128)

Contradicting the descriptions of Bhopal's poor and gas-affected survivors as fatalistic and naive, the poetics of resistance that I've encountered present clear

169 Laughlin and Morehouse in Chouhan 20.

sentiments and persistent demands. Some of the poetics generated by the survivors was available to me through photographs, some through reproductions of artwork, some from collections of testimonials and essays and some from reports issued in connection with survivors' international educational tours.[170] This section will describe those poetics that clearly support environmentally-just solutions for Bhopal survivors, and for the world-at-present which still faces what David Weir and Martin Abraham have termed "the constant fear of a 'Bhopal-without-end'" (in Kolpe 80). I analyze and interpret the roles, efficacy, and iconography of this body of poetics, given the background of situations, perspectives, narratives, and agendas that I've presented in the preceding pages.

I have separated this body of poetics from the previously mentioned chronicles, journalism, essays, and other writings that also advocate environmental justice in Bhopal by two criteria: one formalistic and one related to content in conjunction with subject position. This section deals with images rendered in visual art or short oral or written word; while some of the images have been generated elsewhere, all have some kind of direct relationship to the gas-affected survivors and/or the affected environment. I have attempted to clarify the subject position as it relates to Bhopal survivor representations of all those creating these works when possible. Specifically, I have attempted to respect the degree to which gender plays a role, as experienced by the survivors, according to my reading of the situation. However, I have assumed that an honest lack of conclusion concerning the role of gender, when accompanied by an articulate description of the issue, may be more helpful to the study of gender than a falsely seamless judgement. The same can be said for ethnicity, class, and religion-based issues.

Graffiti on the walls surrounding the UCC plant presents some of the most powerful icons and slogans. A photo from a demonstration on Feb. 16th, 1985, shows a group of demonstrators near the walls surrounding the plant; the painted logo inside clearly identifies Union Carbide. On the surrounding wall, large graffiti letters proclaim (in English) "Down with Imperialism" (in Everest 104). After decades of increasing privatization that disenfranchises the poor in Bhopal, and throughout India, one must assume that whether the graffiti is still there or not the sentiment can only have grown. While most of the graffiti remains anonymous some of the wall slogans have been signed by MORCHA. For instance, on adjacent sections of a wall that reads CARBIDE THRIVES/PEOPLE DIE and BOYCOTT EVEREADY the organization's name is signed. The name is in English script on the

170 Where possible I have identified the source and use of the graphics, however some authors do not credit the graphics they've printed.

Hindi-inscribed walls and in Hindi on the English-inscribed walls.[171]

Ashis Gupta focuses on a graffiti skull face when he describes the abandoned plant: "the slogans and graffiti have all been scrubbed clean off the Union Carbide perimeter walls. The main entrance is padlocked, with not even a sign across the gate to tell one it is the infamous Carbide plant in Bhopal. A crude face drawn on a brick pillar sports the words 'Killer Carbide' written in black below" (Gupta 9). The single calavera commemorating the havoc could be compared to the calavera image in Ester Hernández' "Sun Mad" in its use of the skeletal face to relate environmental racist actions with toxic materials to their deadly effects. The skeleton's eye sockets contain dollar signs. The steaming smokestacks from Bhopal form the skull's teeth. This motif is used repeatedly in the Bhopal images. Jamie Cassels uses the image on the cover of *Promise of Law: Lessons from Bhopal.* The same image is used by UCC itself in their video attempt to scapegoat the victims by laying blame for the leak on a "disgruntled worker." While the appropriation of the wall art by Union Carbide for purposes that oppose the message of the graffiti is condemnable, the image is one of several images in the video that, for the critical viewer, interrupts UCC's intended message.

Bhopal's graffiti articulates clear political messages, and this politics may make it more acceptable to some liberal and even progressive forces in the U.S. who might simultaneously support the anti-graffiti campaigns demonizing graffiti in inner city neighborhoods. The inconsistency suggests that these naysayers have accepted without critique an interpretation of graffiti that scapegoats the graffiti's author for the social ills that the graffiti may expose. While graffiti at the Bhopal site is not given free reign of expression, the images that have been preserved and transported internationally on film remind us of graffiti's crucial place in public art worldwide.[172] While the two nations' graffiti trends cannot be equated, Bhopal graffiti does intervene in the easy dismissal of graffiti as vandalism, in some cases treated rhetorically as akin to murder.

The Union Carbide film *Unravelling* also uses (and manipulates) another repeated image: the photograph of a dead child being buried in a hollow grave. Sanjoy Hazarika uses the same photograph on the cover of his book *Bhopal: The Lessons of a Tragedy.* Neither UCC nor Hazarika credits the photo. To request support for the victims, The Pesticide Trust/The International Medical Appeal for Bhopal created a poster of the photo that also commemorates the anniver-

---

171 Photo by Londoner, Martin Stott (in Jones 77).

172 An outstanding example is the Brazilian film *Abolição* (1988) directed by Zózimo Bulbul who uses graffiti as a powerful cultural tool that portrays and spreads the fight against police killings of street children and other racial violence.

sary of the gas-leak after a decade of suffering. This poster not only credits the photographer but provides a narrative which documents its creation:[173]

> BHOPAL, 3RD DECEMBER 1984. A man is burying a child. He has laid the tiny body in a shallow grave and begun to cover it.
> Then unable to bear the thought that he will never see her again, he brushes the earth from his child's face for one last look.
> The photographer, Raghu Rai of Magnum, cried as he took the picture.
> This little girl died ten years ago today.
> Her death was not quiet, quick or painless.
> She died in fierce pain and unimaginable terror, choking for breath, after an explosion at a pesticide factory owned by Union Carbide spewed a cloud of deadly gases over the sleeping Indian city of Bhopal.
> (The Pesticide Trust/The International Medical Appeal for Bhopal)

This photo comes as close as any Bhopal image to the "starving child" genre that plays on the pity viewers to compel them to action. It may be the fact that it is a photo of an act—as explicated above—rather than simply the image of an anguishing object/victim that saves it from reading as disrespectful. Given the ambiguity, it is worth noting the characteristics shared by some of the contexts in which this photo has been used.

Sanjoy Hazarika's book is one of the few Bhopal chronicles that was published by a US-based mainstream publishing company and, as such, its existence depends on expectations of market appeal. UCC uses the image in its sensationalizing and fictionalizing of the gas-leak. Much as UCC hopes the viewer will perceive of the gas-leak as an artificial construction that did not affect real human beings who are *like* the viewer, the child herself appears doll-like and plastic after her terrible death. Both the Hazarika cover and the International Medical Appeal photos are black and white as presumably the original was. In the UCC video the child's empty eyes are a strange blue, adding to the artificiality and alien feel of the image. "The International Appeal ..." is a commendable project that, upon an international medical team's recommendation, hopes to establish free clinics in the *basti*s for the survivors. Yet the thrust of the poster's narrative, in word and in its use of the Rai image, is to invoke pity for the plight of victims. It is less obviously about just solutions for gas-affected survivors and ecological alternatives to toxic industry than the survivors' organization poetics are. The photo itself reveals the artful and respectful rendering of a tragic mo-

---

173 Upon close examination, it becomes clear that there is more than one photo, taken on the same occasion, but either sequentially by the same photographer or by different photographers. This is evident in the placement of the adult hand in relationship to the child's forehead.

ment.[174] To varying degrees, its use in the above contexts may rely more on its sensation than its depth.

At variance with the sensationalist appeal is a poem from Holland that I found among the items provided by the Bhopal Resource Action Center in NYC. The poet is likely a young girl. The final line in the first stanza suggests the youthful perspective in the poetic voice; the final lines may suggest the poet, like the gas-victim, is a girl.

Flower petals
around her
head
not buried
eyes open
-oh grown-up people-

Bye ...
My sweet
sister, you
and I ...
-oh those opened eyes-

It is not flower petals but small stones and soil that halo the dead child's head. The poet recognizes this in her final lines:

no more
flowerpetals
left in Bhopal
to cover
all my
sweet sisters

Fear of disease was one reason behind disposing of victims so quickly that death warrants and autopsies, not to mention flower petals—a crucial item in Hindu commemoration of the dead—were relinquished. The poet's recognition of the detail—"no more flower petals"—suggests the magnitude of the death fest. The poet applies a mimetic folk imagery in "no more flowers" by drawing

174 I make this assessment, acknowledging that different cultural interpretations may lend varying interpretations. For example, Lee Wilkin's description of the irreverence of photographing the dead within the Bhopal context may be relevant, here.

on the tradition of the anti-war folk song "Where Have All the Flowers Gone?" composed by Pete Seeger in 1955.[175]

Other texts also use imagery with connections to the 1960s in the US. A publication of the Director of Information & Publicity in Madhya Pradesh borrows from the U.S. Civil Rights Movement in their choice of slogan and title: "We Shall Overcome" banners across the bottom of a booklet cover that sports a collage of rehabilitated workers, scientists and people undergoing medical therapies. While there are commonalities between the Civil Rights Movement of the 1960s in the U.S. and the Bhopal survivors' struggle, this state publication may not present them; yet the title makes the document appear progressive, at least to certain audiences. The impulse of appropriation here has similarities to "green" corporate advertising. This said, the origins of the environmental justice movement itself in the Civil Rights Movement has been noted often. For example, Martin Luther King's last public appearance was in support of striking garbage workers.

Another repeated image is a skull that morphs into a funnel cloud of gas, probably rendered originally in pen and ink. This could be seen as a variation on the graffiti skull--especially the row of teeth as smokestacks and the triangular nose repeat the graffiti image. It is also slightly reminiscent of *The Scream* painted in 1893 by the Norwegian artist, Edvard Munch. As H.W. Janson observes of *The Scream*, this graphic "visualizes [nightmarish terror] without the aid of frightening apparitions, and [its] achievement is the more persuasive for that very reason" (Janson 1977, 627). Furthermore, there is a formal resemblance to the expressionist painting in which "[t]he rhythm of the long wavy lines seems to carry the echo of the scream into every corner of the picture" (627); one might add, "just as the gas itself invaded the terrified town of Bhopal." One of the earliest Bhopal images, this Bhopal scream appears on the cover of *Bhopal: a people's view*, but may have been published before December 25, 1984, in the press. In *a people's view* ... graphic, a road sign reads "Welcome to Bhopal" on the skull-bubble and one can see the city at the end of the road. Weir uses a take-off on this image as a title page for the chapter entitled "A Night of Terror." The original bears the signature "Courtesy HT"[176]; this is missing from the image Weir uses; the shape of the skull varies slightly, and the town appears more distinctly, with buildings that resemble

175 Joan Baez who performed the song in the 1960s notes that Seeger was inspired by a verse of an old circular question song about men going off to war that appears in Mikhail Sholokhov's novel *And Quiet Flows the Dawn*. Joe Hickerson added verses in 1960 that solidify it as a circular song like those of the Cossacks of what is now primarily Ukraine.

176 This is likely a newspaper or journal, such as *Hindustani Times or Hindustan Today*; *a people's view* uses such abbreviations for press names but does not indicate HT on its list. On both pictures, an illegible signature including the initials C.D. appears in the lower left-hand corner.

plants and others that could be mosques and temples, or perhaps smokestacks. In the Weir drawing the sign reading "Welcome to Bhopal" has been altered to read simply "Bhopal." Thus, it appears to be a copy of the earlier drawing. While some of the distortion in the early work could come from a less sophisticated copying process, the variation in shape suggests that an original image is being copied by hand and adapted. Like the UFW eagle, such a transferrable image is useful to a movement precisely because it is easy to copy by hand and pass along without much technology or artistic know-how.

A battery/tank blowing its top in smoke which issues a call to "Boycott Killer Carbide" is a remake of the EVEREADY happy cat that appeared on UCC's EVEREADY batteries; UCC- manufactured batteries were more widespread than any other UCC consumer product. A cat—with its face to the audience—leaps through the loop in the top of the number nine that appears on the side of the battery. Its tail—like in the original—is a lightning bolt and there is blood dripping from its fangs onto the Union Carbide logo at its front feet. One version bears the caption: "EVEREADY TO KILL." [177] Many messages are conveyed here besides the obvious: Boycott UCC: don't buy their nine lives batteries. In the changed context, the lightning bolt shaped tail suggests that natural forces (electricity, in this case) are turned into killers by UCC, thus the blood at the other end dirtying Carbide's name. The dripping blood may seem only an archetypal reference to death given that Bhopal did not cause open bleeding wounds; however, coughing up and vomiting blood continues to be a daily reality for many victims. Also, for women whose menstrual cycles were impacted, and menstrual flow increased, blood continues to be a reminder of the gaseous night. Such effects are not merely chronic irritation: the increased loss of blood through menstrual abnormality is likely to cause anemia and increase the inability to work consistently. The image speaks empirically as well as symbolically.

Another cat motif, which refers implicitly to UCC's nine lives batteries, is featured in a simple graphic of a slightly vicious-looking black cat with Union Carbide branded on its forehead. The cat has dollar signs for pupils in its eyes—like those of the UCC graffiti skull—and is lunging forward, tongue extended

---

177 UCC protected itself from consumer boycotts within years of the accident when it sold its consumer products industry to GAF Industries. The battery logo was still used after UCC's sale of Eveready, however after a few years, it seems to disappear. Whether it was changed because of its appropriation by Bhopal activists is unknown. An Appendix in The Highlander Center's *No Place to Run* lists the countries in which Union Carbide had operations and what was manufactured in each (37–40).

toward its milk dish which appears as a half globe with dark shapes of continents swimming in an ocean of milk (Jones 188).

In a poster created by the Kerala Sastra Sahitya Parishad, the smoke cloud contains a very realistic skull lying partially on its side as if resting on the ground of death; the white smoke intensifies to blood red in the sky behind the skull, suggesting the holocaustic results of the gas. In the gas bubble iconography, the artists have used various graphic means to depict the deadliness of a literally invisible substance. This distinctive characteristic of the deadly gas changes the character of the graphics somewhat from those depicting other disasters: earthquakes, hurricanes, tornadoes, bombings etc. all have visible consequences that play immediate and obvious havoc on the environment. A shooting, stabbing, or fist fight all leave visible marks on the body of the victim that are easily recognized when depicted in art. In the absence of visible damage, the Bhopal Poetics may have most in common with depictions of psychic violence and the psychological effects of war upon civilians and structural violence upon communities. The work of Käthe Kollwitz comes to mind.

Another motif that has been used repeatedly came originally from a close-up profile photograph of a young woman's face as she presses her fingers upon her closed eyes in an expression of restrained but traumatic pain.[178] Tears run down her cheek and her mouth is open in a gasp. Her dark hair and shawl halo her face. Morehouse and Subramaniam use the photograph on *The Bhopal Tragedy* .... where it covers nearly the bottom half of the cover; a small photograph of the factory appears in the upper left-hand corner, as if a reminder of the source of the woman's intense pain. The Highlander Center uses the photo on the cover of *No Place to Run* along with two other photographs; in one a woman sits over a dead water buffalo, her hands on its shoulder, as if by comforting the corpse she could comfort herself through the loss. In a third photograph, demonstrators in a first world English-speaking context hold signs reading "Bhopal Scene of a Transnational Crime" and "Union Carbide: Cough Up."

A drawing or print which contains a woman whose gesture and expression borrows from the photographed woman is the graphic for the "Voices of the Victims of Industrial Disasters Permanent People's Tribunal." In the graphic, the expression has been simplified by the large bold lines with which the piece is executed. Her shawl has become ringlets of loose hair and to her left on this horizontally long artwork are two tanks/smokestacks, one emitting black smoke, one white. The black and white smokes define each other as they trav-

---

178 The only source to credit the photo was the Highlander Center's *No Place to Run*; they credit the photography on the cover to Barbara Lounder and the Society for Participatory Research in Asia.

erse horizontally to encircle the profile of the woman's head through the rendition of the black lines of hair. In the poster the woman caught in an instant of excruciating pain by a photographer has been rendered a motif for the victims of industrial disasters worldwide. The Tribunal hears the testimonies of "[w]orkers in hazardous industry in Sri Lanka, Vietnamese sprayed with the Agent Orange herbicide, victims of chemical exposure in Korea and Japan, Filipinos poisoned by gold mining, And the gas affected people of Bhopal." Findings and verdicts from the tribunal, which also includes "jurists, statesmen, litterateurs, academicians and artists" were sent to the UN Commission on Human Rights. Work appears in a variety of genres. A cartoon in *The Nation Review* in Thailand (13-12-84) features a centipede-like insect with the word Union Carbide lettered across its long-segmented body. It is winding across the globe and the oceans appear as the eaten portions as the creature continues to feast on the continents. Above, half eaten leaves replicate the shapes of destruction carried out on the globe. In this image Union Carbide itself is the pest; that this cartoon was published barely a week after the gas leak suggests that the Thai publication may have been previously aware of Union Carbide's callous attitude toward the "Third World." UC Thailand Ltd. was 100% owned by UCC and produced agricultural products and latex in Nondburi (*No Place to Run*).

A memorial sculpture by Ruth Waterman, erected in Bhopal in commemoration of the gas-affected victims, also uses the image of the woman with her hand holding her eyes in anguish. It was built by Waterman "with the cooperation of the victims and supported by the Dutch No More Bhopals Committee" (inside cover: *Union Carbide's Bhopal Tragedy ...*). Photos of the sculpture have been used as cover art and graphics for various publications, including a Bhopal Action Resource Center booklet entitled *Union Carbide's Bhopal Tragedy: A Time for Solidarity: Special Report to American Workers and Communities at Risk* (1989). The sculpture portrays a woman walking briskly, cradling a limp baby in one arm, and holding her face with the other hand. The child is under the cloth of her sari which drapes across the woman's shoulder and up across her forehead and down the other side. The swoop of the sari draws child to mother, and mother to child as in the swoop of the rebozo that the women in Las Madres (MELA) adopted, but in this case the mother and child are drawn together in desperation. The child's limp figure suggests that s/he is near death or already dead. The sculpture depicts victims, the most harshly affected of victims (overall, the young, the elders, and those who fled on foot carrying others were the most severely affected of the survivors.) However, the woman defies the fatalism sometimes associated with the gas victims—running from the gas with her child in hopes that even a lifeless body, if it cannot be revived, must be held with dignity.

Children were often depicted defiantly, rather than sentimentally in the poetics. For example, A Center for Education and Documentation poster, created by Manjula Padmanashan, depicts a baby crawling away from fingers of gas that contain a skull and what appear to be dead animals. The baby's face, arms, and torso are "cute;" the child is plump and healthy-looking, however, the back legs appear slightly deformed, one almost serpentine. Below the striking image in white letters on a black ground is a Hindi phrase (in English script). The English translation is "Poisonous gas is coming—Run;" Below the Hindi is an English quotation: "And we ran—150,000 of us—eyes burning, choking, breathless, vomiting, Leaving even our children behind." This graphic which has a stark, defamiliarizing aesthetic and the fluid line of a stylized print illustrates the horror of the holocaust night. The attractiveness of the baby and the swirling gas in juxtaposition to the written messages produce a disconcerting message. 150,000 people fleeing something so terrifying and terrible that "even [their] children" got left behind. The effectiveness of this powerful art lies in the contrast of elegant style and horrific message (see Weir 1).

A postcard, made from Pablo Bartholomew's photograph of two Indian women has a red band on the bottom which proclaims in white letters "Not Everyone Affected by the Carbide Gas Leak in Bhopal Died." The card is produced by *Bhopal Group for Information and Action* (BGIA) and the image is also used in an article in *The Ecologist* by Ward Morehouse (1994, 165). Except for the eye coverings the women in this postcard would be indistinguishable from the attractive young women who are often featured on postcards in native garb to portray local color and/or a sense of the "exotic." One woman wears a heavy shawl and the other is in a Punjabi dress with extensive jewelry and a metallic scarf—their apparel contrasts disconcertingly with the eye coverings they wear-one has white patches, the other, a dark batik scarf. The young women's attire and attractive features, like the stylistic attractiveness of the baby print, are juxtaposed to eye patches, which literally represent blindness. A more metaphorical interpretation would find that the photographed women with their eyes covered like the eyes of the dead, are themselves "the living dead." Like Bano Bi's description of her family life prior to the gas leak, the esprit and costuming of these women defies the politics of discrimination that is evident in UCC's collaborating medical descriptions, which suggest that poverty and ignorance are the causes of gas-associated problems. The photo caption in the Morehouse' article explains that while "it was initially thought that the major impact of methyl isocyanate gas was on the eyes and lungs of those exposed ... it is now known, however, that the immune systems of victims and other vital organs ... were also damaged" (Morehouse 94, 165). The caption on back side of the postcard is a call for victim solidarity that asks the reader to contact the BGIA. The message dates the postcard to the early 1990s, but it remains salient:

> Seven years after the toxic gas leak from the Union Carbide pesticide factory in Bhopal, 400,000 victims continue to suffer. And die. A study in 1990 showed that while the incidence of spontaneous abortions and untreatable systemic illnesses among the victims is substantially higher, their death rate is twice that of those unexposed to the gas. The Supreme Court of India has, in its final judgement, let the multinational wash its hands off by paying a pittance of $470m. But it has directed that criminal proceedings may continue. Which means that now, as ever, the victims need our solidarity. To help punish the guilty. And prevent any more 'Bhopals'. Anywhere.

A second BGIA postcard contains a similar message on the back. On the front left side is a photo by N. Thiagarajan, a close-up of an older man with a white beard that contrasts with his darker, very wrinkled skin. His eyebrows are still grey and beneath them his eyes are caked shut with white crystals dangling from the lashes. His expression is one of stoic endurance of long-standing pain. On the right side of the postcard whose background is black is a listing of names in small white letters and across the top of the listing bold red letters read: "4000 DEAD. AND STILL COUNTING." 4000 was the most conservative count of those who had died at the time of the Victims Tour in 1989 when a banner and an information bulletin using the same slogan were created. The message on the back of the postcard explains that "[n]one of the names you have just read are of those who died on the night of Dec. 2/3, '84." One wonders if the names that are listed were chosen at random. Were they members of an activist organization or were they people to be commemorated specially for other reasons?

Most of the names are men's names; the majority are Muslim names, although several are "Singhs," a traditional, though not exclusively Sikh name. Ironically, and perhaps politically so, the only mention of Sikhs that I've found in all the Bhopal research I've conducted was in the mention of UCC's initial sabotage theory: that a Sikh terrorist group was responsible for the runaway reaction. A few names could have been nicknames such as Chhoti Bai; (Chhoti means Tiny or Little in Hindi—thus "Little Brother"). Many of the victims have the first names of gods or goddesses: Seeta, Draupadi, Ram, Mohammed; some have the names of plants such as the sacred Tulsi. I make these observations to demonstrate that the simple act of reading the names of the dead may clarify more about the nature of Bhopal's victims than much of what UCC, the government, or even some of the well-meaning chroniclers might say about them. In comparison to "The International Medical Appeal ..." the BGAI postcards appear to be targeting a more modest and analytical audience; their appeal is not for money to buy relief, but for solidarity. The implication here is that solidarity means activism, dialogue and perhaps education. The postcard includes the BGAI's mailing address.

Another set of postcards were made from children's drawings: Amit Kumar, 8 years old and Manju, 10 years old, each produced drawings "[i]n memory of my brothers and sisters who died in the gas tragedy." The title of each postcard is "No More Bhopals" and they are produced by Nagrik Rahat aur Punarvas Committee, Bhopal at National Institute of Design, Ahmedabad. Amit Kumar's card is a painting of fleeing people, a few in vehicles, but most running. Two figures loom large, one is a human perhaps pointing the ways to those who run. The other is more abstract. In the background are triangular-shaped mountains above which birds soar. It is unclear whether they are peacefully soaring hawks or hovering vultures. Manju's picture presents an aerial view of gas victims, lying dead both inside and outside, women with jewelry and makeup lie next to children and dying flora. Inside, a person lies next to his charpoy, various items from the house are strewn about. On the top of the picture there is a line-up of men in suits without arms—a criminal line-up, one presumes, of the corporate administrators. One might come up with other interpretations of these two postcards, but the overall indictment is clear, as is the commanding titles: "No More Bhopals."

Universalizing Bhopal through globe images is a common practice. Susan Siew (who worked on the production of IOCU's version of *The Bhopal Syndrome*) produced a graphic in which the world is a timebomb. The continents appear in silhouette and overlap each other near the fuse which sparks atop a brick chimney. On the periphery of the globe, houses, trees, crosses and industries suggest towns. The message here is clear: Bhopal is a universal threat. A second drawing by Siew portrays the Statue of Liberty in the left foreground and Bhopal in the background. Between the statue and the factory is a high-rise behind which looms a knit brow. In the right front corner, the Bhopal gas-skull rises, almost like an insignia, and above the buildings a few leaves trail down to the edge of the high-rise and a shantytown is tucked into the shadow of the factory. The chapter title is "It Can Happen in America" but the picture not only maps the potential Bhopal in the United States, but it also reinscribes Bhopal's history in New York—Judge Keenan's courtroom and the UCC chartering. A third image from Susan Siew illustrates Weir's chapter "Power and Money." The pen and ink drawing of an aerosol spray, labeled in Spanish, "Pesticida" is crushed by a fistful of bills with U.S. dollar signs and a lot of zeros (Weir 75). The link between "Third" and "first" worlds is clarified in the aerosol spray can and the dollar bills.

Several of the other images that David Weir uses in *The Bhopal Syndrome* also draw attention to pesticide poisoning in varying contexts.[179] The graphics that

179 These illustrations appear only in the copyrighted 1986 version by International Organization of Consumer Unions (IOCU) that was printed by Ganesh in Penang, Malaysia. The 1988 version published by Sierra Club and copyrighted in 1987 by the Center for Investigative Reporting contains no graphics. While the two texts appear to be close to identical, the subtitles of the two books also

Weir chooses, demonstrate that it is not only when there is an "accident" that pesticide plants like the one at Bhopal produce toxins that kill. One graphic, chosen for "The Global Pesticide Industry" chapter, and created by Bill Sanderson, for the IOCU Press Kit (Weir 5) depicts a frightened and crying older male face in a world globe. The image is reminiscent of the man in the moon or maybe a grandfatherly (white) god, even perhaps, the Wizard of Oz. The man's (or god's) hands are held up to protect his face from the shower of poison spray that encircles the globe. Above the earth flies a crop duster, the spray emanating from ducts on its wings. The caption reiterates the presence of a vengeful Supreme Deity in its simple slogan "Spray and be damned." The graphic, then, is an oath against the grower who sprays. Yet, when it comes to the victims who are "damned" in the sense of being doomed by toxins, we know from the Chicana farmworker poetics that to be sprayed is to be damned.

S. B. Kolpe uses the same image on the back cover of his collection *Bhopal: From Hiroshima to Eternity*. On the front cover is a close-up view of a farmworker girl; in this image the crop-dusters have retreated to a horizon, blurred by a long cloud of pesticide spray. The farmworker girl etching also appears in Weir's book on the title page for the chapter entitled "Our Obligation to History." It is signed by artist Carlos Llerene Aguirre and dated 1985; the etching is from the PAN International Press Kit, Public Media Center. The child, who appears to be white or Latina, holds what could be a piece of fruit or even a small dead animal, perhaps a bird—something precious she has found in the field; her hands, cupped beneath her chin, shielding the entity in a protective nurturing manner. Behind her are tilled rows of crops with hat-wearing farmworkers stooped in toil. Above, two crop duster airplanes leave a trail of poison across the sky. The top of the poster image bears its title "Pesticides don't know when to stop killing." Like the BGAI postcard's caption "4000 DEAD. AND STILL COUNTING" the poster caption suggests that deadly toxins, once released, are a virtual Pandora's Box of Poison with uncontrollable consequences.

Carlos Llerene Aguirre's artwork is also on the cover of *The Bhopal Syndrome*. It links the Mexican or Latin American farmworker and the urban Indian pesticide-industry worker through their common exposure to pesticide toxins. The subtitle of this version of Weir's book "Pesticide Manufacturing and the Third World" differs in its central inclusion of the Third World from the later Sierra Club version published in 1987; the original subtitle is reiterated in the colorful cover painting. A poncho-clad campesino stands in a field staring down

---

vary; the first one indicates that it is focused on the "third world" effects of pesticide production. The earlier version was purchased in India, and I have not found it available in the U.S.

at what appears to be a high-rise building writ small amongst the plants that line the slope behind him in rows. To the workers' left side is a city-full of similar high-rises and behind the city looms the pesticide plant. That the plant is the UCC Bhopal one is indicated in the shape of the industrial structure itself and by the geographic relationship of the plant in relation to the city, which corresponds with the maps of Bhopal that show the plant's placement upwind from the city. The brushstrokes in the sky emphasize the focus on the man: everything in the painting seems frozen, solemn, downcast. Oppressive.

David Weir uses these poetics to underscore his message that green revolution pesticides are part and parcel of the problem that preceded Bhopal, that they will continue to create mini-Bhopals, and that they increase the possibility for more bigtime Bhopals; he uses facts and statistics to point this out. For instance, he observes that most of the pesticides used in the "Third World" are used on crops for export, not crops that supplement food consumed at home. He also drives home his point through such convincing and powerful images as I have just described.

A Center for Science and Environment in New Delhi image very literally promotes education and action. A sign which hangs on one side of a pole reads "Bhopal" in both Hindi and English; the letters appear to be dripping blood. On the other side hang three signs of lists under the headings as if it were the outline for lesson plans:

> To Prevent another Bhopal we must
> —ban highly toxic substances
> —stop transfer of all technology not proved to be safe
> —impose strict controls on pollution
> —regulate industry for safety
>
> To do so, we must
> —form people's safety committees, environmental groups
> —take up safety issues through trade unions, in parliament and into the streets
> —insist on people's representation in regulatory bodies
> —demand the right to information about the hazards that can affect us
> What you can do now:
> —boycott all Union Carbide products, begin with Eveready batteries
> —launch signature campaigns against government apathy towards UCIL's victims
> —contribute to relief and rehabilitation of the MIC-affected
> —form or join educational campaigns on health, safety and environment
>
> (in Jones 206)

This statement in the form of a cartoon drawing contains a platform and procedure that can be discussed and adopted by many groups. Jones provides no context for the graphics or pictures and does not discuss where, when, and how widely this graphic was used. Readers are left to wonder whether the lists were also created in Hindi or other Indian languages, where and how it was distributed, and what were its consequences and accessibility. However, the simplicity and straightforwardness of the drawing is impressive.

Elsewhere, I have discussed specific demonstrations in relation to their place in the Bhopal chronology. With those discussions as background, photographs and other documentation give a more complete understanding of the demonstrations, as performance events, and carry the direct and implicit messages in the poetic paraphernalia of the demonstration genre. Women make up a large majority of the crowd in many of the photographs; this substantiates Kumar's gender percentages of attendance that suggests that women predominate (photos in Everest 103, 105). Children participate as well. In a photo taken by the Bhopal Disaster Monitoring Group (PRIEE) from Japan, young boys (preteens) surround a microphone chanting, with their fists raised (photo in Weir 49).

Large banners, sometimes designating the presence of an organization are carried in many of the photos of demos and rallies. Posters and banners are most often in Hindi, but English, or a mixture of the languages, are common too. Many of these banners and posters are more than simple anti-Carbide declarations; some demonstrate critical analysis of global capitalism as it impacts the "Third World." For instance, a woman carries a sign at the February 16th demonstration that reads "why experiment on me?" (Everest 105). In an unidentified demonstration, the Bhopal Gas Peedit Mahila Udyog Sangathan carries a banner which, when translated from Hindi reads "Wake Up [name of major TV station]. Don't take money from multinationals." Here, their analysis extends to the media's susceptibility to corporate collusion.

A Warren Anderson effigy is burnt each year at the demonstrations that mark the anniversary of the gas leak. The effigy pictured from the ten-year commemoration is at least the height of a man pictured beside it, but Anderson's chest is more than seven times the width of the man's chest (photo by TJ Birdi, in Morehouse 166). He wears a suit and top hat; his face has a cartoonish resemblance to Anderson but could also be taken for a clown. Will the effigies created yearly be the only Warren Anderson to arrive in Bhopal, or will the criminal trial succeed in having him and other allegedly guilty parties extradited to stand trial? The activists have created an image so many times bigger than life, just as UCC has created and built on a mess that continues to swell, creating problems many times bigger than life. Yet, even with such monumental imagery, Bhopal passed from global media interest. Still communication with survivors' support groups around the world continues into the 21st Century. The international tours of survivors have also continually prodded the world to remember Bhopal.

Several of the publications of international Bhopal support groups involve Victims' tours that traveled to the US, and several countries in Europe and Asia. Photos document demonstrations and meetings that occurred at the places where touring groups visited. One set of photos reveals the arrest of two of the victims in Houston Texas. The survivors were in Houston while the UCC was having annual meetings there. UCC had hired Houston police who in their enthusiasm for protecting the corporation arrested the men who were passing out booklets, ("UCC 1988 Annual Environmental Report: Union Carbide: 4000 Dead in Bhopal and Counting") to UCC stockholders. UCC had agreed to have the survivors speak to the stockholders, and, reportedly, they were somewhat embarrassed by the Houston police action. Nonetheless, the action parallels the Indian government's readiness to have survivor rights activists arrested in an overenthusiastic impulse to protect the corporation and hide their own duplicity. That the arrests should transpire against visitors in the home country of the corporation only adds to the audacity. As suffering continues, activism continues and as activism continues, harassment too continues. The poetics serve to educate and mobilize and to document the continuous struggle against the chemicalization of poverty in human communities and beyond.

While the only Bhopal-centered novel I came across in my research during the first decades after the gas leak was written in Hindi and not translated. However, this has changed. One notable example of Bhopal-centered fiction—Indra Sinha's *Animal's People* was published in 2007 and subsequently shortlisted for the Man Booker Prize. The bookjacket tells us, "[e]ver since he can remember, Animal has gone on all fours, his back twisted beyond repair by the catastrophic events of 'that night' when a burning fog of poison smoke from the local factory blazed... and the Apocalypse visited his slums." The Editor's Note presents the fictional framework: "[t]his story was recorded in Hindi on a series of tapes by a nineteen-year-old boy in the Indian city of Khaufpur...Apart from translating to English, nothing has been changed." (Sinha np) Though the jacket cover describes his story as "an unflinching look at what it means to be human," the specifics of his "wounds that never heal" recall Gloria Anzaldúa's "herida abrierta," the open wound/borderland "where the Third World grates against the first and bleeds. They reveal the ongoing aftermath of the environmental abomination that is Bhopal, and of other sites of ongoing environmental injustice that won't heal. In particular, in Bhopal, Madhya Pradesh, and in Mission, Texas, the wounds of chemical toxins comprise the collateral damage of the pesticide industry.

Gas-damaged trees are one of the few signs of visible effects on the landscape that are portrayed in the Bhopal poetics. Even in this photograph one would not know, but for the caption, that this was not simply a deciduous tree, lifeless in the middle of winter. On the last page of *a people's view* ... is a photograph, taken by Parivesh Mishra, of a desolate-looking tree that has been affected by the gas leak. Within the year S.B. Kolpe's collection of writings first published in *Clarity*'s August 4 and 11 issues came out; on the last page of this collection is a poem by J. Jothi Kumar entitled "A Lone Tree" (in Kolpe 80). While few of the reports carried within these or other publications, focus on the environmental effects of the gas on nature per se, the tree poem mirrors the tree photo that shares its position as a conclusion. The poem's first lines identify the tree geographically "amidst homes called slums" as the roughhewn shelters at the base of the photographed tree identify its place in one of the gas-affected *basti*s (80). As the title tells U.S. of the tree in the poem, the photographed tree is also a "lone tree;" this may reveal previous pollution or other environmental damage to the area that makes it unlikely to harbor tree growth. The lone tree stands in contrast to the descriptions of wealthier foliage-rich picturesque parts of Bhopal, and thus establishes there was an (ecologically) unfriendly environment even before the gas leak. The next line uses alliteration ("Bare and barren"), and the multiple meanings of "still life" in the context of "a few pale leaves/declaring its still life." The fourth stanza reads alone as a Haiku (at least in the English strain of the genre) that expresses an act in nature that is nearly universal on the land where flora can grow: "And here falls/ another leaf/ To be carried with the wind" (80). The final lines again express a situation that evokes much about Bhopal: "The tree is dumb/ yet it is eloquent/ to express/ the agonies of the sad history" (80). While the order of toxic industry's relations with its victims, be they human or another aspect of nature, often attempts to render them "dumb" often through false representation, the poetics of the people reveals not only their eloquence, but also their wisdom and wit. Their poetics defies attempts to defeat them through scapegoating, prejudice, and misrepresentation. The onus is on us, as outsiders, scholars, artists, activists, and world citizens to, like the poet, "pause/ to learn [their] sore stor[ies]" (80).

7.7 Conclusions: Poetic Justice and the View Beyond

> With over 16,000 people dead to date and over 2,00,000 exposed persons suffering from incurable illnesses the Bhopal Gas Disaster has illustrated the horror of peace time casualties of progress. Machinations of the multinationals, collusion of the Indian government, injustice of the judiciary, the fickleness of the media, and the systemic victimisation of the victims all this and much more, were made eminently visible without the usual verbiage and mystification that go on in modern society.
>
> Satinath Sarangi

275 pages into Salmon Rushdie's novel, *The Moor's Last Sigh*, the protagonist's sister, Mynah, dies from exposure to MIC; the narrator/protagonist, who is called "the Moor," explains that an explosion occurred during his activist-sister's visit to a "chemical factory" where she was "investigat[ing] its maltreatment of its large

female workforce—mostly women from the slums of Dharavi and Parel" (275). "The official report failed to account for the delay in summoning medical assistance, though it did list forty-seven separate counts on which the factory had failed to observe prescribed safely norms" (275–276). Although her detained first aid treatment includes sodium thiosulphate—the drug denied to many Bhopal victims, Mynah dies, as the Moor puts it, "of a shortness of breath" (276, 275). As she had been a successful activist who was thus making rich and powerful enemies, it is conjectured that it may have been an "assassination," covered up by environmental racism, (one of the very issues she was investigating in the factory itself.) Her death appears to trigger a series of events including the Moor's being disowned by his parents, his imprisonment, and the suicide of his mad lover.

By the end of the book, however, the readers know that this interpretation is falsely simplistic. As readers put Mynah's death in perspective in relation to the rest of the 400 plus page novel, they can conclude that the line between intended aggression and accident in events of environmental ruin is seldom well-defined. As in "real life" situations like Bhopal, the clear definition of who and what is culpable for such devastation of human communities and their natural surroundings is clouded by another dominant impulse, that of maximization of profits at the expense of the marginalized.

Rushdie spends only two pages describing environmental justice issues, but the event is an important landmark on the interpretive horizon of the novel just as Bhopal was and continues to be a landmark event both in post-colonized, multinational-corporate India and, more broadly, in the multinational-corporate and post-colonial diaspora. In the factory explosion, Rushdie employs his customary autohistoriographic device wherein events of history are melded onto the events in the lives of ordinary characters. Bhopal is thus writ large in fiction in the death of Mynah, the social activist, and her death is writ large as it evokes the Bhopal gas leak. Mynah's death is a turning point for the Moor, a point that he might have looked back to as the beginning of a slow realization of betrayal, that very little of his life was "as it seemed." The Bhopal gas leak ushered in new dimensions and new understandings of colonial imperialism that have in the last decade shown the malignant weaknesses of "post"coloniality. In the words of Upendra Baxi, "[c]learly, Bhopal must be understood as a symbol of the ruthlessness of the imperialist penetration of Indian state and society. Indeed, one might even say that the ghost of the East India Company stalks through the Union Carbide at Bhopal and it is more fearsome, lethal and daunting than the eighteenth-century persona" (58). Building on the traditions that rocked the country into independence, but also partition, many decades ago, activists were prepared, standing at the UCC gates, and at the doors of the Supreme Court in Delhi, standing worldwide with banners that proclaimed "Hindustan ghulam, Carbide salaam."

Part II: Women Write Environmental Justice: The Literary Tradition in India and Greater Mexico

8 So Close to the United States: Environmental Injustice and the Death of Fe in the "Land of Enchantment"

> We hear about what environmentalists care about out there. We live on dry land but we care about saving the whales and the rain forests, too .... Our people have always known about the interconnectedness of things ... But we, as a people, are being eliminated from the ecosystem, too .... and we are trying very hard now to save ourselves before it's too late. Don't anybody care about that?
>
> Navajo woman character in *So Far from God*

> The implicit suggestion that the erotic and the class struggle may be incompatible in a patriarchal world, when both are made public, places the underclass female in a double bind, since she may be forced to choose between arenas of life that, for her, are intertwined or indivisible. In my view, the speakers in Castillo's work refuse to make such choices ... it is of paramount political importance to identify the textual milieu of culturally marginalized writers such as Chicanas, as well as to clarify the appropriate strategies in the struggle to construct and reconstruct an identity despite its instability, lest a writer appear to speak in a vacuum.
>
> Norma Alarcón in Horno-Delgado, 95–96

8.1 "FALSIES" and the new way to reclaim information

In "Ecocritical Literature: Ana Castillo's 'Virtual Realism'" I suggest that Castillo presents environmental justice historiographies in a kind of "virtual reality" frame by explaining my coinage of the term[180]:

> I apply this techno-art term, recognizing that "virtual reality" of the non-fictional variety has a very different—if not opposite—purpose than this fiction; namely that "virtual reality" is about escaping reality through a simulation of reality, while "Virtual Realism" in fiction borrows from reality in order to create a fiction that commands its readers to confront the political reality of "real life." Thereby, Castillo and Sibal, among others map environmental justice issues, not just in real space, by pinpointing "toxic hot spots" on a world atlas, but also in real time, by pinpointing local struggles against degradation of human/natural habitats. (27)

"Virtual reality" differs from "literary realism" in that it is not about capturing photographic images that naturalize depictions of life, but rather it embodies

180 Parts of this chapter appear in "Ecocritical Chicana Literature: Ana Castillo's 'Virtual Realism'" listed in the Works Cited.

https://doi.org/10.1515/9783111041575-009

artifice, and thus steers the reader to acknowledge the political reality of "constructed" narratives. Before turning to Castillo's novel, I will briefly consider two concurrent performance art pieces by Chicanas who also consider the implications of environmental racism and its gendered effects through "Virtual Realism." Tammy Gómez, a Tejas-based Chicana performance poet, created "FALSIES and the new way to reclaim information about your/my/our body" for a spoken word performance for The Breast Cancer Epidemic and Nuclear Radiation: Action for the Environment Conference held on the UT Austin campus in the early 1990s. The piece juxtaposed falsies—the falsies that women wear to meet a fashion "ideal"—with the lies that deny the links between industrial toxins and breast cancer.[181] The poem begins with a list of names for breasts, some English, some Spanish, each word accompanied by an adjective or phrase that creates alliteration and a sense of a flirtatious reclamation of "Bosom—beautiful/ Peaches—pretty/ Cazumbas—cradle em/ Cenos—sexy/ Bombers—bodacious." The list ends with a twist that identifies the germ of the poem: "Pechugas—pert/ Breasts—bouncy/ Tits—touchable/ Hooters—huggable/ Knockers—*not yours.*/ they're not yours .... no man knows how to breast feed. Feed breasts." Not only do men *not* know how to "[f]eed breasts what's best," they may be the perpetrators of "some misinformations, a few titbits of untruths ... advertising deceits, capitol F FALSIES." In the performance piece, Tammy wears ten "falsies" on her chest, giving the slim five-foot-tall woman, ballooning breasts; she pulls out the falsies one by one and reads them to the audience to "get these things off our chests, so to speak." Some of the "falsies" tie directly to environmental justice issues: "Falsie #4: Nuclear waste is containable; Falsie #5: Cancer is not an environmental disease." Others address issues of representation in conjunction with gendered self-esteem that indirectly affect disenfranchising "environmental" policies of industry. "Falsie #6: Silicon breast implants are a safe and viable option for women; Falsie #10: Better to have falsies th[a]n to be flat!"

181 A common trend among those responsible for pollution is for them to point the finger at the victims of the pollution's detrimental effects and suggest only the potential causes which may be traced to the victim's lifestyle. This is particularly true in issues of health. As Monte Paulsen observes, "Blaming the victim ... simply doesn't hold up against the evidence about breast cancer. It is, however, a convenient way to avoid larger environmental questions" (85). At times, the underlying intent in such situations of blame is brutal and unconscionable. For instance, Breast Cancer Awareness Month which totes the slogan "Don't be an easy target—get a mammogram *now*" is sponsored by an international chemical giant—Imperial Chemical Industries (ICI) which also "cashes in on its message" (Paulsen 8).

Tammy takes risks, pushes boundaries, and exposes social taboos, to disengage euphemisms and name disease, dishonor, and disrespect. Her environmental concerns extend the social justice agendas that much of her work engages by bringing together body-focused feminism, social issues, Latina/o concerns and environmentalism.[182] This is done not only in terms of contents—the presentation of knowledge about environmental toxins and their bodily effects—but also in terms of literary form and style and figurative language. The "titbits of untruths" are life and death matters, as illustrated in the poem's conclusion—a parody of a bra advertisement that sounds like an ominous nursery rhyme: "Cross your heart, Jane Russel. Cross your heart and hope not to die. Cross your heart and hope not to die." As Norma Alarcón suggests of the narrator in Ana Castillo's early fiction, Gómez is a writer who refuses to make the choice "between arenas of life that, for her, are intertwined or indivisible" (Alarcón 1989, 95–96).

Gómez is only one of a growing number of Chicana writers, artists, activists, and performers who are depicting environmental racism as a crisis that their communities face with increasing frequency. Like Gómez, many others who depict environmental degradation depict women's bodies under attack, *and* women fighting back, divulging the "falsies" in mainstream, and commercially sponsored representations of environmental issues.

8.2 "Objects in Mirror Are Closer than they Appear"

Belinda Acosta's "Objects in Mirror Are Closer than they Appear," a multi-media performance art script, transforms 1990's environmental justice issues in Chicano communities—the Govalle oil tank farm; the anencephalic babies born to women along the Rio Grande in South Texas; "La Holly Street Power Plant" in

---

182 Knowledge acquisition and dissemination about/to Latinas and environmentally caused illnesses may arguably be one of the most ignored areas of medicine in the U.S. In the mid 1990s, when a Dominican woman writing an exploratory research paper on possible causes of the high breast cancer rates on Long Island for my class at Nassau Community College discovered there were few statistics on or services for Latinas, she began to inquire. She received contradictory information from the American Cancer Society's Spanish-speaking phone line and when she tried to clarify by double-checking the information in English, was told that the Spanish line attendant was not *allowed* to speak English. When she called a representative of one of the local organizations studying breast cancer, she was told "Check up in the South Bronx where there are a lot of Hispanics." This answer is made more ludicrous by the fact that Suffolk County, Long Island, has the highest percentage of Latina/os, outside of NYC, in the state. My appreciation to Eulalia Ortega for these details.

East Austin; pesticides such as malathion, that, like nerve gas, contain organophosphates and other carcinogens; and the "toxic fumes woman" in California, whose body was so infused with toxins that several medical personnel became ill from being near her—into a presentation that one might call a "feminista teatro of virtual realism."

Acosta's script calls for multiple means of storytelling—T.V. console, video monitor, an actress, and a puppet and sculptural hanging exhibit inspired by the work of San Antonio artist Diana Rodriguez Gil. The written script ranges in form from—info. clips (presumably from activist tracts) and national newspaper headlines on the toxic sites and events to lyric poetry such as its concluding lines:

> I try to imagine the day when I return to my body
> Capture its landscape from a distance
> then close in quick,
> rising over it like a cloud
> ....
> Taste crevices
> sweet with pleasure.
> The day I return to my body will be like no other. (28)

The storyline is deceptively simple, but figuratively, the piece is both condensed and complex: shortly before her death from toxins, a Chicana industrial worker gives birth to a baby girl with an "adult" level of mental development and knowledge. As the high church, the medical profession and the fundamentalists argue over whether the baby is a miracle, a freak, or the work of Satan, respectively, the woman explains it's presence to her child: "I've been thinkin' for a long time, there must be ways to make use of all that frozen anger, all that suffocating silence, all that shame, like a desert inside—all those things that never had a name before—got bundled up into something good and precious and strong. And that would be you. You!" (25)

The complexity of the piece arises from the montage of media that matches a montage of religion, sexuality, environmental, social justice, and feminist issues which layer the meanings of what appears initially as absurdity, but, as the piece unfolds, registers as reality, rationality, and spirituality, coming out of almas de mujeres. As I will show shortly in Ana Castillo's work, events that seem ludicrous or miraculous are made believable, rendered as "virtual reality" in contexts altered by environmental racism. Like Castillo who denies that her work is "magical realism" suggesting instead that it is Mexican Catholic Reality, the video monitor states early in the piece "THIS ISN'T THE MAGICAL REALISM CHANNEL" (5). Rather, figurative reality is often mirrored by empirical events. For instance, near the end of the piece, the baby, whose strange appearance(s) and existence is never completely explained, tells the audience that she is "[t]he longest living [anencephalic] baby" (28); yet earlier the audience has been told "when that baby came down it came born wise" (5). Other events also indicate the baby's unusually well-developed brain: her mother tells the audience "my baby-sweet ... can stay home by herself and tell me what's happened on the telenovelas while I was at work" (10). The baby's condition is explained in a discussion between mother and child that refers to the alarming number of anencephalic births along the border near Brownsville and Matamoras. The baby tells the mother "I read about the others. Those others born with no brain ... And here I am with a big brain. What else makes me 'go?'" (11). The woman answers her child: "*Ganas, míja.* You were born *con ganas.* The way you called the City about that slushy shit behind the house? I just ignore it, but not you."

In the final scene, the baby's *ganas* are given a "spiritual" explanation that transcends the understanding of the "coats and the robes" who the baby's existence is "baffling the shit out of" (28). The materialization of the figurative occurs in the baby's report that the "coats and the robes" are also perplexed by her mother's death: "They buried her today. Buried her without her heart. The coats kept it for evidence" (28). The baby continues her monologue, predicting the reunification of mother and child: "I like to think that the soul rises above the mind and the body to escape what corrupts them both. I'll wait for her to come into me, if that's what's supposed to happen. I'm tired. But I'll wait. I can wait./This is no miracle. This is an act of survival" (28).

Acts of survival in "Objects in Mirror Are Closer than they Appear" are also undertaken by the women's neighbors and co-workers who are shown on the video monitor. They relate the everyday occurrences that are the results of living with environmental racism—rashes, nose bleeds, headaches—and they respond with concern that is often met with defiance, threats, and repression by those in charge. In a scene on the video monitor, concern over proper gloves is met with the lie that the chemicals are "harmless" and the supervisor's threat "Do you want the job, or not?" (4), anticipating the experiences of Fe, Castillo's central character in the environmental justice chapter of *So Far From God.*

Early in the piece, the woman on the stage reads statements from slides, which appear on the video monitor; she becomes "increasingly agitated" (7) with the progression of slides that describes the carcinogenic conditions in which Chicanas live and work. At issue is contamination by illness-causing chemicals that, in some tests, register more than 700 times higher than federal safety limits ... ("Residents are angry because they were not told of the contamination"), the lack of concern by those responsible, and the few, but foreboding, available health statistics ("Hispanic women are twice as likely to die of cervical cancer than are white women") (8). As her pain makes her realize that something is threatening her health, the protagonist takes account of her life. "I have things to finish: That couch to pay off—90-days, same as cash .... The dance at Fiesta Gardens with Mingo Saldívar .... That class at ACC. I have things to finish, The dance with the devil, where *this* time, *I* lead" (16). Such references to folkloric legend are common in texts from both Chicanas and women in India and are tied to "real life" just as the "supernatural" or spiritual is part of "lived experience" for many. As the protagonist departs from the bus at the community college for her class, the video equipment goes off and "the video monitor becomes a heart monitor" (16). While she does not appear to get her chance to "lead the devil," she, rather than the devil, is the one who disappears, at 31, in the midst of her dance of life. After the woman's death, when the doctor on video monitor tells the audience "The patient was in the advanced stages of cervical cancer." The (dead) woman answers "Cancer? *Pues*, I thought I was just crazy!" (20). The exclamation evokes a history of patronizing attitudes about women's health, on the part of many professionals in western medicine, and psychiatry who operated on the assumption that "she is just crazy."

Belinda Acosta's transmedia piece may be the most complexly radical instantiation of transformed family relations in the name of environmental justice creeds that I have studied. It represents an intervention in the tradition of mothering that transposes convention to represent la Causa of the community, as does, for instance, MELA. It also guards against endorsements of the family that simultaneously endorse homophobia, racism, and sexism. The strange arrival of the baby is a transformation of "all that suffocating silence ... all those things that never had a name before," (Acosta 25), things such as "frozen anger" and "shame." The representation of chemical toxins here seems to be tied in with the emotional toxins of family and society. The "longest living [anencephalic] baby" (28) is also the soul, waiting for the woman to "come into [her]" after having escaped what corrupts the mind and the body (28). The woman's sexuality and spirituality merge; birthing and mothering are, in the most profound sense, extensions of the woman. The baby is the part of the woman that, in fact, does the "mothering" and the part that calls the city about the backyard toxic waste. In the unearthing and re-formation of the "suffocating silence," of family, community, and societal toxins, Acosta's piece may, as Ramón Saldívar argues of other "silenced voices of opposition, ... serve to highlight the ideological background of the traditional canon, to bring to the surface that repressed formation that Jameson has called the 'political unconscious'" (Saldívar 1990, 214). In so doing, Acosta's work draws out the connections between the various "environmental toxins" affecting Latinas at the end of the millennium. Acosta's work is not about victimization so much as it is about survival and the courage to stand against and rise above victimization.

8.3 So Far From God

Like "Objects..." and "Falsies," Ana Castillo's *So Far From God* presents oppositional voices that revise conventions, thereby portraying environmental justice issues as life and death matters that transform women's bodies and lives. In all of her early novels, *Mixquiahuala Letters* (1986), *Sapogonia* (1990, 1994), *So Far from God* (1993), Ana Castillo documents social issues and narrates the gendered roles of social injustice in Latina/o and other communities. *So Far From God* represents the issue of workers' environmental health as it affects the "Silicon Valley age" Nuevo Mexicano community employed in the high-tech weapons industry.[183] Castillo draws on the oppositional consciousness and resistance that develops within Latina/o communities around this social environmentalism.

Castillo's involvement with activism in New Mexico enhances her fictional accounts of the area. In her Acknowledgments, Castillo expresses her indebtedness to "the members of the Southwest Organizing Project who assisted in [her] research; above all, for the inspiration [she] received from their consciousness, ongoing commitment, and hope." The Southwest Organizing Project organizes support for economic and environmental justice struggles in the Southwest. Castillo's relationship with them suggests her commitment, as a writer, to these struggles.

So Far From God takes place in and around Tome, New Mexico. Tome can be found on your road atlas, off highway 25, south of Albuquerque. Castillo, Sibal, Viramontes, and Mahasweta Devi all depict places that can be found on maps. Along with a geography that corresponds with reality, they each name organizations that have real life counterparts. The story focuses on Sofia, her gambling, rambling husband, Domingo, and four daughters, each cruelly fated to an extreme situation that leads to early death. Sofia, (nicknamed Sofi), in her youth, has married Domingo against the wishes of her family and friends; she spends most of her married life holding their family together without him. La Loca, the youngest daughter dies and is resurrected at age three. After her resurrection, she stays at

---

183 I have followed the patterns of the authors in choosing whether to italicize "foreign" words and I have chosen the title's capitalization *So Far From God* used in the Plume Books edition published in May 1994 except when referring specifically to a different edition, most of which render the title, *So Far from God*.

home and will let no one, except her mother touch her; she does, however, have a healthy social life with animals and spirits, and with her sisters before, as well as after, their deaths. The three elder daughters, Esperanza, Caridad, and Fe all have relationships with men who abusively reject them, and the termination of relationship is repeatedly a turning point for the female characters in the story.

Esperanza earns a college degree in Chicano Studies and an MA in Communications. After being a local TV anchorwoman, she goes to Washington D.C. to continue her career as a news reporter; this job sends her to Saudi Arabia where she disappears covering the Gulf War. While her physical body is never found, her spiritual/ghostly body returns to visit family and friends. Caridad, meanwhile, attracts but cannot "keep" men; she is married, cheated on, has three abortions, and is brutally attacked in the first chapter. She barely survives molestation by her attacker, but months later she regains her former beauty miraculously. Becoming a clairvoyant and developing a significant lesbian relationship, she leaves her old life behind. Fe is the compulsively conventional daughter for whom things never work out conventionally. Her first fiancé abruptly terminates their relationship causing Fe to scream for years and thus earn the title La Gritona.[184] It is Fe who will die from cancer that she contracts from chemicals used in her weapons factory job. In the midst of the trials of supporting her daughters and her husband—when he is home—Sofia decides to run for mayor of Tome; she wins, and slowly begins to turn the struggling town around with a series of cooperatives and an organization of mothers called M.O.M.A.S.

I offer this summary as a basic grounding in the novel, especially for those unacquainted with the work, but such a linear synopsis is hardly an appropriate treatment for the text of a writer who states that her writing is "never linear" because life is not "that way." Rather, she describes both life and text as "like a freeway:" "You have a million variations and exits, like on the freeway, where you can keep making choices or redoing them" (*Mester* 154). Furthermore, the language of the book is missing from my account of *So Far From God*. With the usual Chicana/o mix of Spanish phrases, and an unusual style of borrowing from the religious language of Castillo's rendition of New Mexican Catholicism,

---

184 Gritona is literally translated as "crying woman" or "woman who cries;" however, La Gritona is also used as a synonym for La Llorona, the mythic woman who cries for her dead children. The stories about La Llorona/La Gritona vary, but the mother is often implicated in the drowning of the children and there is usually a male lover or husband. In Fe's case, she acquires the name after her bout with romance turned sour; nonetheless, the name also predicts her subsequent misfortunes, in particular her miscarriage and the lost opportunity to have the familia she anticipated, the results of exposure to toxins in her workplace.

the language portrays a cultural regionalism largely through almost formulaic caricaturizing.

In the tradition of Castillo's earlier epistolary novel, *The Mixquiahuala Letters*, which provides charts for three different readings of the text, I would like to suggest three possible and predominant readings for *So Far From God*. The readings are: a religious reading that sees the novel as a New Mexican Catholic text; an aesthetic reading that sees the text as an example of magical realism, and the third—the kind I will attempt—a "political" reading of social justice issues viewed through the text. Each of the readings is invested in describing different "representative" aspects of Chicana/o communities. The allegorical depiction of the Stations of the Cross, the religious influence in the language, and the examination of spirituality and miracles are brought into conjunction with social justice and material everyday existence; however, except for their implications for social justice, the religious aspects are largely beyond the scope of my reading.

Likewise, the implications of describing the text as "magical realism" are important, but I do not attempt more than a cursory examination of this. The descriptive category "magical realism" has been used to "ethnicize" the text by situating it in a historical tradition of Latin American Literature; this can, however, assimilate the politico-cultural, historically specific experience of Chicana/os into the larger, Latin American tradition of *realismo maravilloso* that already has been largely de-politicized in the "northern academy." Such misreading of Castillo's text would be ameliorated by José Saldívar's Pan American (post)colonial dialectic; here, I suggest, such a dialect is generated by an environmental justice frame.[185] In an interview published in *io*, Castillo responds to the suggestion that her work is magical realism, as follows: "My style is only magical to a WASP mentality. The women in *So Far From God* are modeled on the martyrs in the history of the Catholic Church. We are made to believe in these miracles. I wasn't making anything up—it's not magical fiction; it is faith" (27).[186] Castillo thus foregrounds the text's religious portrayal of Chicana/o ethnicity, dismissing any interpretation that does not take into consideration a specific understanding of Mexican American religious realities. She thus utilizes the historical specificity of place that José Saldívar describes, thereby re-politicizing the text. Re-politicizing from a feminist-centered perspective, *So Far*

---

185 See José Saldívar in *The Dialectics of the Americas*.

186 The wording of this quotation has been questioned by a thirdparty present at the interview who reports that Castillo was never shown the tearsheets before the interview was published; however, on other occasions she has insisted that "it is not magical realism, it is reality." My appreciation to Elsa Saeta for providing this information.

From God might be considered "Magical Feminism," a term coined by Patricia Hart in 1987 in describing Isabel Allende's work.[187]

There are two extended narratives of environmental justice in *So Far From God*, one that exposes environmental racism, and a second that foregrounds resistance and the development of oppositional consciousness. Environmental injustice plays its most elaborate role in Chapter Eleven, which is entitled "The Marriage of Sophia's Daughter to Her Cousin, Casimiro, Descendant of Sheepherders and Promising Accountant, Who, by All Accounts, Was Her True Fated Love; and of Her Death Which Lingers Among Us All Heavier Than Air." As the lengthy title indicates, the chapter begins with what its protagonist, Sophia's daughter, Fe perceives of as a dream come true at last. She begins married life happily, and for her, this means not only an introduction to post matrimonial bliss but full membership in late twentieth century, consumer culture: "... Fe got the long-dreamed-of automatic dishwasher, microwave, Cuisinart, and the VCR ..." (171), as well as a new weapons factory job to pay for it all. Ironically, after a mere year of married life, the new job, both necessary and responsible for her lifestyle, exacts the greatest price—her death. The reference in the chapter's title to her death lingering "heavier than air" identifies the characteristics of a chemical that she uses in her job at ACME International which, she finds out, is, among other harmful things, "heavier than air."[188] The essence of the air being breathed is important here. The chapter begins with a stereotypical description of the air in New Mexico: "It was that month in the 'Land of Enchantment[189]' when it smelled of roasted chiles everywhere" (170). Two paragraphs later the smell of chiles in the air each year is, for her friends, the recurring emotional connection to both Fe's death and her wedding: "But above all, when the pungent, nostalgic aroma of roasting chiles filled the air again in following years, that month would

187 Gratitude to Kristin Castleman and other students who engaged study of Magical Feminism as a part of our Magical Realism course to the point where I realized the term needs to be applied to Chicana authors, Ana Castillo, in particular.

188 ACME International evokes the language of U.S. popular culture—an early version of such a generic corporation was instituted in the Roadrunners Cartoon in the 1960s. Kurt Vonnegut uses the same acronym for his portrayal of a corporate bureaucracy. Castillo's use of the anonymous acronym acts as a smoke screen to veil the "real life" corporation that figures in an incident of environmental injustice upon which Castillo bases this chapter. At the same time it calls attention to the fact that the story could have taken place within an Anywhere, Corporate USA zone.

189 Castillo has been critiqued for her stereotypes of the region's Latina/o communities; the critique may be warranted but is beyond the terrain of this discussion. Furthermore, the stereotyping is, I would argue, legitimized by her distortions of stereotypes that present a more "realistic" portrayal of the state's Chicana/o inhabitants' "lived experience" of domination.

always be remembered by everyone who had known her as the one in which la Fe died right after her first anniversary" (171). The passage suggests that both the woman, (Fe) and the concept (fe/faith) have died.

The connection between the hot and healthful spice and the chemically hot "cleanser" that Fe used to degrease weapons parts is a symbolic dichotomy that has been synthesized materially. Suzanne Ruta's article in *The Nation* entitled "Fear and Silence in Los Alamos" reports that "traces of plutonium have been detected in chilies" downstream from New Mexico's Los Alamos National Laboratory where 2,400 sites are "suspected of contamination with plutonium, uranium, strontium 90, tritium, lead, mercury, nitrates, cyanides, pesticides and other leftovers from a half century of weapons research and production" (9).[190] In the following passage the novel twists the travel poster "Land of Enchantment" to reflect the actual state of New Mexico that Ruta has described:

> And meanwhile, most of the people that surrounded Fe didn't understand what was slowly killing them, too, or didn't want to think about it, or if they did, didn't know what to do about it anyway and went on like that, despite dead cows in the pasture, or sick sheep, and that one week late in winter when people woke up each morning to find it raining starlings. Little birds dropped dead in mid-flight, hitting like Superball hail on roofs, collecting in yards and streets, and falling on your head if you didn't look out. Unlike their abuelos and vis-abuelos who thought that although life was hard in the "Land of Enchantment" it had its rewards, the reality was that everyone was now caught in what had become: The Land of Entrapment. (172)

Tome, New Mexico, in which the story is set, is on the Rio Grande about 75 miles downriver from Los Alamos. Given Ruta's evidence that the land near the weapons manufactory is becoming poisoned, the fictional description of impending doom does not seem unlikely, even outside of fiction. At such points in Castillo's fiction, there is no need to "suspend disbelief;" "real life" does the job for the writer. In an interview, Castillo reports how "real life" portrayals in her fictions were rejected because of their anticipated "real life" effects.

---

190 Ruta's title evokes popular fiction through its paraphrasing of the title of Hunter S. Thompson's novel, *Fear and Loathing in Las Vegas*. The borrowing from popular media to title articles on environmental degradation is commonplace. For example, "Pulp Fiction" the title of the 1994 box office hit film is the title for a report on the results of irresponsible lumbering in the *Amicus Journal*, Winter 1995. Ana Castillo also uses names that refer to popular media in her fiction. *Fear and Loathing in Las Vegas* has other strong ties to Chicano culture in that the narrator's main sidekick is patterned on Oscar Zeta Acosta, the writer, lawyer, and activist, and in real life, the two writers were mutually influential.

> I am dealing with environmental issues in New Mexico which are very serious for all of us. But they were afraid of the possibility of someone recognizing himself in there and going after the big New York publisher and the rich novelist. I said, "Wait a minute! What rich novelist?" So, I had a telephone conference with my editor and their lawyer and they recommended that one particular chapter had to be redone, to protect them .... They were concerned that one of the characters—and I don't know these people personally—was based on somebody that might say, "This is me ...." (*Mills College Review* 4)

It seems likely that it was Chapter Eleven that Castillo had to rewrite, but it is particularly significant if, indeed, the published version is a "watered down" narration of environmental racism. It is also significant, both to the study of literature at large, and to the study of the political conditions surrounding the creation of literature, when the literary product is partially shaped by the fear of a rich "someone's" potential lawsuit because fictional reality is "too real." While in the interview Castillo is cryptic about who might sue, we can reasonably infer that for many reasons, both economic and strategic, it would be the perpetrators, not the victims, of environmental racism. Therefore, environmental racism intrudes, even in a novel that addresses the issue, to cause a kind of censuring of the fictional representation of environmental racism[191] Nonetheless, as the chapter progresses,

---

191 One might argue that Ana Castillo could have sold her book to a smaller, independent press, and avoided this problem. Amiri Baraka, for instance, took this stand with his late 20th Century writing (Nassau Community College Address, fall 1996). However, Baraka's recent writing that is published by small press is not widely distributed despite his widespread recognition for early work such as "Dutchman." Furthermore, the choice is hampered by economics of corporate capitalism that makes it more expensive to run a small business, and by the fact that historically and even contemporarily women, and all people of color, face discrimination in finding publication for their work at many presses. Historically, work by and/or about women of color has often been unwlecomed by a large spectrum of the publishing industry. Castillo did get a successful start as a writer with small presses: *Women are Not Roses* was published with Arte Publico in 1984, *My Father Was a Toltec: Poems by Ana Castillo* by West End Press in 1988 and she continues to publish with small publishers. *The Mixquiahuala Letters* was originally published with Bilingual Press in 1986, and *Sapogonia* was in 1990. Anchor Books Doubleday published its first edition of *The Mixquiahuala Letters* in 1992. In 1994, Anchor Books published a revised version of *Sapogonia*; while Castillo represented the changes as improvements (Austin, Feb. 1994) to me they popularize the more "literarily" interesting, earlier version. The 1994 Anchor Books version centralizes Máximo as protagonist and simplifies the story, reducing the development of Pastora's counter perspective; the gender/race/class politics involved in the earlier version are diminished. However, Castillo appears to be making strategic choices in her publication history that are not solely based on larger distribution and profits. For *Massacre of the Dreamers: Essays on Xicanisma*, she chose University of New Mexico Press, a choice that presumably allowed her more freedom in her experimental style in scholarly exposition than a commercial press would. It should also be noted that in signing on with Norton, Castillo chose a publishing house that retains an autonomy that most major publish-

Fe's dream job becomes a believable nightmare: she becomes ill, and then finds out that she has developed terminal cancer from toxic exposure in the tasks to which she had been assigned on the job. Meanwhile Fe is investigated by the FBI and is "almost" subpoenaed by the government for having used the deadly chemical, even though she was using it upon the orders of her corporate superior who is not being investigated. She has not been told the potential danger of the lethal chemical, which her ACME superiors had insisted was only "ether." Readers are left to wonder which agent on Suzanne Ruta's list caused Fe's problems. Or was it some unlisted toxin that brought about the surrounding environmental demise, and ultimately for Fe, her death?

By not knowing the specifics, readers are forced to fathom a broad expanse of possible problems: production of industrial toxic wastes seems likely to stop only with the demise of the species who "produce and multiply" them, and in many cases their toxicity far outlasts their use. Fe has been told "Yeah, it'll make you sleepy, but that's all" (182) and she only learns of the full toxicity of the chemical when she is finally allowed to look at its data sheet in the corporate manual. Her fight for the information that revealed the chemical's carcinogenic properties demonstrates much about corporate culpability in environmental racism; in this case, sexism is particularly involved. To obtain this information, the dying Fe had to threaten to sue. We are told that,

> this [obtaining access to the manual] took a lot of determination on Fe's end, calling and coming by and each rotating foreman hiding and telling the girls to tell Fe that he was out to lunch, until she finally left a message for the supervisor in charge of rotating foremen that she knew that the FBI was on her case, so as not to give her no more crap about that chemical having been ether or *she* with her lawyer would sue each little rotating ass there .... (188)

Given Fe's history with male-generated emotional abuse, readers know she will not take ill-treatment quietly, however much she may strive to be a conventional woman. Fe's gender critique in the preceding passage is subtle but important: the fore*men* (i.e. those in charge are a series of males) give orders to those considered their "inferiors" (both in terms of job status and in gender status as is evident in referring to them as "the girls"). But though Fe is just another "girl," who, besides suffering from cancer, has become ACME's scapegoat for the FBI she, nonetheless, turns the tables on the men in charge. In telling the supervisor that "she would sue each little rotating ass" she makes diminutive and slang reference to the men's body parts; she transfers their "rotating" of the responsi-

---

ing companies do not. With Houghton Mifflin, Norton is the only major publishing house that is not owned by a media conglomerate; furthermore, Norton is still cooperative based (Miller 11).

bility to answer her request to their bodies. As both Fe and the reader know, the men "rotate" responsibility in order to "keep their asses covered."[192] In this passage, Fe transforms containment into empowerment; she "uncovers their asses," defies her status as victim, and most importantly, gains access to the truth about the chemical she's been working with—"in fact it was (and this last part really got to Fe) *heavier than air*" (188).

Castillo uses italics not only to emphasize an idea, but to set it off as incongruous to both reader and character expectations. The weight of the chemical is a figurative, as well as an empirical, property of the chemical; this is a point at which what appears to be magical realism is revealed as "virtual realism." The fact of the chemical's toxicity *weighs* upon Fe as the empirical truth about it is finally released to her: the chemical is life-threatening; air—as symbolic of life—is no match for this heavyweight toxin.

Living conditions—especially, in this instance, working conditions—are absurd, but the absurdity is a political indictment. Fe dies spectacularly, but her textual death serves to document "real" world conditions that cause "real" deaths. In *So Far From God*, death comes to each sister on very unusual terms; each death is an allegorical lesson, which is dealt with sinister grace.[193] Fe's death is, on one level, the most "realistic" and probable of the sister's deaths. The description of her working conditions in the novel is not very different from the description of working conditions that are being protested by the environmental justice struggles in many worksites in Greater Mexico. Yet, absurd events, such as Caridad's flying off the mesa to her death/transcendence into another state of being and Esperanza's after-death appearances, happen so often in *So Far From God* that the results of environmental racism are portrayed in the context of what critics and reviewers are enchanted by as "magical realism," and what Castillo calls a Mexican Catholic interpretation of reality.

As Castillo herself has put it, "magical realism becomes realism." It is materialized in the progressive media's reports on high tech industries' abominable conditions, as demonstrated earlier in effects on the environment, and here, for its lowest paid workers. For instance, in "High-Tech's Dirty Little Secret," an article by Elizabeth Kadetsky, which appeared in the April 19, 1993, edition of

---

192 The suggestion has been made to me that this passage is "'homosexually' charged"; while the referent of anal sex is present, I suggest that rather than implying homosexuality, it implies sexual violence, i.e., rape, which, for a man is likely to occur in the anus. The misreading of references to sexual violence for homosexuality occurs frequently in many "fundamentalist" readings of Biblical passages that condemn rape.

193 Grace functions here both as a description of the prose and a description of the Mexican Catholicism that imbues the novel.

The Nation shortly after *So Far From God* first appeared in bookstores, the author reports that, "... electronics assemblers work with a collection of toxic substances that can contain anything from arsenic to cadmium oxide. Medical complications from exposure to these substances range from loss of smell to scarring of the lungs to cancer" (517). In comparison, Castillo depicts a Halloweenesque work scene that produces dramatic, if not immediately deadly, "medical complications:" "[t]he results of working with a chemical that actually glowed in the dark and therefore you could work with it in the dark, with special gloves and cap (and why you did, as a supervisor explained, was to be able to detect if any fingerprints or hair got on the parts) was this red ring around her nose and breath that smelled suspiciously of glue" (181).

While these may be chronic symptoms of chemical poisoning, they are also figuratively significant: the red ring around the nose could be read as an animal's nose ring—the mechanism by which independent-minded animals are controlled. Such a nose ring is how a bull is led around by its master, or—perhaps, in this context, more metaphorically apt, given Fe's persistence in uncovering the facts of her worksite poisoning—a pig is kept from "rooting around." Likewise, the smell of glue signifies the threat of adhesion—being stuck in a job and lifestyle from which there was, ultimately for Fe, escape only through death. It is also significant in the above passage that the limited protective measures recommended by the corporation were aimed at protecting the weapons rather than the workers; herein Castillo's politicized irony is at work.

In discussing Castillo's early writing, Norma Alarcón establishes Castillo's project in terms of its race and gender politics and its complex irony. Alarcón's observations may be effectively applied to *So Far From God* in order to understand the political implications therein. Alarcón states that Castillo's early poetry

> ... ensured her reputation as a "social protest" poet at a time when it was difficult to be anything else. As a result, some of the ironic tones already present in the early work have been easily over-looked in favor of the protest message, which in fact is re-doubled by irony. It can be argued that irony is one of Castillo's trademarks. Irony often appears when experience is viewed after-the-fact or in opposition to another's subjectivity. (94)

It is this very use of *re-doubled* irony that must be decoded to read gender, race, environment, "La Migra", and other political discussion in Castillo's fiction, and it should be underscored that without a repoliticized understanding of the complexity of the irony we don't get full exposure to the fiction's politics. The "redoubling" of protest through irony that Alarcón has recognized occurs repeatedly in Castillo's welding of historico-political events with interpersonal relationship. Castillo shares this trait of environmental justice writing in the fiction under study, most significantly, with Nina Sibal's *Yatra*.

When Fe was given the particularly tough job that leads to her cancer and her trouble with the FBI, she was sent from the upstairs workrooms—where everyone else worked—down to the basement. In the room where she was supposed to clean some large and very dirty high-tech weapons parts, she found ghastly conditions, which she attempted to partially remedy despite the negligent attitudes of her superiors. There was only,

> an excuse for a vent at the far end of the wall. That first day she put her hanky up next to it and it just dropped to the floor. She wasn't given no mask by any of the useless and ineffectual rotating foremen, so she helped herself to the kind used upstairs, and though she realized that in fact it did no good, she still wore it because at least symbolically it made her feel better. She also used the usual orange gloves that they had upstairs, and not only did the chemical eat them up, it dissolved her manicure, not only the lacquer but the nails themselves! ... After she lost most of her fingernails, she was given some "special" gloves for working with ether, they told her. But they could not come up with a mask that helped none, and three months went by and that's just how it was. (183–184)

To the reader who knows that Fe is dying, Fe's attempts to protect herself reveal the nature of the dangerous working conditions—especially for those without means for recourse. For Fe, who naively goes about her job without questioning, the risky conditions merely appear to be an inconvenience. Symptoms like losing not only one's manicure but also one's nails are heightened by the contrast with Fe's fastidious conventionalism; such details mark the illusions of comfort and security created by the lifestyle that Fe has adopted. The dangerous conditions being described seem preposterous, but, again, they are matched in Kadetsky's report: "[A]t a small contract assembly house, U.S.M. Technology [w]orkers handled potentially hazardous solders and solvents with no masks, gloves or safety sheets in violation of state safety and health laws" (517). And, like ACME International, the main offender in *The Nation's* report is a subcontracting company (180). By spreading such work around via a subcontractor, those in command avoid the onus of responsibility, and often, as in Fe's case, blame falls on the victim; thus, the "rotating responsibility" by the foremen that was discussed previously happens in "real life" at the highest levels.

While Fe knew that ACME International was doing the dirty work for other companies who are contracted to build weapons by the Pentagon, with conventional patriotism, she saw her job as "[v]ery important work, when you thought about it" (181). In contrast, her sister Esperanza, the activist turned reporter, seen by most in her community as a mitotera, might have had a more substantial analysis of the deleterious role such work can play in one's world, both personally and politically. Despite ghostly visits to her more spiritual sisters—La Claridad and La Loca—after her disappearance in the Gulf War, Esperanza, as

Hope, does not appear to warn Fe.[194] And Fe had ignored all the signs of looming trouble even as she ignored the "nausea and headaches that increased in severity by the day" that she and many of her fellow workers experience (178). Fe finds out that she had been pregnant only when she miscarries, and when she gets back to work, she finds out that many of her fellow workers can no longer bear children. At this point, she recognizes that "[t]here did seem to be something eerie and full of coincidence about it all" (180). However, it is not until her husband smells glue on her breath that she is really bothered, not until her role as perfect wife is jeopardized that she begins to question whether the job is worth the suffering. By then it is too late. Not only has she lost her chance to produce the "big familia" that they wanted, but the toxins have also occupied her body, and, as a result, cancer has set in with a vengeance (178).[195]

While the titles of both Chapter One and Chapter Eleven refer to Fe's fate, Castillo's use of "fate"—a term that generally depoliticizes—injects unusual politicizing observations of cause and effect. Fe, as a character is held accountable to her "faith" in a system of structural oppression. Fe's labor does not produce seemingly innocent products like grapes, or even computer chips which, to varying degrees, serve useful purposes meeting basic needs. Rather, Fe is involved in the manufacturing of deadly weapons, not unlike those that likely killed her sister, Esperanza during the Gulf War. In addition, they harm workers, civilians, and the environment when industries are unregulated and those in charge are unconscionable. Fe slowly loses her faith in the benign aspect of the system that she had embraced because it had supported her (literal) buying into a related system—mass consumer culture.

While the text critiques Fe's lifestyle, it also implicitly suggests means to productively transforming her unintentional involvement in structural violence. The importance of a progressive education, and of knowledge about appropriate technology to meet the community's needs is foregrounded; the text underscores the necessity of openness to an analysis of the power structures by which

194 Ana Castillo is not the only or earliest Chicana/o author to depict the military's presence as environmental injustice against communities of color in New Mexico. Some of Rodolfo Anaya's fiction beginning with publication of *Bless Me, Ultima*, makes references to the nuclear presence in the state. His short story of a Pueblo community that comes face to face with the gravity of the activities at Los Alamos when a hunter shoots a deformed deer on the national laboratory land offers extensive treatment of the issue. (My appreciation to Jim Tartar for pointing out the history of Anaya's attention to environmental justice issues.)

195 The rapid onset of the environmentally caused cancer may be less realistic, empirically, than most other aspects of Fe's story. However, the rapid succession of changes in Fe's life that lead to her death, all within the year, mirror her sisters' rapid life transformations and subsequent deaths.

the community is dominated. This occurs through events that directly or indirectly expose the structural violence within U.S. policy and practice. As in the critique of Fe's consumerist tendencies, Castillo demands accountability from the community that she depicts as victimized. This saves her fiction from fetishizing the grassroots communities she describes.

Castillo's description of Fe's symptoms and the symptoms of the women with whom she works, reads almost like a case study.[196] However, they also parallel the descriptions—told in narrative lists—of the series of circumstances affecting each member of Sofia's family. In each of the daughter's lives, issues of social justice are prevalent; readers may grapple with these issues both figuratively and literally. Despite her caricatures of the ideal activist (in Sofi) and the epitome of victimization (in each of the sisters) the consequences of their actions are not based on charades but on "real life." Her treatment of Fe as a caricature of "false faith" who naively landed in a corporate-driven consumer economy allows Castillo to critique such a system.

Fe's story, in its allegorical sense, is revealed in her name; it is the story of the demise, the resurrection and the death and final burial of "faith."[197] At the story's outset, Fe's faith in her fiancé's dedication to their relationship is devastated. However, when she recovers from this rejection—remembering it, herself, only as a long illness—she has lost only her voice, or rather a consistent voice. Her vocal handicap means that not all her words are audible; her vocal cords have been damaged by months of screaming. Due to this handicap, she is not given a raise at the bank where she works, another subtle political critique that attends to structurally endemic discrimination. Not seen as fit to deal with customers, she moves instead to ACME International where she is seen as quite fit to deal with chemicals, in fact, the deadliest of chemicals. However, she has faith in

---

196 Castillo used interviews with one Chicana worker, in particular, to inform her writing with the material conditions of environmental racism in the context of the corporate high-tech weapons industry. In some senses Castillo may be able to portray in fiction a situation that cannot yet be rendered "defensible" in a legal court and is limited in its reportability as "fact" in journalism. This is due to difficulty in establishing probable cause in situations of some environmentally caused illnesses. Actual accusations in such situations run the risk of inviting slander suits on the part of the corporation that is allegedly at fault. My appreciation to Elsa Saeda for these details. However, as discussed elsewhere, even the fiction has been limited in the depictions it can "safely" make. None of the papers that accompanied the writing of *So Far From God* are in the publicly accessible boxes of Castillo's archives at University of California, Santa Barbara (as of September 1994 when I researched them). With these papers, readers may see other aspects of the history which Castillo is documenting in fiction.

197 Allegorical interpretations of their stories work with the names of Fe's sisters and mother as well.

the benign nature of the system—in fact she embraces the system—which, as I pointed out earlier, encourages her (literal) buying into the interconnected mass consumer culture. In this sense her lifestyle does not meet with the mandate, issued in the Principles of Environmental Justice, to develop a responsible, and preferably sustainable, lifestyle. Thus, her story underscores the importance of personal responsibility for lifestyle/lifeways in reducing the global vulnerability of environmental destruction. Furthermore, Sofia builds on the lessons that her activist daughter, Esperanza, has brought home, earlier–something Fe was not able to do in her life cut short. Sofia's community work counters several of the traps of victimization into which her daughters had fallen.

In the title of the first chapter, we are set up for a series of strange and fateful events to follow: "An Account of the First Astonishing Occurrence in the Lives of a Woman Named Sofia and Her Four Fated Daughters ...") Each daughter's story, in both empirical and philosophical ways, is tied in with "fate." Castillo has explained that, figuratively, Sofia's daughters represent martyred saints, however, I am not so much interested in matching daughters with saints as determining how the 1980–1990s renditions of the martyrs are involved in issues of social justice. If we focus on Esperanza, we might read the novel as an anti-war novel, whereas Caridad's abusive experiences with men—both supernatural, and (we cannot say) natural—force readers to ponder what is "natural" in heterosexual relationships. In a feminist analysis, her subsequent experiences as a lesbian clairvoyant read as a step toward a "sexualized" sainthood and her new identity as La Armitaña appears to be a more constructive, if not exactly "stable," development in Caridad's life. After Fe's death, the isolated La Loca, who after her inexplicable childhood death and resurrection, allows no one except her mother to touch her, contracts AIDS.

By this point in the novel, some may feel that the author has overstepped the bounds of faith's or magical realism's abilities to make political statements. Indeed Ray González, an editor of Chicano anthologies and a superb writer in his own right, in a scathing review, in *The Nation* terms the book a "reckless fantasy" (772). He claims that the book will "get attention due to the promotional resources of its publisher, W.W. Norton [but i]t will disappoint those who shake their heads every time a writer falls back on romanticizing the best and worst of his or her culture in the name of 'ethnicity'" (772). González states that "[p]redictable figures like the mother Sofia and her daughters ... are too 'ethnic' for their lives to be believable, even in the supernatural world Castillo sets in New Mexico" (772). In this passage, González suggests that Mexican American ethnicity is less believable than "the supernatural." Claiming that rather "[t]here are too many earlier works of fiction that deal successfully with miracles, suffering Catholic women and the clash between Mexicans and Anglos (773)"[198] González's reading misses the fact that while the characters may be caricatures, the social issues they encounter are *very believable*; thereby, Gonzales ignores the abundance of very contemporary issues at stake in the novel's ethnic interactions, which specifically and statistically affect Latino/a communities more heavily than "Anglo" communities—environmental injustice, AIDS, and death on the battlefield, to name three.

Ultimately, the crux of what González misses is that, like the best of Castillo's commentary, the often unuttered, but implicit, political commentaries on social issues like AIDS or environmental justice, function with political irony and through the readers' deductive engagement. For instance, if empirically, positive HIV status cannot possibly be reduced to a causal link to someone's promiscuity or "unconventional" lifestyle; if it is a disease that can affect even those—such as La Loca—who have never experienced a sexually intimate relationship or I.V. drugs, then readers are invited to re-evaluate any response to AIDS that scapegoats its victims and discriminates against certain social communities. Those outside "high risk groups" cannot place themselves apart from AIDS destruction by practicing "safe sex," but must confront AIDS as an issue that has been politically constructed and represented in line with the interests of the different parties involved. Unlike the rhetoric that names as "innocent victims" those with HIV who were exposed to the virus through transfusions of

---

198 González' usage of "Anglo" referring to white people is common usage in Chicana/o Studies scholarship and more broadly in Greater Mexico; I clarify this, because "Anglo" as an identity in the South Asian/Indian context—usually Anglo Indian—has had a different set of definitions. While the review's attention is useful, I question the benefits of González review of Castillo's fiction. González dismisses the novel finally with the kind of statement that those holding up a racist, patriarchal, cultural power structure will happily broadcast: "A novel like *So Far From God* may represent the unfortunate side of the triumph of multiculturalism: One of the dangers today is that glamorous, high-powered agents and publishers place pressure to produce on minority writers who may not be quite ready. New York wants *the* Chicana novel so bad it hurts" (772–773). The strength of "minority writers" is hardly the issue. González, in his patronizing statement is doing injustice, not only to Castillo, but to all Chicana writers. He can think what he likes about Castillo's book, but why did he then choose it as the only Chicana novel he reviews in *The Nation*? (He reviews nine books by Chicana/os—three of which are by women—who, he says, are "leading the pack" of Latino writers because their "universal appeal ... is finally being recognized.") We are led to believe, by deductive reasoning, that there are no other Chicana novels out there worth talking about. Yet when I look at "Ray's List" and then at my own bookshelves, I wonder what chasm all the most recent books by Chicanas, that stand securely on my bookshelves, have fallen into. Is it that he doesn't find that Chicanas "produce work that speaks for us all".

diseased blood, La Loca's disease is untraceable. Like all people living with AIDS/HIV, La Loca is neither "innocent" or "guilty." Thus, Castillo implicitly suggests that the issue of AIDS must be "cured" politically, as well as personally, by everyone, regardless of HIV or presumed risk status.

My reading suggests that Castillo desexualizes and decriminalizes the disease, through fiction, in a way that works "against the grain" [199] of the mainstream media's polarized configuration of "innocent victims" (those who were exposed to HIV through blood transfusions) and the implication that others are somehow "guilty" by circumstance. La Loca's contracting of the virus is inexplicable (by medical knowledge) rather than caused by means of exposure that can be subsequently judged by society. Here, the "Virtual Realism" lens sharpens our understanding of previous photographic reality and images. In *So Far From God* all characters are potentially victims, and all victims are both "innocent" and accountable.

Castillo's somewhat fantastical depiction of AIDS, like the depiction of Fe's exposure to carcinogenic toxins in her workplace makes a more "realistic" rendition—through its deconstruction of social myth via lived experience—than much news reportage.[200] The novel attacks a kind of "fallout shelter mentality" here that is prevalent in both medical fears and environmental thinking. We shall see this played out more specifically in the discussion of environmental racism and the scapegoating of immigrants. The phenomenon of assuming that class or national security protection will buy "fallout" shelters for those in its community is regressive. It leads to AIDS hysteria that calls for quarantines and tattood indictments, rather than for medical research and national health care plans. It leads to dumping toxins in the neighborhoods of people of color rather than monitoring chemical production and waste. It leads to constructing walls across continents and curfew zones and police barricades around inner cities, to

199 I evoke Norma Alarcón's conceptualization of Chicana's working "against the grain" of dominant ideologies; the original phrase is Walter Benjamin's; and Ramón Saldívar uses the concept in *Chicano Narrative: The Dialectics of Difference.*

200 One contemporaneous example of the consciously perpetrated social myth or politicized suspension of disbelief is George Bush's victorious gubernatorial campaign in Texas, which he based on the premise that crime in Texas was skyrocketing, when, in fact, the crime rate in the state has actually dropped. The mainstream media's promotion of Bush's claim to being an "environmentalist" while ignoring his trade of Texas air and water quality (through his refusal to regulate pollution standards for grandfathered industry) for corporate, institutional campaign backing is another example. Another example, in which the media was integrally involved, was the perpetration of myths that scapegoated immigrants surrounding and following the passage of Propopsition 187 in California, and subsequent similar legislation across the nation.

keep the violence of poverty in all its structural and direct manifestations—including environmental injustice— "at bay." The accomplishment of fiction like Castillo's is that it continually asks, "at bay for whom?" Castillo's text implicitly attacks regressive tendencies which impact on environmental justice both immediately and directly and down the road. Castillo productively politicizes the interconnections as a sisterhood of social ills (environmental racism, war, AIDS and patriarchal domestic violence) through the four sisters whose experiences with these social ills contribute to their deaths.[201]

The connections between social issues and the "fallout shelter mentality" drawn in *So Far From God*, have been mapped out more explicitly in a southern hemisphere "third world" context in Ann Danaiya Usher's essay, "After the Forest: AIDS as Ecological Collapse in Thailand." Usher "attempts to look at AIDS as a phenomenon embedded in, and inseparable from other social realities," including environmental injustice, as she examines "the connections between AIDS and the ecological crisis in Thailand" (11). Usher lists parallels including "the sense of urgency and the pressing need for action to reverse, or at least stabilize, the deteriorating situation. Just as the number of people being infected by the AIDS virus rises each day, so ecosystems that took thousands of years to evolve are being fragmented and degraded in one human generation" (11). As with Fe's experience with the infamous chemical and her subsequent death "[t]he sense of crisis is heightened by the apparent irreversibility of the damage being done" (11).

Castillo describes parallel (though more implicit) situations to those Usher reports on in Thailand. The disease and disintegration effect humans (in La Loca's disease,) and environmental degradation on the land. Witness the deteriorating conditions of the two sisters—La Loca and Fe—which occur as the result of AIDS and ecological erosion, respectively. They corroborate Usher's observations that "[i]mmune deficiency, caused by AIDS, which triggers gradual disintegration of the body's defense mechanisms, mirrors erosion of the ecosystem which destroys the natural capacity to regenerate" (11). As Usher explains, systematic parallels exist "between the individual human body with its internal regulatory processes on one hand, and ecosystems in nature on the other, be they forests, swamps, rivers, or fields" (11).

Usher also narrates a situation that resonates with the fictional scenarios that portray resistance to injustice in *So Far From God*. Not unlike Sofia's deci-

201 The metaphorical linking of these issues of structural violence has empirical connections, again, near El Paso in 1997 by the construction of the border wall from portable airport landing materials left toxic by the Gulf War. My thanks for this information to Irasema Coronado.

sion to become mayor to "make some changes around there" (130) the following narration points to the stand of resistance that elder citizens, who know the local community's needs, can take. This parallel between human body and forest is developed extensively by the Chipko Andolan and by others colonialism and environmental attack on forests and native peoples.

> When asked why she was opposed to the dam, an elderly woman in Ban Sai Moon village explained in great detail that she feared that fish migrations would be disturbed, and agricultural land and archaeological sites would be inundated, and then she added: We've seen what happened to the people who were moved away from [a nearby] dam. They can't survive on the resettlement land and all their children have moved away. Our life is good here. We just want to keep the community together. (28)

For this Thai interviewee, like for many environmental justice practitioners, such as those fighting the Narmada dam system, human community is part and parcel of the natural communities with which it coexists. She is concerned about the wellbeing and uninterrupted lifestyles of both fish and people. The similar wisdom Sofia attains through her life experience is basic to the success of the chain of cooperatives that she institutes as mayor of Tome. Laura Pulido in "Sustainable Development at Ganados del Valle," describes the insights of a community in northern New Mexico that has close parallels to Sofia's campaign for a better life. The communities strive to attain self-determination and sustainability and to retain a symbiotic relationship between the needs of the people and the needs of nature. In fact, in the following passage, Castillo tells us that the fictional town's community development is modeled on the Ganados del Valle community:

> There were many community-based meetings in which debates as to what ideas would lend themselves best toward some form of economic self-sufficiency for their area before some people came up with a plan that eventually mobilized everyone into action. It would take YEARS of diligence and determination beyond this telling to meet their goals but Sofi's vecinos finally embarked on an ambitious project, which was to start a sheep-grazing wool-weaving enterprise, "Los Ganados y Lana Cooperative," modeled after the one started by the group up north that had also saved its community from destruction (146).

Laura Pulido reports the significance of Castillo's "group up north," "besides [the Ganados del Valle community's] economic success, is that it has allowed people to develop to their fullest potential" (131).[202] In particular, she notes that "[w]omen who previously saw themselves solely as housewives have acquired

---

202 In 1996, Laura Pulido's *Environmentalism and Economic Justice: Two Chicano Struggles in the Southwest* was published by University of Arizona Press; here, Pulido expands on the significance of her study of Ganados de Valle.

numerous other talents and skills and greatly expanded their horizons. Moreover, they now have a sense of ownership in Ganados, which, more than anything, means they have hope for the future" (131). Castillo's use of the "real" cooperative as a model for the fictional one extends beyond her specific reference to the "group up north." The changes brought about by community development in the novel parallel changes that Pulido attributes to Ganados in her article; and there is a gender critique to be made in both. In both instances, and as we women benefit most from sustainable development. Thus, environmental justice serves not only to curtail increased oppression of women but also functions as a means of gendered empowerment that supports women's and men's work toward a goal of social, political, personal, economic, and gender equality. They are transformed through revision, revamping and subsequent revaluing, rather than dismissing or discrediting women's traditional roles, at least to the extent that they can constructively contribute to both the community and the individual. All scenarios—Usher's and Pulido's, describing "reality," and Castillo's fictional telling—evoke a phenomenon that is happening around the globe: in the name of environmental self-determination women are taking leadership in creating models of resistance to deleterious development that is controlled by exterior forces. Such women are simultaneously constructing alternate models of environmentally and economically sustainable lifestyles. María Varela, who in 1990 won a MacArthur Foundation fellowship for her work as co-founder of Tierra Wool, one of the cooperative branches of Ganados del Valle could be seen as a "real life" model for Sophia's activism. An article in *Vista* (9-22-90) reports that she "has devoted the last 20 years to helping some 100 families in her community achieve economic equality."

In Greater Mexico, there are additional parallels to Usher's description that permit an understanding of *So Far From God* in terms of environmental politics. The connections are the colonization, containment, and manipulation of people's lives, including their symbiotic relationship with the land, for dominating forces to achieve capital gain. For instance, parallels exist in the experience of Anglo's taking of Mexican-owned land in the 19th Century around the U.S. "Southwest" and in earlier Spanish settler colonization of indigenous communities' lands in the same region. Land rights is a basic environmental justice issue, a theme that re-appears in my reading of Mahasweta Devi's stories. As noted in this book's introduction, Native American's land rights battles have been called the first environmental justice battles on this continent, and they continue to be on the front lines, as noted in the People of Color's Environmental Justice Summit's Principles. Native activists and scholars such as Winona LaDuke and Ward Churchill, to mention only two, have written and spoken extensively about this connection, as well. Land rights issues may be categorized under the broader rubric of "environmental justice." Such categorization does not separate or sublimate one issue into another but, rather, marks historical links between them and shows the deleterious continuation of markers of colonialism in post-colonial and colonial contexts.

Usher's description of a Thai resettlement village, due to a dam project, evokes a tone that is reminiscent of the "marvelous" aspects of Castillo's fiction as connected to the description of the Land of Entanglement (described above).[203] The Narmada Dam Project opposition movement has demonstrated that, in India, dams cause some of the most deleterious effects of inappropriate development in terms of environmental justice. Usher describes a parallel situation in Thailand: "[p]erhaps the most absolute, and therefore the most violent, destruction of forests that affects local communities is that caused by the big dams" (Usher 27). There is a sense in which Usher, in her study, describes the parallel phenomenon to what Castillo portrays in "Virtual Realism" as they both present historically specific situations that read as surreal landscapes. Neither situation is merely "magical realism," but each is a very brutal reality, which groups of people face; their experiences are nuanced by their social disenfranchisement, in the clutches of national and international powers. It is an increasingly common situation to which many peoples are responding with proactive resistance: still, too often many lose their land and lifeways to such development. Comparison of Usher's and Castillo's descriptions opens dialogue about the impact of environmental justice and related social issues among women in

203 The following passage, describing a village of people uprooted by a dam project illustrates the parallels to the Land of Entanglement. "In the resettlement village of a later dam, the Sri Nakharind in Srisawat district of Kanchanaburi province, there are roads, electricity, and running water, installed by the Electricity Generating Authority of Thailand (EGAT) as part of the terms of resettlement. But residents can barely afford the utility bills. Because the soil is rocky and dry, it is not possible to grow enough food to eat. They are forced to buy not only rice, vegetables and meat, but sometimes even water .... Clothes hanging inside refrigerators, purchased in the early years with cash compensation payments, are not a rare sight. These villages are eerie places. They are often treeless and barren, with houses built in grid-like rows. But their most striking feature is the absence of young people" (28). The absent young people have migrated to the metropolis to find work that will sustain their families who have been evicted from their previous sustainable lands and lifeways. This move is gendered: Usher observes that often only in sex work, can women earn comparable wages to men. In a broad sense, the women that Usher describes may each encounter and embody almost all the lived experiences of horror that Sofi's daughter's experience, combined; as Usher describes below, they can become the innocent victims of environmental racism/classism, of AIDS, of brutal sexism, and of political aggression.

the "third world" and the "third world within the first world." The world that Castillo describes in Nuevo Mexico, in *So Far From God*, reveals a set of factors that place it as both the "Third world within the first world" and as a border crossing between "first" and "Third worlds." This anticipates further comparisons from this juncture of Chicana realities with South Asian ones, in subsequent chapters.

Castillo's techniques of marking spaces on maps of this world—within which irony plays a large role—also gains dimensions in international comparisons. The title of the book itself marks a politically ironic space. By the end we realize that we, as readers of *So Far From God*, must question where we are: while we hear the land called Nuevo Mexico, we know from the title that we are "so far from God" and we know from the epigraph—if not from our history lessons—that that must mean we are also "so near the United States." [204] If this is the case, then we cannot also be *in* the United States. Thus, deductive logic again plays a role in Castillo's fiction in that she has implicitly denied the legitimacy of the U.S.-Mexican border. Castillo's politically charged remapping of borders is a replay of her mapping of the country of Sapogonia which challenges dominant thought on immigration rights. *So Far From God*, the title, marks a second irony as well: if anything, their strong adherence to Mexican Catholicism suggests that the characters in *So Far From God* cherish and honor their relationship with the spiritual and thus might be much closer to God than many of us.

Near the end of the novel, the town of Tome turns out for a "Way of the Cross Procession" that is as much a political statement on the part of the participants as it is a spiritual one. The symbiotic natures of spiritual and material justice are stressed through transformation of tradition to express the community's lived reality using the occasion of a religious ritual. We are told that,

> [t]here was no "Mary" to meet her son. Instead, some, like Sofi, who held a picture of la Fe as a bride, carried photographs of their loved ones who died due to toxic exposure hung around their necks like scapulars; and at each station along their route, the crowd stopped and prayed and people spoke on the so many things that were killing their land and turning the people of those lands into endangered species. (241–242)

The passage reads like a religious litany that parallels environmental devastation in (mostly) communities of color with the events of the Stations of the Cross. I quote only the passages that deal with specifically "environmental"

204 The epigraph quotes Porfirio Diaz, Dictator of México during the Mexican Civil War, in his cynical reference to México being "So far from God—So near the United States."

issues; related social justice issues—poverty, AIDS, homelessness, unemployment, and the war in the Middle East are mentioned as well:

> When Jesus was condemned to death, the spokesperson for the committee working to protest dumping radioactive waste in the sewer addressed the crowd …
> Jesus fell, and people all over the land were dying from toxic exposure in factories ….
> Jesus met his mother, and three Navajo women talked about uranium contamination on the reservation, and the babies they gave birth to with brain damage and cancer …
> … Livestock drank and swam in contaminated canals...
> Jesus fell for the second time.
> The women of Jerusalem consoled Jesus. Children also played in those open disease-ridden canals where the livestock swam and drank and died from it.
> Jesus fell for a third time. The air was contaminated by the pollutants coming from the factories ….
> Nuclear power plants sat like gargantuan landmines among the people, near their ranchos and ancestral homes. Jesus was nailed to the cross.
> Deadly pesticides were sprayed directly and from helicopters above on the vegetables and fruits and on the people who picked them for large ranchers at subsistence wages and their babies died in their bellies from the poisoning.
> !Ayyy! Jesus died on the cross. (242–243)

The assertive roles that women play in assuring community survival throughout the novel are intensified in the above passage. The women around Jesus console him, but unlike most women in the Biblical tradition, the New Mexican women—whose children are also dying—speak out. This chapter's epigraph about the ecocide of Navajo communities through uranium contamination is the speech of one of the three Navajo women mentioned above. It broadens and builds upon the connection between the spiritual and environmental justice drawn in the passage as whole. The concern over the poisoning of the earth and her people aligns the communities in protest; religious, geographic, and ethnic differences broaden the horizon of the struggle. The litany of issues echo the concerns raised in other chapters of this book and continue their saliency in Greater Mexico, South Asia, and beyond. While conflicts may prohibit a broader mutual alliance among the diversity of interests represented in the procession, concerns for environmental justice unite the people in coalition.[205] Sophia's

---

205 A somewhat similar—though much larger—spiritual gathering of peoples concerned about preserving and defending an earth-and-people-friendly future and engaging the alternate possibilities of an apocalyptic scenario occurs in Leslie Marmon Silko's *Almanac of the Dead*. *Almanac* is only one example of Native American women's fictional rendering of environmental justice and other social issues.

activism which culminates in the procession is crucial in presenting women who suffer from environmental racism as leaders, spiritually and politically.

Castillo's portrayal of environmental justice succeeds at several levels: it portrays, in detail, environmental justice issues, (most extensively, the corporate use of toxins and their effects on workers, especially women); and it portrays resistance in lifestyle/lifeway choices that are modeled on real life community cooperatives, in demonstrations of protest, and in the development of oppositional consciousness. Castillo's text is, therefore, both instructive and foreboding in its depiction of the reality of the "Land of Entanglement," but ultimately it is also celebratory; it celebrates resistance built through alliance. And in doing so, it maps out local environmental justice battles well fought, won, and to be won.

9 India's Forests and the Interconnected Legacies of Environmental Degradation and Colonialism

> The language of the late modernist novel and all subsequent novels does more than simply reflect or mirror a "reality." It produces that reality by a reconstruction and systematic transformation of the older formations of a previous historical moment.
>
> Ramón Saldívar (206)

> Each Chipko protest has demonstrated the special ecological perceptions of women who work daily in the production of survival.
>
> Vandana Shiva SA (211)

> Songs in praise of nature and its gifts and the role of trees and forests in the life of the people have become evocative ecological texts for popular education and mass communication. Here surely is a powerful tool for further organisation for development and for adult education and functional literacy.
>
> Mishra and Tripathi

9.1 Chipko Andolan: Poetry of the Forest

This chapter[206] examines several pieces of Indian literature of environmental justice,[207] beginning with poetry from the Chipko Movement that was discussed at length in Chapter Five. There, I examined Chipko's representations as a new social movement, an ecological movement, and a women's movement through historicization of the movement in the northern Indian context where it began. I investigated its theoretical contributions to a body of work from women organizing around environmental justice issues. Cultural poetics were crucial to the Chipko Movement's spread from community to community in the Uttarkhand of the Himalayan foothills. The poetics show that at times resistance has split predominantly down gendered lines—in these instances most women oppose outside corporate development that many men support. Their opposition is based on the women's recognition of the ways in which development and the global market economy is particularly harmful to them—and through them, to their villages—because of their more vulnerable position in the gender-specific work roles by which their communities operate. As the following investigation of

206 Parts of the following sections appear in "Two Centuries of Environmental Writing in India" *The Literature of Nature: An International Sourcebook*. Patrick Murphy, ed.

207 "Andolan" is a generic term used in India for "the movement." Parts of this section appear in "Environmental Justice and Women's Work: the UFW, Chipko Movement, and Seringueiros" in *San José Studies: A Publication of San Jose State University.* October 1994, 49–62.

https://doi.org/10.1515/9783111041575-010

Chipko poetics will demonstrate the cultural poetics of the movement (or in common Indian parlance, the andolan) also reflect the women's strong participation in it as means to and a form of creative, politically engaged expression.

The first documentation of the use of the Chipko tactic of tree hugging in the 1970s is commemorated in a famous poem by one of the "Chipko poets," Ghanshyam Raturi:

> Embrace our trees
> Save them from being felled
> The property of our hills
> Save it from being looted. (Jain 173; Shiva 73)

This short poem, as well as others by Raturi and other Chipko poets, became the logos of the movement, often chanted, and *performed* by groups of youth, women and men in demonstrations and rallies. Poetry in the Chipko andolan is neither merely an ancient classical text to be read reverently, a sedate event performed by a single poet for an eager but silent audience, nor is it even the performance art or poetry slam spreading across Indian popular culture. The Chipko movement's use of poetry is more radical than any of these applications, for it *requires* poetry to act as a direct means of conducting defiant, sometimes civil disobedient acts against violent perpetrations of environmental and cultural degradation. In the foothills of the Himalayas, poetry is not so much "poesía en la calle," since the streets—or lumber roads—are often the means of the lumber companies' access to the forest rather than home turf to the poet-activist. In this context, "poetry of the forest" is used *in the forest* to protect the forest—with word, song, symbol and, when necessary, bodies.

Political folksingers and poets composed songs that became a popular means of forest support. Thomas Weber explains that school children often learned the songs from singers or tapes. Sunderlal Bahuguna, one of the most visible of the Chipko activists, attributes Chipko's success to the "political folk song," giving "more than fifty percent of credit for the popularity of this movement to the folk-singers, especially to Sri Ghan Shyam Sailani" (in Weber 90). Ghan Shyam Sailani, the folk poet in question, composed the following Garhwali song that demonstrates the relationship between trees and the water with which villagers are familiar: "Do not axe these oaks and pines, nurture them, protect them. From these trees the streams get their water and the fields their greenery. Look how the flower smiles in the forest" (Bharat Dogra "The Response").[208]

208 For Bharat Dogra's continuing work, see https://bharatdogra.in/, http://mainstreamweekly.net/article12217.html and http://mainstreamweekly.net/auteur11.html.

The song is both a personal imperative and a call to action to spread the command. While it personifies aspects of the forest—"the flower smiles at receiving water"—this poetry presents a distinctive, integrated, relationship between human and forest communities, which are in this context, virtually inseparable. This differs from many of the tree-saving projects in the U.S. Northwest, where activists go to a threatened forest and set up a home away from home in the branches of the trees they wish to protect. The practice of singing to protect the natural resources reminds me of corridos composed for Mexican schoolchildren to sing to water in the Mexican state of Coahuila that borders Texas.

One chronicler of the movement, Shobita Jain, explains a vital role in Chipko poetry: communication between geographically distant groups working in close alliance. "The movement spread throughout Garhwal and into Kumaon, through the totally decentred leadership of local women, connected to each other not vertically, but horizontally—through the songs of Ghanshyam Raturi, through 'runners' like Bahuguna, Bhatt, and Negi, who carried the message from one region to another. ... [T]housands of Garhwal women have protested against commercial forestry ..." (Jain 173). Here, Jain's specification that issues of the movement travelled horizontally, not vertically, is important in that it suggests an erasure of hierarchies within the movement. Sunderlal Bahaguna relates an early version of Chipko poetry on the run when he tells of the related struggle against the planting of commercial eucalyptus, which was taking over more diversified plant communities. In this instance, invasive plantings were pulled: "We walked over the hills, using songs to take the message to the people. There is a song which says, 'If you see a eucalyptus tree, pull it out, because it spoils the others; it takes too much water, and is a friend of the capitalist.' I walked 2,500 kilometers at that time" (10).

The personification of eucalyptus' relationship to capitalism as "friendly" may read as humorous in this song, but it refers to a near universal, sobering reality that has destroyed traditional agriculture, as well as forest land, replacing it with a monocultural scheme for fast growth and money. Eucalyptus was introduced broadly in India as a fast-growing commercial crop in the late 1960s and early 1970s. Its devastating effect on polyculture forests and the people who depend on them has been widely documented. [209]

---

209 For instance, see N.C. Saxena's (Navesh Chandra) *India's Eucalyptus Craze: the god that failed*. New Delhi: Sage Publications, 1994. See also Robin Doughty *The Eucalyptus: A Natural and Commercial History of the Gum Tree*. Center Books in Natural History, 2000.

Like the simple narrative on what to do if you see a eucalyptus, the stories of Chipko poetics that chroniclers tell are local ones that narrate popular protests in which women win their battles through performative acts/arts such as embracing the trees or tying the trunks with sacred thread to interrupt the cutting; pulling up (or shutting down) intrusive plants; and singing responses to the local pro-"development" men's retorts. These are the same stories that Krishna, the protagonist of *Yatra: The Journey*, witnesses as she journeys through the Himalayan foothills.

A longer folk song attributed to the folksinger, Sri Ghanshyam Sailani, illustrates through the personification of a tree, the singer's relationship with the forest. While the folk songs, which are attributed to specific writers may not offer the kind of community history that a more traditional folk song might, the fact that these songs were learned and repeated by many in the community demonstrates that they did reflect something of a community spirit that was shared intergenerationally and across genders. Hence, their significance as a community statement goes beyond that of a song composed and performed by an individual artist. The fact that they were used both educationally as didactic learning tools for children, as well as in political demonstrations to protect the forest, also suggests their multi-level community relevance.

"The Appeal by a Tree"

I have been standing for ages,
I wish to live for you.
do not chop me, I am yours.
I wish to give you something in future.
I am milk and water for you.
I am thick shade and showers.
I manufacture soil and manure.
I wish to give you foodgrains.
Some of my kind bear fruits.
They ripen for you.
I wish to ripen with sweetness.
I wish to bow down for you.
I am the pleasant season.
I am spring. I am rains.
I am with Earth and life.
I am everything for you.
Do not cut me, I have life
I feel pain, so my name is tree.
Rolling of logs will create landslides
Remember, I stand on slopes and below is the village.
Where we were destroyed,

Dust is flying there.
The hill tops have become barren.
All the water sources have been dried up.
Do not cut us, save us.
Plant us, decorate the Earth.
What is ours, everything is yours.
Leave something for posterity.
Such is the Chipko movement. (in Weber 89–90)

This first-person *tree narrative* instructs both the singers and the audience on the right relationship with trees and offers many reasons for advocating on the behalf of healthy forests. However, less extensive slogans also spread among supporters of the andolan, influencing audiences in a variety of ways. Women occasionally used shame as a weapon to convince men, often lumber company workers, to have a change of heart about their work. The following satirical slogan reflects such a tactic: "Oh brother-in-law, how brave you are that you lift your axe to trees hugged by your sisters in law" (Weber 55).

Bahuguna relates how one slogan was used to counter another when villagers found it necessary to boycott government nurseries that were not providing sustainable forest plants for local needs but were rather growing eucalyptus and chir pine, "growing trees to grow money." Bahuguna explains that "the programmes are being chalked out by people who don't know what hunger is. By advocating horticulture and eucalyptus plantation, which are money spinners for the affluent few, they are playing a cruel trick on the poor and hungry locals." The poet Ghanshyam Raturi is more specific, siting the World Bank, as a problem. As he explains, afforestation can be merely a deleterious continuation of deforestation. "'In the 1970s people made big money in felling of trees. Today a big opportunity to make bigger money has come through 'planting' of trees, sometimes only on paper'" (in Weber 123). The Chipko activists created a slogan to succinctly illustrate their position: "Trees mean water, water means bread and bread means life" (in Weber 115). Thus, even short slogans can instruct. To give another example, folk poet Ghan Shyam Sailani composed the following Garhwali song that demonstrates the relationship between trees and water with which villagers are familiar: "Do not axe these oaks and pines, nurture them, protect them. From these trees the streams get their water and the fields their greenery. Look how the flower smiles in the forest" ("The Response" Bharat Dogra et al). The song is both a personal imperative and a call to action to spread the command.

The stories of Chipko poetics that chroniclers tell are local ones that narrate popular protests in which women win their battles through performative acts/arts such as embracing the trees to interrupt the cutting, and singing responses to the local pro-"development" men's retorts. For instance, Shiva describes the occasion of the Adwani satyagraha, during which "the Chipko movement became explicitly an ecological *and* feminist movement" (76).

> [t]he most dramatic turn in this new confrontation took place ... [i]n 1977 in the village of Adwani[;] Bachni Devi, the wife of a headman of the village led resistance against her own husband, a local contractor. The Adwani satyagraha created new directions for Chipko. The movement's philosophy and politics now evolved to reflect the needs and knowledge of the women. Peasant women came out, openly challenging the reductionist commercial forestry system on the one hand and the local men who had been colonized by that system, cognitively, economically and politically, on the other (77). Shiva describes their means of poetic resistance: "The women tied sacred threads to the trees as a token of their vow of protection[;] .... a large number of women from 15 villages guarded the forests while discourses from ancient texts on their role in Indian life went on uninterruptedly" (75).

The women created a performative event that duped the forester into participating in their sardonic riddle in which he was shown to be the foolish one.

> The forest official arrived to browbeat and intimidate the women and Chipko activists, but found the women holding up lighted lanterns in broad daylight. Puzzled the forester asked them their intention. The women replied, "We have come to teach you forestry." He retorted, "You foolish women, how can you who prevents felling know the value of the forest? Do you know what forests bear? They produce profit and resin and timber." And the women, led by Bachni Devi immediately sang back in chorus:
> *What do the forest bear?*
> *Soil, water and pure air.*
> *Soil, water and pure air*
> *Sustain the earth and all she bears.* (in Shiva 77)

In the incident described above, the women appear to play a role somewhat akin to the Greek chorus in classical drama. The lanterns in broad daylight seem to indicate that they have come to draw attention to the obvious, doing so in a metaphorical retort that silences the lumber company's belligerence.

In a similar strategy of using objects as metaphors for teaching lessons to development schemers, hundreds of Chipko women gathered in Tehri on World Environmental Day 1979 with empty water pots. They were protesting not only water scarcity but the "failure of water schemes and of a model of science which saw metal pipes and concrete tanks as producers of water, and male engineers and technicians who fitted pipes and designed schemes as providers of that water" (210). When they were asked their grievances, they showed the district collector the empty pots and asked "why, if paper plans and metal and concrete could ensure water, their pots were still empty?" Then they explained their purpose: "We have come to tell you that nature is the primary source of water, and we are the providers for our families. Unless the mountains are clothed with forests, the springs will not come alive. Unless the springs come alive, the taps will be dry. It is the live springs and not the dry taps which fill our pots. If you want to solve our water problems please plan for water, not for pipes" (Shiva 211). Shiva explains how subsequent national plans and water pipe advertisements indicate that India is not heeding such advice as the Chipko women's—and is suffering as a result (211).

As the movement spread and matured the women continued their expressive tactics; localized versions of poetry, songs and chants reveal a common theme: loving protection for a forest that promises daily necessities—and geoculturally distinct details. In 1986, Chipko women of Nahi Kala were protecting their forests for food production. As one of the village women activists, Chamundeyi said, 'We need our forests for growing *mandua, jhanjona, rajma, adrak* and *mirch* to feed our families and ourselves.' And throughout the hill areas, women sing: 'Give me an oak forest and I will give you pots full of milk and baskets full of grain, (Shiva 97–98). As these words demonstrate, "[t]he link between forests and food is clear to the women who produce food in partnership with trees and animals. The patriarchal model, in contrast, sees forestry as independent of agriculture, and reduces the multiple outputs of the forest, including fertilizer and fodder, into a single product—commercial wood" (Shiva 98).[210]

When the women outwitted the foresters at Reni, they played out a series of dramas that bear a more detailed discussion here. Bhatt had been kept out of Reni by interviewers from the opposition (Mishra et al 25). Most of the village men were lured away to Chamoli, an overnight bus ride away, by promises of land compensation payments, which suddenly materialized after 14 years of promises. The communist leader Govind Singh Rawat, still in town "did not have the courage" (Mishra 25) to act when he learned the lumbermen were headed for the area. Some of the male leaders, when they heard of the government set up in collusion with the company wanted to gherao the Gopeshpur forest conservator who had kept Bhatt away to leave the forest open to the lumbermen. However, Bhatt warned the officer, telling him, "[t]hough you did not

210 Shiva explains: "Animals are no longer seen as providing fertilizer and energy for agriculture. And through the 'white revolution', animal husbandry is reduced to the production of milk for the centralised dairy industry. Organic inputs from forests and animals are no longer seen as mechanisms for conserving soil moisture; large dams become the patriarchal option for providing water for food production. Organic manure is no longer a fertilizer; it is fertilizer factories that are seen to be the only source of soil fertility" (98).

hesitate to keep me here on a false pretext, I would not deceive you as I do not wish you to be personally harmed." Thus, Bhatt created shame and panic for the officer. The male activists were responding with varying degrees of panic themselves, unaware of the village women's successful campaign against the lumber company's cutting. A young girl had detected the lumbermen in the forest and had run to Gauri Devi, the head of the women's chapter, an organization of women who helped each other through crises. The organization mobilized quickly, and 21 women and seven girls set off for the forest area where the lumbermen were making camp. The women issued appeals to the men that addressed these laborers from the neighboring state as *brothers* but set themselves as women outside of the negotiating process for forest rights: "*Bhula* ... do not cut this forest. It provides us with cheap herbs. If this forest goes, this mountain would fall on our village. Floods will come and our *bagads* will be swept away. We will be ruined. Please do not cut these trees. You cook your food and eat it, then come down to the village with us. When our menfolk come back, then you can settle this with them" (in Mishra 27).

The men disregarded the women's words; as Mishra phrases it "Seeing the women alone in the forest, their hitherto scared manhood came to the fore. Some tried to take liberties with [the women]. Others shouted at them for obstructing their work. One man threatened that they would be arrested, and a drunk man armed with a gun tried to frighten them." When this lumberman aimed his gun at Gauri Devi, she bared her breast to the lumberman and issued her ultimatum: "Shoot and then only you can cut this forest which is like a mother to us" (27). As Dopti shames Senanayak by offering the sight of her bare breasts to him in Mahasweta Devi's story "Draupadi" so Gauri Devi shames the man who threatens her into lowering not only his gun but also his axe. His sober companions were moved by this action and turned back also.

However, the lumbermen who had been drinking wanted the women to carry them on palanquins. Another group of women also used shame as a tactic when they loaded up one of the men and began to carry him. A "battle of wits" was going on (Mishra 27). Several of the women carried the tools of the drunken men as they all descended from the spot where the tree felling was expected to begin. This act of belittlement later proved quite strategic (27). At a critical point in the road several of the women found it feasible to disconnect the road by using the digging rods they carried to move a cement slab which held a crucial part of the road in place; thus, they insured that the road was unserviceable. Nonetheless, as an added precaution the women sat between the forest and the laborers all night (28).

The next day when the women related what had happened, they did not tell about the gun threat or the drunken behavior because they did not want the workers to lose their jobs (28). Like Bhatt's warning of the gherao, they wanted all their actions and poetics to be focused on the issue at hand rather than diffused into a hatred of the other side. In this context, such a strategy of satyagraha proved effective. Whether it is a strategy that is often transferable to environmental justice struggles elsewhere is perhaps something to discuss, but it is a strategy that, because it relies on open communication, fully utilizes poetic texts and political artwork.

Itwari Devi, who was involved in the Nahi-Barkot chipko demonstrations against mining in the Doon Valley region describes another kind of strength that was distinctive to the context, a strength that Shiva calls "a kind and level of power that no western trained technocrat can have access to"—"participation in nature [as] the source of [that] different kind of knowledge and power" (Shiva 209)

> Shakti (strength) comes to us from these forests and grasslands; we watch them grow; year in and year out through their internal shakti, and we derive our strength from it. We watch our streams renew themselves and we drink clear and sparkling water—that gives us shakti. We drink fresh milk, we eat ghee, we eat food from our own fields—all this gives us not just nutrition for the body, but a moral strength, that we are our own masters, we control and produce our own wealth. That is why 'primitive', 'backward' women who do not buy their needs from the market but produce them themselves are leading Chipko. Our power is nature's power, our shakti comes from prakriti. Our power against the contractor comes from these inner sources, and is strengthened by his trying to oppress and bully us with his false power of money and muscle. We have offered ourselves, even at the cost of our lives, for a peaceful protest to close this mine, to challenge and oppose the power that the government represents. (in Shiva 209)

Itwari Devi's description of the source of the power of the movement illustrates the complex interrelationships of activism and daily life, of physical and moral strength, of poetic power and political power. For Itwari, the strength of the community is threatened by "the power that the government represents." Thus, she ties the interests of outside development to the government. Yet the government plays contradictory roles in the lives of many villagers who are involved in struggles for environmental justice. It is the government that can make forest destruction illegal and thus offer protection under which villagers may be able to resume their sustainable lifestyles. The government has also worked in tandem with villagers in operating reforestation projects. But most often the government has a symbiotic relationship with industry that is rarely willing to consider the desires and needs of villagers, especially, perhaps, the women. Itwari's statement is also helpful in understanding the split(s) in ideological positions that I will discuss in the following subsection.

A second woman quoted briefly above was particularly important to the Nahi Kala; on November 30, 1986, six weeks after the Chipko blockade had begun, Chamudeyi heard mining trucks going up the mountain toward a limestone quarry and past the blockade where the trucks had "attacked the protesters, removed them from the blockade, and driven their trucks through. She … raced down the slope, and stood in front of the trucks; she told the drivers that they could go up only over her dead body. After dragging her along for a distance, the trucks turned back" (Shiva 209). According to Shiva, Chamudeyi's courage and strength of purpose was the inspiration for a new song from the Chipko poet Ghanshyam 'Shailani'(210).

A fight for truth has begun
At Sinsyari Khala
A fight for rights has begun
At Malkot Thano

Sister, it is a fight to protect
Our mountains and forests.
They give us life
Embrace the life of the living trees and streams
Clasp them to your hearts
Resist the digging of mountains
That brings death to our forests and streams
A fight for life has begun
At Sinsyaru Khala

The poet's song in response to the activist's risky act of resistance demonstrates a collaborative event the likes of which are not rare in social movement/public artist circles. Variations on the genre range from ancient to contemporary, from the Himalayas to the Rio Bravo/Grande, from epic to corrido. Since heroines' songs may demonstrate one of the most universal of aesthetic categories, it may not be surprising that environmental justice has its own versions. (Buffy Sainte-Marie's song "Bury my Heart at Wounded Knee" that commemorates Anna Mae Aquash, mentioned in this book's introduction would be an example from North America.) However, it is important to note that in this case of Chipko we don't get the individual tale of heroinism in the song; rather, those who hear the song already know the tales of resistance; they live the "fight for life" daily as they fight to keep the forest in a natural state that will continue to sustain them, and so they are encouraged to act both literally and symbolically by putting their own lives on the line with protest acts such as Chamundeyi's.

The last poetic text I will discuss demonstrates that as the poetic voice of Chipko spreads its message and the poetics themselves, they spread and developed differently from locale to locale as they moved beyond origins in the Himalayan foothills. The Kalahandi district in Orissa/Odisha is a region largely settled by Tribal peoples. During the late 20th Century, Kalahandi was the site of severe drought and famine, ecological conditions created and intensified by human's structural domination. The Development Agency for Poors & Tribal Awakening is a group of professionals serving those who are most impacted by the changes in natural living environment and social inequities. Lawyers, doctors and the like offer their expertise to people who otherwise would not have access to such services. On their project office building in Laxmipur is a mural which depicts Chipko movement women in saris with their arms around tree trunks; they face men in dhotis carrying axes. In a photo, taken by Dwight Platt in July of 1994 "real" trees frame the top and bicycles frame the bottom of our view. Red letters in Oriya script appear horizontally, directly below the picture and are partially hidden by the bicycles. On another wall of the building the achronym DAPTA, the full name of the organization and the identifier "PROJECT OFFICE" appear in English; Laxmipur, Kalahandi, the town and district names also appear in English script. Information was not available regarding who had painted the mural or on what occasion, although the photographer understood from discussion with agency personnel that the artists were local, and members of the organization; he also reported that on the district government building, murals had been painted depicting village-centered development and that these murals, contracted by a former prince of the district had likely influenced the Chipko mural's artists. This is the only Chipko mural I found in my research.

As I study the mural, I ask the following questions. (Further research may answer some; others may go unanswered.) For whom is the mural painted?—seemingly a different audience than the English name painted on the other wall. Oriya/Odia is probably not the first language of the tribal people who are presumably being served, or at least "awakened?" The Oriya script—does not spell out the English in Oriya script, as is often the case in double script signs. Could it be a message in Oriya language or possibly a transcription of an Adavasi or Tribal language? Why is the achronym in English script?

Are the women in the mural from Orissa/Odisha or women from the Himalayan foothills? The fact that they are wearing saris and in one case a sari worn shorter in the Orissan/Odishan village style suggests that they are local. Also, their hairstyles appear to be Orissan/Odishan, and the men's dress also resembles Orissan/Odishan village styles. There are hills in the background of the picture; I wonder if these are Orissan/Odishan hills or represent the Himalayan foothills where the tree-hugging movement originated. There are trees, bushes, and grasses in the picture; the colors and textures blend in the photo with the "real" foliage surrounding the building; does this tell us the mural is set in Orissa/Odisha? If it is a local setting, is it promoting future events or depicting history of a movement happening in Kalahandi? There is no question in this mural but that the women hold the trees and the men the axes; does this suggest that in Orissa/Odisha, the gender divisions are the same as Shiva suggests they are in the Himalaya? Where are the fewer forest-supporting men whom some have called movement leaders? Or runners? Is the Orissan/Odishan movement more of a woman's movement? Or is the picture merely showing the perspective of the artists and their desire to inspire local tribal and poor people, women, in particular, to resistance? Or are we only learning that the muralist(s) and those who work with DAPTA believe that Chipko is a women's movement? I ask these questions because they seem important to consider in interpreting the mural, but also because they have parallels in the debates that have taken place in academic and activist circles concerning the Chipko movement itself.

9.2 *Yatra (The Journey):* Onward From Uttarkhand

> We walked ... to the flat area where so many 'seditious' speeches had been made against the British when Shimla was still their summer capital .... Even her presence, at the very place where so many speeches had been made and morchas begun, was strong .... Two and a half million tonnes of apples were produced per annum. Packing cases for the apple crop came from forest timber. The Kulu Valley, once a picturesque sea of deodars 150 feet in height and 10 feet in girth, was now almost bare.
>
> report of Krishna's speech in *Yatra (The Journey)*[211]

> The fascination of post-colonial writers ... with the map topos can be seen in this context as a specific instance of creative revisionism in which the desystematization of a narrowly defined and demarcated "cartographic" space allows for a culturally and historically located critique of colonial discourse, while at the same time, producing the momentum for a projection and exploration of "new territories" outlawed or neglected by dominant discourses which previously operated in the colonial, but continue to operate in modified or transposed forms in the post-colonial .... The "cartographic connection" can therefore be considered to provide that provisional link which joins the contestatory theories of post-structuralism and post-colonialism in the pursuit of social and cultural change.
>
> Graham Huggan

211 Sibal's italics illuminate English as the "foreign" language.

Not unlike Mira Behn and Sarala Behn, Krishna Kaur, a central protagonist in Nina Sibal's *Yatra (The Journey)*, arrived from outside of the Uttarkhand,[212] but recognized the significance of the local people's model in people-forest relations. The synopsis of *Yatra* is laden with geopolitical significance and personal symbol is usually linked to the political in a post/modernist style that evokes comparison to Salman Rushdie's writing, especially *Midnight's Children*. Krishna Kaur, daughter of a Greek mother and an Indian Sikh father is the central protagonist surrounded, in a nonchronological text, by her past relatives' navigations through their political geographies that crisscross Northern India. The genealogy begins in 1849 after the annexation of the previously Sikh-governed Punjab, by the British. However, the book ends in the same year it opens—in 1984, just before the Indian army in Operation Bluestar, ordered by Indira Gandhi, attacked the Golden Temple where Sikh opposition was barricaded.[213] This took place in Amritsar, which is centrally located in juxtaposition to the three journeys, although not precisely on the path of any of them. While Sibal does not narrate the subsequent years of oppression, revolt, and communal violence that the Punjab has endured, she does give her readers a history of events leading up to the violent, and possibly irresolvable, situation. The Chipko Movement, unlike other political discourses of the time, such as Sikh nationalism, is a struggle with which Krishna can identify; she builds upon it in the development of her own environmental politics. Krishna's decision for environmentally based politics, over nationalist based movements in North India is significant. This may be a more attractive decision to women, or it could be a means in the novel to demonstrate the environmental justice movement's ability to cross the boundaries of political factionalism.

Krishna embarks on a pilgrimage for environmental justice that is central to her socio-political and personal development and her understanding of oppositional consciousness. At the beginning of the book, Krishna's journey is shown on Survey of India Maps that bear a 1987 copyright by the Indian government. These maps show, not only Krishna's *padyatra* (footmarch), but also the demarcations of the nation states of India, Nepal, Tibet,[214] China, Afghanistan, and

212 Uttarkhand is the region in which Chipko demonstrations occurred in the 1970s; I use the name here to mark a cornerstone in the building of the Indian grassroots environment movement.

213 My appreciation to Vik Bahl for the observation of the relationship between the timing of the frame of the novel and Operation Bluestar.

214 No line demarcates Tibet from China; this evokes Tibet's tenuous hold on nationhood. Eliding the line of demarcation marks China's intrusion on Tibet's rights to self-determination.

Pakistan. Thus, readers encounter the scars of partition that mark the subsequent narrative before they encounter the narrative that illuminates this history and its relationship to environmental justice. The maps show that the pilgrimage toward environmental justice is visually contained by international and national boundaries. The map also juxtaposes Krishna's pilgrimage with the yatra, or journey of her ancestors who fled religious persecution, and the journey of her brother and uncle, who are involved in post-independence political movements.

Krishna's journey, through the area where the Chipko Movement is active in community-based protests and projects, begins in Poonch. Krishna chooses the town, "her only personal decision" on the trip; Krishna's choice of the place of departure is "a personal tribute 'to women pressing out against envelopes which hold them'" (155–156). Sibal tells a story of individuals but stresses the communities with which they identify and function; this emphasis is revealed in the form as well as the content in this section, which is written collaboratively by the women on the Padyatra. Such community-based values reflect a lived reality of many of the actors in the environmental justice narratives; yet, as has been demonstrated repeatedly in Part One, these women also engage in critique and reform within their own communities, as well as demanding change from outsiders.

Poonch was the town in which Krishna's "father had been stationed ... during the Kashmir action in 1948,[215] and in the history of women in her family someone called Kailash Kaur was connected with Poonch" (155). A history of the land and the family is interwoven and marked geographically. The pilgrimage ends as the activists stage a successful demonstration to call a halt to an auction for lumber development in the town where Krishna's parents and son live. Thus, her Himalayan pilgrimage is further contextualized, both socio-historically and in terms of Krishna's family history.

Krishna's yatra is initially a journey in search of belonging. The path towards her goal is marked through the stories of her family and ancestors, but it is through sexual and political self-actualization that Krishna reaches the feeling of belonging for which she has been searching. We are told that "Krishna

---

This nuance seems ironic even ludicrous considering "no border" stances reflecting progressive politics on the U.S. México border.

215 Krishna's father was part of the Indian military's movement into Kashmir after Maharajah Hari Singh acceded Kashmir to India in October 1947. Singh was Hindu, but Kashmir had a majority Muslim population; therefore, the decision of accession to India, or to Pakistan, was difficult. His decision was preceded by a large invasion from the North West Frontier Province (Sibal 323).

had now received the secret of *angwaltha* from the *Chipko* women, their spirit of love reaching her as she walked through the *Deva Bhumi* of Uttarkhand on her *padyatra*. And from Ranjit [her lover], who had connected her to a passion for living" (italics, Sibal's, 168). In so doing, she demonstrates her alignment with a contemporary women's movement that strives to move beyond the patriarchal anti-sexuality (and especially anti-female sexuality) stances that held in earlier Gandhian-influenced liberation movements. Her *Bildungsroman* culminates in her discovery of a sense of "belonging" in the sociopolitical fold surrounding the forest-based activism through a coalescence of political and personal factors.[216]

The inspiration Krishna takes from the Chipko women, is, at its foundation, abstract and personal, but it is materialized, politically, in her alliance with their environmental concerns. She is a cosmopolitan, politically connected woman, and her relationship with the Chipko women and her subsequent actions in support of their struggle, could be a blueprint for coalition between academic and grassroots activists, but in the novel, it is left at a spiritual level. Likewise, Krishna's heterosexual relationship with Ranjit appears to be an exemplary relationship in terms of establishing and expressing female sexuality as crucial, though one might cringe when the woman protagonist's "passion for living" comes from a man.[217]

Perhaps the dialectics of gender and class consciousness here are synthesized materially for Krishna in her imbalanced skin pigmentation. This narrative of negotiating social identities is told figuratively in the stabilization of her skin color, which through the novel is a source of consternation and unsettled feelings, first for Krishna's mother, and then for Krishna herself. Krishna's skin has darkened since the time of her birth, when her white skin suggested that her paternity was wholly Greek.[218] However, she darkens, erratically, in patches that emerge in relation to political events in India's history; thus, she embodies, but is also protected from, Indian history that is radiated through her skin. As Vik Bahl observes, "[t]he trope of skin is crucial because it signifies the claiming of

216 The title of Salini Gupta's article, "*Yatra:* Nina Sibal: A Rites of Passage *Bildungsroman*" in *The Commonwealth Review* suggests that *Yatra* is a Bildungsroman.

217 Other Indian women artists, writers, and filmmakers have explored women's sexuality, focusing particularly on lesbian sexuality, more extensively than Sibal does here. For instance, see Pratiba Parmar's films, especially *Khush*, and *Fire*.

218 This could have been possible because, although Krishna's mother, who is Greek, is married to an Indian officer, she had an affair with a Greek shipping owner in Bombay.

Krishna by India as well as the claiming of India by Krishna through the appropriation of significant family narratives" (6).[219]

Like Ana Castillo's novels, Nina Sibal's is not written in linear time; and like Castillo's, Sibal's writing has also been called marvelous realism (Rajan 85). As in Castillo's writing, that marvelous realism often has parallels in "real" life. The novel begins with Krishna's return to India from an activist-business trip to London: "[h]er short visit had been useful in terms of the contact she had made in the Forestry Commission. And an international environmental foundation had committed funds for an important river project in the Gharwal Hills" (1). But environmental concerns are rarely mentioned for the next 154 pages. At that midway point in the 300+ page text, readers are given a narration of Krishna's *padyatra* that is described as a "*report from notes kept by four of us who accompanied Krishnaji from the very beginning, right through the* padyatra" (italics, Sibal's) (155). Thus, the central chapter differs from the rest of the book in that it has collaborative narrators who are identified as characters participating in the pilgrimage while the text that frames this central portion is narrated omnisciently or by single narrators-characters. Thereby, the structure of the novel underscores the textual importance of Krishna's *padyatra*, the sense of it as a collaboration, and its relation to the journeys undertaken before and after the *padyatra*. The novel then begins to foreground gender issues in the Chipko Movement:

> After all, at its heart, the Chipko Movement is very feminist. It consists essentially of a string of spontaneous confrontations, triggered and managed by women of the region, in which none of the so-called leaders were present. In some cases, they were struggling against their own men who saw their immediate economic interests tied up with the decisions of the district administration. In Dungari-Paitoli, for example, the battle was so bitter that it set wife against husband and mother against son. Their men sold off the forest, its destruction would have meant the women walking at least another five kilometres every day to fetch fuel and fodder. The women won and saved the forest … (italics, Sibal's). (156)

This assessment of gender politics linked to environmental concerns and based on both social and biological differences in the experience of environmental degradation in the Chipko Movement is aligned with Vandana Shiva, Jawahara K. Saidullah and many others who have written about the movement. Thus, Nina Sibal writes against the descriptions, largely by men, that efface women's strong presence in the movement (*The Unquiet Woods* is an early example.) The

219 Colleague's scholarship shared (mid-1990s).

Chipko Movement is at the heart of this feminist novel, at least in a figurative sense, although the description of the "real" movement is sketchy in the fictional account. The novel repeatedly parallels the media and academic reports of Chipko organizing. For instance, other accounts of the Chipko Movement suggest a parallel in the self-empowerment through political involvement that Krishna experiences, and that is described as common among Chicanas, particularly the Mothers of East L.A. Jawahara K. Saidullah discusses women's empowerment in her travel narrative based on ethnographic research. She observes that, "[w]ith pride and self-empowerment comes on added burden. In addition to their duties at home, in the fields and forests, the women now spend time and energy saving the forests" (40).[220] Likewise, Krishna takes on a political agenda to support the local people in their struggle to protect the environment.

When *Yatra* is read as a *bildungsroman*, Krishna politically transforms the development of ethical subjectivity that is traditional to the genre by positing, not only a transformation of self, in relation to society, but also an alternative map for re-modeling the social structure in which she works. Here, Krishna begins to establish what Gayatri Spivak has termed "ethical singularity" (1995 xxv) in her political and personal encounters. Krishna's personal subjectivity is tied into a group project. Having taken on the task of creating alternative paths that lead away from neocolonial domination she, like Ana Castillo's character Sophia, in *So Far From God*, is involved in integrating women's empowerment with a traditional cultural discourse. While the women of Chipko are her models, others take her for their model when they join the *padyatra*.

Those who undertake the *padyatra* appear to be primarily urban, probably middle-class women; the narrators report that the group was made up of "*independent social activists who performed the whole* padyatra *without help from any organization or establishment*" (italics, Sibal's) (155). The report of their journey can be read as travel narrative, or as political journal imbedded within fiction; most distinctive is that it is a communal project. The narrators reveal little about themselves directly, except in their descriptions of their leader, Krishna Kaur. Initially, Krishna takes an outsider position in comparison to the communities

---

220 In a study in the Canadian contexts of ecofeminist/environmental activists, Cherylin points out the negative effects (especially on their health) reported by women taking on environmental issues in addition to their other roles and suggests that we miss this downside when women's "caring" is celebrated uncritically (Colleague's sharing: May 13, 2000, Ecological Conversations Workshop, Oregon House, Oregon).

she is walking through. When she does speak at local gatherings, she posits the Chipko women as central; she says she's doing "*[n]othing new. The* Chipko *women had begun the new thing already*" (italics, Sibal's) (155). As she arrives in Simla, the town that was once the British capital, but also the site of strong resistance against the British, Krishna's convictions develop a more active public momentum. As she traverses the area in Uttarkhand where the local women have been active and the three chief incidents of Chipko took place (164), Krishna becomes increasingly less reticent to speak. She has found something to which she feels she belongs and can actively contribute; thus, like Sophia in *So Far From God*, she finds the will to actively promote resistance. She takes on the task of campaigning tirelessly to save the forests from outside development. At this point, her activities, like Sophia's, in her cooperative campaigns, suggest attributes of Spivak's "new type of responsibility for the cultural worker" (IM xxvi).

The *padyatra* enacts a pedagogy of appropriate education and self-initiated/directed learning for its participants and—in a different manner—to its audiences. As the "foot-march" itself stops at the sites of recent environmental justice struggles and earlier resistance against British colonialism, it gives those who participate a radical education. For instance, Krishna's speech, quoted in the epigraph, is given on the very speaking grounds of the oppositional forces in Shimla, the British summer capital. The replacement of the white British male officer with the Indian woman environmental justice activist marks a shift to an optimist model rarely fully enacted in post-colonial contexts. The march serves as a channel for educational dissemination of information, and developing oppositional consciousness, and for spreading news of crises and resistance to the villages through which the women walked. Local and global links are thereby underscored in the narrative. The marchers are met by journalists and politicians, tourists, and well-wishers wherever they stop. Those who greet the pilgrimage, especially the journalists—who are reporting on their journey—spread their message even further (163). While they may not be involved in local politics, the tourists will likely carry the messages of the Chipko Pilgrimage out of the Himalayas with them. Given that Krishna sees the need for a global change in attitude and given that the environmental damage is being caused primarily by outsiders, the journalists' roles, in enhancing the dissemination of information, are important.

Like the people in *So Far From God* who transform the Stations of the Cross ritual utilizing Mexican Catholic tradition for more "material" political ends, Sibal relates the story of Amrita Devi and thereby reminds her fellow activists of the model of the mythic woman who first "hugged" the trees to protect them, hundreds of years ago. The myth serves as a creative source of political action for the Chipko Movement that has built its demonstrations and its name on that myth. Sibal's portrayal of Amrita Devi is brief, but important, in that it lays out a folk-legend-based precedence in protecting the forest, "by any means necessary," including, if called for, the sacrifice of their own lives. Krishna tells her audience:

> I will end with a small story. In the year 1730, a *saka* was offered by a band of Vishnois of Khejadli village in Jodhpur, Rajasthan, when their forest was invaded. They were led by Amrita Devi. She tied the first sacred thread round a tree and offered her head, saying that it was too cheap for the price of a tree. Three hundred and sixty-three men and women hugged the trees to save them, and they were hacked to death. (158)

In a related sense, albeit to a lesser extent, her followers mythologize Krishna who is known as "the woman of the trees" (163). The book ends with her hesitant acceptance of the invitation to engage in party politics as a means toward promotion of a green justice in her country. Sibal's use of fiction as a "creative source of political action" suggests a parallel to the movement's utilization of myth, as depicted in fiction and in other poetics.

Further use of a fictive polemic to support a cause lies in Sibal's description of local organizing. In the novel, the gendered struggle spreads beyond the Chipko context. Readers learn that "[v]oluntary organizations had put out questionnaires asking 'housewives/other women' how they felt they could contribute to protection of the environment" (163). It is significant that the questionnaire is sent out, not to "women," but to "housewives and other women." The focus of this description reverses outmoded assumptions that housewives are not politically pro-active, and it transforms the now derogatory term "housewife" into something "not domestic at all." The household becomes the seedbed for revolutionary change in the forest. This passage resurrects the nexus of (home) economics and ecology that John Cobbs' etymology describes in this book's Introduction.

The *padyatra* culminates in the coalition of the pilgrimage and the local organizing forces of students as well as voluntary organizations to campaign and demonstrate to stop a tree auction that has been scheduled "to award a contract for the felling of 20,000 trees in the Tons Division" (165). Through their local educational efforts, the people are successful in protecting the trees by shutting down the auction, promoting a ten-year ban on tree cutting, and initiating research to further understand what would go into maintaining a sustainable forest. Thus, Krishna's pilgrimage, and indeed the whole novel, weaves together personal and community discourses of resistance that build on historical events to reveal structures that provoke environmental degradation as well as patriarchal domination in both political and personal realms. Sibal thereby situates the "real life" Chipko movement, its ideals, and practical and theoretical bases for organizing, into her fiction to create an ideal for "belonging" that encourages political transformation of nation and self and reconfigures a postcolonial landscape of environmental and gender issues.

10 Chicana/o Poetics: Farm Workers United Against Pesticides and City Dwellers Organized Against Toxins

> Subaltern or subordinate knowledges are composed not only of philosophies that have been assigned a non disruptive place but also of ones that are unrecognizable according to institutionalized systems of meaning. Hence, even though subaltern groups "think" according to the terms of hegemonic discourse, their philosophy manifests itself in the contradiction between thought and action. Rather than being at the forefront of social change academic knowledge lags behind—which is why Gramsci insists that theory not be separated from politics.
>
> Jenny Sharpe (16)

> If God made man in his image, this certainly confuses me ...
>
> María Elena Lucas (Diary, September 20, 1983)

10.1 Chicana/o Poetics: Farm Workers United Against Pesticides: T-shirts

Among the most popular icons of the campaign against agribusiness pesticide use in the U.S. is Ester Hernandez' art piece, "Sun Mad" (1982). Originally a screen print it has been reprinted on postcards, in art books, on Hernandez's business cards, online, and even on a T-shirt; it is now in the Smithsonian Museum of American Art (SAAM).[221] In "Sun Mad," the Sun Maid raisin "maiden" from the raisin boxes has been transposed into a Mexican calavera, reminiscent both of personal/community commemorations of Dia de los Muertos and the political satires of José Guadalupe Posada. The words read "Sun Mad Raisins unnaturally grown with insecticides, miticides, herbicides and fungicides." The image, engages both a pop art tradition and a protest art tradition, with which much Chicano Art, was, and to a lesser extent, continues to be invested. The bright colors are striking on the black T-shirt, and the image is invariably the

221 The SAAM offers the following description online: "In 'Sun Mad,' Hernandez reconfigures the cheerful branding of the Sun-Maid raisin company into a grim warning. In response to her family's exposure to polluted water and pesticides in California's San Joaquin Valley, Hernandez sought to unmask the 'wholesome figures of agribusiness,' such as the Sun Maid. The skeletal figure draws attention to the dangers and adverse effects of the various chemicals listed in the print's lower register." See https://artsandculture.google.com/asset/sun-mad/twG1wEMd-MNBdQ?hl=en.

https://doi.org/10.1515/9783111041575-011

most talked about in class sessions and workshops on environmental justice visual art.[222]

"Trabajando La Tierra" is the title that frames the upper right corner of a T-shirt produced by the United Farm Workers (UFW).[223] The people working the land are stooped over hoeing around small plants. They wear long-sleeved white shirts, hats or scarves and have handkerchiefs through which to breathe. Above them, and ignoring their presence in the field, a crop duster sprays a white mist of pesticide. The background of this painting is an orange red—sunset, fire, holocaust; the same color has been used for a similar doomsday effect by those producing Bhopal's visual iconography. This t-shirt painting also uses many of the same symbols of pesticide poisoning that occur in Bhopal work—the toiling farmworker and the hovering crop-duster. Hence, one begins to recognize these as iconography of a certain aspect of a larger movement; the widespread symbols demonstrate the universality of the threats and the parallels in the effects of toxic substances, as well as similar trends in the cultures of resistance that are developing in much of the world. The relationship between pesticide abuse in agriculture and the risks of pesticide production, especially in the "third world" evokes the historical link between domestic/civilian-use toxins, such as pesticides, and their predecessors produced for war.

Such T-shirts are an important means of communicating environmental justice messages, especially for predominantly Chicana/o groups. The PODER t-shirt offers a case in point; the shirt sports three children from Govalle, the East Austin neighborhood that contained an oil tank farm with facilities belonging to five oil companies. The shirt reads simply, "Save the Children: Close the Toxic Tank Farm."

The tank farm t-shirt's message "save the children" is often repeated in Chicano ecojustice poetics, a poetics suggesting that one of the most consistent concerns of environmental justice practitioners is an ecologically safe environment for the upcoming generation. PODER mission statement T-shirt, mentioned in this book's introduction, sports a globe on the front of it, thus suggesting that the world is at stake in their struggle and the universal importance of promoting environmental justice. Videos, too, address the universal and local

---

222 Some images discussed in this chapter (and other chapters) are pictured and discussed in my article, "Feminist Visual Poetics of Environmental Justice" at Women's Eco Artists Dialog: https://directory.weadartists.org/feminist-poetics-of-eco-justice.

223 The painting is not signed, and I have not found reference to an artist, but its style resembles paintings executed in support of the Bhopal Gas Victims, and their anti-pesticides stances. Search, for instance, the International Organization of Consumers Unions edition of David Weir's *The Bhopal Syndrome* (1986) to see the cover.

importance of redressing environmental issues affecting farm worker communities. The United Farm Workers (UFW) videos *Wrath of Grapes* and *No Grapes* provide further examples of the universal importance of children in the iconography of the movement. Examining farm worker poetics, including videos, music, fiction, drama, and testimonio, we can better understand the concern for children's health and other environmental justice-related issues, with which farm workers in the U.S. contend.

10.2 Chicana/o Poetics: Farm Workers United Against Pesticides: Videos

No Grapes, (1992) a UFW-produced video, presents both vignettes in current farmworker situations and shocking statistics (300,000 farmworkers are poisoned each year; eight million pounds of pesticides are used annually on U.S. grapes alone, one third of them known to be carcinogenic). Life (and death) stories, mostly of farmworker children who are dying due to pesticide exposure as a side effect of their families' professions, are told in painful-to-watch soundbites that punctuate the short video, between quotes from celebrities like Martin Sheen, Edward James Olmos, and Emilio Estevez. The title, in its concise, clear call to join a boycott is indicative of much of the language of the film. Phrases like "Don't use the future generations as guinea pigs" and Lind Langdil's plaintive plea to "Love you children enough to boycott grapes" have the memorable aspect of commercial advertising, but the message is an anti-commercial. Videos are available from UFW offices free of charge to those who will show them as an educational tool for the public. At the end, the video tells how to obtain a copy to help publicize the effects of pesticides used by growers and the need for support of the rights of Farm Workers. *No Grapes* has produced resources for a spawning ground between popular Chicano culture and public service announcement geared at grassroots boycott organizing. A musical example is Doctor Loco's audio recording entitled *Movimiento Music*; the cassette recording creates a music video that publicizes the Farm Worker grape boycott, through direct audio footage from *No Grapes* with the song "el picket sign."

No Grapes and its forerunner, *Grapes of Wrath* (1986), share footage of many scenes including fields being sprayed by crop dusters, pesticide-affected children and the testament and mandates of celebrities: don't eat grapes. The videos are both geared toward consumers whose actions make or break the grape boycott. The videos were made to gain support for the grape boycott that was undertaken to ban growers' use of several particularly toxic pesticides, rather than to gather farm workers as union members. They are venues by which farm workers whose families have been attacked by pesticide poisoning may confront consumers with the facts of the most deleterious results of an industry that the consumer is buying into. The majority of testimonios in both videos are farm worker women whose children have birth defects or cancers. Like in other environmental justice contexts, the role of mothering is politicized in these videos.

The tears of the women whose children became ill because of their mothers' labor in poisoned fields are made public, publicized.[224] As viewers we are in the homes of the families that are speaking out, and we view what are arguably very personal, private tragedies. The women who choose to speak do so for the public good—so that what has happened to them can be prevented for others. Some of the women indicate the guilt (as well as the powerlessness) they feel in what has happened to their children. As they speak, their personal guilt is not only shared on film. With the knowledge of the ramifications of the farm work the silent consumer becomes an accomplice and the personal guilt is transformed into a societal accountability.

No Grapes is clear about the consumers' role, and thereby puts forth a proactive agenda for the viewer disturbed by the video images. The jacket tells readers that "[i]n small farming communities across California, children are dying ... The cause: the 8 million pounds of unnecessary toxic pesticides used on table grapes each year ... But we as consumers can fight back ... Cesar Chavez and a host of celebrities, farmworkers, and parents show us how in this must-see video." The film is both a summons and a crusade publicized by celebrities; it is a declaration of war—the UFW's bandstand and battle is the boycott, and the reason is pressing—children's lives are at stake.

The title *Wrath of Grapes* bears literary allusions rather than the staccato slogan of *No Grapes*. The video's purpose and information are much the same as *No Grapes*; the differences in tone, format and style may simply reflect editing for a different decade. A few of the child stars include Juan Chabolla who died from cancer; Salvador De Anda, who developed inoperable cancer at 4 years of age; Amalia who was born with a piece of her spine missing (her mother worked in the fields during the first months of pregnancy); Filipe—born without legs and arms; and Ramona, poisoned by captan. Not only do the farm worker chil-

---

224 In the videos and other cultural production, the suggestion has been that the poison is transferred from mother to child in utero, through breast milk, through residue on produce, and through toxins brought home from the surrounding environment. Given documentation of Gulf War Veterans, both male and female, whose civilian families have become ill from exposure to the substance the man was exposed to at an earlier time, a new precedence is set. Some of the poisonous effects of pesticides, to which children are most vulnerable, may happen through exposure routes that have not yet been determined.

dren whose families are directly exposed at work suffer—pesticides seep into the ground water (and thus the drinking water) in cancer cluster towns like Fowler, Earlimart and McFarland. While the narratives are the most compelling aspects, the videos rely on statistics to warrant the stories, an iconography developed over several decades, and celebrities' voices to lend weight to the cause. The final listing of the names of the child victims (expanded in the second video) clinches the solemnity of the imperative to support the farmworkers' crusade against pesticides, and for healthful and fair working conditions.

Safe Food & Justice for All made by UFW Volunteer Staff in 1991 stars, among others, Martin Sheen who has offered support for the farmworkers on many occasions; Dr. Marian Moses, who works to protect the health of farmworkers is interviewed. The film presents UFW demands for the suspension of use of five of the most dangerous chemicals sprayed in the fields. César Chávez explains that risks are present for the unsuspecting consumer as well as the poor workforce. Like the *Grapes* videos, the film ends with a list of names of those children who have died because of pesticides.

Another aspect of the relation between children and environmental justice, found repeatedly in environmental justice imagery, draws attention to the role of childrearing in tandem with environmentally just protection of communities. One of the best testaments to childrearing as an occupation that lends itself well—both symbolically and empirically—to environmental justice organizing may come when it works across genders and in nontraditional settings. *Homenaje A Cesar Chavez*, which offers a good video synopsis of the UFW, reports that Cesar Chavez and his wife, Helen Fabela, had an arrangement in the early days of the movement in which she worked in the fields while he combined care for their eight children with his organizing work.

The video *Fighting For Our Lives*[225] presents UFW history that provides a context for the development of contemporaneous poetics. For example, a "Don't Eat Grapes" poster with bunch of grapes represented as a skull from the early seventies prefigures the iconography used today to popularize the danger of the pesticides on grapes. Musicians of color such as Joan Baez, who went to every major U.S. city to publicize farmworker strikes and lettuce and grape boycotts by speaking and singing songs such as *Deportee*, and Taj Mahal, who, on *Fighting For Our Lives* performs for a farm worker Mass, lent support from early on. Mexicano and other Latino musical groups such as Los Terribles del Norte performing "El Deportado" are common on farmworker videos. Photography and video, as well as organizers' narratives from the sixties and seventies show

225 See https://www.imdb.com/title/tt0072982/ for the 1975 documentary film site.

that cultural icons such as Virgen de Guadalupe banners and Mexican flags have been used by farmworkers for decades.

In the 2021 documentary film, *A Song for Cesar*, filmmaker Abel Sanchez and film editor, Andres Alegria, both activists, compile the music and art of the Farmworkers movement with interviews with the people who were part of the movement, bringing the legacy of the movement's people, stories, and expressive networking processes to a 21st Century audience. The documentary was made under the "direct orders" of Maya Angelou who, upon hearing the six-minute piece in tribute to Cesar in 2004, said it must be a documentary. Her testimonial makes the important point that movement art and Cesar and the farmworkers' stories are a universal legacy: "I can't wait for it to be in the clear possession of everybody, Black, and White, Latino, and Asian, Native American, all of us we should have it."[226]

Such cultural iconography melds the political, spiritual, linguistic, and cultural aspects of a heritage; songs such as "El Deportado"/"El Deportee" present the narratives of struggle that are enmeshed in the cultural history of "La Raza." Most farmworkers' situations have consistently been tied to their status as immigrants. *Nuestra Lucha: Our Struggle for Justice*, a video produced by PCUN which describes the situation for farmworkers in Washington state who pick tulips, berries, and other northwestern crops describes a phenomenon that is common for undocumented farmworkers as well as other undocumented workers in factories and service industries. Cepriano Ferrel, PCUN president, explains that labor contractors would not pay workers and then threaten to call La Migra if the workers would file wage claims. The video cites a 1989 study that showed that 50% of the workers were not making minimum wage; the estimate is that workers are underpaid a total of over $2 million a year. Immigrant communities, and particularly immigrant workers, are vulnerable to environmental racism practiced by industry for precisely the same reason they are cheated on wages—the threat of deportation or denial of continued legal status can be held against the immigrants' demands for a healthful, affordable working and living environment.

Another video presents the profundity of these immigrants' dilemmas through the camerawork as well as the content. The narrator speaks to "Maria Gonzalez" who has been working for many years at wages she considers "an abuse." The camera never shows "Maria's" face of but rather focuses on her hands and on her little girl as the girl puts away a rack of dishes in their kitchen. "Maria" explains how the work demands increase and yet there is little organiz-

226 See https://songforcesar.com/.

ing among workers because to say anything is risky—people are afraid of being laid off or fired or worse—the INS has come to the nursery where she works. She has three girls to take care of and so cannot see herself joining farmworkers who demand justice—not as long as growers beat, fire, kill, retaliate. The English voiceover disguises so-called Maria's voice as she tells her story in Spanish. For her, to say anything face to face with her video audience, is too risky, but the views of her hands—working hands, wringing hands, hands holding her child—and the absence of her face, based on her fear, makes her message even more compelling and powerful.

Over the years, several videos on the farmworking conditions, the infringement of farmworker rights, and environmental hazards of migrant farm work have been produced by farm worker support organizations, consumer interest groups, progressive, and Spanish-language and even mainstream media. Most have been produced in English with voice overs for Spanish-speakers but a few such as *Mama Porque Me Muerto?* are produced in Spanish with voice overs for English interviews. As the title indicates the video revolves around the story of a young child with a cancer that the family believes was caused by pesticide-contaminated groundwater.

The farm worker organizations have repeatedly used news media to publicize their issues and to encourage support, further education on farmworker issues, and boycotts to influence growers. The relationship with media, as for most environmental justice groups, and indeed many social movements, runs the gamut from a supportive polemic on the part of some progressive and Spanish-language media to ignoring or misrepresentation, often by the mainstream. The UFW and other organizations use good coverage as publicity and attempt, when possible, to increase coverage of key issues through press conferences and similar strategies. Although it is beyond the sphere of this study, the relationship of media to pesticide issues and farmworker resistance is important research that might aid both activist and scholar. UFW calls for support have also gone out on the Internet, especially in listservs that publicize immigrant issues.

In the extraordinary long-term decades of organizing that these organizations have accomplished (and which will be described further by María Elena Lucas), women have, from the beginning, been key players. While only later achieving the monumental status of Cesar Chavez (and understanding that this fact would require, most importantly, an extensive gender analysis) Dolores Huerta is a familiar name to anyone who has followed progressive media, not to mention the UFW's development, over the years. She was a co-founder of the National Farmworkers Association which, after merging with the Agricultural

Workers Organizing Committee, became the UFW Union and she has become well known outside of UFW supporter circles. In the mid 1990s, her photo appeared on a marquee poster in the New York subway system, among several Latinas pictured on a wall of posters and nearly three decades later, in her 90s, now, she continues to be an active, influential Chicana spokesperson on human rights issues and political campaigns.[227] Like women in the Narmada and Bhopal demonstrations, Dolores Huerta has suffered at the hands of the police.

Especially on the pesticide issue, Dolores Huerta, and other women in the UFW, FLOC, the Farmworker Justice Fund, Inc., the National Farmworker Ministry, and other farmworker support organizations have increasingly taken the lead. Rebecca Flores, director of the Texas UFW chapter, and later vice president of the national organization is one example. María Elena Lucas, whose testimonio I study, is another. Another example is Dr. Marion Moses, whose work has been of vital importance not only to understanding the effects of pesticide poisoning, but to the dispersal of knowledge among workers. She has appeared on numerous radio programs and videos to explain in laypeople's terms how pesticides affect the human body, and she has written numerous documents concerning pesticide dangers. Most interesting to my study because it is one of the few texts written for farm workers themselves is *Harvest of Sorrows/Dolorosa Campesinos y Pesticidas*, a two-part video and book set available in English or Spanish, illustrated by Vincent Perez and published by Pesticide Education Center in 1992. The video narrates the story of the death, by pesticide poisoning, of a 25-year-old worker, as well as the stories of older workers and children who have died of cancer or been born with birth defects. This video, unlike the UFW's grape boycott videos, is directed toward farm worker education, and explains how pesticides enter their bodies, and the ways in which farm workers can reduce the effects of pesticide exposure. The film discusses a farm worker organic cooperative in Texas and other positive changes to provide farm workers with a safer, more enfranchised future.

Farm worker organizations have produced books such as *Ministry of the Dispossessed: Learning from the Farm Worker Movement* by Pat Hoffman, buttons, bandannas and pins with the easily replicable black eagle, and canvas shopping bags with the image of Los Peregrinos to remind us, as we buy groceries, to heed the boycott and at the same time to protect the environment further

227 See her Library of Congress Library Guide, for example: https://guides.loc.gov/this-month-in-business-history/april/dolores-huerta-born. For a current film-in-the-making by Laura Varela and Anne Lewis , on Rebecca Flores, see trailer 1 for *Under the Texas Sun* on conditions for women farmworkers at: https://www.voxfem.org/rebecca-flores-short-film.

by reducing the use of plastic and paper bags. The UFW has created greeting cards and sponsored poetry contests. Numerous drawings and paintings of Cesar Chavez circulate in grassroots circles, but perhaps the most famous and impressive is one that has been made into a poster sold by the UFW. The Mexican folk artist, Octavio Ocampo, creates Cesar's image in his metamorphic style—when viewed up close, the viewer sees rows and rows of farmworkers picking produce.[228] Painted images, however, are not relegated only to canvases and posters. Painted images of the farm workers' struggles have also appeared in public art executed by acclaimed muralists such as Judy Baca and Raúl Valdez.

On April 29, 1993, at least 35,000 people marched in the funeral procession for César Chávez, demonstrating the commitment that farm workers, Chicano/as, and progressive people of all races, ethnicities and walks of life, felt for La Causa that César Chávez led for over 30 years. As Elizabeth Martínez points out in her tribute article, "Walking With César," César Chávez, unlike other leaders like Gandhi and King, to whom he has been compared, died "long after the height of the struggle he led" (21).[229] Martínez notes that "[a]t one time 17 million Americans boycotted grapes not picked by unionized farmworkers. In response, the Pentagon bought almost half a million pounds of the fruit for troops in Vietnam. But even that could not break the boycott's power and finally the growers yielded" (60).

I am not interested, here, in exploring the deleterious effects of creating individual movement stars, or the intriguing question of why such stars are so often men. But I am interested in establishing the importance of the relationship between the heroes of nonviolent resistencia/resistence—and those who worked with them, and/or were inspired by them, and went on themselves to lead struggles in environmental justice, people like Mira Behn, Sarala Behn, Dolores Huerta, María Elena Lucas, Susana Almanza of PODER, who was a Brown Beret in her youth, and the many Indian and Mexican American women and men

---

228 "Portrait of La Causa" https://chavezcenterstore.org/product/ocampos-portrait-of-la-causa-poster/ (viewed March 30, 2023) For a historical study of Judy Baca's work and SPARC, see https://escholarship.org/content/qt5hj7f3r9/qt5hj7f3r9_noSplash_f5c4353fbfffcd0008950e2cb43ea92a.pdfFor Raúl Valdez' website with mural archives, see: /www.raulvaldez.net/.

229 While not termed "environmental justice" at the time the farm workers preceded the environmental justice movement in struggles in common. A fellow proto environmental justice figure is Martin Luther King, given his support for workers' and family's rights to environmental health, the subsequent environmental justice work, by African Americans, especially in the South, Louisiana's "Cancer Alley," and in urban settings such as Chicago and NYC; his last public event offering support for the Memphis garbage collectors' struggle is often evoked to illustrate the significance of his environmental justice concern.

who've left footmarks if not inkmarks or brushstrokes, who've chanted Si, Se Puede and Embrace Our Trees.

Specific worker rights issues have changed over the years, with pesticide poisoning becoming increasingly important, as the pesticide industry has expanded. Yet, basic calls for justice remain foundationally the same. And some of the means of publicizing the cause remain consistent, as well. Such an example of cultural expression is the political button. Alliances with other organizations or institutions are represented in buttons. Such buttons show connectedness of issues that the environmental justice movement in Latina/o communities recognizes and the interest groups with whom they wish to coalition. One button sports the scientific sign for female with the Eagle inside the circle and reads "Viva La Mujer," suggesting a coalition of feminism and farm worker union support. Buttons with the eagle superimposed on the Tejas flag reads "César Chávez Presente!" In another with the drawing of Chávez (wearing a button on his shirt) the eagle and the Tejas Lone Star commemorates the 1994 12th Convención. The text on the outside reads "en tu memoria César Seguiremos Adelante." The phrase is familiar to anyone who has listened to Musica Tejana on the radio: the sentimental affection singers feel for their lovers is transferred to the political figure en memoria for César Chávez. In another love-related political alliance, the farmworker eagle is superimposed on the pink triangle adopted by gay and lesbian activists to show solidarity with the LGBT... community's call for equal rights and an end to homophobia, heterosexism and related forms of bigotry; it reads "Solidarity Boycott Grapes."

In addition to the grassroots cultural poetics such as T-shirts and buttons and the popular forms of culture such as video and música, Chicana writers—novelists, poets, testimonio collaborators and playwrights—have lent their artistry to voice the need for an ecologically safe work and home environment for farmworkers. The resulting writing combines the poignant clarity of the farmworker videos and songs with the aesthetics of Virtual Realism to produce creative texts with both a narrative and a mandate.

10.3 *Under the Feet of Jesus*

In *Under the Feet of Jesus: a novel,*[230] Helena María Viramontes shows how sentiment and collective strength develops in Estella, a young Chicana farmworker

230 "The title of the book refers to birth certificates and other important documents kept in a portable statue of Jesus that moves with the family to each new location along the agricultural production cycle." https://fyp.uoregon.edu/under-feet-jesus.

who battles poverty in league with her family, and gives support to her young novio, as he battles the life-threatening illness brought on by pesticide poisoning. Alejo, Estella's prospective novio/developing love-interest, is sprayed by a pesticide duster plane, while in a tree, picking peaches for himself; during the horrendous experience, he fleetingly thinks of the spraying as punishment for stealing. Such internalized acquiescence stands in comparison to the consciousness-raising of the United Farm Workers who distribute "white leaflets with black eagles on them" that Estella tucks away to read later because "her eyes hurt too much" (84). But it is through characters, like Estella and Alejo, who finally will not be defeated, that the Farm Workers' collective task is carried out.

Alejo does not recover from his exposure, but rather becomes weaker daily. Estella's mother takes in the young man who is across the country from his only living adult family, a grandmother, but it is the young girl who takes him into her heart. Their affection grows, but the strength of youthly attraction is paralleled by the poisonous takeover of pesticide residue in Alejo's body.

Alejo defies the stereotype of the uneducated, disenfranchised farmworker—he has an interest in geology, and the will to go to college, after a few summers of farm labor, to make further education financially feasible. Furthermore, the romance between Alejo and Estella is predicated on an intellectual, as well as an emotional, physical connection. In a tender scene, before he is too weak to work, he and Estella have found refuge from the searing sun and the hard field work by laying in the shade of one of the trucks. A leaking oil tank above them leads Alejo to tell Estella about tar pits, the source of fossil fuels. "The bones lay in the seabed for millions of years. That's how it was. Makes sense don't it, bones becoming tar oil? Estella felt Alejo's hand take hers and she could feel the wet of sweat rolling down the side of her breast" (87).

Viramontes punctuates her narrative with the details of day-to-day existence in pastoral poverty. She describes in intimate and precise renderings of the sensory awareness, through which nature gives soulful comfort, but she indicts the harsh conditions exacted by the growers from the workers in the fields. Alejo's "daño of the fields" (93) is one of the many extreme prices that the farmworkers pay in the face of their labors. Human and environmental degradation go hand in hand, dealt out callously by the growers, who care more about consumers' money than about the sustainable wellbeing of workers, or land. The extent to which the farmworkers' work-related suffering is left untreated is illustrated as Alejo's condition worsens. When, without medical treatment, Alejo's death seems eminent, Estella convinces her family to take him in their old station wagon to a town with a clinic.

It is in the clinic—where the family is most removed from their familiar outdoor domain, and where the elder generation is alienated by their lack of English language skills—that Estella most dramatically comes of age. The nurse tells them that Alejo will need to go to the hospital in Corazón, a town 20 miles away, and then she demands ten dollars for the preliminary examination she has given. Estella hands over all the money they have—nine dollars and seven cents. But, immediately after doing so, she realizes that without this money they will not have the gas to get to the hospital. The family offers to barter fix-it services in exchange for the bill and when this fails, Estella, desperate but determined, brings a crowbar into the clinic, and demands the money back. In smashing the crowbar onto the nurse's desk, she demonstrates that she has learned "their language,"—she strikes to intimidate; she commits a symbolically violent act that challenges the structural violence inherent in the agribusiness and health care industries that she is confronting.

In the car, afterward, on the way to the hospital, Alejo asks Estella if she has hurt the nurse. Estella does not answer directly, but replies, "They make you that way....You talk and talk and talk to them and they ignore you. But you pick up a crowbar and break the pictures of their children, and all of a sudden they listen real fast" (151). When Alejo becomes emotional and tells Estella "I'm not worth it, Star. Not me." Estella replies "'That's a stupid thing to say.' She forgave him because he was sick," but she tells him "*you* don't make it so easy for *them*" (153).

Under the Feet is a story of continuous struggle, struggle for the basic rights of food, shelter, and health, and struggle against those whose domination make these basic rights unattainable. Such justice struggles are consistently juxtaposed to the idiosyncrasies of nature and human relationship that give the farmworkers the strength to rise to the fight and do so with the grace and dignity that "doesn't make it easy" for the oppressors of human and natural communities.

10.4 *Heroes and Saints*

Young women, like Estella, who begin developing their consciousness for justice as children or adolescent farm workers, have long been key players in farm worker justice issues. While never having achieved the monumental status of Cesar Chavez (and understanding that this fact would require an extensive gender analysis) Dolores Huerta, United Farm Workers vice president, is a familiar name to anyone who has followed progressive media, not to mention the UFW's development, over the years. That she has become the female icon of the movement, second to Cesar Chavez, is demonstrated eloquently in Carmen Moreno's "Corrido de Dolores Huerta #39" recorded on the album *Si Se Puede!*

The song connects Huerta's identity as a woman to her successful contribution to la causa: "Su sentir de mujer/ dirigió por buen camino/ del mejor por venir/ al humilde campesino. Su sentir de mujer/ le presto a la union la fuerza/ te has ganado la flor de la paz."[231] Huerta has been with the UFW from its inception, and she is becoming increasingly known outside of UFW support circles. For instance, her photo appears on a marquee poster in the New York subway system, among several Latinas pictured on a wall of posters.

Like women in the Narmada and Bhopal demonstrations, Dolores Huerta has suffered at the hands of the police. In fact, the police beating of Dolores Huerta in San Francisco was one of the 1988 events which brought "growing visibility to the United Farm Workers' grape boycott in protest against pesticide poisoning" (Moraga 89) in response to which, Cherríe Moraga wrote the play *Heroes and Saints*. Other events that influenced the play's inception were Cesar Chavez' 36-day fast, to stop growers' pesticide ab/use and the "cancer cluster" in McFarland, California. (89).

Heroes and Saints parallels the South Asian and Chicana fiction in that environmental devastation of human community is experienced by protagonists as inseparable from ethnic, class, and gender oppression. *Heroes and Saints* dramatizes the response of a community that has become a cancer cluster in the San Fernando Valley of California. Like Sibal, Moraga patterns her description of resistance on "real life" environmental organizing—in this case, the UFW's campaign for Agribusiness Growers to halt their use of toxic pesticides. The cancer and the reproductive and infant health problems in the novel are patterned after "real life" consequences of pesticide use, and the town, McLaughlin, is a "fictional town" whose model is the "real life" town of McFarland, where Moraga traveled to research the play. Furthermore, "real life" small town conservatism and homophobia are presented as part of the broader range of social issues to be confronted in the struggle for environmental justice.

Cerezita, arguably the main protagonist in this Chicana teatro, has been literally disembodied (from birth) by the effects of pesticides used in her mothers' work and environment. Cerezita is an intelligent and attractive adolescent who, from birth, has lived without a body. Cerezita's mother uses religious fervor to cope with her trials—a deformed daughter, a dying grandchild, and the desolation of her hometown that is slowly being poisoned. She hides Cerezita from all but the family and the priest and does not allow her participation in political events. However, the mother's comadre and neighbor, Am-

231 Streaming: https://soundcloud.com/aurora-grajeda/corrido-de-dolores-huerta-39.

paro, aided by Juan (her nephew and a priest) are engaged in demonstrations of active resistance. These struggles take the form of consciousness-raising, education, and demonstrations to enact the symbolic crucifying of the bodies of children who die of pesticide-induced cancers.

On one level, Cerezita's story is a traditional coming of age story. However, in her growing up, Cerezita must not only choose her rebellion against parental norms, but she must face her own loss/difference. As a woman, she finds her life contained, both by her physical deformity, and by the deformity of her patriarchal society's mores. The two replicate each other and are at points indistinguishable. Cerezita chooses the activist life modeled by Amparo and diligently, if less perfectly, by el Padre, Juan. Her relationship with Juan, one of the few outsiders allowed to spend time with Cerezita, culminates in a sexual encounter, which is aborted, but because of Juan's ambiguity between desire and guilt, control, and tenderness, not by Cerezita's physical shortcomings. Later, Cerezita tells Juan, "All I wanted was for you to make me feel like I had a body because, the fact is, I don't. I was denied one. But for a few minutes, a few minutes before you started thinking, I felt myself full of fine flesh filled to the bones in my toes .... I miss myself. Is that so hard to understand?" (144). This scene brilliantly demonstrates the social constructedness of the limitations of difference. Cerezita's life presents an unusual parallel to the protagonist in Mahasweta Devi's story "Dhowli," which I discuss in the following chapter: Dhowli, the title character's integrity remains intact even as her body becomes her means of physical survival through prostitution.

In a very different context, but through a similar trajectory, Cerezita shows that the severe containment that is situationally forced upon her sexual expression is more about patriarchal oppression than about her own bodily hiatus. While internally prejudice based on sexuality issues pollutes the town, the outside environment, itself, exemplifies the situation of a community under siege. The play is punctuated by planes dusting fields and community with pesticides. Clean fresh water is a gift brought into the community from the outside. The reading of the names of the dead in a church service echoes the listing of the names of children who have died from toxic pesticides in the UFW's *No Grapes* video. Given this state of perpetual siege, and after the death of her infant niece from yet another case of childhood cancer, Cerezita decides to use her bodiless self as a means for political action. Her mother allows this, not through rational convincing, so much as through her own decision that Cerezita is La Virgen, holy because she is without body. The fact that Cerezita's saintliness is expressed most fully after her sexual experience with Juan (unbeknownst to others) registers the politicized irony and critically nuances the mother's religious conservatism. Cerezita is dressed as la Virgen de Guadalupe and is finally allowed out of her family's home, out into the fields where, with Father Juan, she carries out the sacred and political "crucifixion" of her dead niece, as a demonstration against pesticide use by growers.

Moraga links issues of sexuality and body to environmental health effects in another character as well. Exploration of the human body in relation to dysfunctional aspects of the society and the demise of the earth that sustains the community is expressed through the town's treatment of Cerezita's brother Mario. Mario leaves the dying town, as a gay man, a medical student who cannot find constructive personal development in the conservative atmosphere. At the end of the play, he returns to attend the wake of his niece, only to realize that his appearance to his family, as a man, himself, dying from AIDS, is too difficult. Instead of the family visit he intended, he finds voice in politicized community performance/appearance. In the play's culmination, during the "crucifixion" of Mario's young niece—who died from cancer—by the "Union of Campesinos," a helicopter passes over the solemn crowd, distributing machine-gun fire. Mario, home from the city—unbeknownst to his family—jumps up in the fields, his fist in the air, shouting "Burn the fields." Like Castillo's appraisal of Fe's consumerism, and, as we shall see in subsequent chapters, Mahasweta's evaluation of the Indian bourgeoisie, Moraga critiques community (in this case, the Mexican American community) for its narrow religious and sexual values; this critique is issued alongside her broader analysis of agro-business, its influence on the larger society, and the resulting oppressive effects on the communities of farm and agricultural industry workers.

At stake in these deadly situations is the need for community reevaluation of values. In the case of environmental demise, the community is under attack from without, and a change in the national value system is necessary for the community's environmentally healthy survival. In the case of Mario's departure, illness, and impending demise, the attack is more subtle and implicit, and is, at least partially, the community turning upon its own who are different.

As audience for these texts, we are brought face to face with the oppressive realities of environmental demise that structurally disenfranchised communities confront in daily life. Hence, the literature of environmental justice is potentially a powerful tool in mobilization that raises the conscientiousness of its readers and gives not only publicity but support to struggles taken on by communities under attack through empathetic portrayals and critical analysis. María Elena Lucas' discussion of sexuality issues, discussed in the next chapter, might serve as a first step in opening issues of sexuality in a heterocentric and homophobic community, such as Moraga's play describes.

11 A Farm Worker's Blue Cape: Testimonio and Teatro

11.1 Testimonio as Socially Engaged Literature

Testimonios have been a means for many "third world" women to describe their communities-in-struggle for outsiders, often those of "other—usually 'first'—worlds." Probably the most canonized is *I, Rigoberta Menchu,* in which Menchú, a Guatemalan K'iche' activist and 1992 Nobel Peace Prize winner, narrates the oppression and violence done to the indigenous people of Guatemala. Carolina Maria de Jesus, an Afro-Brazilian favelada and writer who exposed the unhealthy environment of the favela and the government's lack of concern for the favelado/as basic civil rights in her 1960 testimonio-like text *Quarto de Despejo* offers an earlier, distinctively different, but similarly famous example.[232] Such testimonies offer local historical narratives that chart a space of overlapping social concerns. They offer a community narrative—intrinsically tied into a personal one—of suffering as the result of environmental poisoning or destruction. These toxic events range from gaseous poisoning of neighborhoods, such as the UCC explosion in Bhopal and pesticide poisoning on the job, experienced by farmworkers in the U.S. and elsewhere, to destruction of lifestyle/lifeways, means of livelihood, land, and shelter, as has happened globally due to damming and mining projects and other corporate development. Testimonios develop strategies for resistance, education, and community empowerment that share knowledge and equitably redistribute access to empowerment. These strategies help the reader to understand the role gender plays in these movements and to understand the relationship of activist work, both practical and theoretical, to academic work—both in the areas of conflict and in the potentials for alliances. Academics have become eager consumers of testimonio texts, but finally, what have we taken with us from what we have read?

As a means of education for the "first world" reader, testimonios have proved invaluable. Although John Beverley points out the contradictions that arise when several interlocutors with their own political agendas adapt, trans-

232 Soon after publication, *Quarto de Despejo* was printed in many countries and sold record-breaking numbers of copies. It is important to point out, however, that Carolina María de Jesus' text is different from most testimonios, like Menchu's and Lucas' in that de Jesus does not see herself as representative of the favela in which she lives, and in fact, she distinguishes herself, both racially and socio-economically from those around her, who, for the most part, she sees as uneducated and uncultured.

https://doi.org/10.1515/9783111041575-012

late, and/or edit an original text, he finds positive potential in these relationships that seems to outweigh the problems in most contexts.

> ... the production of a testimonio can function as an ideological figure or ideologeme for the possibility of union of a radicalized intelligentsia and the poor and working classes of a country. To put this another way, testimonio gives voice in literature to a previously "voiceless," anonymous, collective popular-democratic subject, the pueblo or "people," but in such a way that the intellectual or professional, usually of bourgeois or petty bourgeois background, is interpolated as being part of, and dependent on, the "people" without at the same time losing his or her identity as an intellectual... (19)

Testimonio is a direct means of access to the theory and praxis of grassroots activist "Third World" women (in the "first" or "Third Worlds)." I turn now to María Elena Lucas' 1993 testimonial to investigate, from the perspective of one Chicana farmworker, the conditions that perpetuate the oppression and the organizational resistance against those conditions, in particular the fight against pesticide poisoning.[233]

11.2 Narrating Pesticide Poisoning

Forged Under the Sun/Forjada bajo el sol: the Life of María Elena Lucas is the text in which María Elena Lucas, a Chicana farmworker, documents her organizing work in the U.S. American Southwest and Upper Midwest, for the Farm Labor Organizing Committee (FLOC) and the United Farmworkers (UFW); both groups made up of predominantly farmworkers of the Americas. In addition to describing her life in testimonio form—growing up in South Texas, working in the fields and factories, and becoming politicized and involved in organizing and support work—Lucas' book includes her original creative writing, such as poetry and a play *Flor Campesina*, diary entries, and ink or pencil drawings. Much of her expressive work has served as organizing tools. That Lucas' book is mixed genre is paralleled by her public life in which she organizes performance events that range from boycotts to dance teatro; both are integrally political and cultural.

Both Lucas and Fran Leeper Buss (who transcribes and edits the testimonio and prefaces it with an introduction, consisting of "library" information on

---

233 The United Farm Workers Union's first national grape boycott in 1965 brought growers to the tables to sign major contracts with the UFW in 1970. Farm Labor Organizing Committee (FLOC) was formed in the Midwest in 1968; it conducted negotiations three-ways between farm labor unions, growers, and processors (Buss in Lucas 22).

Tejana/o farmworker history) analyze gender politics and women's leadership struggles within farmworker organizations. They explain what the farmworker videos visually document: because pesticide poisoning can interfere with healthy human reproduction, women who are exposed to toxic pesticides and their children are at particularly high risk of suffering the often-deadly consequences of this dangerous agricultural practice. Thus, in recent years the environmental justice issue of most importance to the farmworker rights struggle has been the fight to attain regulations on pesticide usage by growers. Lucas, herself, has been living with the after-effects of Sonalan poisoning, sprayed on her by an aerial crop duster.

Basic to the marginalization experienced by farmworkers is the legalized suspension of their civil rights which was put into effect by the Wagner Act. As Buss explains in her introduction to Lucas' book:

> The National Labor Relations Act (Wagner Act) passed in 1935, guaranteed United States workers the right to organize and bargain collectively. However, alarmed by the possibility of migrant labor unions, agri-business lobbied Congress and excluded farm laborers[234] from the act. Farm workers were also excluded from the Fair Labor Standards Act, which governed minimum wages and child labor, and from the Occupational Safety and Health Act, set up to maintain health and safety in the workplace. (Buss 14)

When she learned of these legal exclusions of rights, Lucas understood the brutal and racist implications of these "legal" acts, ratified by her years of lived experience, and she describes her feelings of outrage. After Olgha Sierra Sandman, her mentor and organizer colleague, explained the labor law to her, she wrote the following in her diary:

---

234 The argument could be made that this law's exclusion of agricultural (and domestic) workers was, in part, a precipitating factor in California's turn of the century economic crisis. As David Avalos has pointed out (Austin, 3-94), farmworkers are the labor backbone without which a $23 billion dollar a year industry (at the time) in perishable crops in California would itself parish. David Avalos along with Elizabeth Sisco and Louis Hock countered misrepresentations of undocumented workers perpetuated by state and local government, media, and business for San Diego area communities, in the late 1980's/early 1990's, in a conceptual artpiece entitled ART REBATE ARTE REEMBOLSO. As a part of the larger Border La Frontera Project, ARTE REEMBOLSO was designed to underscore the economic contributions that undocumented farmworkers made to the California economy. The artists signed $10 bills and offered them as symbolic tax rebates to undocumented workers/taxpayers. However, if farmworkers were receiving just compensation for their labor, including insured health care and education, the entire region would, theoretically benefit (under either a capitalist or a socialist economic model). That political leaders such as Pete Wilson constructed immigrant farmworkers as the downfall of the California economy is ludicrous, dangerous, and reprehensible.

> I made a dreadful discovery. I read the National Labor Relations Act that was passed in 1935. It stated that "all people have the right to organize for collective bargaining except for the farmworkers." All of a sudden, for the first time in my life, I realized what I really was, due to the law, a farmworker in bondage, a legal slave as inconspicuous as an earth worm. I laughed and laughed and laughed, and then I cried as I never did before. I felt bitter and resentful. No wonder I've never been able to eat or live decently. (Diary, April 9, 1983)

Lucas' response to her learning was rooted in her foundational analysis of the structural oppression of farmworkers passed down by her mother, who she reports in her diary, told her daughter, she was "a slave girl .... My mother told me I was a farm worker slave woman. I knew she was right, for no woman could have suffered more or worked more—Diary, July 26, 1982" (69). What she has been told as a child strikes Lucas hard when she reads about the discriminatory labor divisions legally upheld in the Wagner Act. Like in this case, most of Lucas' political identity formations come directly from other women, usually her elders. Her grandmother gives María Elena a figurative image of their self-identities as farmworkers. In reference to the transience of the farm worker's life, she offers María Elena the description of their life style informed by nature: "My grandmother would tell me we were Farm worker flowers and she would call me 'My Dandelion' because she'd say we were like Dandelions, that the wind would blow us into the drifting winds and we'd go all different directions and go land somewhere, only to start all over again.—Diary, July 20, 1984" (51).

While this might read as endearing conversation between an older woman and young girl, does it read as a symbol of resistance or transformation? It suggests a lack of autonomy, and the ability to adapt to, rather than to actively resist, oppression—dandelions are flowers, but they are most often seen as weeds. Yet, they also serve as food—sustenance and persistence; in some cultures, their role as food prevails.[235] In this context, though clearly celebrative of their nomadic survival, the description of children-farmworkers as dandelions seems conflicted. (Yet, in the 21st Century, the dandelion representing strong, precarious existence has spread.)[236]

---

235 I was reminded of this when I posted on social media a photo of early spring dandelions on a nearby street corner and received admiration and Lebanese village recipes remembered from childhood from friends—gratitude to Nadine and Imane Saliba.

236 For example, *SOME WHERE WE ARE HUMAN Authentic Voices on Migration, Survival, and New Beginnings*, edited by Ryena Grande and Sonia Guiñansaca (2022) sports dandelion blossoms on the cover; the flowers were discussed in similar terms to Lucas' story, though as representative of immigrants, by the editors in a *Fronteras* interview on TPR, June, 2023. https://www.tpr.org/podcast/fronteras/2023-06-02/fronteras-undocumented-and-formerly-undocumented-migrants-document-themselves-in-somewhere-we-are-human.

In terms of utilizing the symbol of the "pest" that will survive, as symbolic of the will of a dominated people, Oscar Zeta Acosta's use of the maligned insect trope in *Revolt of the Cockroach People* is comparable. In that the dandelion materializes a derogatory image into beautiful, Nature imagery, the dandelion image compares with the concept behind a San Antonio mural entitled "Barrio Jungle." The head muralist of this San Anto Cultural Arts project conceived of the mural as a response to those who called her community, a jungle; "People call our neighborhood a jungle. Well, I'm going to give them a jungle." [237]

María Elena's grandmother has given her granddaughter a nickname that seems the likely inspiration for artwork too—the title of Lucas' play *Flor Campesina*; as such it transforms a passive image into active resistance. Considered alongside another statement from the grandmother, the dandelion image offers a rootedness in self-knowledge and lifestyle that draws upon nature as a model and allows for self-expression against oppression. Lucas writes in her journal that "My Grandmother taught me that the fields was a place of worship where we could sing and rejoice and also where we could cry out our anger at God and nobody would care" (51).

Buss marks the effect of María's grandmother's beliefs when she summarizes what Lucas narrates.

> María Elena's deep mysticism, which informs all her actions and fuels her strength, was profoundly influenced by her grandmother's indigenous religious beliefs. María also learned the dominant Mexican folk Catholicism of her mother .... This intensely spiritual belief system taught that faith and life are one, that health comes from harmony with the environment and other people, and that manifestations of the divine ... are accessible and immediate to the most humble of people. (17)

Buss underscores the importance of these cultural belief systems in informing both María Elena's poetics and politics:

> Remnants of indigenous traditions and of the new mestizo culture that had been forged from Spanish and native backgrounds appear in the religious beliefs, folk traditions of sharing and cooperation, and the songs, stories, and prayers of María Elena's childhood. Together they form the major substance of the interpretive system from which her creative efforts and political undertakings have evolved. (17)

In her introduction, Buss further analyzes Lucas' discourse, noting that "[h]er writing was almost always disrupted so the works she created are in segments—fragments of attempts to explain and record her world and to give directions for

237 See http://www.sananto.org/9---barrio-jungle.html .

resistance" (26). In reference to Lucas' poetry, Buss cites Audre Lorde's observation that time limitations and space constraints may make poetry a more viable option for poor and working-class women than more lengthy writings would be (26). Lucas often wrote at night "with a flashlight under a blanket" (26).

Both her family and her husband's family suspect that her written creativity is the work of the devil (99). Despite this opposition, Lucas, herself, continues to relate her religion and politics in dynamic interaction, through her creativity demonstrating the fortitude with which she sustains her commitment to self-expression in politics, art, and religion. In the poem, "The White Crack in the Sky," which, she says, took her 30 years to complete, she describes the anguish she felt as a child when she heard her father declare, in despair, that "God is Dead." In the poem, she prays that her children will never see her give up hope/faith and like her father "raise [her] tight fist up in anger, to cause a white crack in the sky" (49).

For Lucas, la lucha seems intrinsically involved in a religious faith even if at points this causes ironical contradiction; the symbiotic relationship is unwavering (Austin, 4-24-94). In this she is not alone but has perhaps vocalized the relationship more extensively than other Chicana activist-writers. For example, her use of the Virgin of Guadalupe, as farmworker and organizer, is preceded by the UFW's carrying of the Virgin's banner in their marches (58). Denise Chávez notes that "Our Lady of Guadalupe is often a symbol for justice .... The cry, *Que Viva La Virgen de Guadalupe!* has heralded farm workers' strikes as well as other local and national marches." She continues,

> As *La Morenita* spoke to the *nativo,* she now speaks to the artist struggling at his craft, to the prisoner, the domestic or farm worker, the migrant worker, the politician who represents the people, to young people, to the elderly, to minorities, to people who have traditionally suffered the pain of conquest. The political and social justice dimensions of the story are crucial to many people throughout the Americas. (58)

The name "La Morenita" and the term "nativo" underscore the indigenous ancestry of La Virgen. In Chávez' explanation, there is a shift, from the nativo *of the past* to the artist, prisoner, domestic or farm worker *of the present*. However, Lucas, herself of mixed Mexican American, American Indian, and Anglo background, incorporates the perspective of the nativo/a with that of the farmworker/artist/activist, all in the present.[238]

---

238 Her father's mother was a "Yaqui or Tarahumara or Tarascan woman" (51). Her paternal grandfather was an Appalachian Anglo from Kentucky (52).

> ... When Rosamaría is attacked by the people carrying the signs of her suffering, she falls and cries to God. Then a woman comes from behind. This is Mother Mary. She's dressed as a farm worker. She wears her blue cape, but underneath she wears old pants and a shirt, old tennis shoes. She's got a scarf and a basket next to her, and she's carrying something red in her hands. Two angels wait for her where she entered so everybody can tell who she is. But Rosamaría does not see the angels. (185)

The intense visual description that Lucas offers of La Virgen in the play she writes, brings to mind Chicana artist's renditions of La Virgen de Guadalupe in various nonconventional contexts such as Ester Hernández's "La Virgen de Guadalupe Defendiendo Los Derenchos De Los Xicanos" in which La Virgen is a performing martial artist.[239] Lucas has drawn her own visual reinterpretation of La Virgen in a Christmas card entitled "Un Eco Navideño;" the Virgin of Guadalupe as farmworker stands on a globe with a basket of produce on her head. In an accompanying poem, Lucas merges her farmworker identity with that of the Virgen through their common experience with nurturing and birth: "Era María, mi cara, la suya. / En su vientre, un hijo, en mis manos, una semilla-/nace un amanecer." In the poem's conclusion, however, the relationship is predicated on a common grito: "Queda su eco, soy yo—-/su grito sale del alma mía. / Yo soy campesina!" (214). Lucas uses a communal icon of Mexican Catholicism, but the soul of her imagery is her personal experience and identity formation.

Lucas portrays her own lived experience in this dramatic scene, when she states: "In a way, Olga came to me almost like the Virgin comes to Rosamaría in my play" (185). In the message from the Virgin, the UFW symbols replace Catholic ones: the UFW banner is the Virgin's flag. Lucas' use of religion is consistently both figurative and political:

> You will find him (César Chávez)
> where the sun sets
> and the beast falls,
> where a black eagle flies in my flag.
> In the fields
> where they sing "De Colores."
> There, reigning you shall find
> Justice, Peace, God, and César Chávez.[240] (185)

---

239 Etching, 1976. Contemporary Chicana artists transpositions of such traditional images have been discussed at length by Ramón Saldívar and others.

240 Richard Chávez, in his keynote address, "The UFW Today & Tomorrow" noted, that his brother César had represented many different things to different people; to the religious, he said, César represented "righteous living," (some religious folks even felt Chávez was "close to the

Lucas explains how she uses tropes from Judeo-Christian religion in her conversations and as an explanatory tool in organizing and convincing people who share her sense of the sacred to join the cause:

> I tell them how I think that it really started way back in the beginning, that Adam and Eve were the first farm workers. But then I explain how Moses was the first activist who tried to get, how do you say it, who tried to get *un descanso para la gente*. He was the first bricklayer leader, organizer, and he asked the Pharaoh for a break for the people ...
> Then I explain what I believe about Jesus. I tell them that at first Jesus Christ organized all the people in Galilee. He taught them a different way of life. Now this is my own theory, but what I believe is that he thought and he studied and said, "What is wrong? These people now have learned a better way of living, but the situation doesn't change. They're still poor. They're still hurting." So he got the idea that *el mal*, the problem, was coming from over there with the politicians. He thought, I've already organized these people, so now I have to go to Jerusalem and start with the politicians. Then, of course, I tell the people that Jesus went to Jerusalem and fought with the politicians and died for us in the process. (298)

The play demonstrates Lucas' own political conscientização process as a blueprint for her farm worker audience. The *religious* role models, with whom the farm workers are already familiar, are put forth as *political* role models. Lucas plays the role of translator, codeswitching between religious and secular language. Near the end of the book when Lucas speculates on the future, the role of her religious understanding and framework for action in support of her politics are synthesized:

> I think that someday when I have my home or a better trailer, what I'd like to do is form a women's organization and say we're open for services. I'd also keep on organizing people in general, teaching them about the union, showing them the video about pesticides. But I'd especially like to have a place where I can invite women over and teach them about a differ-

gospel)," and to the farmworkers' "hope" (Austin 4-24-94). In her play, María Elena places César Chávez in relationship with God, Justice, and Peace, a trinity of values that builds on the Christian holy trinity. Given the endless problems that have been identified in deifying an individual leader, one might become uncomfortable with the figurative implications of this dramatic setup. However, it seems important in discussing this, to remember that Lucas does not consider Chávez to be beyond failing, as a man, and she feels comfortable in expressing her doubts about the sexist dynamics she experienced in farmworker organizing. The healthy tension between worshipful respect and constructive critique is played out on another level in a statement which weaves through her writing in the constellation of relationships between justice and religion: "I wrote to God. I fought with him... I fought with the Virgen de Guadalupe. I fought with all the holy people in heaven." It is perhaps the empowering egalitarian nature of Lucas's relationship with what she considers holy, then, that allows her to both eulogize and critique Chávez, in ways that break down the deleterious hierarchical structures upon which Christianity, like Capitalism, very often thrives at the expense of those on the bottom of such hierarchies.

> ent Christ, the kind of Christ that's an organizer, and a different *Madre de Cristo*, the kind that would come to us in our present times. Not the Mary from way back then, but the kind of mother that we need now and that would stand up for our rights and be with us. (287)

In this statement, other priorities in her organizing are clarified alongside religious ones; in particular, the pesticide issue and the lived experience of women of color, as Latina farmworkers in the U.S. and within farmworker organizations. The Madre de Cristo that Lucas describes seems reminiscent of Sophia as mayor of Tome, and as organizer of the Stations of the Cross Procession.

It is through the church that María Elena organizes outside support as well. Sometimes this involves threatening situations, but fear does not sway her. She reports that,

> What I started saying shocked people all around the state. I think I was called to the churches in practically every small rural area because especially the women, the wives of the growers, wanted to see me personally and find out what was going on. Sometimes I'd go into a small community church, and everybody would be so tense. It would seem like everybody had a rifle in their hands and was ready to go to war. But when I finished talking to them, some of them would cry and say, "we didn't know." They'd come and hug us and say, "We're glad that we heard it from you." It seemed like each place I left a sister behind. (194)

Lucas' ability to give her audience the benefit of the doubt may have allowed her message to be heard, if not heeded, by women involved in agribusiness, but, in at least one case, she realizes, too late, that she may have outdone herself in zealous outreach and inclusion.

> But one time I was in a church meeting, and this woman came up and said, "I want you to know there are Ku Klux Klan members in this community, and I've been told to tell you to lay off because they're going to pay you a visit."
> I said, "What do you mean?"
> She said, "They're very upset with what you're doing."
> I didn't know what the Klan was, so I said, "Well, tell them if they want to pay me a visit, fine. I'd be glad to talk with them." I wasn't scared until afterwards when I found out about the Klan. I learned they ... belonged to one of the churches. (195)

In a sense, Lucas' forthright response to the admonition that the clan would "pay her a visit" is, in its innocence, a brilliant strategical mechanism that offers a non-premeditated (in this case) act of nonviolent defense. The fortitude of the defense may depend, however, on a "normalized" sense of propriety among the Klan members that may or may not extend across the racist containment of Klan ideology. Could a Chicana farmworker safely invite the KKK into her home for café y pan dulce and a chat? Would the KKK be caught off guard enough to question their own motives, as appeared to be happening among church women from agricultural growers' families? Lucas' narrative begs that we consider the implications of such unlikely circumstances, because she relates successes in other—not quite—such unlikely circumstances; however, her statement "I wasn't scared until afterwards..." shows that, although she was initially ignorant of the danger of the Klan in the area, she was not naive about it. That they "belonged to one of the churches" illustrates that while the church was an important base for organization for Lucas it was not hegemonic or benign. Her roots in Mexican Catholicism gave her common points of reference with many, but not all others of differing denominations and cultures within the larger rubric of the Christian faith.

11.3 *Flor Campesina* and Pesticide Poisoning

Between a proposition (187) and an agreement (NAFTA) is a very difficult place. For the privileged corporate economic community, NAFTA has remapped U.S. Mexico border relations onto a "post-border" space. That remapped space, already a "Limited Entry Zone" for those who do not control corporate capitalism, underscores the demarcation of the U.S. border region of "Greater Mexico" as a "No Trespassing Zone" for the "undocumented" worker from the South. The passage of Proposition 187 in California and federal anti-immigrant and anti-welfare legislation that followed in 1996, and state and local legislation moves toward English only, and against immigrant and worker rights further sealed this deal. Political art and artistic politics, both Chicana/o and other, has provided alternative cartographies to that "No Trespassing Zone." The Zapatista Rebellion in Chiapas, initiated in an uprising (January 1994) timed to correspond with the inauguration of the NAFTA Agreement, is a clear example. Teatro Campesino is a long-standing example of Chicano/a response to immigrant, class, nation, and ethnicity issues in U.S. farmworker communities, begun more than a generation ago. Separate from the tradition/genre/theatrical movement initiated by Luis Valdez in the 1960s, María Elena Lucas staged Teatro Campesino actos in the 1980's in the upper Midwest. *Flor Campesina*, an acto by María Elena Lucas, farmworker and organizer, poet and playwright, involves audience participation as political action that presents, and protests, injustice to workers, often without U.S. documentation.[241] The play is included in its English version in an appendix to Lucas' testimonio.

241 While *Flor Campesina* has three acts, an unusual attribute for an acto, it is quite short, the acts resemble scenes, and the play as a whole, resembles the actos developed in earlier Teatro Campesino.

Like Ana Castillo, Lucas emphasizes religion—specifically Mexican Catholicism influenced by the Native American religion that she inherits from her grandmother—in her writing, as a channel for engaging her audiences in politics, and gender as a key point at all levels of political interaction. Thereby, she engages a common agenda with her audience, when it is composed of predominantly farmworkers, many of whom are women. Like the earlier Teatro Campesino, Lucas' teatro is performed primarily as a means of consciousness-raising among farmworkers and potentially supportive communities, such as the audiences for the UFW videos. Such works use communication and information dissemination through art to promote enfranchisement of "undocumented" communities. She challenges audiences to address discrimination and structural racism, which Latinas/os face and draws her audience from inside and beyond migrant worker communities. María Elena discusses her play, in the text of her testimonio:

> Part of my play is about all those things, the sadness and the happiness, we people in the fields went through together ....
> I tried to have the characters act like the real people I knew. In the second act, Rosemaría, her husband Miguel, their kids, and their many farmworker friends were in the field picking tomatoes. Some of them were talking and laughing and others were singing, and in the distance, you could hear the noise of an airplane.
> The airplane gets louder and it comes over the farm workers, spraying them with pesticides, and the farm workers rub their bodies with their hands trying to clean up a little, and they go back to picking. (211)

The real-life situation, as narrated in the following passage, corresponds precisely with the scene written in her play:

> One day, when I was out in the fields organizing I saw a crop-duster airplane heading at all the people, then it began spraying right directly over them. They were just dressed with flannel shirts and handkerchiefs across their faces to protect them. I got so upset I climbed up on the roof of my car and started yelling up at the airplane. I started screaming and hollering and shouting, "Hey, don't do that! They're not animals! Don't you spray on top of the people!"
> The guy in the plane must have seen me because instead of coming back, he just kept circling and circling, and finally, he took off. The people, everybody, were so submissive, so accepting, that I started hollering at several people. "Hey, don't let that guy spray you! It's dangerous."
> And one guy said, "But what can we do? They don't listen to us."
> I said, "Get out of the field."
> He said, "But, the *patrón*, he'll fire us." (227)

As with other social justice and racism issues discussed in the text, Buss, in her introduction, presents us with a description of the pesticide issue that historicizes the farmworkers' experience.

> ... since the late 1940s, the vast majority of commercial crops have been sprayed with pesticides, which are presently available in about thirty-five thousand different commercial products or formulations. Among these is the herbicide Sonalan with which María Elena was poisoned.
>
> Agricultural workers are repeatedly exposed to these toxins, resulting in such immediate effects and long-term consequences as damage to the nervous system, disorders of the skin, severe allergies, cancer, birth defects, neurobehavioral deficits, neuropsychological changes, and reproductive and fertility problems. (15)

Lucas narrates several cases of poisoning besides her own, beginning with her childhood memories of her sister's probable poisoning when she was a young working child:

> [O]nce, when we were working in the fields and she was about four, she ate something that had been in a container, then she ate some of our lunch and went back to the fields. I think she was trying to climb a tree to pick some fruit when she had an attack. She started foaming from the mouth. The doctors said it was food poisoning, but I think that the field was being sprayed and someone left the containers out there. Norma had convulsions after that. (73)

Given this history, with its beginnings in childhood, it is not surprising that Lucas identifies even the midwestern landscape with the inhumane conditions faced by the farmworkers: "It's true, Illinois is beautiful. Beautiful trees and flower farms and all kinds of vegetables. But behind every flower, fruit, or vegetable, I see a human being, doing stoop labor, taking cuttings from shrubs or trees, out in the bitter cold and snowy fields of winter.—Winter, 1991" (165). Ironically, in this description, nature itself is a signifier of abusive human labor demands, similar to the moment in Mahasweta Devi's story discussed in Chapter Twelve, when Dhowli "feels hurt, wounded by nature's indifference to her plight" (translated in Bardhan).

Lucas' descriptions detail the carelessness with which the growers use dangerous chemicals, the necessary information they fail to dispatch to the workers, and the lies the workers are told concerning the results of pesticide use on their health.

> And the workers don't know what we're doing with the chemicals. I myself was spraying chemicals, and at first, I wasn't even curious enough to worry. The chemicals came in something that looked like a butane gas tank. It was hooked onto the water system, and it would go through the water hose. Then we'd disconnect the hose from the chemical tank, let clean water run through it, then drink what we thought was clean water and use it to wash our faces ... (166)
>
> Then I saw what was happening to Don Lupito. I think he'd got the chemicals in his boot, and it was like his foot was rotting away. They told him he had leprosy, but I began to think it was the pesticides or chemicals. (166)

Like in the case of her sister's poisoning, Lucas, and presumably other farmworkers, do not believe the doctor's prognosis; given that, in addition to her experiences with them, doctors very rarely have any extensive training in the health effects of environmental toxins, and that the research has not been conducted on the health effects of many environmental toxins, Lucas' suspicions are germane. Lucas' narrative of her own nearly fatal poisoning is, not surprisingly, one of the most compelling sections of her text, not only for the drama of the life-or-death situation in which she finds herself, but also in the recognition that her near-death experience and her subsequent suffering only magnify the level of activism to which she is committed. Lucas, in simple and straightforward language, puts forth her position on the use of chemicals.

> Chemicals are bad, and we don't need a nuclear bomb to destroy us. The people that are creating these chemicals, they are destroying us, and they are so powerful. I think they've got control of everything because there's so much money involved .... With all this destruction of human beings and the earth, it's going to be too late to change it. I keep wondering how come we on the bottom can see that and they can't. These people must be super-intelligent to be able to make so much money and to be able to accomplish so much, yet there is something missing in their brains or hearts or whatever. Think what greed can do. (252)

This statement asks for our solidarity based on a somewhat abstract generalization: "Chemicals are bad." However, the fact that the tone of Lucas' language in the above statement is not cynically bitter but informed with a gentle sardonic humor ("these people must be super-intelligent ...") and an informed recognition of their disastrous shortcomings ("there must be something missing") defines her political philosophy as critically complex and deep-rooted. Simultaneously, her sarcastic comment underscores the complex role of (corporate) greed in the destruction of the earth. Lucas summarizes, in accessible language, the crux of the problem brought to bear upon those disenfranchised by environmental and economic racism, as illustrated repeatedly in the texts examined in this study.

Her words are more powerful when read in juxtaposition with the paragraph that precedes them, in her text, in which Lucas tells us about the struggle of trying to decide whether she should return to organizing after the poisoning incident, given that her doctor has told her that returning to the fields, and risking further exposure to the chemicals, is risking her own death. María Elena also writes about the physiological results of the poisoning that are also still with her: "The worst part was when I was writing everything backwards ..." (252). The very creative act that has been at the crux of her development of active political work is damaged by her poisoning, yet she continues her political work—despite setbacks and the risk of death. Her testimonio, by nature of the collaboration involved, gives Maria Elena voice she might have not had capacity for after the poisoning. After its publication, María Elena also expanded her audience when she began to speak and read poetry in academic settings.

The audience is crucial and definitive in her acto because the work promotes changes that require audience participation and assumes preconceptions and beliefs as grounds for those changes. Lucas requests political response, in terms of union involvement and support, from her audience of farmworkers and potential allies. *Flor Campesina*'s Act Three is more immediately audience-participatory: the scene is a Farmworker Convention and the play's audience represents the body of farmworkers present at the drama's conference. Thereby, she directly involves the audience in artful expressive portrayal, as well as in response.

For Lucas, artistic creation and performance was a means of addressing issues even when a "bias against women" had "prevented her from exercising her full leadership potential" (Buss 24). The audience participation her teatro, poetry and questions promote may aid in this. Utilizing religious imagery like what Cerezita's mother bestows upon her "virgin" daughter in *Heroes and Saints*, Lucas' play transforms a farmworker woman into the Virgen de Guadalupe and César Chávez into Moses. Lucas' audiences—often, other Mexican Catholic farmworkers—respond to the revamped religious icons in the portrayal of adverse working conditions and unjust compensation based on lived experience and familiar iconography.

Lucas also uses other more conventionally "depoliticized" artforms and cultural and social institutions besides religion, for progressive ends. For instance, she reports that a Mexican Folk Ballet performed at a U.S. bicentennial celebration was an assertion of Mexican nationalism, which, in this case, gained the group the respect and support of their non-Latina/o neighbors. Lucas calls their dance "[i]n some ways ... the start of my organizing." Before she knew the meaning of the word "boycott" Lucas had organized a boycott of a grocery store that was treating the farmworkers unfairly. As Lucas became more involved in farmworker organizing for social services and her folk ballet group began doing *Teatro Campesino* performances, Lucas developed questions to "get the audience in the right kind of mood."

> ... Have you ever been a farm worker in your life? If so, raise your hand .... How many people do we have from Mexico ... If our audience was middle-class but they used to be farmworkers, I'd do it another way. If they were college kids I knew most of them were studying La Causa and would have some knowledge. If they were church people I'd try to use Christian or spiritual ideas. And if they were growers, I'd hit hard. I'd say, "How many of you have ever gone out there and seen what's really happening? Have you thought about being pregnant or on your period out there in the snow and having to make a hole to go to the bathroom? (189)

Lucas uses the audience response to such questions as catalysts for disseminating information and mobilizing organization among her audience-members, even when the male leadership was not ready to allow her to organize for them on a large-scale basis. Lucas confronts growers with the lived experience of the farmworkers and demands change; *Flor Campesina* and her other performances confront all her audience members with farmworker realities and the necessity to transform these realities through a struggle for justice. What Gayatri Spivak has termed "a new type of responsibility for the cultural worker" (IOW xxvi) Lucas encourages through a link between realism and lived experience. María Elena Lucas describes this realism, citing a scene in which workers are poisoned by aerial pesticide spraying which is narrated both in the drama and the testimonio of her "real life." (211)

In the farmworker convention scene mentioned above, a farmworker/martyr presents a statement about farmworkers' justice issues to César Chávez in front of the gathered farmworkers, i.e., the play's audience. Following the list of injustices, the statement turns to resolutions. The first set of resolutions mandates a nonviolent fight against "injustices and bad laws;" the second set is a men's resolution to terminate sexism against the women within the farmworker community. Not only does Lucas present gender issues to her audience, but she also articulates women's justice issues as convention agenda and presents a model for audience members to do the same in real life conventions.

While Lucas' portrayals of lived experience encourage audience consciousness-raising through identification, *Flor Campesina* reiterates societal rituals in new contexts. Like *Flor Campesina*, the boycott calls for audience collaboration to facilitate the event's work/political action. Thus, picketing and not buying from boycotted businesses, rethinking gender relationships in political organizing, rethinking the economic, international, and environmental implications of border relationships as a community are all events that lend support to the enfranchisement of the migrant worker, undocumented, and border communities. Like other activist-artists, part of Lucas' role as a social poet is to be an "educator."

Art that educates can play a profound role in finding and breaking open schisms and fractures in structural oppression. An art performance or conceptual art piece can do this in several ways as, for instance, a means toward mobilization, as in *Flor Campesina*, or as means to establish dialogue and thus propagate new relationships, as Lucas does when she speaks and reads her poetry. Such artists' performances compare with other political performances on related issues. Lucas' teatro engages an oppositional consciousness that intervenes in the rhetoric of "performance events" sponsored by the far-right sector of the dominant culture's continuum. An overview of the political landscape of contemporaneous border performances demonstrates this relationship when White Supremacist Hate groups employ such theatrics in the Light Up the Border Campaign. Another such event, the wall constructed—presumably with taxpayer money—in bits and pieces along the Mexico-U.S. border, is portrayed as theater by Leslie Marmon Silko: "Like the pathetic multi-million-dollar 'antidrug' border surveillance balloons that were continually deflated by high winds and made only a couple of meager interceptions before they blew away, the fence along the border is a theatrical prop, a bit of pork for contractors." [242]

A related symbolic event is revealed when we consider the intents behind Proposition 187; Prop 187 was largely unconstitutional and court cases against sections of it were launched within hours of its passing. While despite those court injunctions, ramifications of the proposition resulted in vigilante enforcement, the proposition has a figurative impulse that goes beyond its effects on individual immigrants' lives. As a proposal to cut off school and health services, it can be argued that 187 was more about creating a public space for domination—response through abhorrent audacity—than about actual or immediate enforcement. Simultaneously, there were immediate consequences for undocumented individuals and others "marked" as immigrants, which escalated with the enforcement of the judicially uncontested portions of the proposition.[243] However, the other face of 187 was the momentum of the resistance that was provoked. The prominent role of high school students' demonstrations and the coalitions that crossed ethnic and class barriers are signs of hope that expressive response to the likes of Prop 187's repressive nature crystallizes in progressive coalitions and alliances.

In October 1994, one of L.A.'s largest demonstrations, ever, figuratively countered the hordes of tourists who visit the state's attractions without regard for the rights of the state's service industry workers, many of them immigrants. Examining the media representations of multiple sites of resistance to 187 is useful in understanding the counter-narrative. For instance, English-language representations, in the mainstream press, have repeatedly demonized Mexican flag-flying during pre-voting demonstrations against 187. Unlike the bicentennial celebration where Lucas' organizing began with a Mexican dance perfor-

242 Quoted in *The Nation* (October, 1995, 416).

243 It is symbolically significant here that 187 is the police code for murder; rap artists, graffiti artists, and muralists have appropriated this code in their art; such symbolic usage resonates for an audience that is all too familiar with its significance. Juan Felipe Herrira's "*187 Reasons Mexicans Can't Cross the Border: Undocuments 1971–2007* references such connections in the title of this hybrid, mixed genre collection.

mance, the audience is portrayed as responding vehemently against the demonstration of Mexican loyalties—specifically, flags. In the wake of continuing attempts to make racism structurally legal, despite its unconstitutionality, it is vital to identify the resistance inherent in Lucas' work that challenges scapegoating and injustice, as she shows that the impulse behind immigrant bashing is clearly ethnic and class discrimination that denies human rights to those it scapegoats.

Proposition 187 asked for a judgment against the undocumented worker, parent, and child, just as the subsequent Welfare Bill in 1996 asked for a judgment against economically disenfranchised (predominantly) women and children. Both judgments refuse to consider either lived experience or the economic contributions of labor communities that Lucas portrays.

11.4 Narrating Sexist Discrimination

For Lucas, gender issues are at points foundational, but she recognizes the complexity of crosscutting strains of domination—intersectionality. Lucas calls for a revamping of systems of morality in light of the desperate situation facing many Tejanas. Lucas lists the avenues of support that women pursue and the systematic patriarchal oppression which keeps them from self-sufficiency; she repeatedly underscores the extensive marginalization women face:

> I feel real bad for some of the young undocumented women, girls really, the ones who came here and can't get asylum or papers or find any kind of work, and they don't even have a home to go back to. Many of them are working as prostitutes for old men. They're so desperate they say to the old men, "I'll work for you, I'll cook, I'll clean, I'll rub you, I'll do anything that makes you feel good, just please, Señor, give me a place to stay."
> Then all the women turn against these girls. They call them *putas* and say they're breaking up the family. I tell the women that it's not the women that it's not the girls, they're desperate; it's the men. And the system. The immigration barriers. But lots of people just say I'm crazy. (286)

Lucas trusts the reader to not be among those who "just think [she's] crazy;" her security in the correctness of her position thus seems firm. That others think she is crazy because she articulates the impossible situation these women face only illustrates the community's adherence to the dominant ideologies of racist patriarchy. The situation described above brings to light the stereotype of sexuality issues as largely middle-class, white feminist issues. Yet the right to determine one's own sexuality is a basic and crucial human right and should be protected. When these rights are not in place, other infringements follow, as Lucas describes:

> And the other danger for all of them is AIDS. They warn about AIDS on television, tell people it will kill them, but then they don't tell them exactly how it spreads. So there are lots of rumors, but people don't have information. And poor women can't afford condoms, even if the men would agree to use them. Men can get real mean about that, and the women are so desperate thinking about tomorrow. How are they supposed to think about something that might happen in a bunch of years? Like one young woman I know, she's supporting four sick kids and a mother at home by trying to work as a maid. If a man gives her a little help, how's she supposed to force him to use protection? (286)

Lucas' description of the AIDS threat, as in Usher's observation below, simultaneously heightens the imperative for structural change and links communities in similar dire situations. Lucas' question here is not merely rhetorical; its contextual specificity categorizes it as the kind of questions around which ethnicity-based AIDS action organizations such as Informa Sida in Austin Texas have formed. That the numbers of HIV exposure and AIDS-related deaths were growing rapidly among Latina/os and African Americans and women, relative to white men in the U.S., may illustrate that—in addition to a lack of adequate health facilities—questions, such as Lucas' have not been dealt with adequately by most AIDS service and education organizations.[244] The relationship of AIDS to environmental racism via prostitution—undertaken for personal survival and/or family survival—is detailed by Ann Danaiya Usher in "After the Forest: AIDS as Ecological Collapse in Thailand" when she traces "how the processes of degradation in the human body, the community and the ecosystem are linked physically, politically, and metaphorically, each reflecting and shedding light on the others." She talks about "the fate of women in Thailand [like in Greater Mexico], who are being infected with AIDS, but appear to be insufficiently armed to protect themselves" (12). The issues are also interrelated in *Heroes and Saints* in the difficulties faced by character of Cerezitas' brother Mario, mentioned in the previous chapter.

Fran Leeper Buss describes another kind of difficult decision that Lucas faced in analyzing the implications of offering a critique of sexism in the movement in *Forjado*—Lucas decided to discuss issues for which she does not have final answers, issues that may be less likely to split movements if they are brought onto the negotiation table, rather than sequestered away to harm those who engage in an internalized imposition of silence.

---

244 To my knowledge, the roles of class and gender in HIV spread have not been adequately studied either.

> After agonizing over the decision, María Elena has decided to speak out about the gender discrimination she experienced from the leadership of FLOC. While considering her decision, María Elena felt trapped in a condition faced by a multitude of women in progressive movements. To criticize aspects of the movement is to risk that these criticisms will be used by forces wishing to discredit the movement itself. However, to remain silent is to sentence other women activists in similar situations to the belief that they are alone, and to blunt the potential for equality.
> Virtually all modern social change movements that include both men and women, such as the civil rights movement and the new left, have marginalized their female members... (Buss 23)

Lucas' indictments of sexism are consistently couched in respect for the men's work toward a shared political cause. In one of the few passages in the book that is in Spanish, Lucas explicates the gender problems she faces in farm worker organizing, and her doubts about men, even those men whose leadership she respects and lauds:

> I think, sabrá Dios UFW cómo será. Me pongo a pensar, siempre he alabado a César Chávez. Siempre lo he visto como un Moses y no nomás a César Chávez pero a otros hombres que, como a Jesse Jackson también, que yo veo a estos otros hombres como un Moses también. Como unos discípulos de Cristo .... A veces me pongo a pensar que las mujeres que anduvieron con ellos, que andan con César Chávez y con Jesse Jackson, si también a veces ellas no tendrán los mismos problemas como tenemos acá con FLOC. (259)

The use of the Spanish language here, may indicate the intimacy, the private nature of the ambivalent feelings that were behind her decision to speak about gender issues and a means to hide the issues from Spanish-impaired outsiders. The strength of her convictions about sexism is indicated in that she even brings religious figures (for whom we know she has great reverence) "como un Moses" and "como unos discípulos de Cristo"—into her analysis.

Along with narrating her concerns about women organizing with men, Lucas tells us that it is important that the women leaders be visible for other women to have role models for participation:

> During the convention, I got to just talk a little when they introduced the chemical resolution to support César Chávez and Dr. Marion Moses. I got up and gave a testimony, what happened to me, but other than that I just sat with the board members. But it's important that we show female participation, so we, the women, were very rowdy from up there, chanting and clapping. I think it's very important for the rest of the women to see us. (258)

She narrates the hardships, both within the political group, and within the family, for women involved in organizing, and she registers specific complaints, but always with great diplomacy.

> I think that Balde and Fernando [FLOC leaders] think they're trying real hard for women and to make the union into an equal thing, but I don't really think it happens that way. I'm not sure they understand there's a great need for the female influence or input for female freedom .... I think the presence of a woman in a major decision-making staff is very important, women that have been around, that know how to communicate, to deliver a message.
> And, of course, it's just harder for a woman .... most of us women have to work against our husbands and all the services they expect.
> There's been times as a woman with FLOC that I've felt swatted like a fly, and as a woman, I think that's wrong. It's not good organizing for that to happen. One by one I've watched the top women leaders leave, and in June 1989, I was the only woman board member left, and I wasn't really there anymore. No one ever contacted me. (258)
> ... I'm just asking them [men] to give us a fair chance that we may be able to operate. After all, we make things roll and work, so why do they put us down? I know that Balde is a good man and that he's trying and I know that Fernando Cuevas, oh God, he's an angel, but women need to be allowed to be more important in final decisions. (259)

Lucas repeatedly expresses frustration over feelings of internal contradiction given her dedication to the struggle of the farmworkers and her admiration for its leaders as opposed to their patriarchal functioning. This battle is exacerbated by the fact that she realizes that sexism is "not good organizing," yet as the only woman representative, she does not have support in demanding restructuring, especially when she is not even contacted for decision-making meetings.

She relates how she holds off from full scale organizing among workers against her better judgment because she is waiting for OK's from above. When she sees another woman resign "for health reasons" in a situation that she knows stems from a conflict with the male leader, she is distraught: "I was so frustrated I cried, and then I called her and said, 'Sister, I know what's really happening. I want to tell you I love you. When will we women ever be free to say what really happens?'" (259). The women cope by supporting each other emotionally when structural change within the organization to combat the sexism seems unfeasible. Lucas realizes her organization is not alone in facing these patriarchal problems and she visualizes (this time in English) various grassroots groups right up to the president's cabinet in a similar bind.

> As a woman, I feel powerless, and I wonder if this is the way it is all over the world or all over America or like with the president and his government. I wonder if women like us who are trying to be part of growth and development, of a better life, I wonder it it's like this all the way through. It seems like every time a woman tries to express herself or say, "Well, that's not right," "Well, that's wrong," or, "If we do it this other way it might work," we're put down. (259)

Lucas' discussions serve as a culturally sensitive starting point for sexuality and gender discussions in small towns such as she and Cherríe Moraga portray. Her discussion could be an opening point for imagining marginalized women sitting at tables of power, such as the MELA women envision. Such a transformation would not come without work—even among the women themselves. Lucas describes her own coming-to-terms with lesbian relationships through her political work with other women. When she hears two lesbians who identify with a coalition of women as "lesbians" Lucas registers initial shock, but then describes overcoming her prejudice through recognition of their common grounds and political dedication, and her own "provincialism."

> And there may be ways of living that I don't even know about. Once I was at a women's conference, and people were being introduced, and I was sitting there watching, Some women said, "We represent black women." Some said, "We represent welfare women." Others, "We are Indian women." Then two women came forward, and they said, "And we represent lesbian women."
> My mouth just dropped open, I was so shocked. I couldn't believe it. I'd never heard anybody say something like that before. Boy, did I have a lot to think about when I left the room! But the more I watched them, the more I thought, well, these are really strong women, and they are really working hard for our cause. How can I think anything against them? It just really opened my mind. (285)

Lucas' passage, read in conjunction with Moraga's play, *Heroes and Saints* describes a way out of homophobia. Lucas' initial encounter with the lesbian organizers is educational, and gives her "a lot to think about," but it is in considering their common dedication to the cause of environmental and economic justice that Lucas does battle with her own hetero supremacy. Such occasions demonstrate the mediating and bridge-building role of a coalitional issue such as environmental justice.

11.5 Narrating International Power Dynamics

Much of the racial/ethnic prejudice and discrimination that Lucas discusses is complicated by issues of nationality.[245] These occur on the figurative level, in

245 Another way in which migrant farmworkers are discriminated against and experience environmental vulnerability can be explained by understanding the concept of "sedentarism, and the idea, which is prevalent in many dominant ideologies even the environmental movement that nomadic lifestyles are less healthy for people or the earth." Beyond the scope of this study the parallels with the experiences of the Romany and the Irish Travellers among other nomadic or semi-nomadic groups nevertheless should be noted.

terms of personal prejudice, as well as in structural racism. Discrimination based on nation status occurs on the very literal, and legal, level when U.S. citizenship is at stake and is repeatedly a problem that only exacerbates other issues such as environmental racism for the farmworkers, who for many reasons, including poverty, may not have U.S. documentation.[246] In reporting on the 1988 farmworker convention, Lucas assesses the importance of international contact, in particular, with "Third World" sites where corporate injustices were linked to the farmworkers' own struggles:

> And we had some people from Mexico, which I thought was very good. You see, these companies are international now, and we're preparing for that, for the future. The companies practice the international tactics of business. In Sonora, Mexico, they have a Campbell's company, a tomato processor, that is exploiting the people. They produce them over there ,.. and they bring them to the United States. This way they pay real cheap labor, and they come and sell it at U.S. prices. What we're doing is we're having meetings with representatives from over there. We've been saying that we should demand contracts for the employees there, too, so that the companies know that this is not just a U.S. thing—it's international, and we're going to be fighting to end the exploitation of those people too. (257–258)

Lucas' concern for understanding how the U. S. struggle crosses borders and for establishing alliances and linked struggle with "third world" groups is increasingly salient. U.S. corporations have taken advantage of more lax environmental laws to cheaply manufacture products and use processes that have been outlawed in the U.S. The blatant disregard for human wellbeing has provoked an outcry from the United Farm Workers and other progressive organizations in the U.S. for years, yet the practice has not been abated. Mira Shiva, in her article, "Environmental Degradation and Subversion of Health" reports the disastrous effects of this phenomenon in India, effects that have economic, environmental, social, and psychological ramifications that cause extensive disenfranchisement and even death for the disempowered:

> The extensive use of pesticides, many of which are banned in their country of origin, has made cultivation more capital-intensive and also seen the perverse effects of pesticides in

---

246 Ana, the woman who takes care of María Elena as a child has never gotten documentation. Lucas says that Ana would have no problem getting the documentation because she's lived on this side of the border for 30 years, but she needs $300 to become documented. Ana has survived partially by sleeping with men who would feed her; neither she nor her friends have had the money for the documentation fee. Activists have increased their discussion of the ways in which immigration prejudice has played out in environmental and environmental justice debates, especially against women, and others facing gendered disempowerment.

> the food chain. Pesticide resistance is beginning to appear, failed crops make livelihoods perilous, and the consequent indebtedness has led to some tragic fall-outs. In 1987 over 69 cotton farmers in India's prime cotton-growing district of Prakasam (Andhra Pradesh) committed suicide by consuming pesticides. (in CTH 69)

The act of suicide becomes metaphorically charged by politics when the material cause of one's desperation—the deleterious results of the corporate promotion of dangerous pesticides—becomes the source of one's self-inflicted death.[247] The voice of metaphor becomes a choir of opposition when one death is echoed by many more in the same disenfranchised occupational community. The discussion of subaltern—academic communication, evoked in Spivak's 1988 essay, "Can the Subaltern Speak?" might be used to thinking about the cotton farmers' suicides. What could be misinterpreted as death due to personal desperation (as the young woman's death in Spivak's story was blamed on "illicit" love), may, by a more scrutinous reading—both politically and, in this case, formally—be hailed as a call to arms, extended from those, whose arms are bound by corporate imperialist power, to those who might act. Another event that Mira Shiva narrates in her discussion of pesticide poisoning in the "Third World" is laden with figurative meaning, albeit less intentional on the part of the victims when a communal love feast becomes a feast of death for participants. The accidental ingestion of pesticide caused the Basti tragedy of 1990 when food distributed in recycled pesticide containers was distributed at a wedding. Two hundred people died as a result (Shiva 70).

Like her younger sister's first poisoning in Lucas' testimonio, we assume if "care is taken" contamination should not mix with food; only children, in their ignorance, are potentially vulnerable. However, the assumption does not stand, especially when one considers the degree of toxicity that would be required to kill people, not by direct consumption of a chemical but through food that came in contact with a container that had come in contact with that chemical. As is repeatedly underscored in the cultural poetics of environmental justice, the separation of toxic waste from life-sustaining elements is impossible; the dichotomy is a false one. Containers (or hands) that have been used to disperse poison, in disregard of others' health will never come clean, even with the most carcinogenic of cleansers.

247 Vandana Shiva has spoken and written extensively about farmers' suicides in South Asia. In a 2006 interview on *Democracy Now*, she notes it is a new development in conjunction with debilitating aspects of industrial farm products and sees India's "cotton belt" becoming a "suicide belt." https://www.democracynow.org/2006/12/13/vandana_shiva_on_farmer_suicides_the.

Lucas' discussion of farmworker organizing for environmental and social and economic justice introduces several issues that are echoed in the Third World sites outside the first world as well as in other sites from the Third and Fourth Worlds within the first world. Her narrative suggests that being denied basic human rights to a healthful environment, sustainable work, and lifestyle/lifeways is commonplace for those within farmworker communities, and that such injustices are most often brought on by outside corporate, interests. Such trajectories exist worldwide.

Like María Elena Lucas, Mahasweta Devi carries the word artistry of "real life" a step further by the fact of her own activism which informs her writing. Mahasweta has been a well-known activist for years; she advocates not only through her fiction, but also through her journalism and other forms of writing and in extensive organizing and social work. It is her activism, rather than her subject position, which brings her close to her characters. Unlike Castillo, who writes about communities in Greater Mexico that are not unlike those that she grew up around and lived in as an adult, or Sibal, who was a cosmopolitan upper-middle class Indian like her character Krishna, Mahasweta Devi's stories focus on characters who, unlike herself, are tribal and lower caste villagers. The following chapter will demonstrate that Mahasweta is, nonetheless, familiar with these communities through her activism, and as an outsider who has put herself into the rural landscape about which she writes. She has literally "walked the walk" from rural village to village. Like María Elena Lucas, she has committed herself to a lifework of promoting the wellbeing of the groups she portrays in her texts.

12 Mahasweta Devi's Short Stories: Tribal and Peasant Peoples in Environmental Struggles in Bihar and Bengal

in the hands of your land, your sentence
is as extraordinary as a poet's dream.

Pramila Venkateswaran

I believe that even if we have to starve, we must get the guilty officials of Union Carbide punished. They have killed someone's brother, someone's husband, someone's mother, someone's sister—how many tears can Union Carbide wipe? We will get Union Carbide punished. 'Till my last breath, I will not leave them.

Bano Bi (*Voices From Bhopal*)

María Elena Lucas' call for social and environmental justice coalitions that bring together activists and allies across national boundaries has been reiterated by many. Sometimes the writer may bring home the struggle that appears to be far removed from her audience. For the "first world" audience, ecojustice writing may point to intimate, empirical links to the environmental racism perpetuated around the globe. Such is the case in Pramila Venkateswaran's poem "When they hang a poet," which Venkateswaran dedicates to "Ken SaroWiwa, environmental activist and writer who was hanged by the Nigerian government in 1995." In the poem, Venkateswaran speaks to SaroWiwa, who was also a poet, implying her relationship to the crime against him, through her relationship to the corporate world:

I see your blood
in my quiet hands, in the hands
of my country, in the hands
of every human being caught
in the clamor of living,
in the hands of corporate souls
on whom desire sticks like sin

As an Indian emigrant teaching in the U.S., Pramila Venkateswaran has published the poem, in the U.S. Assumably, the phrase "of my country" refers to her adopted country, the country shared with her audience, for the U.S. is also the nerve center for the corporate connections and international policy-building that laid out the contextual groundwork for the assassinations by the Nigerian government. The poets share a vision and sense of relationship to the earth: "You spoke of a green earth—your dream / a filament of the earth's / desire."

https://doi.org/10.1515/9783111041575-013

While Pramila Venkateswaran condemns her country's corporate sin, she also observes—in gendered metaphor—that SaroWiwa critiqued his continent's role: "You wrote of Africa pillaging/herself, a prostitute 'choosing'/her destiny." Nature imagery saturates her description of the impact of the hanging of the Ogoni activists—"They hanged SaroWiwa: syllables shock the air/as leaves weep on the cold, cold dirt"—and the continuing impact of SaroWiwa's words, words that "spread like a rain storm, /filling decrepit croplands of the Ogoni."

It is then, words of nature and of conscience that bring the two poets into relationship. Pramila Venkateswaran writes of SaroWiwa with an impassioned reverence that channels his influence and furthers his lifework. SaroWiwa's textual relationship to the Ogoni people bears some resemblance to Mahasweta Devi's relationship with the tribal people of Bengal and Bihar[248]. Both writers have chosen language, written (and sometimes, performed) to relay the concerns of a group of people who have been little noticed outside their remote communities, and hence are vulnerable to capitalist (often corporate) interests. In the case of Mahasweta Devi, two of her translators, Gayatri Spivak and Kalpana Bardhan, bring much of her creative writing to the English-speaking "first world."

Taken collectively, Mahasweta Devi's translated short stories utilize experimental fiction to provide a historiographic deconstruction of environmental, race, class, caste, indigenous, gender, and national politics in rural Bengal and Bihar. The translated short stories that I discuss—"Dhowli," "Draupadi," "The Hunt," "Paddy Seeds," "Pterodactyl Puran Sahay & Pirtha" and "The Witch-Hunt"—offer refutations of the common binary articulations of feminism, nationalism, and race identity that mark self and other as two-dimensional polarities. This is accomplished through complex diagramming of individual social issues by overlaying the specifics of regional, rural, feudal, and postcolonial contexts. Additionally, Mahasweta, like Castillo, Sibal, Viramontes, and others, treat literature as contemporary feminist historiography. In the Epilogue, I briefly consider the pedagogical implications of this aspect. Mahasweta's work complicates the paradigm of hegemonic "Third World" as monolithic victim, and demonstrates the implications of class, caste, gender, and race/ethnicity that operate in systems of oppression—such as environmental racism—functioning in specific geopolitical sites in South Asia. I examine Mahasweta Devi's short

---

248 This study is limited only to English translations of the original Bengali/Bangla texts and to literary criticism in English of Mahasweta's work. Earlier versions of portions of my study of Mahasweta's fiction appeared in my environmental justice cultural poetics conference papers and publications in the late 1990s.

stories[249] via the rubric of *third world feminism* utilizing the writings of Vandana Shiva and Gayatri Spivak, who, in terms of their philosophical groundings that guide their readings, have been described as an ecofeminist/deep ecologist and a deconstructivist Marxist feminist, respectively.[250]

Mahasweta Devi breaks with both traditional realism and popularized versions of postcoloniality to create texts that are layered with complexities in form and content, and that expose multiple layers of domination and resistance. Yet, Mahasweta's stories may be placed in the socially engaged Bengali/Bangla tradition in literature that has been impacted by colonial and postcolonial, political, and social upheaval in the last century.

Mahasweta's storytelling reveals, often in the interaction of large and diverse casts of characters, the enabling, as well as the oppressive, aspects of gendered identities, in conjunction with the impact of race and caste identities for the rural peoples of Bihar and Bengal/Bangla. Through extensive readings of several short stories, I will demonstrate how Mahasweta constructs social commentaries that inform and instruct those "first world scholars" and other readers interested in the current and historical formations of feminisms, nationalisms, and race identities in South Asia. By means of introduction to stories of rural life, I would like to go back to Bhopal (Chapters Six and Seven), as an urban environmental justice site. I will briefly return to discussion of testimonio from Bhopal, Madhya Pradesh, to compare Mahasweta's story from the decade following the Union Carbide gas leak—that continues to affect thousands of (mostly poor) citizens—to make a comparison with the thoughts of Mathur, an academic character, researching tribal friends, in Mahasweta Devi's story "The Witch-Hunt."

12.1 "The Witch-Hunt:" Women, Fate, and Outside Representation

In comparing the epigraph from Bano Bi that heads this chapter to another comment Bano Bi makes regarding her fear for her children in the case of her possible death, we learn that while she fears the medical operation that might

249 Gayatri Chakravorty Spivak translated "Draupadi" and "Breast-Giver" in *In Other Worlds: Essays in Cultural Politics* and "The Hunt," "Douloti the Bountiful," and "Pterodactyl, Puran Sahay, and Pirtha" in *Imaginary Maps*. Kalpana Bardhan translated "Paddy Seeds," "Dhowli," "The Funeral Wailer," "Strange Children," "The Witch-Hunt," and "Giribala" in *Of Women, Outcastes, Peasants, and Rebels: A Selection of Bengali Short Stories*.

250 Colin MacCabe suggests the common use of the phrase for Spivak's work in his Foreword to *In Other Worlds*.

take her from her children, she is nonetheless determined to face all odds—even starvation—to bring Union Carbide Corporation officials to justice. Her reasoning here is consistent: behind wanting the "guilty officials ... punished" is the fact that they have killed so many people's family, family members that are in positions that are least "replaceable." Her fear, too, rests in the possible loss of another familial relationship for her children—having already lost their father, her apprehension is that her children will become orphaned upon her death. For Bano Bi, then, people's worth lies not in their ability to produce capital—the formula by which most government and corporate programs figure familiar remuneration; rather, she finds that supreme worth lies in peoples' familial relationships. How does one compensate for a lost sister, brother, husband, mother? One cannot. In asking the rhetorical question "how many tears can Union Carbide wipe?" Bano Bi not only personifies the corporation but portrays it as a comforting "mothering" figure in counter-position to the corporate administration's de-personification of its victims. Thereby, Bano Bi's demand for justice shifts the discussion to human/e terms. In doing so, she represents a consistent aspect of the Bhopal poetics—the continuing demand for reparations. However, not all respondents retain this fortitude; certainly, many people were overwhelmed by situations like the one narrated in the following passage.

> In the shadow of Union Carbide's pesticide-producing Bhopal plant in India, 45-year-old Neelam Bai and her four young children sleep under an open sky. They are too poor to afford even one of the ramshackle huts located nearby, and survive on leftovers shared by their almost equally destitute neighbours.
>
> Their only possession of potential value in the world are three slips of green paper—the death certificates of Neelam Bai's 50-year-old husband, mother-in-law and sister-in-law—all of whom perished in the Bhopal gas-leak tragedy ....
>
> The green slips list Body no. 96, and Body no. 245, all [sic] identified at the time of their 'disposal' by rescue workers in the aftermath of the Bhopal catastrophe. As the next of kin, Neelam Bai and her children are supposedly entitled to relief measures from the Indian Government; but as of June 1985, they had not received a single rupee in compensations. (Weir and Abraham in Kolpe 73)

Their *plight* is shared by thousands of others. Stories such as Neelan's may help readers understand some of the socio-ethical issues at stake in the first decade of Bhopal—issues that Bano Bi and other victims have also tackled in the *Voices of Bhopal* interviews and the Carbide workers accounts in *Bhopal: The Inside Story*. We might never truly empathize with the desperation of Neelam Bai's situation, but considering her story read in juxtaposition, helps clarify the following story which concludes Claude Alvares' *Afterward* to David Weir's book *The Bhopal Syndrome: Pesticide Manufacturing and the Third World*, one of the first major studies of Bhopal and the negative effects of pesticides on the "third world."

> Throughout history, terrible disasters have often spawned mythologies that capture the total helplessness of the victims. In the *bastis* of Bhopal today, an old woman is said to visit houses unannounced. She knocks at the door and asks for food. If she is given it, she throws it at the house, and all the inhabitants die. If she is refused food, she curses those who live there, and all of them will die.
> The newspapers report that recently, in the old part of Bhopal, frightened residents join together to take part in a beating. Their victim was an old woman. (Alvares in Weir BS 102)

Like Neelan, elder begging women, survive on the "leftovers of her almost equally destitute neighbors." Neelan's desperation may forewarn of the presence of the myth of the old woman. The story of desperation leading to scapegoating the most disenfranchised in society is common. Certainly, the discussion of environmental racism's intersection with the scapegoating of immigrants resonates here. Likewise, relevant, is Mahasweta Devi's story "The Witch-Hunt" in which the local landowner suggestively creates a "witch" in the minds of his neighbors in order to retain social control in the face of a drought, and to cover up his own son's rape of a "deaf and dumb" servant. Two points in this short story bear consideration in comparison with discussion of "women and fate" in Bhopal. The first is the perspective of Mathur, the graduate student and teacher who has become friends with the Pahan[251] of Hesadi, partially out of an intention to write a dissertation on Pahan's ancestors who had fought the British. Through his connection to Pahan, Mathur becomes involved with the culmination of the witch-hunt. In the following passage, Mathur's thoughts are revealed as he follows along on the final hunt; he has seen the witch and knows it is actually a woman, but the villagers ignore him in their excitement.

> Listening to them Mathur suddenly understands a crucial and terrible truth about their life. He sees that these people have no place at all in the economic world. They are left out of all the economic progress surrounding them—the steel industry and the coal mines, the lumber business, the rail ways, the grain-laden irrigated lands. They are totally excluded from the man-made bounty and control of technology and abandoned to nature at its most fickle. ... So when nature's breasts turn dry, they blame it on the witch because they don't understand their man-made deprivation .... The chasm between him and them cannot be bridged: the gulf between those holding the gun and those at whom it is pointed, between caste Hindus and the tribals. No magic can ever unite the firing squad with its target. (268)

Mathur's analysis seems fatalistic; without a place in the economic system of the country at large, the low caste Hindu and tribal villagers have no worth outside their own homes. Should their way of life be threatened by "man-made depravation" (which we have learned from the Chipko movement most likely

251 The Pahan is the tribal religious leader in the village, in this case, the village of Hesadi.

affects even so-called natural events like drought) Mathur believes they face a "firing squad." He implicates himself as an academic with the "man-made bounty and control of technology," the firing squad. Perhaps this is why he decides not to pursue the Ph.D. and academic life in the west that previously was his dream. But as Mathur realizes, he cannot understand the villagers, nor they him. In the conclusion of the story, the villagers defy Mathur's (and their own) fatalism through an act of resistance against the Brahmin landlord who has bought up all the industry in the area. The witch-hunt has culminated in the Pahan's realization that the vicious female witch, at whom they have been throwing stones in the forest, is the pregnant, deaf, and dumb daughter of the Pahan of Tura who has given birth in the cave into which the village men have chased her. When the Pahan of Hesadi comes out of the cave and the men ask, "Where's the witch?" the Pahan divulges the scapegoating to which the villagers have been gullible. When he replies, "Ask the Brahman in Tahad. After his son ruined her, he threw her out. Then he told us that there's a witch, that we must stone her away" (270).

> Subsequently, as Pahan and Mathur walk back to the village, Pahan tells Mathur, "I want you to go to Hanuman Misra and take back our appeal. We won't work for him, not one of us. We won't let him bring outside coolies." ... With the oppressive cloud of terror lifted from his mind, the Pahan of Hesadi realizes that nature is not at all different from any other drought year. Only his fear made him think otherwise. He speaks again to stress his resolve, "We won't work for him. We won't let anyone else work for him either." (271)

Here, we might compare the myth of the elderly woman beggar in the Bhopal *bastis* to the witch. The elder women who have no sustenance other than what they can attain by door-to-door begging are no different than before, though there may be more of them. And it is the after-effects of the gas that is killing the people. But just as the begging woman will stop at every household, so the gas has hit every household with death. In "The Witch-Hunt" it is no one from the outside, but rather the villagers themselves who have the will and the tools to fight the oppressive structure of feudal capitalism.

In concluding with the story of scapegoating the most vulnerable of victims, Claude Alvares, as journalist, is, like Mathur, in Mahasweta's fiction, making a pronouncement of futility—in Alvares' case, against the Bhopal victims' futile chance of recovering from the structural oppression that caused the leak and the aftermath. Yet they also expose a nearly universal phenomena—that of scapegoating society's most vulnerable—here, homeless, vulnerable women surviving in bureaucratic patriarchies. Demonizing mythologies that target women as the spirit of the most wanton destruction cause attacks on real women, who usually embody none of the characteristics for which they are metonymically being attacked. Finally, we can look to the Bhopal survivors, themselves, to find the spirit of resistance that intervenes in such phenomena—the spirit that ultimately Mahasweta Devi's villagers of Hesadi exhibit. The epigraph from Bano Bi illustrates the will to such resistance. Her spirit of opposition is also evident in the iconography present in the mobilization of Bhopal survivors over subsequent decades, and others involved in bringing about environmental justice in empirical and fictional "virtual realities."

12.2 Transforming Language/Language that Transcribes and Transposes

Gayatri Chakravorty Spivak, who has written about Mahasweta's work, extensively, demonstrates how Mahasweta's use of language transcribes social realities.

> Much third world fiction is still caught in realism (whereas the international literatures of the First World have graduated into language games) is a predictable generalization. This is often the result of a lack of acquaintance with the language of the original. Mahasweta's prose is an extraordinary mélange of street slang, the dialect of East Bengal, the everyday household language of family and servant, and the occasional gravity of elegant Bengali. The deliberately awkward syntax conveys by this mixture an effect far from "realistic," although the individual elements are representationally accurate to the last degree. (I have not been able to reproduce this in the translation.) (IOW 267)

Gayatri Spivak observes that Mahasweta's writing is not simply "realistic" in the literary sense. My approach finds that rather than the literary genre of "realism," Mahasweta Devi, like the authors I've discussed previously, works in the realm of "Virtual Realism." Hence, her use of language does not "naturalize" her narration, but rather it exposes, lays open in all its "awkwardness" and grit, what other more conventional, literary language smooths over.

Spivak generalizes Mahasweta's project in a productive way when she observes that, "the word 'India' is sometimes a lid on an immense and equally unacknowledged subaltern heterogeneity. Mahasweta releases that heterogeneity, restoring some of its historical and geographical nomenclature" (OTM 78). Stories such as "The Hunt" and "Paddy Seeds" narrate the social struggles over land and resource access which are basic to the mere physical and ecological survival of many of the tribal and lower caste communities. Mahasweta identifies the source of these communities' disenfranchisement, thereby tracing the tracks of oppression and naming oppressors: multiple structural repressions are set in place by higher caste landlords often from other states and are kept intact by corrupt and inefficient government actions. Several stories, including "Dhowli," "The Witch Hunt," "Girabaldi," "The Funeral Wailer," "Breast-Giver," "The Hunt" and "Douloti the Bountiful" primarily foreground the gender struggles of Indian women.

Spivak summarizes Mahasweta's project in gendered terms when she observes that "Mahasweta displaces the woman's body even from the reversal logic of labor and capital" (OTM 86). In *Outside the Teaching Machine*, Spivak explores three "events" that occur in Mahasweta's stories: "(1) inscription of displaced space, (2) social investment of bonded labor, and (3) the woman's body as last instance, and elsewhere" (OTM 86). In *Imaginary Maps*, Spivak adds to her list of "events" when she remarks that "... the stories in this volume are not only linked by the common thread of profound ecological loss, the loss of the forest as foundation of life, but also of the complicity, however apparently remote, of the power lines of local developers with the forces of global capital." Here, Spivak evokes the large picture described in environmental justice poetics: "This is no secret to the initiative for a global movement for non-Eurocentric ecological justice. But this is certainly a secret to the benevolent study of other cultures in the North" (IM 198).

Spivak identifies the very issues in Mahasweta's work on which my study focuses. I demonstrate how Mahasweta represents these "events" specifically and will thereby illustrate the centrality of her work to environmental justice poetics. Of these issues—ecological loss—including the indigenous inhabitants' loss of land rights and natural resources—lies at the crux of my project. However, intersectional ties mean this facet cannot be seen alone. Utilizing an intersectional lens that acknowledges the specific subject position politics of the area, I am primarily interested in the gendering of both environmental loss and the resulting struggles for economically and otherwise disenfranchised people, and how these struggles compare to the larger body of gendered struggles that Mahasweta represents in her fiction. As Spivak points out, in engaging environmental issues even at local levels, one must contend with global capitalism. Likewise, as Mahasweta demonstrates in a rural Indian setting, environmental issues are linked with issues of bonded labor and the "displaced space" where both women and forest have been conscribed by forces of feudal and capitalist control. Having established these specific claims about Mahasweta's work, let me turn to an overview before further examining specific stories, themes, and characters.

Late in the 1970s, Mahasweta published her only novel that was immediately translated into English. *Hajar Churashir Ma (No. 1084's Mother)* was written in the "sentimental idiom of the Bengali novel of [preceding] twenty-odd years"

(Spivak IOW 180). Her following work changed 'significantly' in a subsequent novel, *Aranyer Adhikar (The Rights [or Occupation] of the Forest)* in which "Mahasweta begins putting together a prose that is a collage of literary Bengali, street Bengali, bureaucratic Bengali, tribal Bengali, and the languages of the tribals" (180). *Aranyer Adhikar* was thus a precursor to the style of the short stories that have been translated. Spivak further historicizes the significance and placement of Mahasweta's writing in terms of Bengali social and political contexts.

> Since the Bengali script is illegible except to the approximately twenty-five percent literate of the about ninety million speakers of Bengali, a large number of whom live in Bangladesh rather than in West Bengal, one cannot speak of the "Indian" reception of Mahasweta's work but only of its Bengali reception. Briefly, that reception can be described as a general recognition of excellence; skepticism regarding the content on the part of the bourgeois readership; some accusations of extremism from the electoral Left; and admiration and a sense of solidarity on the part of the nonelectoral Left. Any extended reception study would consider that West Bengal has had a Left-Front government of the united electoral Communist parties since 1967. Here suffice it to say that Mahasweta is certainly one of the most important writers writing in India today. (IOW 180–181)

While Mahasweta Devi has been long established as a Bengali novelist and leftist intellectual, English-language response to her creative work, available in the U.S. through the 20th Century that I located, were almost exclusively limited to the writing of her translators.[252] The MLA computerized catalogue (in 1994) listed only one article on Mahasweta Devi—Gayatri Chakravorty Spivak's theoretical treatment and translation of "Draupadi" which appeared initially in *Critical Inquiry* and was later incorporated into *In Other Worlds*. Since its publication, *Imaginary Maps* has been the subject of seminar and conference papers, and, as these are published, her reception in the West may evolve, but before *Imaginary Maps*, critical work aside, the academy in English had little access to Mahasweta's fiction itself. Besides the translations by Bardhan and Spivak I found only three other translations. a novelette "Operation?—Bashai Tudu" was translated by Samik Bandyopadhyay and published in *Bashai Tudu* along with Spivak's translation of Draupadi. Pinaki Bhattacharya offers a compelling translation of a short story "Shishu" (Children) in the twentieth century volume of *Women Writing in India*. The children to whom the title refers are actually a

252 Exceptions (circa 2002) included a study by Jia-Yi Cheng-Levine entitled "*Mahasweta Devi's* Imaginary Maps" published in *Pheobe: Journal of feminist scholarship theory and aesthetics* (Volume 9, Number 1/Spring 1997 and my essay "Two Centuries of Environmental Writing in India" in *The Literature of Nature: An International Sourcebook*. Patrick Murphy, ed.

village of tribal adults whose growth has been stunted by malnutrition; when the villagers steal food in the night, Singh, the protagonist, and a famine relief officer, comes face to face with his own complicity in the crime of world hunger.[253] "Salt" is the captivating story of resistance against the most extreme social deprivation, undertaken by an isolated rural community that has been politically disempowered by outside structural oppression. The community struggles to maintain access to its most basic needs—in specific, salt. According to an English Literature Guide, "It represents the plight of the tribal deprived of arable forest land by the traders who came there after the Kol Revolt in 1831." Given this history, the story offers an example of the long reach of environmental racism in South Asia. I found the story in an anthology of Bengali protest literature in Ann Arbor circa 1988, but have not been able to relocate it, though I've found a lot of secondary discussion of it, including study guides online.[254]

Following *Imaginary Maps* published in the mid 1990s, several collections of Mahasweta's works have been published in English by Seagull Books in Calcutta in a series under the title of *The Selected Works of Mahasweta Devi*. The press statement on the series establishes Mahasweta's importance in several arenas: Mahasweta Devi has made important, broad contributions to literary and cultural studies. Her empirical research into oral history as it lives in the cultures and memories of tribal communities was a first of its kind. Her powerful, haunting tales of exploitation and struggle have been seen as rich sites of feminist discourse by leading scholars. Her innovative use of language has expanded the conventional borders of Bengali literary expression. Standing as she does at the intersection of vital contemporary questions of politics, gender, and

---

253 The absolute deprivation the indigenous villagers face is apparent in the following passage that compares their situation with that of the officer; such descriptions in Mahasweta's work serve to break down the false hegemony of "Third World" contexts, often suggested in "first world" treatment. "Somgh's cerebral cells tried to register the logical explanation but he failed to utter a single word. Why, why this revenge? He was just an ordinary Indian. He didn't have the stature of a healthy Russian, Canadian, or American. He did not eat food that supplied enough calories for a human body. The World Health Organization said that it was a crime to deny the human body of the right number of calories.

But he could not utter a single word in his own defense. Standing still under the moon, listening to their deafening voices, shivering at the rubbing of their organs against his body, Singh knew that the malnourished and ridiculous body of an ordinary Indian was the worst possible crime in the history of civilization." (250) The same story is translated as "Strange Children" by Kalpana Bardhan.

254 For example, see https://www.journalijdr.com/voicing-unvoiced-mahasweta-devi's-salt and study guide: https://www.englishliteratureguide.com/2021/08/salt-by-mahasweta-devi.html.

class, she is a significant figure in the field of socially committed literature. (Paraphrased from preface statement to the series books).[255]

Imaginary Maps is dedicated "for all indigenous peoples of the world," a dedication which indicates the placement of the three stories in indigenous communities whose rights and needs have been long ignored both within India and externally. Though the issues of the indigenous peoples of India have rarely been discussed in academic models of oppression, the consistent disenfranchisement perpetrated against India's tribal peoples is centuries old. Mahasweta documents the effects of internal settler colonialism[256] and the after-effects of British colonialism against the indigenous tribal peoples in India. Revisions of colonial histories have rarely considered the cultural genocide, disenfranchisement, and denial of basic needs and rights that tribal peoples in India have faced. Mahasweta extends the postcolonial map of India to include the places of tribal ethnic groups, places which remain un-inscribed on many maps of postcolonial India.

Mahasweta's gendered renderings of tribal and dalit community struggles based on her exposure to, and support of, these struggles inform Bengali/Bangla, South Asian, and international audiences by beginning to remedy the lacunae of knowledge that occur at all these levels.[257] We can witness her focus

255 Some of the books in the series include *Five Plays: Mother of 1084/Aajir/Bãyen Urvashi and Johnny/Water* (1986), the novel *mother of 1084*, (1997) both translated from the Bengali by Samik Bandyopadhyay. *The Armenian Champa Tree* (1998) Nirmal Kanti Bhattacharjee translator, *rudali: from fiction to performance*, translated by anjum katyal (1997), and *Dust On The Road: The Activist Writings Of Mahasweta Devi* edited by maitreya ghatak (1997).

256 While use of the term "colonialism" might be questioned in these circumstances, and I take precautions against its rampant application, advisedly, I find that the historical relationship of the indigenous peoples of India, the "tribals," to the elite of the occupying peoples, who immigrated onto the continent is repeatedly, a colonial one; often the parlance, "settler colonialism" that Spivak utilizes is most applicable (OTM 79).

257 Mahasweta Devi has lived in West Bengal and Bihar's tribal and outcaste communities in rural areas "where capitalist exploitation combines with feudal oppression." She became involved with these communities "as a participant-observer and political-anthropologist in the late 1960s ...;" she collected information from "the rural and urban underclass," many of whom were Naxalites or supporters. In 1984 an early retirement from her Calcutta teaching post allowed her to devote more time to "writing, reporting, and social activism ..." (Bardhan 24). In an editorial note, Kalpana Bardhan tells the reader that "Mahasweta pointed out to me that in a village of tribals and outcastes in Bihar, like the one here, the groups generally coexist in neighborly harmony, aware of, but not really divided by, the differences in their customs and rituals" (163). Bardhan further explicates the complex social structure in Mahasweta's stories:
The socio-economic situation is polarized, agitated and violent with the capitalist forms of exploitation reinforcing the old forms of oppression by high-caste landlords and moneylend-

on tribal communities whose rights are rarely mentioned even by opponents to the Hindu secularism currently threatening Muslims and others of non-Hindu belief. In *Outside the Teaching Machine*, Spivak notes the implications of Mahasweta's focus on indigenous world views in the context of the denial of religious freedom to indigenous groups.

> That scene of strife, again not to be ignored—especially today as India is on the brink of Fascism in the name of Hindu nationalism—is still within the hegemonic struggle over so-called national identity—still, that is to say, in the space of the empire-nation reversal. No Indian, expatriate or otherwise, could bypass the issue of violence in the subcontinent in the name of religious identity. *But we must also keep our eye on the differences, where tribal animism does not even qualify as a religion.* (Italics, mine. OTM 80)

Mahasweta exposes several levels of class struggle that interact with, and reinforce patriarchy, ethnic and caste discrimination, and racism in historically and geographically specific ways. Kalpana Bardhan explicates this in her description of the setting of most of Mahasweta's stories that she translated in *Of Women, Outcastes, Peasants, and Rebels: A Selection of Bengali Short Stories*: "[t]he five stories [that she translated] ... are set in southeastern Bihar during the mid-1970s, in a belt of semilandless tribals and untouchables effectively denied the rights guaranteed by the Constitution, even a legal minimum wage, and marginalized by the process of economic development" (25). Bardhan draws a comparison between Bengali literature and Latin American literature that could appropriately be extended to Chicana/o literature when she claims that these literatures "reflect the turmoil of a society in flux." She decided to translate a collection of "socially focused literature" from Bengal partially [258] because of "a doubt [on the part of Western readers] that such a literature could exist in Bengal" (2). This suspicion seems to be part and parcel of the heritage of the West that Edward Said, in his seminal text, identified as "Orientalism," or that which reiterates "European superiority over Oriental backwardness, usually overriding the possibility that a more independent, or more skeptical thinker might have

ers ... The tribals and the untouchables, tyrannized and exploited by landlords and money-lenders, deceived and let down by double-dealing officials, patronized by educated radicals, are beginning to wage their own struggles (25).

258 Bardhan acknowledges "the insistent curiosity of my non-Bengali Indian friends about how social change and transition have been reflected in Bengali literature, especially compared to their respective languages" (2). Additionally, she was "increasingly drawn to take stock of and collect Bengali stories dealing in one way or another with the gender aspect of oppression." She was "[s]truck by the parallels and connections between the forms of oppression—by gender, class, caste, and tribal ethnicity ..." (Bardhan 2–3).

had different views on the matter" (7). That Bardhan's critique is directed at those scholars with an interest in the Western hemisphere's "Third World,"—specifically Latin American socially-engaged literature—reflects the pervasiveness of Orientalism.

12.3 Gendered Subaltern Voicing Survival as Resistance: Theorists Respond

Gayatri Chakravorty Spivak's interest in Mahasweta Devi's work has spanned many years from her early article in *Critical Inquiry* to the re-publication of *Imaginary Maps* "companion essays" (197) in *The Spivak Reader* (1996) and beyond. Spivak identifies an element which may be overlooked in much of the cross-cultural, international reception of Mahasweta's work outside of South Asia, but which is of interest to my study. She finds that Mahasweta offers a critical discussion of post-Independence internal "feudal imperialism" and thereby affronts the upperclass nationalist.

> ... Mahasweta Devi lingers in postcoloniality and even there in the space of difference on *decolonized terrain* in the space of difference. Her material is not written with an international audience in mind. It often contains problematic representations of decolonization after a negotiated *political* independence. Sometimes this offends the pieties of the national bourgeoisie. (OTM 77)

This updating and expansion of Spivak's earlier survey (in IOW) of Mahasweta's Bengali reception suggests both a growth in Mahasweta's international exposure and increased national, critical attention in the intervening years between the two appraisals. Spivak contextualizes the response to Mahasweta's "offensiveness" by praising the extensive and persistent breadth of Mahasweta's project: "The sheer quantity of Mahasweta's production, her preoccupation with the gendered subaltern subject, and the range of her experimental prose—moving from the tribal to the Sanskritic register by way of easy obscenity and political analysis—will not permit her to be an isolated voice" (OTM 77). The detailed articulation of the very postcolonial moment that makes the national elite uneasy is precisely the moment that must be clearly rendered, with all the diverse facets of its contextual complexity intact, to visualize environmental justice resolutions in India.[259] While the exquisite prose that Spivak lauds may

259 Mahasweta's complex and critical rendition of postcolonial relations implicates native elites in hierarchies that disenfranchize the poor and the "ethnic" other. This work compares to make Mahasweta's work more interesting to a broader political spectrum of English- and Bengali-speaking Indians, another great aspect of Mahasweta's significance lies in the depth and distinctiveness with which she treats issues that face social environmentalists in both the South and the North.

The "offensiveness" for the elites on which Spivak remarks, may be caused by their defensive reactions to Mahasweta's radical process of complexification. Her ambitious interlinking of issues such as postcoloniality, class, caste, gender, and race invariably implicates that elite as part and parcel of the disenfranchising forces, she describes. That the national bourgeoisie would take offense at Mahasweta's work is ultimately a reactionary move on its part, by which it attempts to protect itself from self-critique, for Mahasweta's analysis reveals a nationalist duplicity with imperialism and environmental racism. As Spivak observes in discussing "Stanadayini" ("Breast-Giver"),

> Mahasweta's text might show in many ways how the narratives of nationalism have been and remain irrelevant to the life of the subordinate. The elite culture of nationalism participated and participates with the colonizer in various ways. In Mahasweta's stories we see the detritus of that participation. (IOW 245)

This nationalist continuation of colonialist domination is particularly salient in environmental justice issues, such as the caretaking of India's forests, the termination of feudal bond-slavery, and the encroachment of multinational corporate capitalist "globalization." Additionally, the "first world" academic reader's lifestyle and lifework are revealed as complicit in shaping the "Third World" subaltern's dire situation. In speaking specifically to the "migrant intellectual" from the east Spivak notes the connections between global capitalism and environmental racism that are ultimately relevant to all progressive academics. In their ignorance about this association of domination, Spivak finds, "a strong connection, indeed a complicity, between the bourgeoisie of the Third world and migrants in the First [that] cannot be ignored" (IM 198). Reminding us that "[w]e have to keep this particularly in mind because this is also the traffic line in Cultural Studies," Spivak suggests that Mahasweta offers an antidote: "Mahasweta's texts are thus not only of substantial interest to us, but may also be a critique of our academic practice" (IM 199).[260]

Ana Castillo's treatment of environmental racism in *So Far From God* in which Castillo demonstrates that Fe, the victim, also initially believes in the system which causes her demise.

260 This might be seen as reiterating an updated version of Spivak's decision to translate "Draupadi" for its antagonist, Senanayak, whom she compares to the "first world" scholar viewing the "Third World."

I find that elements of the academic critique, to which Spivak points, recur repeatedly in much of the cultural production that warns of the need for a gender-sensitive environmental justice. Furthermore, Mahasweta's texts become more critically and theoretically accessible, and relevant to international audiences through the work of environmental justice practitioners (such as Vandana Shiva) who draw further attention to the international linkages of oppressive power structures as they operate in rural India.

Unlike in the academic discussions of subaltern subjectivity, to which Spivak refers, the voices of subaltern women are not silenced—either literally or figuratively—in Mahasweta's stories; nor are they silenced in Vandana Shiva's telling, as witnessed in the chapters on the Chipko movement. We can observe the distinctive nature of Mahasweta's renderings of subalternity through a comparison with Spivak's discussion of how gender is discussed in "Subaltern Studies: Deconstructing Historiography."[261] As Jenny Sharpe observes, Spivak finds that the Subaltern Studies Group's approach has eclipsed the subaltern woman from its discussion.

> She shows that upon deriving a subaltern "will" from the text of open revolt, the Subaltern Studies group produces a model of agency that cannot accommodate the sexed subaltern ... Spivak goes on to demonstrate that an academic writing of the subaltern as insurgent is a tropological move that displaces the sexed subaltern. The symbolic exchange of women appears at crucial moments in the historiography of the Subaltern Studies group for explaining the mobilization of peasants across villages. Yet, the collective does not raise questions about the absent text of subaltern women's consciousness as it does about peasant insurgency in elite historiography. Spivak notes that the project of writing a history from below repeats the subaltern male's indifference. (Sharpe 17–18) [262]

There are many interesting comparisons and contrasts between Spivak's enumeration of the tenets of subalternity in Mahasweta's work, and Spivak's analysis of the Subaltern Studies Group's positing of subaltern subjectivity. Spivak's work on women in "Subaltern Studies: Deconstructing Historiography" (in IOW) reveals that while "[t]he group is scrupulous in its consideration towards women" in terms of their recording of "moments when men and women are joined in

---

261 This is Spivak's introduction to *Selected Subaltern Studies*.

262 Sharpe prefaces the comment with the observation that "[i]n 'Can the Subaltern Speak?' Spivak makes a distinction between tropological representation and political representation in order to demonstrate that the absence of a match between consciousness and its representation-as-trope means that any political articulation of subaltern subjectivity is always an act of reading 41" (17). While it seems unnecessary to evoke such a basic poststructural tenet, it is worth the reminder that my political articulation is, as well, is just such a reading.

struggle," when women's conditions of work or education suffer from gender or class discrimination they "overlook how important the concept-metaphor woman is to the functioning of their discourse" (Spivak IOW 26). Conversely, Mahasweta remains consistent in her vigilance on the ramifications of gender issues. In many of Mahasweta's translated stories, women are the primary protagonists and gender oppression's role in the domination of the tribal and lower caste people is treated prominently. Mahasweta remedies the "subaltern male's indifference" in her fiction, to the extent that such amelioration is possible; Spivak describes the process by which we can "learn from below" in Mahasweta's work: "we draw out from literary and social texts some impossible yet necessary project of changing the minds that innocently support a vicious system" (IOW 200). Though Spivak does not explicate this, I would suggest that one main difference between the outcome for women in Mahasweta's projects, as opposed to the Subaltern Studies Group's, lies in the "difference of degree" between historical and literary events that Spivak comments on elsewhere.[263]

This countering of the dominate culture's images and ideologies with stories that stir "against the grain" analysis is basic to all the environmental justice writers I have discussed. Furthermore, the subaltern women characters Mahasweta portrays bring lessons for the "first world" reader. Mahasweta demonstrates that gender oppression is not inscribed equally across race, caste, and class lines; rather, it is evoked doubly upon the disempowered groups, sometimes even by other women—almost always by the upper class.

Sharpe demonstrates a similar point theoretically; her reminder of the necessity of looking for dislocation and difference is important as we critically consider Mahasweta's stories in relationship to the texts I've examined in previous chapters.

> Inasmuch as feminism calls attention to gender as a category that cuts across the discursive field of colonialism, it can be a force in displacing the binarisms of colonizer/colonized, Self/Other, oppressor/oppressed, and East/West. Yet unless we see that gender itself is overdetermined by other relations, we risk reducing colonialism to a narrative of sexual difference. To read social contradictions as overdetermined involves seeing how the axes of race, class, and gender are "linked through their differences, through the dislocations between them, rather than through their similarity, correspondence or identity." An analysis that begins with difference and dislocations between them, rather than identity and correspondence is crucial if we are to perform the race, class, and gender analysis that continues to elide feminist studies. (Sharpe 11)

263 "That history deals with real events and literature with imagined ones may now be seen as a difference in degree rather than in kind. The difference between cases of historical and literary events will always be there as a differential moment in terms of what is called 'the effect of the real'" (Spivak IOW 243).

In her contextually informed gender critique, like in her critique of the Indian class/caste elite, Mahasweta Devi posits "feudal imperialism," a moment of disenfranchisement within the nation. However, in a broader sense, as Spivak claims, Mahasweta is drawing attention to "the rural subaltern scene that is paying the price of (the failure of) decolonization" (OTM 255). In observing women in this scene, Mahasweta shows that even within this space, "the woman's body is the last instance, that it is elsewhere" (OTM 79). It is important to observe, though, that in examining women's displacement and sometimes almost complete and literal deterritorialization, Mahasweta never portrays women solely as victims; they are always already survivors, and they are often the initiators of extensive resistance against their oppression.[264]

12.4 Women Survivors Fighting Ecocide

Draupadi is a character who appears in more than one of Mahasweta's stories and offers a consistently strong "feminist" model of resistance.[265] The short story "Draupadi," was published originally in *Agnigarbha (Womb of Fire)*, which Spivak describes as "a collection of loosely connected, short political narratives" (IOW 180). "Draupadi" portrays a woman protagonist named Draupadi, and known less formally as Dopdi, who is a member of the Naxalites,[266] a Benga-

---

264 Almost every story has numerous references to literal loss of land, due to feudal concerns. At times, this loss of land is gendered. For instance, Dhowli's mother loses the lease to the land that sustains the family when her husband dies and the landlord refuses to reinstate the lease to a woman. Loss of home is also a related gender phenomenon: in "The Witch-Hunt," Somri is driven into the woods when she is impregnated by her employer's son, and Somni in "Douloti the Bountiful" is driven out of her home in the brothel, and into the street to beg with her children, when her work as a prostitute is no longer profitable.

265 I use the term "feminist" here as an adjective, conscious that placing it in a subaltern "Third World" context problematizes the often-hegemonic implications of its usage in the "first world".

266 Spivak quotes Marcus Franda, "unlike most other areas of West Bengal, where peasant movements are led almost solely by middle-class leadership from Calcutta, Naxalbari has spawned an indigenous agrarian reform leadership led by the lower classes." Spivak notes that the Naxalite resistance which surfaced with a successful rebellion in the spring of 1967 includes "tribal cultivators." She situates the importance of the organization. "This peculiar coalition of peasant and intellectual sparked off a number of Naxalbaris all over India. The target of these movements was the long-established oppression of the landless peasantry and itinerant farm worker, sustained through an unofficial government-landlord collusion that too easily circumvented the law" (IOW 181). Arundhati Roy's *Walking With the Comrades* (Penguin Publishing, 2011) is a highly acclaimed, first-hand account of spending time with Naxalites in

li resistance movement that united the struggles of rural peasants and members of the urban middle-class Left. "Operation?—Bashai Tudu," the novelette translated by Samik Bandyopadhyay, precedes the story "Draupadi" in the two-story collection entitled *Bashai Tudu.* It situates Bashai Tudu in a cast of characters from the rural Bengali left community including "Draupadi." This grouping gives readers background on the character Draupadi and fills in more details of the political struggle in which she is involved.

Draupadi is not the only character with the same name and similar traits to reappear in different stories. A character by the name of Sanichari, usually an "herbal medicine woman" or community health/social worker or promotora/curandera appears, with similar attributes, in many of Mahasweta's stories. Sanichari is the prime example that lower class/caste women can and do resist the constraints of oppression they and fellow villagers experience. Sanichari demonstrates a dynamic quality that intervenes in the static cycle of repressive control. As Bardhan explains, "Sanichari in ['The Funeral Wailer'] and 'Paddy Seeds' is probably the same individual in two different stages of her life. Sanichari in ['The Funeral Wailer'] is in an earlier stage in the process of weathering the public misfortunes before she becomes a public personality ready to fight for others" (206).

In "Dhowli," Sanichari plays an advocate role mediating the conflict between the land-owning Misra family and Dhowli as she attempts to contain and counter the brutal disenfranchisement the wealthy family is imparting upon the mother of their "illegitimate" low caste grandson. She also defends Dhowli who has been ostracized by the other landless villagers because she fell in love with a Brahmin. Misrilal, the Brahmin son who had fallen in love with Dhowli, the young, low-caste widow, communicates through Sanichari and finds out that his mother lied when she told him his lover and son have been provided for. While this does not lead to reunion, it does lead to negotiation between the forcibly estranged lovers and it provides a moment in the story when the forces of economic and social hierarchy are exposed as the criminal elements that allow for the pillaging of the love affair. Here, as elsewhere, Sanichari is the character who most consistently untangles the complexity of social forces to expose, not only the sources of oppression, but the channels by which it circulates. She has power in this situation because "[t]he Misra matriarch" is dependent on Sanichari since she is "her secret supplier of the medicine for holding onto her old husband, who is addicted to a certain washerwoman" (trans. in

---

Chhattisgarh jungles. She discusses aspects of gender in conjunction with resistance movements. Ecofeminist comparativist studies drawing on such work would be valuable.

Bardhan WOPR 197), but, in fact "[e]very family in the village, rich or poor, needs Sanichari. Nobody can do without her help with the medicinal herbs" (WOPR 203). Sanichari illustrates the significance of empowerment retained through knowledge.

Sanichari's profession as an herbalist aligns her with the forces of nature and illustrates her extensive knowledge of the complexity of interconnecting, natural forces; this is precisely the knowledge that has not been acquired by outside "developers" who fail to recognize the ecological demise that their "development" projects bring with them. Spivak sees this kind of relationship to nature as a "cultural conformity," which indigenous groups use "precisely to mobilize for ecological sanity as well as against historical injustice" (IM 199).

In "The Witch-Hunt," readers are told that "[e]very village in the area has a woman named Sanichari" (WOPR 258) who embodies reason and a sense of the "sacred" or what Spivak has identified as "a sanction that cannot be contained in reason alone" (IM 199). At the beginning of the story, Sanichari of Murhai offers a voice of reason and respect for the villagers' belief system. However, the Sanichari of Hesadi is subsequently attacked in the woods, and readers, along with the villagers, are led to believe that the witch has been the attacker. Sanichari of Hesadi dies of her festering wounds. The doctors at the town hospital say she "had a disease that prevented the healing," but the local people know that "[n]o one lives after being scratched by the nails of death" (WOPR 265). At the end of the story, a different explanation for the attack emerges for attentive readers, when the witch materializes as a mentally disabled teenager who was thrown out in the woods by the Brahmin landowner, for whom she was working, when she became pregnant by his son. Possibly, the young woman understands that Sanichari, the herbalist, could help her and approaches her, but when she is misrecognized as a witch, responds by attacking. Sanichari is portrayed in this story as a "feminist" force that is a threat to the feudal, capitalist patriarchy. As a character, she had to die for the story of disenfranchisement to be played out. As in "Dhowli," the Sanicharis in "The Witch-Hunt" "represent the most viable hope in female form that the people have of breaking the stranglehold of structural violence that contains and manipulates their lives. She is, in one sense, a force that opposes the witch who Misra, the Brahmin priest reports to be "a dreadful female, dark and completely naked, flying atop a blood-red cloud and saying 'I'm the famine.'" (WOPR 243). Yet Sanichari of Hesadi's death also validates the people's belief in a witch, making it more than merely ignorant superstition that Misra manipulates into a scapegoat to hide his own repressive tactics. Ultimately, Misra is revealed as the demonical aspect of the witch, the force that works violence against natural and human communities.

Thus, indigenous belief and social critique coalesce to expose yet another form of "environmental racism."

While Sanichari is the most sustained feminist character, both "Dhowli" and "Douloti the Bountiful" illustrate Mahasweta's sustained focus on extended gender issues, especially in relation to the economy of feudal structures, and in "Douloti," to bonded labor. Spivak and Bardhan agree that gender issues cannot be subsumed under scrutiny of the Indian feudal system. Mahasweta Devi is one of the few writers to expose the complexities of the integral links between these issues.

> Some feminists have described the broad spectrum of women's issues—from anorexia as resistance in the United States to the dowry system in India—as subsumable under the feudal mode of production. Such gestures are, I think, incomplete. The woman is fully implicated in the mode of production narrative and, at the same time, also distanced from it. To quote Kalpana Bardhan again: In a stratified society, discrimination of wages and jobs/occupation by caste and sex is not a feudal remnant but perfectly consistent with the play of market forces ... If the wage-and-access differentials follow the lines of traditional privilege, then attention gets conveniently deflected from the adaptive dexterity of capitalist exploitation processes to the stubbornness of feudal values, when it is actually a symbiotic relationship between the two. (OTM 86)

"Dhowli," illustrates in fiction the "symbiotic relationship" between dominating impulses within a rural Indian context that can be read as a *tragic* love story that demonstrates that ties to the economic hierarchies—be they feudal or capitalist—and caste hierarchies and patriarchy are stronger than the bonds of affect or "love." However, a parallel reading could find that "Dhowli" narrates a woman's regression to the point where her body has become means for the "absolute sexual and economic exploitation" that Spivak finds in the embodiment of the bonded prostitute. The first reading, the love story—turned tragic by systematic factors outside the relationship—resonates with Cerezita's and Estella's situations, in Moraga's and Viramontes' writing, respectively. The second description evokes Lucas's descriptions of the situations among immigrant women forced into prostitution to feed themselves and their families in South Texas—and as described by Ann Danaiya Usher, among those women forced into prostitution due to environmental and ultimately economic displacement caused by dams and other development projects, in Thailand. The contrasts between these interpretations raise important questions about the position of women's subjectivity in the context of the ideology of heterosexuality. Such questions apply on both local and global (or "universal") levels. For instance, the story of "Dhowli" proposes a shift from the passive paradigm of *woman as nature* to a view of *relationship and nature as a space of interaction—an active habitat for woman and man.*

The issues raised are salient to the links between feminisms and environmental justice. Mahasweta professionalizes the traditionally "female responsibilities" of nursing babies and providing sexual experiences for men. Spivak identifies this phenomenon in Mahasweta's story "Breast-Giver:" "Mahasweta introduces exploitation/domination into that detail in the mythic story which tells us that Jashoda is a *foster*-mother. By turning fostering into a profession, she sees mothering in its materiality beyond its socialization as affect, beyond psychologization as abjection, or yet transcendentalization as the vehicle of the divine" (IOW 265). However, it also occurs—in the context of prostitution—in "Dhowli." Likewise, when sexual practice becomes professional practice, sexuality is exhibited "beyond its socialization as affect." In "Dhowli," the definition of the sexual encounter is marked as crucial at several moments in the narrative.

When Dhowli becomes pregnant, Misrilal's family is enraged at the couple's indiscretion, and he does not have the courage to stand up for his eloquently spoken love. Kundan, Misrilal's older brother who operates the family's land is bent on killing Dhowli through slow starvation. Misrilal's family sends Misrilal away and manipulates him with lies to the point that he succumbs to their pressure. He does not return for his lover after one month as he has promised. When he does return, it is to marry the bride provided by the family.

Meanwhile, even the other villagers, peers of the same social status, turn on Dhowli and her mother because she has loved a Brahmin and "turned down those from her own caste" (198). Had Misrilal raped her she would have had the others' empathy, but because they have consummated a mutual desire, Dhowli is shunned by her peers. Sanichari remains firm in her support, but nonetheless Dhowli finds herself faced with the desperate socio-economic choice between prostitution and suicide. The village has turned against the mother and daughter, and they can get no work. When there is nothing, but gruel left to eat in the house the mother tells the daughter "If you can't find something to keep alive, better kill yourself." The daughter agrees; the next night she opens her door to the men who have been soliciting her for sex. Thus, Dhowli begins her career as a prostitute, a career that allows her to feed and clothe herself and her family, and a career that further instills the wrath of the Misra family against her. Kundan Misra is angry because she has outsmarted his plan to starve her to death; in revenge, the older Misra brother challenges Misrilal about his manhood, given that his son is being raised by a prostitute. Dhowli, in different circumstances, has already told Misrilal that he is not a man, and Misrilal, in response to his brother's taunting, turns against Dhowli, and "to prove his manhood" asserts his caste/class, gender, and race status over her: he has her sent out of the village to become a "public whore" in the city.

Mahasweta's story engages a "naturalized" construction of sexuality as well as a "materialist" construction of sexuality and the two seem to exist at odds. The naturalized paradigm is created through a description of nature that takes on anthropomorphic characteristics that parallel the "nature" of Dhowli's sexual encounters.[267] Dhowli and Misrilal consummate their mutual attraction for the first time in the forest which, even at that moment, plays a role in convincing Dhowli to become involved with Misrilal: "The forest in the early afternoon is primitive, gentle, and comforting. The Misra boy's voice was imploring, his eyes full of pain and despair. Dhowli was unguarded in mind and body. She gave in" (trans. in Bardhan 192). As the relationship develops, the forest continues to set the tempo: "In the solitude of the forest, the Misra boy was dauntless, telling her of his plans, and his words seemed to mingle with all the myths associated with the old forest, taking on an enchanting and dreamlike quality" (in IOW 192).

In Dhowli's period of waiting, after Misrilal has been sent away by his family, the forest takes on an aura of foreboding: "The woods looked horrible to her, the trees looked like ghoulish guards, and even the rocks seemed to be watching her" (194). When Dhowli's situation becomes unbearable, and she first considers suicide she intends to use pesticide: "She knew that she could fall asleep forever with the poison for killing maize insects" (trans. in Bardhan 187). In contemplating death by a synthetic anti-natural element—a pesticide—Dhowli figuratively equates herself—the human shunned by her lover, and subsequently, by her community—with the creatures of nature that are despised, and thus poisoned by men. This symbolic gesture evokes the accounts over the decades of Indian farmers who have committed suicide by ingesting pesticides (Shiva). But Dhowli's decision not to carry out the suicide reaffirms her self-respect as she recognizes her own ambivalence toward her lover's betrayal, based on the vexed complexity of the situation.

Descriptions of nature are suspended in the middle of the narrative, but return at the end when Dhowli has been sentenced to become a "public whore"—when she is on the bus to the city, having been exiled, evicted from the village by her lover:

> The sun rises, and Dhowli watches the sky, blue as in other days, and the trees, as green as ever. She feels hurt, wounded by nature's indifference to her plight. Tears finally run from her eyes with the pain of this new injury. She never expected that the sky and the greens would be so impervious on the day of turning Dhowli into a public whore. Nothing

---

267 As the land/nature's role develops, in relation to Dhowli's changing situations, a comparison could be made to Lucas's use of landscape to connote foreboding that warns of the oppression against the people working the land.

> in nature seems to be at all moved by the monstrosity of what is done to her. Has nature too gotten used to the Dhowlis being branded as whores and forced to leave home? Or is it that even the earth and the sky and the trees, the nature that was not made by the Misras, have now become their private property? (in IOW 205)

Nature plays the role of surrogate lover: it is the "imperviousness" of nature, not of Misrilal, that finally brings Dhowli to tears. Yet through this shift of applied metonymy, nature plays a further role in this passage: in questioning the motives for Nature's indifference, Dhowli draws attention to the connections between gender abuse and the economic and environmental subjugation of "feudal capitalism."

Dhowli evokes the brutal relationship between affect and economics when she tells Misrilal "I spit on your love. If you had raped me, then I would have received a tenth of an acre as compensation" (trans. in Bardhan 199). Thus, the elegant respect Misrilal paid Dhowli (even when he must break hierarchical barriers to do so) that reads as progressive, even radical, resistance, at the beginning of their love affair, ultimately results in adding injury to insult when he fails to love up to his feelings. It is not only Misrilal's inability to "be a man" and stand up to his family's brutal classist patriarchal prejudices that destroys the couple's ability to love each other, betraying their relationship. Subjugated, and materially contained, Dhowli articulates only that she deserves monetary support from him. Finally, the couple fails to identify the role that the structural violence of the feudal social structure plays in the demise of their relationship. Placed in such unseemly circumstances, romantic love cannot survive.[268]

Dhowli has gone from being a child widow—one of the lowest gendered positions that one can hold, in terms of civil rights, in much of Indian society—to being the lover and prospective wife of the son of a rich Brahmin landowner (though whether the actual ritual of Hindu marriage could have been carried out in their context is doubtful) to being a prostitute for the lowest caste men. What reads as a pendulum swing in Dhowli's "fate" is tempered by a gigantic consistency: In each instance, her status is based almost exclusively upon a sexually-charged definition of Dhowli as female body and her sexualized body

---

268 Western critics must recognize that romantic love in the Indian context is influenced by different traditional and commercial factors than in the west, and that—try as we might, through the incorporation of historical specificity, to read the story as "authentic" to its setting—we will always finally apply our own trace constructions of "romantic love" in our rendering of the narrative's implications. Thus, it is most honest simply to acknowledge that, despite familiarity with and ambivalence about both systems, my reading of the romance is itself necessarily a cross-cultural construction.

reads as her only available means of empowerment, albeit a dangerous one. When Dhowli suggests that she and her mother could go to the city and become beggars, her mother tells her "You think men will see you as a beggar? They'll be after your body" (trans. in Bardhan 201). And because of her ostracization in the village, the men will not hire her to do day labor but will pay to fuck her. Thus, as in "The Witchhunt" and other stories, Mahasweta deconstructs "fate" and re-presents it as vulnerability to sexualized, gendered, and class, caste, and ethnicity/race-based discriminatory forces of disenfranchisement.

"Dhowli" is a tragedy of affect that portrays a rural feudal system in a patriarchal structure reinforced by capitalist values that creates gendered experiences of extreme poverty and depredation. Mahasweta foregrounds classist and sexist manifestations of blame and punishment for sexualized experiences and documents the patriarchal co-optation of lifestyle and lovemate choices in rural Bihar. The economic infrastructure of patriarchy manifests itself in the disembodiment of basic human rights from the female body. Despite such disenfranchisement, Dhowli, as characteristic of Mahasweta's female protagonists remains intelligent and pro-active in her decision making. Thus, when they fail in their struggles, these women protagonists, nonetheless, expose the magnitude of the oppressive forces they face. When they win, they are successfully resistant role models who do not separate the interests of individual from community or human from nature. Two stories in *Imaginary Maps* offer both a continuation of and a response to the gender and nature issues voiced in "Dhowli." However, before examining them, I turn to Mahasweta's short story "Paddy Seeds" to offer an interpretation of Mahasweta's narrative of "natural selection" as "self-determination" in the context of the reproductive rights of land and seed.

13 Contested Seeds and Imaginary Maps

13.1 "Paddy Seeds" and Seed Patents: Mahasweta Devi and Vandana Shiva Write about Contested Seeds on Corporate and Community Grounds

"Paddy Seeds" identifies internal colonialism and environmental racism, which, as Mahasweta demonstrates, are two of the most distinctive of the many forms of rural India's racial patriarchy. "Paddy Seeds" foregrounds class, caste, and race power-relations played out largely by men. This narration of dominance is inscribed onto the life of the low caste Dulan Ganju, the male protagonist who, like many of Mahasweta's women characters, exposes what Spivak has identified as "the space of difference *on decolonized terrain* in the space of difference" (OTM 4). By incorporating Vandana Shiva's theoretical and cultural analysis into my interpretation of the story "Paddy Seeds" I utilize methodologies that consider the spectrum of local to global implications of the struggles of predominantly rural Tribal and Dalit (outcaste/low caste in 20th Century translation) largely Hindu agriculturalist villagers in central to northeastern India.

"Paddy Seeds" demonstrates that the oppressive nature of the postcolonial, rural, feudal system negatively impacts male lives—albeit in differently extensive ways than it affects female lives. Dulan's central struggle is his attempt at autonomy of his land utilization; for many of the female characters in Mahasweta's stories, the struggle for autonomy is at the site of the sexualized and/or reproductive (physical) body. Bardhan suggests that "Paddy Seeds" "is the story of rebellion against tyranny at several levels, personal and social, economical and cultural" (WOPR 26). The story begins with the description of a barren piece of land outside "Kuruda and Heradi, the twin villages of outcastes and tribals" (trans. in Bardhan WOPR 158); on the barren land there is a spot of green—weeds and thistle—that is fertilized by the corpses of martyred victims—those who initiated struggles for fairer pay and working conditions during the harvest, those who the local landlord/moneylender has had killed. The barren land, nourished into fertile production by the corpses, belongs to Dulan Ganju, who is forced to keep the secret of his landlord's macabre use of his land.

The story of "Paddy Seeds" reveals how Dulan Ganju breaks out of this impossible situation of domination, and it demonstrates the psychological torture and material and physical distress Dulan's family and village endure at the hands of their landlord. The narrative is both a dire critique and a hopeful tale in that Dulan can break the reign of terror—at least temporarily—and thus he manages to feed the village (figuratively, and the story suggests, in the long

https://doi.org/10.1515/9783111041575-014

run, literally) with paddy nourished by the remains of his murdered family and neighbors. Herein, Mahasweta politicizes the modernist trope of the regenerative forces of nature by charting them over environmental racism and other class, caste, and ethnicity issues. (The regenerative seed trope further begs a transnational reading through a Sustainable Agriculture lense—a main tenet of Vandana Shiva's raison d' être and ongoing life work.) Paddy (rice) seeds are of figurative and literal importance to the story "Paddy Seeds" just as they are literally the traditional bulk food sustenance of much of India, including the region that is the site of most of Mahasweta's work.[269]

In conjunction with Vandana Shiva's charting of the co-optation of regeneration by multi-national corporate interests, "Paddy Seeds" reveals a regenerative seed trope that is multidimensional in its revolutionary markings. Shiva's comparative model of theories of seed reproduction traces a shift from mythologically-informed ideology toward an ideology of "patriarchal capitalism" that bears resemblance to the ideological shift that followed British colonization of India's forests, discussed in the Chipko Andolan chapters. Shiva illustrates her model through seed paradigms: "While ancient patriarchy used the symbol of the active seed and the passive earth, capitalist patriarchy, through the new biotechnologies, reconstitutes the seed as passive and locates activity and creativity in the engineering mind" (in CtH 129). She suggests that the *progression* of the sequence is a *regression* into increased economic disenfranchisement for the rural "Third World" peasantry, in particular the women.

Vandana Shiva empirically illustrates what Mahasweta critiques in global corporate capitalism and its effects on indigenous "Third World" peoples. She shows that paddy seeds, and other seed grains are the latest sites of contested territory to fall victim to a global "capitalist patriarchy." Seed grains developed over the centuries as sites of production that are most compatible with local conditions; seed grain sites, which have been *village commons* since their beginnings in early agriculture, are being invaded by multinational, corporate capitalism.

> Where technological means fail to prevent farmers from reproducing their own seed, legal regulation in the form of intellectual property rights and patents is brought in. Patents are central to the colonization of plant regeneration and, like land titles, are based on the assumption of ownership and property. A vice president of Denentech has stated, 'When you have a chance to write a clean slate, you can make some very basic claims, because the

269 The story indicates that, in this context, however, rice, is something of a luxury. Largely because of the tyranny of landlords such as Lachman Singh, the people have little (of any food, even rice) to live on.

> standard you are compared to is the state of the art, and in biotechnology there just is not much.' Ownership and property claims are made on living resources, but prior custody and use of those resources by farmers is not the measure against which the patent is set. Rather, it is the intervention of technology that determines the claim to their exclusive use, and the possession of this technology then becomes the reason for ownership by corporations and for the simultaneous dispossession and disenfranchisement of farmers. (Shiva in CtH 133)

Common village property is thus seized by corporate thieves who patent it for their own profits. This silent techno-colonial war is another geopolitical condition that India, Chicana/o communities and Mexico and Latin America (as well as many other "Third World" sites) experience in common. Faxing seed genes to theU.S.to obtain patents and patenting gene materials from indigenous peoples threatened by genocide are rumored to be endeavors of the techno-imperialism of U.S-based multi-national corporations in Latin America. Vandana Shiva sees this techno-war as yet another colonial war in a (not so post)-colonial world: "Technological development under capitalist patriarchy proceeds steadily from what it has already transformed and used up, driven by its predatory appetite, towards that which has still not been consumed. It is in this sense that the seed and women's bodies as sites of regenerative power are, in the eyes of capitalist patriarchy, among the last colonies" (in CtH 129).

Of these two struggles over the life-generating reproductive forces and the sites of struggle—seeds and bodies, and land, one struggle is largely feudal, one largely neocolonial; however, as Mahasweta demonstrates, they are inextricably connected, and both are being fought over the boundaries of seed walls. While both are environmental struggles, we cannot conflate the differences of the locally defined struggle of Mahasweta's characters with the globally determined struggle over genetic and intellectual patenting. Nonetheless, I find the parallels significant in providing both metaphorical and literal links between the "first world" power structure, which has our tacit support and "Third World" disempowerment.

If we map the aggressions of Lachman Singh, the landlord/moneylender, we find that throughout the development of most of the story, he has under his control all the mechanisms, which might allow village circumvention of his power; thus, he can indefinitely keep the villagers in a lifestyle of virtual slavery. As a Rajput landlord and moneylender, Singh is "an ethnic outsider in Bihar, usurping the lands of the area's native peasants" (Bardhan 174). The villagers have no access to their own plots of land on which to grow food to subsist thus avoiding the capitalist economy; nor do they have any workers' control or unionization to alleviate the militant economic aggressions carried out against them by the landlords who monopolize access to the cash economy and remuneration for the workers laboring in the fields of the richly landed.

At one point, the omniscient narrator observes that "Lachman Singh's paw is poised over him (Dulan) with its pointed claws barred" (trans. in Bardhan 175). Mahasweta's trope, in which a predatory human is represented as a predatory animal, reverses the conventional figure of peasant as animal. She uses the comparison of dominator to animal to reverse the damage done by those who see the "other" as less than human in order to legitimate violence against them. The reversal is activated by the fact that the violence that Dulan perpetrates against Singh operates as resistance—it is, in effect, an act in self-defense *and* in defense of the other villagers. Shiva's discussion of the linguistic battle over land, marks how this kind of literary naming (which promotes a concept of nature as passive, thereby facilitating domination) has affected indigenous peoples, such as tribal communities of "Paddy Seeds."

> The patriarchal construct of the passivity of the earth and the consequent creation of the colonial category of land as *terra nullius*, served two purposes: it denied the existence and prior rights of original inhabitants and negated the regenerative capacity and life processes of the earth. The decimation of indigenous peoples everywhere was justified morally on the grounds that they were not really human; they were part of the fauna. (Shiva in CtH 130)

The idea of "active habitat" that interacts with men and women, mentioned in discussion of "Dhowli," might be applied here as a conceptual means of resistance. Dulan is not initially one to challenge this kind of systematic oppression either figuratively or literally; rather, he is described as a "complex, dark-natured, inscrutable," man who is always "busy working on tricks for survival," but not necessarily for resistance (trans. in Bardhan 160). Here, Mahasweta reverses the dark/light, evil/good western dichotomy; his dark nature reads as intelligent rather than foreboding. By modifying Dulan's cunning with the phrase "for survival" his action gains a subaltern credibility. Furthermore, Bardhan parallels Dulan's subaltern struggle against structural tyranny with women's gendered struggles when she notes that his "crafty personal battle of wits with the powerful, his manipulative obsequiousness, is not unlike the strategies of indirect personal power that women learn to deploy to counteract patriarchal domination" (25). Furthermore, Dulan is aided in his resistance to tyranny and his fight for survival by women, in specific his wife, and his fellow villager, Sanichari.

It is Sanichari who comes up with the idea of how to get money from the unproductive land that Dulan has been given by his landlord: "Dhatua's father should go down to Tohri, to the *Biddi* [Block development] office. The government will give him seed and a cash loan to cultivate the land!" (trans. in Bardhan 161). In the narration of how Dulan initially got the land, we receive a critique that illustrates the manipulation of the good intentions of the Bhoodan workers who were attempting "wealth redistribution by means of moral persuasion rather than through class struggle or state intervention ... announcing the amounts donated in different areas to arouse a kind of contest for goodwill" (Bardhan 161). Here, landlords, who gave away uncultivatable land, prospered from unexamined praise. Sanichari critiques the situation with an insider's wisdom, and, perhaps, the fatalism created in popular stereotyping of the Bengali "babu" which Bardhan defines as "urban, educated gentleman" (161). When the well-intentioned, educated, and relatively empowered class is seen as inept against landlords (or earlier in the century, against the British colonizers), the dominating force gains symbolic strength.

> Sanichari was quick to size them up, saying that they were the crazies from the babu class; they thought they were going to make the landlords repent and say what a shame it was that they had so much land and others none at all and give away their land. Sanichari said she would know when that was going to happen because she would then find herself seated in a chair drinking buttermilk and cooking rice for two meals a day. (trans. in Bardhan 161)

Sanichari's cynicism is proven correct—she has, perhaps, even underestimated the scheming of the landlords. The land redistribution allows the landowners to get rid of land that was not giving them a monetary profit and it simultaneously improves their reputations in the eyes of the outside/dominant society.[270] However, as Sanichari had predicted, it did little for the peasants. Mahasweta's narration evokes cynicism about the Bhoodan movement. Kalpana Bardhan mentions in an editorial note that the Bhoodan Movement, initiated by Vinoba Bhave, was led by Gandhian Sarvodaya workers who had other campaigns including "ecological protection movements" (163). The initiation of the 20th century Chipko Movement illustrates a moment in which Sarvodaya workers were productive and successful, not only in serving the rural poor by interven-

---

270 The landlords' "giving" of the land, which is useless in terms of producing capital, is somewhat analogous to the US "giving" reservation land to Native American nations in areas that the government deemed at the time to be the least productive; much of that land was later decimated for uranium, or as storage for toxic waste and later for lithium (for batteries related to *renewable energy* development). Likewise, Singh retains control over the land that he has given Dulan. Because Dulan is dependent upon Singh's goodwill to keep his family's agricultural jobs and the access to revenue on the thorn-producing land, Dulan must obey Singh's orders about what is to happen to the land.

ing in the destructive power structure, but in gaining the respect of local communities by laying out a means to protect forest lands.[271]

Mahasweta—in a style reminiscent of Ana Castillo's—offers imbedded criticism of the state and federal governments' roles in the rural system, as well. For instance, while Dulan is successful at obtaining the seed and money, to do so he must go back to Singh to request Singh's lawyer's endorsement of his application—without a command from those in higher "real" authority the government office won't consider the low caste Dulan's request as valid. Mahasweta exposes the government hierarchy that denies civil rights to those on the bottom of its scale (trans. in Bardhan 164).

The rural structure of environmental domination is further mapped out through other, often reoccurring, characters in Mahasweta's stories: in addition to Lachman Singh and other competing landlords, there is Hanuman Misra, the priest in the village of Tahad, whose malevolent power and influence penetrate many of Mahasweta's stories. The sometimes corrupt, sometimes charitable, government officials who arrive and depart, always at the most opportune times for the landlords, are, at best, ineffective in their bid to aid the outcastes and tribals.

The model change agent in "Paddy Seeds" is Karan Dusad. Upon his return from jail where he was serving time for his involvement in a controversy with the landlord over wage rates, he successfully organizes workers who obtain a small wage increase at harvest time. However, immediately following the harvest, the landlord terrorizes the people by setting fire to the village, in which the most vocal of the harvesters live, and he has Karan and his brother killed. The two brothers are the first of the victims that the landlord, Lachman Singh, brings to Dulan's land for burial in the middle of the night. With his actions, Singh unwittingly participates in turning Dulan's inaccessible, fallow land into figurative productivity as a memorial ground for those killed in resistance.

Simultaneously, these two events—the burial, on Dulan's land, of those who led revolts and the revengeful arson at the workers' homes signal that Lachman Singh is escalating his economic dominance into a reign of terror. As

271 The critique of the Bhoodan movement should not read as Mahasweta's condemnation of social action groups. Bardhan sees such characters in Mahasweta's works as "patronizing," but they also try to "forge links" and "change the exploiters' hearts" (25). Mahasweta was deeply influenced, both politically and literarily, by her association, early in her life, with the Gananatya, a group that Bardhan describes as "highly accomplished, keenly political actors and writers, who took the revolutionary step of bringing theater to the villages on themes of burning interest in the thirties and forties in rural Bengal" (24). In some parts of the country the Bhoodan Movement itself was much more productively effective than Mahasweta describes.

Dulan surmises, "Lachman knew he did not need to hide the removal of the bodies. Those who witnessed it could not open their mouths. They had read the warrant in his silent glare: whoever talks is dead too" (trans. in Bardhan 168). The reasoning behind Singh's violence is versed in vicious classist, caste-biased hyperbole.

> From time to time, with flames and the screams of the massacred leaping into the sky, the lowly untouchable must be made to realize that it meant nothing at all that the government had passed laws and appointed officers to enforce them and that the Constitution held declarations. They must not forget that the Rajputs remain Rajputs, the Brahmins remain Brahmins, and all the Dusads, Ganjus, Chamars, and Dhobis remain under their feet... (trans. in Bardhan 168)

Further grounds for the government's ineffectiveness are raised when a leftist S.D.O. (subdivision officer) who seems to be genuinely interested in the people's welfare is transferred to the remote region as punishment for his leftist tendencies. Simultaneously, a government circular informs the people of their fair wages—fourteen times what they have been receiving. With sardonic irony, Mahasweta writes that his transfer notice, "written with impeccable logic" states that "[t]he most important problem of the region is the deep-seated distrust of the farm laborers toward the landlords. Thus, there has been no agricultural growth, and the per capita income has not risen. Income, consumption, health, education, and social consciousness—everything has remained backward, subnormal as a result" (trans. in Bardhan 170). Mahasweta illustrates the results of ineffectual government intervention; readers already know that the basis of "mistrust" and the listed ills are due to the tyrannical control the landlords keep over peoples who have no access to channels of justice that are upheld—in name only—by law. The S.D.O. with the likely option of moving on to other work, accepts the risks of helping the people organize a campaign for a pay raise before the upcoming harvest. However, this too results in violence. The S.D.O. takes Singh to court, but Singh is acquitted, and the S.D.O. is "demoted for inciting farm laborers and disturbing the traditionally harmonious[272] relations between landlords and laborers in the area" (trans. in Bardhan 173).

Mahasweta describes the full complexity of land-based struggles in a time when "[t]error reigns under the cover of Emergency rule. The hoodlums working for the Congress party have become contractors procuring outside laborers" (trans. in Bardhan 173). One of these contract laborers appears "with four lack-

272 Mahasweta's sardonic comment is implicit here and the effect is not unlike that achieved by Ana Castillo's politicized irony, as discussed earlier.

eys, all dressed like him in polyester clothes and dark glasses. Speaking in the style of the movie star Amitabh Bacchan" (trans. in Bardhan 173) he accomplishes what the villagers and the government officers could not, telling Singh, "Your monopoly is over. Breaking strikes, contracting labor, managing the harvest, everything is now going to be in the hands of professionals. I am the *mercenary* supplier of this service .... Even if you don't want me, I'm still your supplier. So pay up the advance of five thousand rupees ..." (trans in Bardhan 175). [273] However, later in the story even the contractor is jailed; thus, Singh retains unbroken control.

At harvest time following a strike, Dulan's son Dhatua is shot by one of Singh's men and is buried in his father's plot of land. Two levels of crisis ascend to a climax at this point—one is the horrific physical crisis of the villagers who are being pressed into increasingly dire material straits with no means for recourse against their aggressive oppressors. The other is the psychological crisis that builds within Dulan with the weight of more and more bodies being buried on his land. The communal struggle and the martyrs of that struggle gather figuratively inside Dulan as he suppresses the secret of their memorial grounds. At the point when he can no longer bear the psychological pressure, Dulan begins to prepare the field for planting. Rather than eating the seed grain, as has been their family's habit over the years, Dulan announces that he is going to plant it. In his planting ritual he speaks to his dead son: "I'll not leave you as thorn bushes anymore. I'll turn you into paddy. Dhatua, I'll make you all grow into paddy!" (trans. in Bardhan 180). Thus, a circular relationship emerges between the assassinated villager's bodies and the new rice that grows even better than "the fertilized fields" of the landlords. This relationship culminates at the end of the story when Dulan gives the rice as seed grain to the other villagers. The reference to "costly" fertilizer (i.e. bodies of villagers) is evoked both in Dulan's interaction with Singh and with the other villagers.

The issue of "costly fertilizer" is foregrounded differently by Vandana Shiva when she explicates the relationship of traditional farming practices to the Green Revolution that would have likely affected the area beginning in the decade before the story takes place. "Fertility," she explains "was no longer the property of soil but of chemicals" (SA 131). In Dulan's fields, however, the "fertilizer" represents the property of the soil which has been removed from his control; in a different sense, it is the embodiment of the villagers themselves. Dulan literally grows his rice through the "bodily labor" (through decomposition) of

273 Mahasweta inserts popular culture into the conflict; Bacchan was a leading actor in the world's largest film industry.

his son and the other martyred villagers. Dulan prepares the soil, containing the body of the son he had helped conceive years earlier, to make a bed for the conception of the seed grain. Desperate for the figurative reclaiming of both his son's life and the distribution of the awful secret he keeps, Dulan creates life out of Singh's waste of life. He refuses to harvest the ripe rice, but saves it for strategic, figurative, and psychological reasons. He knows Lachman Singh will hear about the rice and come to rebuke him for growing it. Dulan wants this to happen—and he wants to save the seed for the village as seed grain so that he can turn the body of his son and the others into "seeds for us to plant and grow over and over again" (trans. in Bardhan 184).

Vandana Shiva uses Jack Kloppenburg's description of the seed to discuss it in similar, circular, (economically materialist) terms:

> ... it [seed] is both a 'means of production' as well as a 'product.' Whether they are tribals engaged in 'shifting cultivation' or peasants practicing settled agriculture, in planting each year's crop farmers also reproduce the necessary element of their means of production. The seed thus presents capital with a simple biological obstacle; given the appropriate conditions, it reproduces itself and multiplies. Modern plant-breeding has primarily been an attempt to remove this biological obstacle, and the new biotechnologies are the latest tools for transforming what is simultaneously a 'means of production' and a 'product' into mere 'raw material.' (Shiva 132)

The capacity for the seed to self-generate its reproduction introduces an element into the capitalist equation that capital is unable to control; it is this quality that will—at least, figuratively—defeat Singh's feudal reign of power. In "Paddy Seeds," not only is the seed regenerative, but the human bodies at either end of the seed's growth cycle are interlinked *with* and *through* the seed in a cycle of regeneration. This is a component of the hopeful elements worked out in the story. Furthermore, Dulan's rice-planting, analyzed in conjunction with Shiva's discussion of the seed patenting's role in promoting global capitalism meets Gadgil's and Guha's charge (discussed in Chapter Three) that "modes of production [be supplemented] with the concept of modes of resource use" (13). However, before this cycle can complete itself, Dulan must destroy what is devastating him, himself, his family, and his neighbors. He kills Singh, who as he expected, has appeared at his field to reprimand him for planting paddy.

Singh is on horseback and Dulan, standing beneath him, can reach up and pull him off—Dulan, again acting both empirically and symbolically, topples the enemy from below. Dulan grabs Singh's gun but does not shoot Singh; rather, Dulan knows that beating will bring the most shame on Singh as he dies. Another reason Dulan beats—rather than shoots—Dulan, is perhaps his dissonance with killing, which the narrator describes through a comparison with Singh's violent lifestyle:

> He pounds Lachman Singh's head with a rock. He keeps pounding. Lachman Singh was skilled at murder. He knew the value of bullets, and he was never moved inside by the act of killing. In Dulan's situation, he would have killed with a single bullet. Dulan is not a skilled murderer, and rocks have no value, and this act of killing is for him the culmination of a very long and hard battle inside his mind. So, he goes on pounding Lachman Singh with the rock, long after he is dead. (in Bardhan 182)

Singh is rendered helpless unto death in the face of the fearless fury that Dulan feels; Dulan has nothing to lose because, as he points out, "And your people? Maybe they'll hit us back and kill us. When haven't they done so, malik? When have the police not beaten us?" (in Bardhan 182). It is important here that Dulan's killing is, in a sense, "justified" by the fact that he has thought long and hard about it, because this runs counter to the legal premise, in the U.S., and elseswhere, that premeditation increases the severity of the crime. As Mahasweta illustrates in this story, this precedent is erroneous when long-standing violence has been perpetrated by the "victim" upon the one who kills. The most obvious parallel example of a moment in which the legal premise should be reconsidered in contemporary U.S. society would be in "crimes" against an abusive partner that have been precipitated by that spouse's/domestic partner's abuse. This is most often a gendered situation in which women, who make up most abuse victims, like Dulan, rebel against an unbearable situation. Thus, Dulan's rebellion might read as a parallel to what Bardhan notes as deployment of women's "indirect power" against the patriarchy; here, in the moment of rebellion "strategies of indirect power" are used to assert directness. As demonstrated in both contexts, the moments of greatest vulnerability and greatest power, are simultaneous, for those in the disenfranchised position. Dulan's unfamiliarity with killing might read as conventionally "feminine." His ritualized caring for the dead and nurturing of the rice plants further bend many conventional gender expectations.

Ethnicity and caste conflicts insert themselves during the death scene of Lachman Singh, as well. For example, we read that "[e]ven in the grip of the fear of death, however, a Rajput in this part of the country can never beg for mercy from an untouchable. And, even if a Rajput could beg an untouchable for life, the untouchable may not grant it. Dulan cannot now" (in Bardhan 182). Dulan tells Singh, "Such a shame, malik, that you have to die at the hands of a Ganju!" To shame the landlord further, Dulan styles his killing to disgrace the Rajput landlord more intensely; he does so in accordance with his interpretation of his act through the ideological paradigm of ethnic, hierarchical valuation. Dulan continues this conscious reversal of hierarchies as he buries him: "He rolls the body into the ravine and rolls rocks after it. Many, many rocks. A gleeful laugh rises inside him. So, malik parwar, now you've become just like one of the Oroans and the Mundas those you so despise! Your own funeral is burial under stones in a ravine!" (182) Bardhan explains the significance of Dulan's actions which add insult to Singh's death, "In being killed by an untouchable and buried like a tribal,[274] the high-caste Lachman Singh is doubly disgraced. Dulan's gleeful remarks signify, in Mahasweta's interpretation, his satisfaction in avenging their common oppressor" (in Bardhan 182).

While Singh's death ensures a momentary release for the villages, the fact that Singh's son is waiting in the wings to step into his father's shoes demonstrates that his carefully crafted structure of violence has been merely disrupted, not overthrown. Nonetheless, the expansive regenerative value of the paddy seeds continues to allow for optimism. However, that hopefulness reiterates the grim realization of the severity of the loss of local control of the regenerative value of the rice paddy—that Shiva notes—for those who are the victims of corporate crimes that are broader in scope than Singh's local ones. The relationship of global and local struggles is marked by Spivak's observation of the opportunist inclinations held by the World Bank, in specific, the impulse to capitalize on indigenous peoples' knowledge of nature. The World Bank's dubious, self-serving offers of "assistance" are embedded in the hierarchical relationships that Mahasweta critiques (IM 199). As Shiva notes: "Violence, power and ecological disruption are intimately linked as life-processes ... and their sundering becomes the source of the creation of value and wealth—when invasion into the space within (seeds and wombs) becomes a new space for capital accumulation and a new source of power and control which destroys the very source of control" (Shiva, Mies 33). The tribals and outcastes, as subaltern, speak out of the multi-layers of oppression and disenfranchisement; both figuratively and materially, the voices Mahasweta portrays are even, (or rather especially), in the age of the (bio)technological revolution, the most insightful for envisioning a revolutionary turn toward justice.

"Paddy Seeds" eloquently illustrates the domination of the feudal system and its connection to other forms of oppression, while "Dhowli" (like "Doulhoti the Bountiful" discussed in the next section) provides a synthesizing focus on gender issues. In the final sections on Mahasweta's work, I will contrast the stories in *Imaginary Maps* by examining how patriarchal, capitalist, and feudal

274 Bardhan explains: "Tribals traditionally bury their dead in a chosen common ground and mark the grave with a rock; the untouchables customarily cremate their dead" (182).

forces combine "symbiotically" to create systematic havoc in environment and body that disproportionately disrupts the lives of the poor, of women, of the Dalits, and of the indigenous tribal groups.

13.2 Imaginary Maps: A Fictional Survey of Forest on Foot

In *Imaginary Maps*, a short story collection, the cover, title page, and the first page of each story contain the same map: a map of the South Asian subcontinent, labeled in Latin that appears to have been drawn around the time of Alexander the Great's campaigns. I found no credits for this map anywhere in the book. However, the map gives the appearance of being one of the earliest topographical documents of colonial exploration into South Asia. As it was a result of Alexander's mis-mapping that the area became known as India, the map seems to mark a beginning point of foreign misrepresentation in the geopolitical history of the subcontinent. In this marking, the text is graphically scored as a postcolonial revision that extends the history of the country of India far before 1948. Historical borders are deconstructed by such moves. Indeed, the text is consistent in this impulse: the written narratives—Mahasweta's short stories, Preface, Afterword, and Gayatri Spivak's interview of Mahasweta Devi—also dissect and revise geo-historical borders repeatedly. In Mahasweta's stories, the displaced tribal woman's body is re-placed onto maps and calendars. This is most extensively illustrated in the death of the character, Douloti, a bonded prostitute and protagonist of "Douloti the Bountiful."

In discussing "Douloti, the Bountiful," Spivak draws on the ending of the story in which Douloti, a dying prostitute, has lain down in the courtyard of the school which has been inscribed with a map of India in preparation for an Indian Independence Day celebration.[275] The last two lines of the story are saturated with figurative significance which Spivak decodes through an explanation of the multiple meanings of the original Bengali. Douloti, having vomited blood upon the map, dies sprawled across the subcontinent. "The story ends with two short sentences: a rhetorical question, and a statement that is not an answer: 'What will Mohan [the schoolmaster] do now? Douloti is all over India'" (OTM 94). Spivak suggests that "[s]uch a globalization of douloti, dissolving even the proper name, is not an overcoming of the gendered body. The persistent agendas of nationalisms and sexuality are encrypted there in the indifference of superexploitation, of the financialization of the globe" (OTM 95). Spivak further

275 Douloti means "wealthy", furthering the ironic significance of the title (88).

proposes a movement in the last sentence that "can push us from the local through the national to the neocolonial globe" (OTM 95).

That Douloti dies on Mohan's carefully drawn map, prepared in the courtyard of the school for the Independence Day celebration, is of further importance given Mohan's political character development through the story. He has met Douloti twice before during his work against bonded slavery. He has been moved with the desire for creating change in a system he finds reprehensible, but he is ineffectual in his work because he is unwilling, or does not understand how, to risk revolutionary change, as is evident when he asks his fellow worker about response to bonded prostitution in another region. The friend replied "They are shooting guns in Bihar to keep the honor of the harijan women in Bhojpur. They are not putting a fresh coat of clay on the schoolyard, painting a *map* of India with *chalk* dust, planting a flag, and singing 'May the flag remain high,' like you" (85). [276] Thus, as she dies on his map, Douloti underscores the implicit accusation that Mohan's friend has made: the ineptness of the "Mohan's" on the Left leaves the most extreme systems of oppression unexamined and does not attend to the disenfranchisement unto death that the "Doulotis" face.

Bonded labor is one of many markings of the links of colonial and feudal exploitations of indigenous peoples. Mahasweta Devi and Spivak explain that, in India, the far-reaching bonded labor system had its origins under British rule: "They [the British] created a new class, which took away tribal land and converted the tribals into debt-bonded slaves" (IM xii). Mahasweta maps out the extensiveness of the bonded labor system noting that "in every state, there are districts marked as bonded labor districts because there are more than forty thousand bonded laborers in each of them" (IM xii). Mahasweta remarks that the district she writes about in *Imaginary Maps* she has "covered ... on foot" (IM xii). She writes maps of such oppressions on paper, only after having literally surveyed on foot, the regions she portrays.

Spivak describes the significance of the bonded labor system in parts of "modern" India in which families' "[o]nly means of repaying a loan at extortionate rates of interest is hereditary bond-slavery" (OTM 82).

> Below this is bonded prostitution, where girls and women abducted from bonded labor or *kamiya* households are thrust together as bodies for absolute sexual and economic exploitation .... Women's body is thus the last instance in a system whose general regulator is still the loan: usurer's capital, imbricated, level by level, in national industrial and transnational global capital. This, if you like, is the connection. But it is also the last instance

276 Spivak italicizes all words that are in English in the original.

> on the chain of affective responsibility, and no thirdworld-Gramscian rewriting of class as subaltern-in-culture has taken this into account in any but the most sentimental way. (OTM 82)

Her observation that class and ethnicity-based readings (even the work of the Subaltern Studies Group) have not adequately addressed this gendered deferral, stands as a mandate that is met in Mahasweta Devi's fiction, even while not being addressed adequately in theoretical analysis.

Mahasweta not only observes gendered deferral, but she also describes the facets of its effects. Douloti's physical dissolution under the brutality of the bonded labor system—to the point where she dies at age 27 of tuberculosis and venereal disease—empirically reiterates and extends the relationship between AIDS and environmental disintegration we've drawn from Ann Danaiya Usher's article and María Elena Lucas' description of the South Texas landscape. Women's bodies under the physical siege of forced prostitution—i.e., rape—are set into a cycle of deterioration that is furthered by a lack of respect and nurturance for their emotional and intellectual selves. Likewise, in the forest, the scourge of environmental desecration—i.e., "the rape of the land" in conjunction with an absence of the respectful nurturance of ecological balance carried out by those who, like the Chipko women, hold tenets of reciprocity with their forest homes—sets a cycle of disintegration into effect that poisons the land, destroys its potency for reproduction, and causes the breakdown of linked/symbiotic relationships within habitats. In Douloti's story, like in "Dhowli," but unlike most of the other narratives we've examined, Nature, as the female protagonist's homeland, remains unharmed—it is the woman's body that is ravished, as "Nature" is elsewhere.

Douloti's definition of "natural" sanctions her integrity as a "country girl" (71), charts her forced removal from the "natural" world of the rural countryside to the urban-based world of bonded prostitution, and articulates her desire for Nature as an antidote to her life of imprisonment. When she is first kidnapped, she encounters new kinds of food, clothing, shelter, and other lifestyle changes that she considers luxurious, however she is not impressed by being enclosed and away from Nature. This is particularly evident when the indoor latrine is discussed, as is made clear in the following passage. Douloti wonders whether she will be kept,

> [i]n this kind of room with brick walls all around and clay tiles on the roof? Douloti's own place is much better. You can see trees and sky if you stand at its door. The latrine is by the door. O how much better it is to "go" in the fields. When one of Douloti's uncles went to the field as a child, a tiger took him. Douloti has seen wolf, hyena, and fox. She has never seen a tiger. (IM 52)

Despite the story of the threat of a tiger's attack, Douloti remembers the wild animals as symbols of contentment and fulfillment in the face of the threats of the "civilized" havoc in which she finds herself. As in "Paddy Seeds," Mahasweta uses animal metaphors here to present and endorse alternate indigenous/low caste world views.

Likewise, Uncle Bono's visits offer a means for contrasting Douloti's lived experiences before and during her bonded imprisonment. The last time that she sees her uncle he comes with his comrades who are conducting a survey of the "*Incidence Of Bonded Labor*" (85). After answering their questions, Douloti turns her full attention to her uncle requesting a personal emotional connection to her past, as opposed to political strategies of resistance. She remembers the natural world of her childhood as follows.

> Remember that banyan tree in Seora village? Speak of it. I swung myself on its branches when I went to graze the goats ... When winter came to the Nagesia neighborhood we would sit by the fire ... At night you beat on *cans*, made a great uproar to chase away tigers.
> Then I didn't know, Bono Uncle, that the world had so much liquor that it held Baijnath, that it had so many clients. I lost those days long ago. I get all of it back when I see you. (IM 87)

Douloti again recalls her idyllic youth in nature when, her *career* is ended by disease, and she is turned away from the hospital and told to take the bus to the medical center in a larger city. At this point, she faces precisely the same dilemma that Alejo faces, in *Under the Feet of Jesus* when Estella's family is told that the health center can do nothing for the poisoned young man, and he must be seen in the hospital in a larger town. In Alejo's case, however, Estella, and her family, intervene in the systematic absence of health care for the rural poor when Estella takes back the money that they have given the nurse to buy gas for the trip. Conversely, Douloti, forcibly separated from her family, is dependent solely on her own waning strength to get care. When the trip for medical care appears unfeasible, she decides to attempt to walk back to the countryside that she had "lost," so that she may die there. Thus, the World of Nature represents a paradigm of resistance against, and escape from, her urban, bonded, sexually exploitative containment. Yet, it is an antidote that she fails to obtain, and Nature remains an elusive ideal to which she cannot return.

The forest that Douloti yearns for is the backdrop for Mary Oraon's resistance in "The Hunt." While Douloti extends Dhowli's situation of forced displacement from self-determination of body and environment, Mary Oraon, in "The Hunt" offers an alternative model of capable resistance where both women and the forest are under the siege from local feudalism and global capitalism.

Both she and the planted timber are partially the result of earlier Australian colonization in the region. Parallel plots are narrated in "The Hunt"—one tells of Mary's revenge against male sexual power that allows her to determine her own life mate and escape the kind of contained lifestyle to which Dhowli and Douloti have fallen victim. The other plot develops around the illegal cutting of the sal forest by an outside contractor who lies and cheats and bribes so as to carry home an immense profit from organizing the cutting of a forest he has no right to cut. The contractor is also Mary's stalker. To retain her choice in her sexual partner/companion with the Muslim man, Jalim whom she has chosen to marry, Mary uses the festival of the women's hunt in order "to make the biggest kill"—the contractor (IM 17). She thereby adheres to the "virtual meaning" of the tradition that the communities carry out in symbolic ritual. As Mahasweta explains in "The Author in Conversation,"

> [t]he tribals have this animal hunting festival in Bihar. It used to be the Festival of Justice. After the hunt, the elders would bring offenders to justice. They would not go to the police. In Santali language it was the Law-bir. Law is the Law, and *bir* is forest. And every twelfth year it is Jani Parab, the women's hunting festival in Bihar. Every event narrated within that story is true. What Mary did that day has been done in that area again and again. Among the tribals, insulting or raping a woman is the greatest crime. (viii)

Mahasweta explains that the tribals' songs are their documentation of history and through their songs she learned the story of "what [Mary] had done on Jani Parab day in order to marry the Muslim boy" (xxviii). However, as Mahasweta's conversation with Gayatri Spivak tells us, the significance goes beyond Mary's own self-determination in romance, and in reprisal for male harassment: "The real point is, Gayatri, that it was Jani Parab, the woman's hunting festival day. She resurrected the real meaning of the annual hunting festival day by dealing out justice for a crime committed against the entire tribal society" (xxviii). Thus, in this story, the tribal woman is the proprietor of justice.

As Mary prepares for her own marriage which will follow the hunt, she also prepares grounds for a marriage of gender and ecology issues. When the contract broker insults Mary with his unsolicited attentions, she reveals his crimes against the community to the people he is cheating. She kills him at the end of the tree harvest, after damage has been done to the forest, but nonetheless her actions prevent him from returning for the next stand of trees to mature, as he intended. Furthermore, her detective work and organizing have prepared the local community—from the landowners on whose "property" the sal forests stand to the manual laborers who carry the cut lumber—to resist the illegal deforestation that took their resources and failed to remunerate them fairly. Thus, figuratively, following the symbology of the tribal traditions, and sociopolitically, by offering strategies for fighting the lumber contractors' intrusion, Mary Oraon appropriates and transforms conventional responses to threats in order to defend both her autonomy and the forest environment upon which her community depends. She acts, from a different tradition than the Chipko women to the north; though in sync with community tradition, she acts in singular, and with violence. However, the aim of her actions accomplishes a parallel goal—protection of her community's forest-centered lifestyle and women's autonomous choice for shaping the future of their own lives and the forest itself.

13.3 Mapping the Pterodactyl: Impossible Mandates and Indigenous Spaces

As Puran Sahay prepares for a journalistic foray into a famine-ravaged tribal area, he consults a survey map of the region. Readers are told that "[t]he survey map of Pirtha *Block* is like some extinct animal of Gondwanaland. The beast has fallen on its face. The new era in the history of the world began when, at the end of the Mesozoic era, India broke off from the main mass of Gondwanaland. It is as if some prehistoric creature had fallen on its face then" (99). Thus, the myth of the pterodactyl is figuratively rendered as a map of indigenous India. Later in the story we read of the roads that have penetrated this map. The portrayal of the reasons for and effects of these roads illustrates Mahasweta's narration of cultural genocide.

> Whenever they [tribals] come up [to the market] they see the broad arrogant roads. These roads have been built with the money sanctioned for tribal welfare so that the owners of bonded labor, the moneylender, the touts and pimps, the abductors, and the bestial alcoholic young men lusting after tribal women can enter directly into the tribal habitations. (109)

In a note at the end of the story "Pterodactyl, Puran Sahay, and Pirtha," Mahasweta writes "I have deliberately conflated the ways, rules, and customs of different Austric tribes and groups, and the idea of the ancestral soul is also my own. I have merely tried to express my estimation, born of experience, of Indian tribal society, through the myth of the pterodactyl" (196). In "The Author in Conversation" she tells us that "[i]f read carefully, 'Pterodactyl' will communicate the agony of the tribals, of marginalized people all over the world" and, furthermore, "'Pterodactyl' wants to show what has been done to the entire tribal world of India..." (xxi). The task that Mahasweta lays out for herself in this story is an enormous one.

My brief treatment of the story will merely mark some of the moments when environmental racism and, to a lesser extent, gender issues, figure in the immense content of this epic-styled narrative. Initially, however, the following short synopsis is necessary to contextualize my comments: Puran, a journalist, leaves the woman he cannot bring himself to marry, to investigate a famine and alleged incidents of poisoning in a remote tribal region. During his trip, he meets a mute tribal boy who brings him face to face with the pterodactyl, which is known in the region through ancestral myth. When Puran writes his report, however, he includes none of the sacred and mythical aspects of his visit, but simply documents the exploitative practices on the part of the government, global interests, and the national elite, which have led to the people's near-extinction. The voice of Saraswati, the woman he leaves behind, emerges occasionally, most often to offer a "feminist" reading of whatever situation he is struggling to comprehend. Communication, or rather the impossibility of communication, surfaces often in the narrative. This impossibility seems to be a trope that comments on the situation of the tribal community, vis-á-vis, the "mainstream" of India. The differences that cause such a lacuna in communication are seen as differences of degree, rather than absolutes, in "Pterodactyl." Perhaps because Mahasweta has combined and conflated the local specifics of tribal differences, the tribal community reads as monolithic in some respects, here.

In first encountering the pterodactyl, the narrator speculates on the issue of communication. "What do its eyes want to tell Puran?" (157). The rhetorical question is answered with a universal list of man-made means and indications of extinction that recall "The Way of the Cross" litany in *So Far From God* both in the contents, and the liturgical form.

> What does it want to tell? We are extinct by the inevitable natural geological evolution. You too are endangered. You too will become extinct in nuclear explosions, or in war, or in the aggressive advance of the strong as it obliterates the weak, which finally turns you naked, barbaric, primitive, think if you are going forward or back. Forests are extinct, and animal life is obliterated outside of zoos and protected forest sanctuaries. What will you finally grow in the soil, having murdered nature in the application of man-imposed substitutes? "Deadly DDT greens,/ charnel-house vegetables,/ uprooted astonished onions, radioactive potatoes/ explosive bean-pods, monstrous and misshapen/ spastic gourds, eggplants with mobile tails/ bloodthirsty octopus creepers, animal blood-filled/ tomatoes? (157)

By the end of the list, the referents begin to seem absurd—perhaps protogenetically engineered, bizarre mixtures. Yet given that nature, when distorted with pollutants, by definition, creates absurdities, the reader can assume each item on the list is an alias for an empirical entity that has developed into something that is "virtually real."

The list of the universal problems extends beyond the exploited indigenous communities. As Puran questions the pterodactyl in his mind, a procession of images emerges. He focuses first on indigenous history, and then on the environmental crimes, which play a major role in that history.

> The collective being of the ancient nations is crushed. Like nature, like the sustaining earth, their sustaining ancient cultures received no honor, they remained unknown, they were only destroyed, is this what you are telling us?
> The dusky lidless eyes remain unresponsive.
> Have you come up from the past to warn us, are you telling us that this man-made poverty and famine is a crime, this widespread thirst is a crime, it is a crime to take away the forest and make the forest-dwelling peoples naked and endangered? Are you telling us that it is a crime to grasp in a stranglehold the voice of protest, and the arm of combat. (IM 157–158)

While the pterodactyl brings to bear issues that are community-wide for the indigenous people, Puran, as academic scholar, confronts these issues through personal crisis. Puran struggles with himself in front of the creature because he finds that there is "*No point of communication*. Nothing can be said or written" (IM 158). Communication as knowledge becomes a focal point for sardonic comment on Puran's life in subsequent passages: he struggles with his academic approach to the subjects about which he writes, his faith in the written word, and his failure to come to terms with his relationship with Saraswati.[277]

> How little he understood when he traveled in Ranchi district from one Munda village to another till he finally learned about them from S. C. Roy's book. Saraswati says, "Perhaps you have not been able to know me after so many years spent close together, because there is no book about me."—No I have not, Saraswati. Hominidi—hominidi—homo sapiens—mapiens—the human being, modern man is afraid to know life by entering life. It is much safer to know life by reading books, reading theory." (IM 158)

In this passage, dysfunctional communication in a heterosexual relationship is treated with humor, but it simultaneously speaks of a serious hiatus, not only between genders, but almost universally between humans whose value systems, perceptions of the world, and levels of autonomy differ extensively. The passage might be compared to the moment of crisis that Mathur, also a scholar, faces in "The Witch-Hunt" "when he realizes that he has been alone in the way he perceived of the events that the whole village witnessed.

277 Saraswati is the Hindu goddess of knowledge and as such she plays a metaphorical role for Puran the scholar of life. Yet Saraswati, the woman, Puran's potential life partner, does not allow her influence to be limited to the divine muse role her name suggests. Puran seems hesitant to deal with her on either level, but unable to let go of his attachment to her.

The trope of the *removal* of theory—and even of language itself—from life is used, earlier in the story, to represent removal from the synesthesia between language and life experience; furthermore, it exemplifies the displacement of indigenous experience in the context of colonial and post-colonial India. The following conversation between Puran and his friend Shankar suggests that there are moments—such as the moment of intense exploitation—when common ground cannot be found, even through translation.

> Shankar says his say in Hindi, but the experience is a million moons old, when they did not speak Hindi. Puran thinks he doesn't know what language Shankar's people spoke, what they speak. There are no words in their language to explain the daily experience of the tribal in today's India. Pashupati Jonko, of the Ho tribe of Singhbhum, a native Ho-speaker, had said with humble amazement at the time of translating Birsa Munda's life into the Ho language, There are no words for "exploitation" or "deprivation" in the Ho language. There was an explosion in Puran's head that day.

Puran, in his own mind, carries Saraswati's analysis into the gender issues that stand between them; gender issues and indigenous rights issues are conflated in the following sentence: "He must understand Shankar's words, otherwise no justice can be done to himself or Saraswati in the Saraswati affair" (IM 119). Puran thereby attempts to draw parallels between the personal crisis of understanding in which he is a main player and the larger crisis of understanding between communities in which he is struggling to be a "participant-observer." As is her style, Mahasweta relates this theoretically relevant piece of language trivia with a historically specific manifestation of the "exploitation." She remarks on the foreignness of the concept of exploitation in the Ho community.

> That was during the Sagwana (teak) movement: "Away with teak, save the Sal." Forest Singhbhum was washed over with turbulence. There was firing at Gua .... in the site of the unfinished Sagwana struggle the word "exploitation" cannot be explained. Then in Ilyagarh, in the resistance against the damming of the Kharkai, the fearless Kol tribal Gangaram Kalundia died. In Gua, Bidar Nag is ruthlessly beaten to death, and Pashupati Jonko says, "Brother! The word "exploitation" is not in the Ho language. (118)

Saraswati intervenes in this listing of ecological resistance on the part of indigenous communities to keep the discussion from stereotyping the tribal people as monolithic "noble savages." Kamal, the theorist—"who sticks to the tribal area, [and yet] even he can't jump over the glass wall of book-learnt theory in his head"—reports that class differences among tribals are creating an exploiting elite. Saraswati, indignant at his ignorant insensitivity, complicates his comment.

> —Oh yes, in our society one person can swindle others and make millions in black money, keep it abroad, that you can accept. And we have taken away everything that is their own, we are imposing our rotten value-system upon them, and then if one of them makes a bit of money, or becomes like us, we abuse them from a safe distance. We say, Look, look! How that man's nature has changed, he is no longer a tribal. (IM 118)

Saraswati's interventions, which are apparently only in Puran's head, are moments in which as Gayatri Spivak observes, "[w]oman is in the interstices of 'Pterodactyl.'" (Yet, we don't experience the thoughts or presence of the tribal women to any substantial extent, here.) Spivak's analysis names other instances of such appearances that take us beyond fiction and into other areas of cultural production and activism such as has been examined in my study.

> If the non-Euro-centric ecological movement offers us one vision of an undivided world, the women's movement against population control and reproductive engineering offers us another. And here too Mahasweta shows us the complicity of the state. The bitter humor with which she treats the government's family planning posters shows us that the entire initiative is cruelly unmindful of the robbing of women and men of Pirtha of the dignity of their reproductive responsibility. (IM 201)

Spivak finds an answer for "the inter-nationality of ecological justice in that impossible undivided world" that can be potentially reached through learning what she names "ethical responsibility in singularity" or in its "simple name" love (200); Puran, she believes, learns this lesson. "Nature, the sacred other of the human community, is, in this thinking, also bound by the structure of ethical responsibility of which I have spoken in connection with women's justice. The pterodactyl is not only the ungraspable other but also the ghost of the ancestors that haunts our present and our future" (IM 200).

Through readings of Mahasweta's work that intervene in cultural relativism, Spivak "attempts to open the structure of an impossible social justice glimpsed through remote and secret encounters with singular figures; to bear witness to the specificity of language, theme, and history as well as to supplement hegemonic notions of a hybrid global culture with this experience of an impossible global justice" (IM 197). She believes that "we must *learn* to learn from the original practical ecological philosophers of the world, through the slow, attentive, mind-changing (on both sides), ethical singularity that deserves the name of 'love'—to supplement necessary collective efforts to change laws, modes of production, systems of education and health care" (200–201). She posits this mandate to "*learn* to learn" as "the lesson of Mahasweta, activist/journalist and writer" (201). Spivak suggests that,

> [t]his relationship, a witnessing love and a supplementing collective struggle, is the relationship between [Mahasweta's] "literary" writing and her activism. Indeed, in the general global predicament today such a supplementation must become the relationship between the silent gift of the subaltern and the thunderous imperative of the Enlightenment to "the public use of Reason," however hopeless that undertaking might seem. (201)

This model may be useful as a transformative answer to Puran's ambivalent feeling about relying on the written theoretical word over the lived experience. As the story ends, Puran makes decisions to mediate the crisis he experiences and witnesses; he does so by acknowledging that he is accountable to those with whom he crosses paths. In accepting the responsibility of encounter, Puran's identity crisis comes to a productive head. Having witnessed the intensity of the tribals' struggles and the futility of language in the face of their exploitation, he ultimately recognizes that, for himself, the weapon that can best serve is, nonetheless, the pen.

> [L]et Puran be able to keep his faith in the pen. he is not a tribal .... his ancestors' soul does not become unquiet, he is not the prey of man-made famines every year.
> How can he have faith in their faith? Puran must keep unshaken his faith in paper, pen, and the printing machine. Puran has nothing else.
> If there is no pen there is no Puran. (IM 185–186)

Puran reinstalls his faith in the efficacy, or at least the necessity, of his writing by realizing that it too will play a direct role for the tribals' struggle. He thus finds his niche in the immensity of their cultural resistance project.

> How will fifty-nine million six hundred and twenty-eight thousand, six hundred and thirty-nine people capture and put together their history and their culture from the storm winds of areas ruled by twenty-five states and the central government? Will they too finally seek shelter from mainstream writer? If Nagesia has to learn from the writings of some anthropologist, he has to get that much education in order to read that material. If he wrote his own story!
> Even educated tribals don't do that.
> Puran picks up his pen. (IM 186)

Having come to a personal resolution, he sits down to write a report that lays out the operative structure of oppression and follows up with suggestions for political resolutions. In a sense, his report is his offering to the pterodactyl, just as the illiterate village boy Bikhia, he encountered early in the story, has worshipped the ancestral myth with his wall paintings. The alliance of the two projects is expressed in the story's ending:

> Love, excruciating love, let that be the first step. Now Puran's amazed heart discovers what love for Pirtha there is in his heart, perhaps he cannot remain a distant spectator anywhere in life ....
> Oh ancient civilization, the foundation and ground of the civilization of India, oh first sustaining civilization, we are in truth defeated. A continent! We destroyed the primordial forest, water, living beings, the human. (IM 196)

As Spivak notes, the protagonist in each of Mahasweta's stories creates a part of the model that is needed to promote the "impossible global justice" that she posits as an imperative.

As audience for these ecocritical justice texts, we are brought face to face with the oppressive realities of environmental demise that structurally disenfranchised communities confront in daily life. Hence, the literature of environmental justice is potentially a powerful tool in understanding, communication, expression, and mobilization. It may be able to raise the consciousness of its readers, and to give support to struggles taken on by communities under attack. Or it may at least "link ... theories in the pursuit of social and cultural change" (Huggan 128) so that we may better discern and learn about the facts and subsequent representations of environmental and human loss.

In the Epilogue, I propose roles that productive pedagogical transformation might play in utilizing the "Virtual Realism" of environmental racism and the social movements and poetics that resist it. We look to Draupadi for a shift in learning to listen, attempting to comprehend. Readers tussle with what Gayatri Spivak posits as our "circumscribed task"—recognizing our complicities alongside our connections. Past and future coalesce, as we global citizens distinguish the many languages, literally and figuratively, that subaltern women use in assuming leadership to face increasing climate cacophonies. The Afterword alerts 21st Century readers to the reverberations of environmental justice moving across Greater México, across the Americas, across the South Asian subcontinent, along rivers and arroyos, and in border cultures, in between.

Epilogue: The Pedagogical Implications of Studying Environmental Justice Literary and Cultural Poetics

> Read dialectically, narratives indicate that language and discourse do affect human life in determining ways, ways that are themselves shaped by social history. Giving rise to questions concerning language itself, the sovereignty of our identity, and the laws that govern our behavior, they reveal the heterogeneous systems that resist the formation of a unitary base of truth.
>
> Ramón Saldívar

> I suspect that among other readers there is a hunger for journalism and art to make visible the passion for freedom and dignity that has moved men and women of every color and class, again and again, to challenge seemingly immutable power. It's not a question of offering us saints and icons. It's a question of making vivid the human face of social change, as well as the abuses and violent opposition of entrenched power.
>
> Adrienne Rich[278]

In discussing discourse which portrays struggles for environmental justice, I have made figurative and descriptive use of topographical metaphors to envision the writing as cartography—a cross between power-mapping and connecting the network of expressive culture with capability to transform. Thereby, I've discussed the discursive relationship to "real life" maps that offer a path through "Virtual Realism." I've talked about the presentation of a topography of environmental justice and mentioned the relationship of literary texts to other more directly practical/pragmatic genres of environmental justice discourse. We have looked at the form that fiction takes, particularly in terms of its adaptation of a marvelous or magical realism with an underlying polemical, often decolonial agenda. I've also mapped out the theoretical implications of the environmental justice narratives in relation to their postcolonial and new social movement contexts and the expressive and movement thinking in relationship to other theoretical stances on environmentalism, ecology, and related social issues such as immigration and feminisms.

Implicit to this cartographic framework is the necessity of learning to read the keys to the maps. Thus, in concluding, let us briefly pay heed to the pedagogical methodologies mandated by this eco-historiographic literature and the

278 Adrienne Rich in letter in "EXCHANGE: The Chavez Legacy" *The Nation*, November 22, 1993, p. 635 and Saldívar in *Chicano Narrative: The Dialectics of Difference* 1990, 207.

https://doi.org/10.1515/9783111041575-015

environmental and eco-justice organizing that has inspired it. How do we learn to key these maps? How do we learn to pay attention so that through the poetics, the maps are ours, as active, politically conscious readers, students, teachers, and researchers, to follow? And how do we learn to teach what Gayatri Spivak, borrowing from colloquial Bengali, has termed "*anushilan,*" in English "attention, concentration" (IM 197)? To address these questions, we must take up further inquiries (some raised initially in this book's introduction) into how to develop pedagogical methodologies that resonate with the literary, graphic, and expressive artworks and grassroots progressive struggles for the cultural poetics of environmental justice.

Interventions through different cultural discourses have the potential, in moments of pedagogical crisis, to erupt at the epicenters of predominantly "Western" paradigms and disrupt their *naturalization* of colonization, patriarchy, capitalism, and environmental racism. (This phenomenon is related to the concern that Gayatri Spivak raises repeatedly as she presents Mahasweta Devi's work in an international, North-centered context.) Investigating poetics for environmental justice themes across distinct historical contexts may intervene in the regressive impulses of dominant systems of homogeneity. To demonstrate this, I would like to return to a memorable convention keynote.

Mary Louise Pratt in "Comparative Literature and Global Citizenship," delivered at the 1993 MLA Comparative Literature Forum suggested that Comparative Literature should be involved in three—then, and I suggest, still now—current historical processes: democratization, globalization, and decolonization. In discussing how these would occur within language, literature, and cultural studies classrooms, she suggested that as we acknowledge new perspectives, we must shift our priorities and accountabilities so that we may remain competent comparativists and teachers in our multicultural academy of the 1990s. The imperative still rings true decades into the new millennium.[279] "[I]f

279 A pedagogy of Post/De-colonial American Encounters might begin with the recognition that mono-English language instruction is incomplete in the multi-cultural, post-colonial classroom of the Americas, U.S. and otherwise. Literature in Spanish, English, Spanglish, Portuguese, Patois, Ebonics, Creole, French... as well as the continents' indigenous languages, the Diaspora languages from South Asia and other regions and their many written scripts, could become accessible through the diverse language legacies and abilities in many modern classrooms. A democratization process in American academia could be initiated through the multi-lingual, multi-ethnic studies of cultural poetics within the classroom that was previously mono-lingually contained. I am not suggesting that professors need to become multi-lingual to be competent to teach composition or World literature, but that we acquaint ourselves with the

one begins working beyond a handful of European languages, the issue of translation versus original language relates to a different set of priorities. These are things that can only be done via translation which are too valuable and important not to do" (61).

As Pratt points out, multilingual material presented in a classroom with one shared language of primary instruction means more "collective and collaborative work" (61). In multicultural—and I add, interdisciplinary—classrooms, students and teachers are already engaged in cultural translation in sharing perspectives with each other; why not acknowledge this fact and open our translating to include language as well? Pratt suggests "updating our rhetoric," disposing of the Anglo-centric term "foreign languages" and fostering, instead, bi or multilingual people who engage in a study of "expressive culture." These changes would help us shift and clarify priorities in changed academic contexts. Such shifting priorities would help us, as teachers, to respond to the diverse strengths in our classrooms. Not long after rereading Pratt's talk, Lawrence Hart, a family friend who is a Cheyenne peace chief described to me the research being done in his community to study, document, and revitalize their language. I noted the many parallels to a Comparative Literature postdoctoral project and the comparison brought me back to Pratt's proposal. Is there a place for Indigenous languages such as Cheyenne, and Diasporic languages, such as Bengali/Bangla to be studied in the academy, on the terms of their practitioners, and in service to their communities?

While Pratt's audience seems primarily to be those involved in traditionally privileged Literature and Language Programs, attending the elite/expensive convention (and meat market) of the Modern Language Association, with its own legacies of exclusion and continuing discriminatory practices, the democratization involved in re-visioning the teaching and learning comparatively, in a multilingual, multicultural classroom, is also applicable—and maybe more vital—in the community college ESL classrooms in which I had been teaching for two years when I heard Pratt's talk. If we consider multi-lingual/cultural experience a privilege and means of contribution to a collaborative pedagogical effort, how do we go about shifting priorities and accountabilities? What will this entail in the classroom?

Our relationship to environmental justice in postcolonial, decolonizing contexts shapes our pedagogies and classroom space. In open diverse classrooms, students and teachers are already translating at least a minimum amount of

---

linguistic/cultural/paradigm-shifting resources available in our students, our colleagues and our communities.

culture to share with others. Through teaching environmental justice texts this exchange is expanded trans-disciplinarily to include languages and histories as well. Concurring with Mary Louise Pratt's suggestions for "updating our rhetoric," to nurture bilingual or multilingual people engaging in study of "expressive culture" (1995 61), I believe that applying environmental justice theories helps shift and clarify priorities in fluctuating academic contexts. Such strategies are particularly fruitful when both the classroom and the curriculum are decolonial and multicultural; in literature, cultural, social studies, composition and other classrooms, a post/decolonial studies curriculum, built around the theme of exposing environmental racism and promoting justice, links the local and global, yesterday and today, community and academy, thus bringing together the concerns of activists, artists, scholars, and teachers to envision the world as transformed by the textual production of a network of environmental justice practitioners.

Much of the literature that this book examines has not been previously discussed in-depth as post or decolonial discourse or environmental literature.[280] However, these texts do establish what Graham Huggan terms a "cartographic connection," that is, they provide "that provisional link which joins the contestatory theories of post-structuralism and post-colonialism in the pursuit of social and cultural change" (128). Thereby, they engage in a decolonial remapping of environmental concerns that interconnect with issues of gender, race, postcoloniality, and immigration. In the exchange between literature and theory,

---

280 Contemporaneous critical exceptions that address ecological destruction as part of postcolonial situations include Gayatri Chakravorty Spivak's "companion essays" to the Mahasweta Devi stories she has translated (1995, 197). Both Kalpana Bardhan and Spivak, Mahasweta Devi's predominant, early English translators, both discuss postcoloniality in the short stories that they translate. Additionally, in "Mahasweta Devi's *Imaginary Maps*: Colonial Legacy and Post-Colonial Ecology in India" Jia-Yi Cheng-Levine discusses Indian colonial and postcolonial ecological situations in light of Mahasweta's work. Critical work on Mahasweta in other languages may address postcolonial issues but was not available to me. Vik Bahl's paper, "Interrogating the National Narrative: Re-Imagining History in the Contemporary Indian Novel in English" delivered at the "Writing History: Narrative Strategies for the 21st Century" panel entitled "Imagined Communities: Recreation of Identity in Modern Fiction," on October 20, 1994, and his dissertation discuss *Yatra* as a postcolonial text, in a broad sense of the term. Rajeswari Sunder Rajan addresses some issues of postcoloniality in *Yatra* in his article, "The Feminist Plot and the Nationalist Allegory: Home and World in Two Indian Women's Novels in English" in *Modern Fiction Studies*, Vol. 39, #1, Winter 1993. Susan Comfort discusses Ken Saro-Wiwa as a environmental justice writer portraying a neocolonial context in a forthcoming article entitled "Struggle in Ogoniland: Ken Saro-Wiwa and the Cultural Politics of Environmental Justice in *Organization and Environment*.

further agendas become evident as well: rural/urban, caste, sexuality, LGBTQIA..., religion, nation, immigration status, sense of place, and sedentarism are a few of the additional identity issues that have direct bearing on the portrayals of social environmentalism of the cultural poetics, I examined.

In *The Dialectics of Our America*, José Saldívar provides one of the most extensive mappings of postcolonialism in the Americas in the 20th Century. He proposes a "new critical cosmopolitanism [that] neither reduces the Americas to some homogeneous Other of the West, nor does it fashionably celebrate the rich pluralism of the hemisphere" (4). Saldívar finds that for Latin American, Ethnic American, and Caribbean texts, read within a context of a Pan American Postcolonial Studies, the mapping of "the common situation shared by different cultures... allows their differences to be measured against each other as well as against the (North) American grain" (4). For instance, Gabriel Garcia Marquez's work, when read in its Pan American (post)colonial context, presents a dialectic that has "no inconsistency between aesthetics and politics," (José Saldívar 25) while dominant Anglocentric readings that focus on non-dialectical formalism fail to uncover the historical detailing of colonialism and imperialism in the Americas that Marquez presents. The dominant Anglocentric American critical approach misreads, not only Marquez and other conscientious practitioners of *lo realismo maravilloso*, but also Latina/o and Caribbean writers (such as Ana Castillo and Helena María Viramontes) who are influenced by them.

For further illustration of the global and historical limitations of many current practices of Postcolonial Studies, let me turn to the Caribbean. Courses in English language that examine sites of colonialism in their post-Independence eras often introduce texts from the Caribbean, including what were previously British, French, and less frequently, Spanish, and Portuguese colonies. How often, however, on such a syllabus, do we see a Puerto Rican text that represents the lived reality of U.S. colonialism and environmental racism currently in practice? Activist texts have cited the bombing of Vieques as environmental racism, but how often have we examined this issue in the humanities classroom? How often do we see texts from Cuba that explicate its "postcolonial" reality? (Cuba's groundbreaking work in organic and low technological/eco-appropriate agriculture could lead the world in adopting agricultural methodologies that are less detrimental to the climate and to human and environmental communities.) How often do we see South Asian Diaspora Studies of the Americas? And when will we develop regionally defined courses that foreground the coloniality (both post and neo) and the resulting environmental and social detriment in the Caribbean, North, South and Latin Americas? Or how often do we look to Indigenous nations within any continent for our eco-justice storytelling?

These are rhetorical questions that allow us to examine both the forced—as in the increasingly common book banning's and the U.S. embargos against Cuba—and the more subtly programmed decision-making that goes into syllabus building. I present these questions also as propositions to consider as we re-examine, tinker with, and perhaps dismantle our canon building. In concluding my study, I propose that looking at environmental justice as a mimetic, historicizing, linking *and* transformative theme may be one way to counter some of the flaws that are common to both Post-Colonial and Ethnic American Literature and to pedagogical and, sometimes, scholarly approaches in contemporary academe.

Focusing on such situations, in the historically "colonial" aspect of a "post-colonial" moment can make us miss the more recent nuances of the story. For example, when a Guyanese, creative writing student of South Asian descent presented me with a descriptive narrative of racial conflict between the African and Indian communities in her hometown, I realized that neither of us had the knowledge to deepen the sociohistorical significance of the pronounced struggle. While British colonialization had shaped the context and informed the content of the racially defined conflict she had remembered, in eloquent prose, the British presence was missing, no longer central, though haunting her autohistography, in ways yet to be uncovered. Through innovative, critical vigilance, and the establishment of a canon of "Post/De-colonial Poetics of the Americans," we can create pedagogies that intervene in the more regressive impulses of British post-colonialism and U.S. multi-culturalism as often practiced. Our pedagogies can uncover a Pan American Poetics and a means to collaborative translation that democratizes and decolonizes the global classrooms in which we find ourselves, establishing a foundation for understanding multiple, discerned perspectives on environmental justice. While the environmental and climate racism that invades South Asian, Chicana/o and many other communities has colonial roots, interdisciplinary approaches to our teaching can lend more multi-faceted, clearly articulated descriptions of present manifestations. Through social movement study and local stories, their specific instantiations of global corporate impositions on local communities can be heard replete with supportive poetics.

In the U.S., Ethnic American literary studies also often fail to recognize the global connections and socio-historical facets of our inquiries. For instance, two trends in undergraduate anthologies and readers predominated in publishing house textbook catalogs and exhibits at the close of the millennium: multicultural and environmental collections. Diversity and ecology were timely campus topics, however, none of the environmental readers that I've examined contain essays about environmental issues that have been addressed primarily by people of color, issues which fall under the rubric of "environmental justice." The textbooks reveal an absence that demonstrates the trendy shallowness with which issues of multicultural diversity, environmentalism, and indeed feminism, are often engaged. They *efface* what environmental justice poetics *demonstrate*—environmentalism is an issue with direct ties to social justice, colonialism, imperialism, patriarchy, globalization, climate justice and more. The absence of textbook writing on environmental justice illustrates how pervasive environmental racism and Eurocentrism continue to be in academic institutions.

Investigating environmental justice poetics contributes to our understanding of the development of theoretical, artistic, pedagogical, and practical bases of oppositional consciousness that act in alliance to discern and counter environmental racism. Analysis of such consciousness provides us with an understanding of the larger political and pedagogical ramifications of the cultural products of environmental justice. Research on and curriculums of environmental justice poetics are one means of sharing the insights and creative expression of women most directly impacted by degradation of Earth's homes and habitats.

Old pedagogical approaches often don't fit the literatures that we teach. For instance, the paradigm of western periodization of literature that conventional anthologies have used erases literary aspects that do not fit the predetermined periods. Therefore, it is necessary to create new, more appropriate, pedagogical methodologies that resonate productively with the issues foregrounded historically or in current geopolitical and cultural contexts. The study of both South Asian and Chicana/o texts on their own, and in comparative terms has intervened in the constrained paradigm of western periodization. Such studies work "against the grain" of dominant, interpretive ideologies that do not lend themselves to an inclusive and constructive classroom. Working against the grain may entail contextualizing the texts we teach, on their own terms, even, and especially, when they conflict with conventional terms and resonate with less-exposed perspectives.[281]

To talk about Chicana/o literature as post or decolonial literature broadens the parameters of postcolonial issues and establishes useful international parallels and contrasts with which Chicana/o literature engages. To discuss literature from India as texts that describe a multi-cultural nation—India—resonates with

281 For a study of the related issues, specifically in Chicana/o literary study in a comparative context of cultural history and identity, see Louis Mendoza's *Historia: The Literary Making of Chicana & Chicano History*. College Station: Texas A & M Press, 2001.

the U.S. discussion of multi-culturalism in ways that politically reactivate both fields. To trace social issues such as "environmental justice" and "feminism," through literature, in conjunction with more aesthetic ideological issues, raises questions that impact both aesthetics and politics and everything in between and entangled in both. Kalpana Bardhan emphasizes one role that Bengali/Bangla (and I would argue, other) socially engaged traditions of literature and culture, can play in analyzing the structure and functioning of society.

> The power relations and modes of oppression in society must be seen at multiple levels, in their many-faceted and interconnected patterns. Both oppression and the resistance of the oppressed are structured by gender, class, caste, and ethnicity, usually in combination. If we want to understand modes of oppression and modes of resistance and rebellion in relation to each other, then literature was a good place to look. (3)

Bardhan observes literature's relation to the multi-valiant natures of disenfranchisement and, conversely, self and community empowerment.

> Like many others trying to understand social processes, I turn to the literature of the society I study—Indian generally, Bengali specifically—for insights and for affirmation or negation of observations that have been made with statistical, sociological, and anthropological methods. Literature as social commentary helps us gain valuable insights not only into behavior, but also into the thoughts, beliefs, and motives underlying behavior. Literature helps me understand the microsociology of behavior within the layers of social relations: relations between individuals, between groups variously situated in society, between individuals and the group, and the contradictions in these relations. In a society characterized not only by hierarchical structures of privilege and oppression but also increasingly by class differentiation and class conflict, literature reflects and grapples with the tensions between these structures. These tensions, crucial to understanding social processes, are extremely hard to discern and measure with the standard methods of the social sciences. (Bardhan 3)

Bardhan assumes a division here—between the literary study and other fields of study, which is nuanced by the following observation from Gayatri Spivak. "That history deals with real events and literature with imagined ones may now be seen as a difference in degree rather than in kind. The difference between cases of historical and literary events will always be there as a differential moment in terms of what is called 'the effect of the real'" (Spivak 1988 243). Given the important relationship between the historicizing of literature and the literature of social and environmental history, what lessons can community historiographies—like the ones that portray environmental and gendered histories—offer through progressive pedagogies? All texts are laid out in arenas in which formal, linguistic, and socio-political concerns all contribute to a crosshatching of power and identity relationships in the cultural product. The texts resist, replicate, and describe gendered and racial oppression, and they strive for, imagine, or describe social justice struggles on a range of issues. While genre and methodology affect the politics of the text, they do not determine it; rather that happens in the social engagement that occurs between writer and reader. In examining those hierarchical engagements, we may discern the relationships between an environmental justice text, its varied contexts, and its diverse audiences.

An example involves my experience of finding over 20 copies of books by the Nigerian writer, and social and environmental justice activist Ken Saro-Wiwa on the shelves at Columbia University the weekend after his execution. A week later, almost all his works were checked out. While it is deplorable that despite a Goldman Environmental Award and a Nobel nomination, it was Saro-Wiwa's death that appears to have prompted recognition of his people's struggle in Ogoniland and his writing, his death should make us face our "first world" accountability. The Ogoni struggle is rooted in European colonialism, and as such, it is a postcolonial struggle. However, inherent in the "post" of post colonial is an implicit relationship to imperialism and global capitalism. In the Ogoni' people's case, Shell Oil was not only the perpetrator of environmental racism, but the corporation also initiated repression against those who resisted their exploitation. Saro-Wiwa's words, like those of Rigaberta Menchu, Subcomandante Marcos, Mahasweta Devi, Chico Mendez, and others may be the vanguard of late 20th Century postcolonial studies precisely because all these writers link a colonial past with a present that is dominated by capitalist imperialism.

In *Outlaw Culture,* bell hooks reminds us that after Malcolm X was assassinated, "Bayard Ruskin predicted that 'White America, not the Negro people, will determine Malcolm's role in history'" (155). For hooks, history confirmed what had seemed ludicrous thirty years previously: Malcolm X became a "hot commodity" on the "white supremacist" consumer-capitalist market (155). Similar phenomena of 'white [moneyed] determination' develop in literary canon formation and in popularized ethnic cultures of the Americas. How do we identify and resist such trends? José Saldívar in *The Dialectics of Our America: Genealogy, Cultural Critique and Literary History* promotes "canon expansion" by questioning "not only the canon of American literature (as it is usually understood in the Anglocentric model prevalent in our normal curricula), but the notion of America itself" (xii).

The study of postcolonialism in the Americas must repeatedly be both scrutinized and subsequently promoted with what bell hooks terms "critical militancy." One way to do this is to teach literary texts that deconstruct naturalized monolingualism and that historicize our eco-colonial past. Chicana and South Asian ecojustice texts do both. Bi/Polylingualism, in the U.S. classroom, when viewed as the asset that (academically) it is, may re-fashion stereotyping constructs in dominant culture, and cultivate respect for diverse expressive culture, thereby broadening and deepening understandings of social identities and, conversely, their commodification.[282] Deconstruction of naturalized linguistic representations of global capitalism and patriarchal and racist stereotypes, which contribute to environmental racism and ecological dilapidation may be undertaken via language, literature, and cultural study. Hence, language, literature, and cultural studies classrooms may be an avant-garde space in which to unlearn our participation in environmental racism and to learn to re-comprehend an environmentally just lifestyle, both figuratively and materially.

David Avalos has called multi-culturalism "the handmaiden of global capitalism." [283] This gendered metaphor, which acknowledges multi-culturalism's effacement of class issues, describes the power relations between the multi-cultural subject and the academy as an assimilatory function in which ethnic literatures are used by (and to serve) the dominant consumer culture/educational system; in return, they receive "servants' quarters" on the same premises with the "master's" mansion. Thus, ethnic literature gains token entry into "traditional" canons. But how does this new, likely transitory, home affect our readings of *ethnic* texts?

At this point, let us return to further examine one of Mahasweta Devi's short stories as we consider pedagogy's link to women's environmental justice in literature. Returning to the most celebrated figure of resistance in Mahasweta's stories, as received in the English-speaking classrooms in the West, (with special regard for Gayatri Chakravorty Spivak's work), Draupadi offers another lesson about pedagogy. Despite less interest in the short story's title character, Dtaupadi—in lieu of the villain, Senanayak as the base for Spivak's theoretical work on the story (IOW 179)—Draupadi's character has evoked numerous class-

282 I do not mean to conflate "bilingualism" in all contexts; certainly, for instance, many in the wealthy Mexican or South Asian "jet set" are fluently bilingual, with very different consequences than I describe here.

283 Communication and Art Conference, University of Texas at Austin, 3-5-94. This critique of multiculturalism functions figuratively, as well as economically. Avalos explained his view of multi-culturalism by referring to William Crevin's comment in 1993 that the undocumented were at the "lower end of the scale of humanity." Crevin later claimed that he was not racist but was rather referring to their economic position. As Avalos observes, one problem with multi-culturalism is that it applies to race and gender and not class—so it makes it OK to deny rights to those at the bottom of the economic scale. This merely changes the names by which groups of people are disempowered and protects the perpetrators of disempowerment. The structures of oppression remain in place; because of racism and sexism in the economic system, discrimination continues against largely the same groups.

room readings. As we have seen, Mahasweta's work is crucial for her portrayals of women as role models of organized community, as well as individual resistance. Spivak identifies another means by which Mahasweta complicates her female characters that parallels Nina Sibal's (and the Chipko Andolan's) use of the legendary Amrita Devi. Mahasweta "mobilizes the figure of the mythic female as opposed to the full-fledged goddess" (IOW 265). Characters such as Draupadi and Jashoda (the foster-mother/professional wetnurse in "Breast-Giver") have names that suggest associations with mythic characters in Hindu tradition. Mahasweta uses these names as an implicit platform upon which she can build, by situating the mythic in a contemporary politicized contextualization. Similarly, one might look to Chicana reinterpretations of La Lorona, Malatzin, and even the Virgin of Guadalupe (in Yolanda Lopez's artwork and decades of farmworker banners at marches, for starters) as "mobilized" mythic women in Mexican Catholic tradition.

Spivak suggests that "Mahasweta herself relates that "'Stanadayini'" [in the story of Jashoda, the 'breastgiver'] is a parable of India after decolonization. Like the protagonist Jashoda, India is a mother-by-hire..."[284] (IOW 244). Draupadi/Dopdi demonstrates a similar mythic status as Jashoda (IOW 265), but she represents a different aspect of India: the tribal resistance fighter, like the mythic Draupadi in the epic Mahabharata, Draupadi cannot finally be stripped—at least figuratively. Draupadi/Dopdi, having been apprehended, raped, and brutalized by her captors, is summoned to come before Senanayak, the man responsible for her apprehension. She refuses to put her saricloth back on and approaches Senanayak unclothed:

> Draupadi's black body comes even closer. Draupadi shakes with an indomitable laughter that Senanayak simply cannot understand. Her ravaged lips bleed as she [begins] laughing. Draupadi wipes the blood on her palm and says in a voice that is as terrifying, sky splitting, and sharp as her ululation, What's the use of clothes? You can strip me, but how can you clothe me again? Are you a man? (IOW 196)

Spivak's work on subaltern resistance contextualizes this scene: Draupadi, as a character, *speaks* loudly and oppositionally, and Spivak offers a comparison to the woman, Bhuvaneswari Bhaduri who was involved in the "armed struggle for political independence" to further nuance apprehension of their power. Spivak

284 Spivak uses Mahasweta's stories in contexts that are indirectly related to the author's stated or "intended" audience; however, Spivak also informs us of Mahasweta's motives. Thereby, through Spivak's readings we get a multi-layered discourse which seems appropriate for the complexity of the politicized characters in the texts.

posits Bhuvaneswari Bhaduri's story at the end of "Can the Subaltern Speak?" (1987 307) as an answer to the question in the title of the essay. Bhuvaneswari's attempts to speak through her blood—she had waited until menstruation to commit suicide, and thereby, she proved she was not suiciding due to an illicit pregnancy. Yet, as Spivak discovers, her political voice is not heard in contemporary oral historiographies. Despite her signaling that she died to cover up political information for the struggle, she is remembered as a victim of illicit love. In comparison to Bhuvaneswari, an urban woman whose family is of "modest" means, Dopdi/Draupadi is more truly "subaltern" and thus a conventional reading suggests it would be less likely that her voice, as one involved in resistance, would be heard. However, to insert Draupadi into Spivak's narrative on subaltern voice in place of Bhuvaneswari Bhaduri would change the course of that narrative *and* the "circumscribed task" with which the female as intellectual is faced. There is no ambiguity to Dopdi's actions and voice at the time of her capture and most probably eminent death. To describe the connection, I quote Spivak in her critique of what she labels "liberal feminism's" approach to the gendered subaltern.

> [A] certain version of the elite vs. subaltern position is perpetuated by non-Marxist anti-racist feminism in the Anglo-U.S. toward Third World women's texts in translation. (...I will call the ensemble "liberal feminism" for terminological convenience.) The position is exacerbated by the fact that liberal feminist Third Worldist criticism often chooses as its constituency the indigenous post-colonial elite, Diasporic or otherwise. (IOW 254)

For Spivak, "Mahasweta's text... calls into question this liberal-feminist choice. It dramatizes indigenous class-formation under imperialism and its connection to the movement towards women's social emancipation" (IOW 254). She further explicates the role Mahasweta plays in relation to the liberal feminist dynamic: "The critical deployment of liberal feminist thematics in Mahasweta's text obliges us to remember that we "might be parasitical not only upon imperialism (Haldarkarta)[Senanayak] but upon the gendered subaltern (Jashoda)[Dopdi/Draupadi] as well" (IOW 256). Spivak again nuances Bardhan's assertion that literature in tandem with social science/history produces a depth of study that neither approach can accomplish alone.) The lesson Spivak draws from this observation is that "[f]iction and its pedagogy can here perform the ideological mobilization of a moral economy that a mere benevolent tracing of the historical antecedents of the speaker might not be able to. The two must go together as each other's 'interruption,' for the burden of proof lies upon historical research" (IOW 256).

Given that it is in the work of the teacher, theorist, translator, and/or critic to see that fiction and history coalesce with, *and* interrupt each other, those of us who go to texts by "Third World" women to inform our work have the opportunity, as well as the mandate, to guard against the perpetuation of the "elite versus the subaltern" phenomenon that, in yet a new context, subjugates the gendered subaltern, even, one might conjecture, on her own grounds. Forced de-territorialization of the subaltern by the elite has been the "norm" that history, as well as the literary/storytelling, has too often naturalized. In our analysis, we, as educationally privileged workers, teachers, critics, theorists, artists, authors, and yes, activists, find ourselves, by definition, in the position of that elite. It is our work to discern where we are, resituate ourselves, and remap our relationships to the makers of the history and fiction that we study.

Let me then turn to a brief narrative of my own. About six weeks after the passing of proposition 187 in California, I was to deliver a paper on Chicano/a Performance/Conceptual Border Art at the 1994 MLA Convention in San Diego. I felt some trepidation about my role as cultural critic venturing into a border zone that was fast becoming a mine field to speak in, as one colleague put it, "the belly of the beast." At the time I made the following observations, which I have edited slightly for this context.

> For me, going to San Diego, breaking a boycott I support to give a paper on border issues in Chicana/o art underscores the complex duplicity that we as scholars and teachers face. Like in Maria Elena Lucas's *Flor Campesina* we as the MLA audience become actors in the California drama enacted against immigrant communities. We do however have some choice in the roles we take on. What is the most effective means to perform under protest? As consumers we have grown up with the daily choice to participate in boycotts against California grape growers, among others. As MLA participants, we are forced into the role of "tourist," in California, at a moment, when, to be a tourist here is to support a system that scapegoats immigrants to hide political blunders and crimes that fuel violence and racism and that threaten to deny basic human rights to many of the states' inhabitants. Our dilemma is only a magnified version of the conflicted choices that we as professors and students, artists and organizers must confront daily. As socially concerned artworks, the cultural work I discuss, lays open such contradictions; the artists, in engaging their audiences, take initial steps toward re-zoning art, politics, and cultural critique through historicizing that begins the conceptual dismantling of structural borders.

I include these observations because I believe that the cultural poetics, I have investigated for its representations of the *Virtual Realism of environmental racism* lays open such contradictions as well. In concluding, I want to situate environmental justice figuratively in a contemporary cultural context—one that has penetrated globally though still serving primarily the *first world North*—by reminding us that poetics that present environmental justice presents local historiographies in a kind of "virtual reality" frame. The ramifications of this cartography are important for anyone with an interest in literature, the environment, and/or justice.

As we read, study, and teach environmental justice texts we must realize that we are workers assembling representations. Our impact on the significance of the final product is based on what we piece together from the parts that are passed to us. The relation between the pieces in the assembly of any cultural expression produces effects on all sides. When we turn to representations, and in particular, self-representations of gendered subaltern and marginalized people in fiction, drama, poetry, history or testimonio to inform our critical or theoretical work, we are establishing a creative interlude, or channel, that has the potential to break through the barriers of disinformation and displacement caused by colonialism, environmental and other racisms, feudalism, capitalism, patriarchy and the miriad of phobias and bigotries. However, without what Jenny Sharpe and Gayatri Spivak have termed a "philosophy of vigilance" we may do the disservice of reinscribing the hierarchical discriminations that we have inherited.[285] Yet, texts like Mahasweta Devi's, Castillo's, Viramontes', Moraga's, and Sibal's, and characters like Draupadi, Sophia, Estella, Cerezita, and Krishna, can facilitate students with the wherewithal and understandings to face our "proscribed tasks."

Environmental justice writers are representing "el otro lado," "the other side" of nation, technology, development, colonialism, capitalism, and patriarchy, as grounds upon which we must all, as readers, take a stand because, as these stories show, environmental toxins do not stop for La Migra. Gloria Anzaldúa's often-quoted description of the "U.S. Mexican border [as] *una herida abierta* where the Third World grates against the first and bleeds" (1987 3) evokes Sanichari's wound in that it is a wound that does not heal. In Mahasweta's story, whether the healing is halted by the witch, as the villagers first believed, or by disease, as the western tradition doctor suggests, is not at issue, so much as the contradiction at stake for Mathur, the academic in league with the subaltern community. In the case of the bleeding wound that creates the "border culture," the dialectic that allows for communication in, and of, "border

---

285 Sharpe's passage reads, "[t]he critical transformation of an impossibility into a condition of possibility means maintaining "subaltern consciousness" as both irreducible and irretrievable to a discourse that can only be inadequate to its object. This is the "philosophy of vigilance" that Spivak proposes for negotiating the double bind of either producing subaltern groups as the objects of academic knowledge or else disavowing an intellectual responsibility by granting them self-representation" (Sharpe 18–19).

culture" is the representation of the environmental toxin, the environmental racism, which, in metaphor and fact, contributes to the continuously bleeding wound.

Meanwhile, academic, activist, and artist all contribute to expressing, discerning, interpreting, and teaching these representations. Specifically, the half of the bookcover painting that features the folks running upstream holding a sign against toxic dumps is inspired by a community mural painted by environmental justice activists near the Texas-Coahuila border. La Paz, an agreement between the U.S. and México signed in 1983 has been offered as solidarity against placing toxic dumps in our shared borderlands, in places like Sierra Blanca, Texas.

Let me give a postscript to my previous small narrative about the ambivalence I felt in going to San Diego. I returned home to find a letter from Maria Elena Lucas, one of the artists/activists I was speaking about in California and have written about here. About proposition 187, she wrote, "We have been awakened by a time-bomb. Now, our oppressors are going to see how effective we can be as deactivators."[286] The cultural poetics I have studied has illustrated that, though the substances may vary from chemical toxicity, to radioactivity, to climate change vulnerability, to racism, sexism, xenophobia, and gender expression bigotries, the task of combating environmental racism invariably begins with the act of "deactivation."

286 Personal correspondence dated 12-28-9[4].

Afterword: Environmental Justice Cultural Poetics, a Blueprint for Climate Justice

> Today we are faced with a common issue of survival and a crisis of life for this living planet Mother Earth. Any threat to the environment endangers all of us.
>
> PODER, Austin website, 2022

Since 2000, when I completed the bulk of my manuscript, scholarship on cultural response to environmental justice has increased, but critical attention has not kept up with the cultural response to environmental threats to our planetary wellbeing, and future sustenance, such as global warming. *Environmental Justice Poetics* connects 20th century cultural poetics to 21st century calls for Climate Justice. Publishing my book in hopes that lessons from the 20th century environmental justice poetics might be built upon in the 21st century is a big reason I persisted with pursuing publication plans for this manuscript even while it sat in a box on a top shelf of my study as paper copy and was transferred from one computer hard drive to the next as electronic copy, over two decades of hectic, contingent/adjunct teaching positions punctuated by the reprieve of developing The Meadowlark Center for community arts, education, environment & social justice on the land where my grandmother had built Meadowlark Homestead, a healing refuge in 1950s Kansas..

In this Afterword, I suggest that women's poetics for just and ecological change speaks to the transformations necessary to better address the inequity and chaos of our rapidly warming climate. Some of those who created the poetics of environmental justice in the last millennium are now on the front lines of growing climate chaos, some have a solid, sustained standing on the front lines of transformation or are creating and documenting the expressive poetics—the blueprints for climate justice, as las luchas continuas. Their work reveals ways that the humanities and social sciences are involved with and reshaped by the rethinking and reworking of our relationships to nature, planet, place, and to each other. T.V. Reed proclaims "[b]ringing environmental justice into environmentalism, and into ecocriticism, must lead as well to a fundamental rethinking and reworking of the entire field."[287] This mandate extends social envi-

287 See https://culturalpolitics.net/index/environmental_justice/memo. The significance of the statement, the ending of his essay, is apparent in the history he gives to the online essay: "Environmental Justice Ecocriticism: A Memo-festo": This essay was originally published via the online conference, "Cultures and Environments: On Cultural Environmental Studies," held at Washington State University and in cyberspace during June 1997; an expanded and updated

https://doi.org/10.1515/9783111041575-016

ronmentalism into expressions of climate vulnerability and protection—thus synthesizing transformations in interdisciplinary study and praxis in conjunction with societal transformations of our relationships with power, culture and nature made in a movement toward ecological and climate justice.

In centralizing narrative, image-based, and performative means of expressing toxic invasion, climate catastrophes, and other inequitably experienced reverberations of environmental destruction, we see how the poetics both anticipates and spreads the movement. This process is steered by the will to prevail of artists, activists, authors, and planetary citizens who maintain and sustain both planetary and local health and eco-cultural balance. My process of choosing poetics has been guided by the Principles of Environmental Justice using the same process I ask students to take in choosing environmental justice paper topics. We read through "The Principles" and see which might apply to the situation we have in mind to study. These criteria are valuable in addressing dilemmas of exponentially expanding environmental and climate-related inequities, vulnerabilities, and calamities. While not mentioning climate justice, verbatim, "The Principles" and other environmental justice discourse resonates with *reciprocity* and rejects *extraction* as encouraged by 21st Century environmental justice groups such as the Canadian, indigenous women-led *Idle No More*, whose explication of these terms in conversation with Naomi Klein deepens my comprehension (Klein, Naomi & Leanne Beatasamosake Simpson. 2013).

Much of the discourse from the last four decades historicizes environmental issues by tracing back across centuries of ecological and cultural displacement and land and nature destruction. It identifies colonial/imperial roots in capitalist accumulation as well as ways that access to natural places and the rhetoric of relationships with place are historically determined or denied in relationship with social identities. These historical aspects are mapped in my study in postcolonial theory largely from South Asian scholars.

Resonating arguments in 21st Century scholarship from indigenous, of color, and persons in other marginalized vantage points have extended these discussions. In the Preface of Carolyn Finney's *Black Faces, White Spaces*, she argues that "[in] the case of race and the environment, it's not just who we imagine has something valuable to say. These assumptions, beliefs, and perceptions can be

---

version of this essay was published in the collection, *Environmental Justice Reader: Politics, Poetics, and Pedagogy*, edited by Joni Adamson, Rachel Stein, and Mei Mei Evans (University of Arizona Press, 2002), and the final version was published in T.V. Reed, *The Art of Protest* University of Minnesota Press, 2005. In the interests of history, the text below is the original 1997 version."

found in the very foundation of our environmental thinking...how we think of ourselves in relationship with the environment."

Latinx 21st Century decolonial and environmental discourse is especially generative. *Latinx Environmentalisms: Place, Justice, and the Decolonial*, edited by Sarah D. Wald, et al, is a long overdue compendium. The historical grounding and cultural specificity of such discourse speaks a distinctively calm logic in the face of climate and other chaos. Priscilla Solis Ybarra's concept of "goodlife writing" in *Writing the Goodlife: Mexican American Literature and the Environment* offers a foundation of specificity and logical grounding. "Goodlife" writings of "simplicity, sustenance, dignity, and respect... implicitly integrate the natural environment as part of the [Mexican American] community" (WTG,4 & 5). Among South Asian thinkers, Arundhati Roy has made singular, often foundational offerings pertaining to many of the areas of study we have examined; her writing is consistently wise and inspiring.

Ecojustice Literature from both South Asian and Chicana authors grows in abundance. Of special relevance to Chicana activism of environmental justice (in San Antonio) that packs a love story to boot is *Luz at Midnight* by Marisol Cortez. As I describe on a back cover blurb, "Cortez has crafted a literary montage... Puro San Anto at its environmental and social justice core..." Published by Flower Song Press at the end of 2020, *Luz* was described in the *San Antonio Report* in the midst of Winter Storm Uri as "The shape of things to come: San Antonio author Marisol Cortez foresaw the rolling blackouts now plaguing the city." Cortez' novel made the news again that Spring as the 2021 Winner of the Texas Institute of Letters's Sergio Troncoso Award for Best First Book of Fiction. In 2022, *Luz at Midnight* won the Association for the Study of Literature and the Environment's (ASLE) *Creative Book* award.[288]

Another ASLE winner is a South Asian environmental justice multi-genre text, that describes an environmental justice struggle and *win* in the community of Plachimada on the border of Tamil Nadu and Kerala; they won against a nearby Coca Cola water plant that had destroyed the community's water. In 2015 ASLE's Translation grant was given to translate *Mayilamma* (2012). Translated as *MAYILAMMA The Life of a Tribal Eco-warrior (As told to Jothibai Pariyadath)* from the original Malayalam by Swarnalatha Rangarajan and Sreejith Varma who describe it as an "oiko autobiography." The book resonates in many ways with work from the 20th Century discussed, here—formally it relates to Maria Elena Lucas testimonio, and it includes powerful poetry (by Jothibai Pariyadath). Mayilamma was supported by and joined in protest with Vandana Shiva and Mehda Patkar. Her

288 See https://mcortez.net/luz/ for Marisol Cortez' website.

translators write in the introduction: "Mayilamma's words speak to the history of environmental disasters in India like the Bhopal Gas Tragedy (1984), pollution of life-giving rivers like the Ganga and the Yamuna, ill-conceived mega dams that spawn developmental refugees and man-made floods, shrinking of the commons, nuclear contamination and a host of other problems" (xxxvii). Mayilamma's forthrightness comes out in their narration:

> On becoming the recipient of the prestigious Speak Out Award and Sthree Shakti Award, Mayilamma's world expanded from Plachimada to India's capitol city where she got to meet important politicians like Ms Sonia Gandhi. However, this glittering political arena is always informed by the oikic as far as Mayilamma is concerned. She confesses that she had just one thing to tell politicians like Ms. Sonia Gandhi: "There is a small well in front of my house. We were drinking water all these days from that well. Now the water is not good. We are not against you giving any company a permit or an award. But can you bring the good water back to our well?". (xxxvi)

Mayilamma's book also represents a significant 21st Century development-- the increase in Adivasi and Dalit authors speaking and writing, themselves, on environmental justice and social identity and marginalization.

Another example of this is another autobiography/testimonio: *Mother Forest: The Unfinished Story of C.K. Janu* (2004). More recently, *Father May Be an Elephant and Mother Only a Small Basket, But...* (2022), a collection of short stories by Gogu Shyamala, which "dissolves the borders of realism, allegory, and political fable" is translated to English and German and "hailed as a landmark in Telangana Dalit literature. Gogu Shyamala is "a philosopher, poet and prolific story writer in the Telugu Language." These works speak to the fact that women in *subaltern spaces* are speaking and writing literature that challenge readers to conceive of just, eco-cultural spaces, globally, in new ways, while connecting with and building on the 20th Century work presented here.

Women have made films with international distribution about environmental justice for decades, and comprehensive film study in this field is desperately needed, but here I will mention just two films because they expand on two luminaries—Mahasweta Devi and Vandana Shiva's monumental lives are documented in *Mahananda* and *The Seeds of Vandana Shiva*, respectively.[289]

---

289 See trailers for *Mahananda* at https://www.youtube.com/watch?v=-giLL8dXmmU and https://www.youtube.com/watch?v=XqrVtiikQb0 Praising the work and contribution of Bengali writer and activist Mahasweta Devi, director of the Bengali film 'Mahananda', Arindam Sil said that like the River Mahananda, her principles should flow from one generation to another. (Outlook, 2022 https://www.outlookindia.com/art-entertainment/arindam-sil-principles-of-mahasweta-devi-should-flow-from-one-generation-to-another-news-240452) See the trailer https://www.you-

Throughout the world, women are acting in league with the earth, striving for an "earth democracy" as Vandana Shiva describes, being "good citizens" to use Winona LaDuke's self-descriptive term in the 21st Century. Decades after the Chipko Andalan protected trees from logging through women-led activism that spread from the Himalayan foothills across much of India, Indigenous-led water protectors are spreading the concept of "protection" across North America in the wake of Standing Rock's resistance encampment to stand against oil pipeline invasions in 2016. Climate action activists are allied with the water protectors for "keeping fossil fuels in the ground." Now, in South Asia, protected forests are a valuable means of reducing carbon, hence slowing planetary warming. "Protection" as basic to, or in some cases, replacing, protest, is increasingly important in climate actions and organizing, especially among indigenous communities. Water Protectors continue to work, walk, pray, holding vigilance in threatened watersheds. "Protection" resonates for Indigenous, Chicanaox, and other 21st Century North American environmental justice groups standing against oil pipelines and infrastructure on their lands to extract fossil fuels within them that increase global heat.

During these last decades, storms advanced the sea inland several times, destroying homes and agricultural land in areas such as the east coast of Odisha, India, not so far from the Chipko mural depicting women embracing trees, painted circa 1990 that inspired part of Mary Agnes Rodriguez' painting for this book's cover. Women bear the brunt of the fallout of such chaotic weather, but the last two decades have seen women in Odisha challenge climate and ecological injustice in unprecedented ways. They've saved their communities not unlike how they kept local weavers making traditional fabrics under the British by refusing to do their pujas except in locally made designs of saris, like the Barpali/Sambalpuri ikat weaving. Through diversifying crops, planting kitchen gardens, and improving the soil organically in "Grow Your Own Food" campaigns that counter genetically modified seeds, chemical pesticide, and synthetic, fossil fuel-based fertilizer use. For instance, working with gaia education "Koraput women developed their own kitchen gardens, and were trained in integrated sustainable farming practices and agroecological approaches—particularly how to develop new climate-resilient agricultural approaches, rooted in the traditional methods of food growing."[290] Perhaps most significantly, tribal women have formed the Odisha Nari

tube.com/watch?v=o9usfYeY5vU and the film's website: https://vandanashivamovie.com/ for *The Seeds of Vandana Shiva.*

290 See https://www.projects.gaiaeducation.uk/empowering-and-buildingcapacity-of-tribal-communities-in-india.

Samaj, a state-level federation of 54 tribal women's organizations and have organized protests to keep native seeds for cultivation and harmful land amendment ordinances at bay. [291]

In my current hometown of San Antonio, protection of river and arroyos, a karst aquifer, and what was once a vibrant underground system of springs and streams, has for decades been embattled. Indigenous activist-educators, Matilde Torres and Gary Pérez, illustrate how in Indigenous cosmologies the "terrestrial constellation" of waters, here resembles a "celestial constellation" in the sky. For their peoples, it was and is the cormorant, like the white herons and egrets for Chican@s, that signified their homelands.

A largely women of color-led group, including emigrants of the Americas and beyond, has built a protection movement, replete with poetics that is standing up for heritage trees and migratory water birds like egrets, cormorants, and herons in city parks where they are now being banished. Bird Island, the Westside San Anto's *Aztlan*, Mexican homeland in the North, continues to bring white egrets, cormorants, and herons in persistent defiance of pyrotechnic gun explosions, lasers, sirens, and habitat and nest demolition. Beneath the attacks on nature by city powers, USDA Wildlife Services, and powerful real estate development groups, are largely unexamined legacies of segregation, slavery, and capitalist imperialism addressed by historic and ongoing environmental justice struggles. Expressive art extending ecocultural legacies and relationship is vital to these struggles—Alesia Garlock's photography and film-making, dance/movement in city parks by Rosie Torres and Fabiola Torralba are examples. (My firsthand experience with these efforts is thus far expressed predominantly in my poetry and mixed genre work.)[292]

Recently, I received a call from a Westside Chicana friend, distraught that the city parks department had mowed the slopes along the westside arroyos of "tiny yellow flowers that cover the field like a painting." With burgundy in the center of the blossoms? I asked, and with her answer "yes!" I knew the Plains Coreopsis fields had been mowed. They were barren of flowers and of butter-

291 See https://siddharthvillage.org/about-us/ and listen to the women here: https://www.youtube.com/watch?v=igeFZ77xQXU.

292 See https://www.facebook.com/friendsofMigratorybirds and https://www.youtube.com/watch?v=VlJE6W-6cdI for examples of Alesia Garlock's photography and advocacy, https:// fabiolatorralba.wordpress.com/about/ for Fabiola Torralba's website and projects; for Rosie Torres, https://events.getcreativesanantonio.com/artist/rosa-rosie-torres/ and for my Bird Island Diptych, see https://directory.weadartists.org/emotional-numbness-the-impact-of-war-on-ecosystems and scroll down through *Emotional Numbness: The Impact of War on Ecosystems Exhibit* curated by Atefeh Khas and Raheleh Minoosh Zomorodinia. WEAD Women Eco Artists Dialog & Platform 3 Exhibit.

flies, when my dog and I went out the next morning, but we found a patch still blooming on a nearby neglected road tucked away near railroad tracks. Despite small homes nearby someone had dumped garbage there, but in the short moments before the stench overwhelmed us, we saw more butterflies, and other pollinators than during the whole hours' walk along the trails where the wildflowers had been mowed. Sadly, a week later it too had been mowed, likely at the behest of Code Compliance, which is currently targeting our council district even at many elected officials and leaders' chagrin. The yards and gardens of several San Antonio women mentioned in the pages of this book have been threatened, this year.

Near my home we've built a Garden of Good Trouble which continues to be such a place for people, finches, doves, cardinals and mockingbirds—to name the currently most common avian visitors—to forage volunteer and selected plants, and to nurture soil communities, wildflowers, native grasses, and a few perennial plants, a return to the southern end of a prairie that sweeps down the center of our continent; it has survived despite code compliance threats of abatement, extreme, chaotic weather, and plant theft. However, the day I sent my nearing CRC chapters to De Gruyter, I received the city's code compliance threat of "abatement"—by city code 'uncultivated' vegetation cannot be over 12 inches. My sustenance work did not count as cultivation, in their eyes. The sunflowers after May rains are 12 feet, the amaranth is catching up on them, and I live in a barrio that receives more notices of property condemnation than elsewhere in a city, where, a recent study shows, we demolish more endangered homes than other major cities in Texas combined, several times over.

When I went outside that next morning, there was a new passionflower blossom in my front yard, also full of sunflowers, as well as Turk's Cap and Eve's Necklace and wild oregano and the accompanying Gulf Fritillaries, Red Admirals, skippers, immigrating Monarchs and Checkerspots in their seasons, and many solitary and honey bees, hummingbirds, and other pollinating critters. I remembered passionflowers from gardens in India as well as at El Valle's resacas and refuges to the south when I taught in the Rio Grande Valley for five years, but I had not recognized the leaves of this volunteer plant in my yard and had almost pulled it out. The rose light of the rising sun filled the pale lavender for a second before a cloud intervened and suddenly my distress was lifted by the color I saw. The poetics of Bhopal survivors, farmworker children, Himalayan foothill communities came back to me: and I began to plan a message to artists, storytellers, dancers, songsters I knew—come out to the Garden of Good Trouble—commemorate Juneteenth, remember our aquifer and constellation of rivers with your commemoration of land under threat of "abatement."

Just as 20th Century women were on the frontlines of environmental justice struggles, they/we are now also in the frontlines expressing the need for transformative change, traditional wisdom of land work, and leading campaigns for the climate justice struggles. I hope that *Environmental Justice Poetics* emboldens readers to listen for and learn from these women and their expressive wisdom. I hope, worldwide, our progeny will retain the sense of awe at self and community expressions that mark each hue's distinctive glow of life and light. That generations of all genders will "water Tulsi daily," that water will return to the springs and rivers and moisten seedbeds for change.

In presenting concepts of environmental justice that promote equity and equality across communities in environmental decision-making, Susana Almanza, co-founder of People Organized in Defense of the Earth and her Resources (PODER, Austin, TX) often draws a metaphorical comparison between the star-studded cloak of the Virgen de Guadalupe and the ozone layer of the earth to suggest that toxins are destroying the protective aura of the sacred. She draws on a synthesis of locally grounded Chicana culture and related experiences of nature to discuss the impetus for social transformation, common in vernacular and literary representations of environmental justice from the turn of the millennium. Almanza's analogy represents a core of images that identifies, and initiates paradigm shifts which, leaders (increasingly, young people) listening to climate scientists, advocate in the name of climate justice. Such current work frames and furthers the legacies and wisdom of the 20th Century environmental justice cultural poetics.

When I mentioned to Graciela Sanchez, director of the Esperanza Center for Peace and Justice in San Antonio, where I have been part of the "Buena Gente" for many years that my environmental justice book had found a publisher, I expressed concern that it had sat so long while ecological justice travesties had increased, manyfold, and yet the world had moved on. Graciela responded with the observation that the book will have accumulated the contextualizing stories and relevance of the intervening years—to launch the book now will mean implicating the actions and insights that would not have yet developed, earlier. In bringing the 20th Century environmental justice poetics into the 21st Century context of intensifying climate justice concerns that have been called the most pressing existential concern of our age, this book serves the purpose of helping establish foundational directions in proceeding in equitable, sustainable, and environmentally and socially conscious ways. If there is even a small bit of transdiscursive influence that comes from this, the impact—both within stakeholder communities and at large—would make the work and the wait worthwhile.

Works Cited and Selected Bibliography

Acosta, Belinda. *Objects in Mirror Are Closer Than They Appear.* Unpublished manuscript, 1994.

Alarcón, Norma. "The Theoretical Subject(s) of This Bridge Called My Back and Anglo-American Feminism." in *Making Face, Making Soul: Haciendo Caras: Creative and Critical Perspectives by Women of Color.* Gloria Anzaldúa, ed. San Francisco: Aunt Lute Foundation Books, 1990. 356–69.

Alarcón, Norma. "The Sardonic Powers of the Erotic in the Work of Ana Castillo" in *Breaking Boundaries.* Asunción Horno-Delgado, Eliana Ortega, Nina M. Scott and Nancy Saporta Sternbach, eds. Amherst: The University of Massachusetts Press, 1989.

Alvarez, Claude. "Afterward" in *The Bhopal Syndrome: Pesticide Manufacturing and the Third World.* David Weir, ed. Penang, Malaysia: International Organization of Consumer Unions (IOCU), 1986.

Alvares, Claude and Ramesh Billorey. *Damming the Narmada: India's Greatest Planned Environmental Disaster.* Penang, Malaysia: Third World Network – Asia-Pacific Peoples Environment Network, 1988.

Anzaldúa, Gloria, ed. *Making Face, Making Soul: Hacienda Caras Creative and Critical Perspectives by Women of Color.* San Francisco: Aunt Lute Foundation Books, 1990.

Anzaldúa, Gloria. *Borderlands La Frontera: The New Mestiza.* San Francisco: spinsters/aunt lute, 1987.

Avalos, David, Louis Hock and Elizabeth Sisco. "Art Rebate Arte Reembolso Artists' Statement." 1993.

Avalos, David, Louis Hock and Elizabeth Sisco. "Media Packet: Collected Articles on 'Art Rebate Arte Reembolso'".

Avalos, David. Communication and Art Conference, University of Texas at Austin, 3-5-1994.

Bahl, Vik. "Interrogating the National Narrative: Re-Imagining History in the Contemporary Indian Novel in English." paper presented at Narrative Strategies for 21st Century, Historical Symposium. Fall, 1993.

Bandyopadhyay. J and Vandana Shiva. "Asia's Forests, Asia's Cultures" in *Lessons of the Rainforest.* Suzanne Head and Robert Heinzman, eds. San Francisco: Sierra Club Books, 1990.

Banerjee, Brojendra Nath. *Bhopal Gas Tragedy: Accident or Experiment.* South Asia Books, 1986.

Bano Bi. in *Voices From Bhopal.* Produced by Rajiv Lochan Sharma, Kim Laughlin, Satinath Sarangi, Arun Kumar Singh, Vinod Raina and Rex D. Rozario. Bhopal: Bhopal Group For Information and Action, 3-12-1990.

Bardhan, Kalpana, trans. & ed. *Of Women, Outcastes, Peasants, and Rebels: A Selection of Bengali Short Stories.* Berkeley: University of California Press, 1990.

"Better to be Poor" *Ebony.* December, 1966. 100–104.

Bhopal Action Resource Center. *Union Carbide's Bhopal Tragedy: A Time for Solidarity: Special Report to American Workers and Communities at Risk.* 1989.

Bordewich, Fergus M. "The Lessons of Bhopal" in *Atlantic Monthly,* March 1987. 30–31.

Bullard, Robert. *Confronting Environmental Racism: Voices from the Grassroots.* Robert D. Bullard, ed. Boston: South End Press, 1993.

Bullard, Robert. *Dumping in Dixie: Race, Class, and Environmental Quality.* New York: Routledge, 1990.

https://doi.org/10.1515/9783111041575-017

Canel, Edward. http://www.yorku.ca/ecanel/profile.html.

Cassels, Jamie. "The Uncertain Promise of Law: Lessons from Bhopal" in *Osgood Hall Law Journal,* 29.1, 1991. 1–50. https://digitalcommons.osgoode.yorku.ca/ohlj/vol29/iss1/1.

Castillo, Ana. *So Far From God.* New York: W.W. Norton & Company, 1993.

Castillo, Ana. Interview in *Mills College Review: A Publication of the Walrus Literary Magazine,* Vol. 2 # 2, December 11, 1992. 1–4.

Castillo, Ana. Interview in *Mester,* Vol. XX, #2, Fall, 1991.

Castillo, Ana. *Sapogonia.* Tempe Arizona: Bilingual Press/Editorial Bilingue, 1990.

Castillo, Ana. *Sapogonia.* New York: Anchor Books, 1994.

Chavis, Benjamin F. Foreword. *Confronting Environmental Racism: Voices from the Grassroots.* Robert D. Bullard, ed. Boston: South End Press, 1993. 3–5.

Chávez, Denise. "Our Lady of Guadalupe: She Infuses Culture with Life and Hope" in *New Mexico Magazine,* December, 1986. 55–63.

Chisti, Anees. *Dateline Bhopal: A Newsman's Diary of the Gas Disaster.* Foreword by Sumitra Chisti, South Asia Books, 1986.

Chouhan, T.R. and others. *Bhopal: The Inside Story Carbide Workers Speak Out on the World's Worst Industrial Disaster.* New York, NY: The Apex Press, 1994.

Cortez, Marisol. *Luz at Midnight.* McAllen TX: Flower Song Press, 2020.

Cuomo, Christine J. "Unraveling the Problems in Ecofeminism." in *Environmental Ethics,* Vol. 14 #4, Winter, 1992. 351–363.

Dakin, Susanna. "Bhopal Disaster: A Personal View" in *Bhopal: From Hiroshima to Eternity.* S. B. Kolpe, ed. Berkeley: University of California, 1985.

De Grazia, Alfred. *A Cloud Over Bhopal.* Kalos Foundation, 1985.

de la Torre, Adela and Beatríz M. Pesquera. *Building With Our Hands: New Directions in Chicana Studies.* Berkeley: University of California Press, 1993.

Diamond, Arthur. *The Bhopal Chemical Leak.* Lucent Books, 1990.

Dogra, Bharat. *Forests, Dams and Survival in Tehri Garhwal.* New Delhi: Bharat Dogra C-27, Raksh Kunj, Paschim Vihar, 1992.

Eklavya Bhopal. *A peoples view of death, their right to know and live.* Bhopal: Arera Colony, 1985.

Everest, Larry. *Behind the Poison Cloud: Union Carbide's Bhopal Massacre.* Banner Press, 1985.

Ferree, Myra Marx and Patricia Yancey Martin, eds. *Feminist Organizations: Harvest of the New Women's Movement.* Philadelphia: Temple Univ. Press, 1995.

Ferree, M. M. (1992). "The political context of rationality: Rational choice theory and resource mobilization." in *Frontiers in Social Movement Theory.* Aldon. D. Morris and Carol. M. Mueller, eds. New Haven, Conn.:Yale University Press. 29–52.

Fine, Gary Alan. "Public Narration and Group Culture: Discerning Discourse in Social Movements" in *Social Movements and Culture.* Hank Johnston and Bert Klandermans, eds. Minneapolis: Univ. of Minnesota Press, 1995. 127–143.

Finney, Carolyn. *Black Faces, White Spaces: Reimagining the Relationship of African Americans to the Great Outdoors.* Chapel Hill: UNC Press, 2014.

Finney, Carolyn. "What's Race Got to do With It? Climate Change, Privilege and Consciousness" in *Whole Thinking Journal,* January, 2009.

Freire, Paulo. *Pedagogy of the Oppressed.* Myra Bergman Ramos, trans. New York: The Seabury Press, 1970.

Gaard, Greta, ed. *Ecofeminism: Women, Animals, Nature*. Philadelphia: Temple University Press, 1993.

Gadgil, Madhav and Ramachandra Guha. *This Fissured Land: An Ecological History of India*. Berkeley & L.A. CA.: Univ. of CA. Press by arrangement with Oxford Press, 1993.

Gamson, William. "The Social Psychology of Collective Action" in *Frontiers in Social Movement Theory*. A. D. Morris and C.M. Mueller, eds. New Haven Conn.: Yale University Press, 1992. 53–76.

García, Arnoldo and Nancy Stein, "Scapegoating Without Borders" in *Crossroads*, November 1993. 5–7.

Gilliam, Angela. "Women's Equality and National Liberation" in *Third World Women and the Politics of Feminism*. Chandra Talpade Mohanty, Ann Russo and Lourdes Torres, eds. Bloomington: Indiana University Press, 1989.

Gómez, Tammy Melody, "Falsies" in Seis *Huesos*. Austin: Tejana Tongue, 1995.

Gómez-Quiñones, Juan. *Roots of Chicano Politics 1600–1940*. Albuquerque: University of New Mexico Press, 1994.

González, Ray. "A Chicano Verano" in *The Nation*, June 7, 1993. 772–774.

Gray, Ann and Jim McGuigan, eds. *Studying Culture: an introductory reader*. London: Edward Arnold: A division of Hodder & Sloughton, 1993.

Guerrero, Monique. "Ana Castillo: Una Voz A Despecho De Definicion" in P*alabras Chicanas: an undergraduate anthology*. Lisa Hernandez and Tina Benitez, eds. Mujeres en Marcha, Berkeley: University of California Press, 1988.

Guha, Ranajit and Gayatri Chakravorty Spivak, eds. *Selected Subaltern Studies*. New York: Oxford UP, 1988.

Gupta, Krishna Murti. *Mira Behn: Gandhiji's Daughter Disciple Birth Centenary Volume*. New Delhi: Himalaya Seva Sangh, 1992.

Gupta, Shalini. "Yatra: Nina Sibal: A Rites of Passage Bildungsroman" in *The Commonwealth Review*, New Delhi, Vol. 1 # 1, 1989. 124–129.

Gupta, Ashis. *Ecological Nightmares and the Management Dilemma: The Case of Bhopal*. Dehli: Ajanta Publications, 1991.

Harjo, Joy. *In Mad Love and War*. Middletown, Connecticut: Wesleyan University Press, 1990.

Hofrichter, Richard, ed. *Toxic Struggles: The Theory and Practice of Environmental Justice*. Philadelphia: New Society Publishers, 1993.

Hooks, Bell. *Outlaw Culture: Resisting Representations*. New York: Routledge, 1994.

Huggan, Graham. "Decolonizing the Map: Post-Colonialism, Post-Structuralism and the Cartographic Connection" in *Ariel*, 20, October, 1989. 120–131.

Jain, Shobita. "Standing up For Trees: Women's Role in the Chipko Movement" in *Women and the Environment: A Reader Crisis and Development in the Third World*. New York: Monthly Review Press, 1991.

Jaising, Indira and C. Sathyamala. "Legal Rights ... and Wrongs: Internationalising Bhopal," in *Close to Home: Women Reconnect Ecology, Health and Development Worldwide*. Vandana Shiva, ed. Philadelphia: New Society Publishers, 1994. 88–91.

Janson, H. W. *History of Art*. Upper Saddle River, NJ: Prentice Hall, 1977.

Jawahara, Saidullah. "A Chipko Journey" in *The India Magazine of her People and Culture*, Vol. 13, #10, 1993.

de Jesus, Carolina Maria. *La Favela*. La Habana: Casa de las Americas, 1965.

de Jesus, Carolina Maria. *Quarto de Despejo diario de uma favelada*. Sao Paulo: Livraria Francisco Alves, 1960.

de Jesus, Carolina Maria. *Child of the Dark: The Diary of Carolina Maria de Jesus*. David St. Clair, trans. Boston: E.P. Dutton & Co. Inc., 1962.
Johnston, Hank and Bert Klandermans, ed. *Social Movements and Culture*. Minneapolis: Univ. of Minnesota Press, 1995.
Jones, Tara. *Corporate Killing: Bhopals Will Happen*. London: Free Association Books, 1988.
Kadetsky, Elizabeth. "High-Tech's Dirty Little Secret" in *The Nation*, May 19, 1994. 517–520.
Kahrl, William L. *Water and Power: The Conflict over Los Angeles' Water Supply in Owens Valley*. Berkeley: Univ. of California Press, 1982.
Kelly, Petra. "A Very Bad Way to Enter the Next Century". Acceptance Speech, Right Livelihood Award.
Kerr, Mary Lee and Charles Lee. "From Conquistadors to Coalitions: After Centuries of Environmental Racism, People of Color are Forging a New Movement for Environmental Justice" in *Southern Exposure*, Winter 1993. 8–19.
Klein, Naomi and Leanne Betasamosake Simpson. "Dancing the World into Being: A Conversation with Idle No More's Leanne Simpson" in *YES Magazine*, March 6, 2013.
Klor de Alva, J. Jorge."The Postcolonization of the (Latin) American Experience: A Reconsideration of 'Colonialism,' 'Postcolonialism,' and 'Mestizaje'" in *After Colonialism: Imperial Histories and Postcolonial Displacements*. Gyan Prakash, ed. Princeton: Princeton UP, 1995.
Kolpe, S. B. *Bhopal: From Hiroshima to Eternity*. Berkeley: University of California, 1985.
Kumar, Radha. *The History of Doing: an Illustrated Account of Movements for Women's Rights and Feminism in India, 1800–1990*. New Dehli: Kali for Women, 1993.
Kurzman, Dan. *A Killing Wind: Inside Union Carbide and the Bhopal Catastrophe*. McGraw-Hill (Original from University of Michigan), 1987.
Laughlin & Morehouse in Chouhan, T.R. and Others. B*hopal: The Inside Story Carbide Workers Speak Out on the World's Worst Industrial Disaster*. New York: The Apex Press, 1994.
"Life in a Garbage Room" in *Time*, Sept. 26, 1960. 43.
Linkenbach, Antje. "Ecological Movements and the Critique of Development: Agents and Interpreters." in *Thesis Eleven*, 39 (1), 1994. 63–85. https://doi.org/10.1177/072551369403900107.
Lopez, Elsa. *Letter to The L. A. Times*. Oct. 2, 1994. https://www.latimes.com/archives/la-xpm-1994-10-02-op-45492-story.html.
Lucas, María Elena. "Flor Campesina," in *Forged under the Sun/Forjada bajo el sol The Life of María Elena Lucas*. Francis Leeper Buss, ed. Ann Arbor: The University of Michigan Press, 1993.
Mahasweta, Devi. *Imaginary Maps: Three Stories by Mahasweta Devi*. Gayatri Chakravorty Spivak, translator and introduction. New York: Routledge, 1993.
Mahasweta, Devi. "Operation?—Bashai Tudu" in *Bashai Tudu*. Samik Bandyopadhyay, translator.
Mahasweta, Devi. in *Of Women, Outcastes, Peasants, and Rebels: A Selection of Bengali Short Stories*. Bardhan, Kalpana, trans. & ed. Berkeley: University of California Press, 1990.
Martínez, César Augusto. "Citings from a Brave New World: The Art of the Other Mexico" in *New Art Examiner*, May 1994.
Martinez, Elizabeth. "When No Dogs or Mexicans Are Allowed" in *Z Magazine*, January 1991. 37–42.

Martinez, Theresa A. "Toward A Chicana Feminist Epistemological Standpoint: Theory at the Intersection of Race, Class, and Gender" in *Race, Gender & Class in The World Cultures: An Interdisciplinary & Multicultural Journal*, Vol. 3, No. 3, 1996. 107–128.

Marx, Gary T. "External Efforts to Damage or Facilitate Social Movements: Some Patterns, Explanations, Outcomes, and Complications" in *The Dynamics of Social Movements: Resource Mobilization, Social Control, and Tactics*. Mayer N. Zald and John D. McCarthy. eds. Cambridge, Massachusetts: Winthrop Publishers, 1979.

Mayilamma: The Life of a Tribal Eco-warrior (As told to Jothibai Pariyadath) Swarnalatha Rangajan and Sreejith Varma, translators. Hyderabad,Telengana, India: Orient Black Swan Pvt. Ltd, 2018.

McClintock, Anne. "The Angel of Progress: Pitfalls of the Term 'Post-Colonialism.'" in *Social Text*, No. 31/32 (Vol. 10 no. 2&3), 1992.

McCully, untitled account in *The Times of India*, 8-7-1993.

McMohan, Martha. *Engendering Motherhood: Identity and self-transformation in women's lives*. Guilford Press, 1995.

Melucci, Alberto. "The Process of Collective Activity" in *Social Movements and Culture*. Hank Johnston and Bert Klandermans, ed. Minneapolis:Univ. of Minnesota Press, 1995.

"Memórias de Carolina de Jesus," in *Nós Mulheres*, No. 4 March/April, 1977.

Menezes, Taimundo. *Dicionário literário brasileiro*. 2nd. ed. RJ: LTC Livros Técnicos e Cien tícos, editora S.A.: 1978.

Mendoza, Louis. "Making History: Generational Constructs, National Identity, and Critical Discourse in Twentieth Century Chicana/o Literature." Ph.D. Dissertation in English, University of Texas, Austin, 1994.

Mendoza, Louis. *Historia: The Literary Making of Chicana & Chicano History*. College Station: Texas A & M Press, 2001.

Mies, Maria and Vandana Shiva. *Ecofeminism*. United Kingdom: Fernwood Publications, Zed Books, 1993.

Miller, Mark Crispin. "The Crushing Power of Big Publishing" in *The Nation*, Vol. 264, No. 10, March 17, 1997. 11–18.

Molotch, Harvey. "Media and Movements" in *The Dynamics of Social Movements: Resource Mobilization, Social Control, and Tactics*. Mayer N. Zald and John D. McCarthy. eds. Cambridge, Mass: Winthrop Publishers, 1979.

Moraga, Cherríe. *Heroes and Saints & Other Plays*. Albuquerque: West End Press, 1994.

Moraga, Cherríe. *The Last Generation: Prose and Poetry*. Boston: South End Press, 1993.

Morris, Aldon D. and Carol McClurg Mueller, eds. *Frontiers in Social Movement Theory* . New Haven Conn: Yale University Press, 1992.

Mujeres Activas en Letras y Cambio Social. *Chicana Critical Issues*. Norma Alarcón, Rafaela Castro, Emma Pérez, Beatriz Pesquera, Adalijiza Sosa Riddell and Patricia Zavella, eds. Berkeley: Third Woman Press, 1993.

Omvedt, Gail. "Green Earth, Women's Power, Human Liberation: Women in Peasant Movements in India" in *Close to Home: Women Reconnect Ecology, Health and Development Worldwide*. Vandana Shiva, ed. Philadelphia: New Society Publishers, 1994.

Omvedt, Gail. *Reinventing Revolution and the Socialist Tradition in India*. Armonk, New York & London, England: M.E. Sharpe, An East Gate Book, 1993.

Pansing, Cynthia, Hali Rederer and David Yale. "A Community at Risk: the Environmental Quality of Life in East Los Angeles" A Client Project for the Mothers of East Los Angeles, Masters Thesis, Architecture and Urban Planning, UCLA, 1989.

Paulsen, Monte. "The politics of cancer: Why the medical establishment blames victims instead of carcinogens" in *Utne Reader*, Nov./Dec. 1993. 81–89.

Pineros y Campesinos Unidos del Noroeste (PCUN). "Homenaje A Cesar Chavez." Washington, 1993.

Pardo, Mary. "Doing It for the Kids: Mexican American Community Activists, Border Feminists?" in *Feminist Organizations: Harvest of the New Women's Movement.* Myra Marx Ferree and Patricia Yancey Martin, eds. Philadelphia: Temple Univ. Press, 1995. 356–371.

Pardo, Mary. "Identity and Resistance: Mexican American Women and Grassroots Activism in Two Los Angeles Communities" Ph.D. dissertation in Sociology, UCLA, 1990.

Paulsen, Monte. "The politics of cancer: Why the medical establishment blames victims instead of carcinogens" in *Utne Reader,* Nov./Dec. 1993. 81–89.

Peña, Devon G., ed. *Chicano Culture, Ecology, Politics: Subversive Kin*. Tucson: University of Arizona Press, 1998.

Peña, Devon G., ed. *The Terror of the Machine: Technology, Work, Gender, & Ecology on the U.S.-Mexico Border*. CMAS Books, The Center for Mexican American Studies, University of Texas, Austin, 1997.

Peña, Devon G., ed. *Environmental and Food Justice*. website. http://ejfood.blogspot.com/

Perrow, Charles. "The Sixties Observed" in *The Dynamics of Social Movements: Resource Mobilization, Social Control, and Tactics*. Mayer N. Zald and John D. McCarthy, eds. Cambridge, Mass: Winthrop Publishers, 1979.

"Latina/o Environmental Justice Literature." in *Oxford Research Encyclopedia of Literature. Oxford University Press*. Article published February, 2019. http://dx.doi.org/10.1093/acrefore/9780190201098.013.649

Platt, Kamala. "Feminist Visual Poetics of Environmental and Climate Justice" in *New Feminism of WEAD (Women Eco Artists Dialog) Online Magazine*, Issue 8, winter 2015–2016. http://weadartists.org/feminist-poetics-of-eco-justice.

Platt, Kamala with Irasema Coronado. "Cultural Poetics of Environmental Justice: Where Borders Meld" in *Gateways: Northeastern Mexico and South Tejas, One Region, One Culture: An Anthology of Essays*. San Antonio: Guadalupe Cultural Arts Center, 2009. 120–133.

Platt, Kamala. "Proposal for Graduate Seminar: The Poetics of Environmental Justice" *Women's Studies Quarterly: Earthwork: Women and Environments*. Diane Hope and Vandana Shiva, guest editors. The Feminist Press, Vol. 29 # 1 & 2, Spring/Summer 2001. 254-260.

Platt, Kamala. "Ecocritical Chicana Literature: Ana Castillo's 'Virtual Realism'" substantially revised. In *Ecofeminist Literary Criticism*. Greta Gaard & Patrick Murphy, eds. University of Illinois. 1998. 139–157.

Platt, Kamala. "Two Centuries of Environmental Writing in India" in *The Literature of Nature: An International Sourcebook.* Patrick Murphy, ed. Chicago: Fitzroy Dearborn, 1998. 315–324.

Platt, Kamala. "Chicana Strategies for Success and Survival: Cultural Poetics of Environmental Justice from the Mothers of East Los Angeles" in *Frontiers: A Journal of Women Studies*, vol. xviii, Number 2, 1997. 48–72.

Platt, Kamala. "Environmental Justice: Multicultural by Definition" in *Ecofeminism? Ecocriticism. Phoebe: An Interdisciplinary Journal of Feminist Scholarship Theory and Aesthetics,* vol. 9, # 1, Spring 1997 SUNY/Oneonta Women's Studies. 21–29.

Platt, Kamala. "Environmental Justice in Chicana and South Asian Poetics" in *Multicultural Environmental Writing Conference Proceedings Phoebe: An Interdisciplinary Journal of Feminist Scholarship Theory and Aesthetics*, Vol. 9, #2, Spring 1997.

Platt, Kamala. "Ecocritical Chicana Literature: Ana Castillo's 'Virtual Realism'" in *ISLE Ecofeminist Literary Criticism Special Issue*, Spring 1996, Vol. 3.1.

Platt, Kamala. "Pedagogies of Environmental Justice" in *Greening the Campus Conference Proceedings*, Ball State, Indiana: Spring, 1996.

Platt, Kamala. "Tracking La Migra in Ana Castillo's *Sapogonia*." Texas College English, Spring, 1995. 28–30.

Platt, Kamala. "Environmental Justice and Women's Work: the UFW, Chipko Movement, and Seringueiros" in *San José Studies: A Publication of San Jose State University*, October, 1994. 49–62.

Platt, Kamala. "Race and Gender Representations in Clarice Lispector's 'A Menor Mulher do Mundo' and Carolina Maria de Jesus' 'Quarto de Despejo'" in *Afro-Hispanic Review: African- Brazilian Culture Special Issue*, Vol. XI, #s 1-3, 1992. 51–57.

Platt, Lavonne. *Barpali After Ten Years: Observations Made in Revisiting Barpali in 1971*. American Friends Service Committee, 1973.

PODER. *Sacred Waters: Life-Blood of Mother Earth: Four Case Studies of High-Tech Water Resource Exploitation and Corporate Welfare in the Southwest*. Southwest Network for Environmental and Economic Justice and the Campaign for Responsible Technology, 1997.

Pratt, Mary Louise. "Comparative Literature and Global Citizenship" in *Comparative Literature in the Age of Multiculturalism*. Charles Bernheimer, ed. Baltimore, MA & London: John Hopkins University Press, 1995.

Pulido, Laura. *Environmentalism and Economic Justice: Two Chicano Struggles in the Southwest*. Society, Environment and Place Series. Tucson: University of Arizona Press, 1996.

Pulido, Laura. "Sustainable Development at Ganados de Valle" in *Confronting Environmental Racism: Voices from the Grassroots*. Robert D. Bullard, ed. Boston: South End Press, 1993. 123–140.

Pulido, Laura. Laura Pulido Educator Author Activist. https://www.laurapulido.org,

Quinn, Guadalupe. Personal interview, January 2000.

Reed. T.V. *Fifteen Jugglers, Five Believers: Literary Politics and the Poetics of American Social Movements*. Berkeley & Los Angeles: University of California Press, 1992.

Reed. T.V. *Cultural Politics Resources for Critical Analysis*. http://culturalpolitics.net/index

Rich, Adrienne. Letter in "EXCHANGE: The Chavez Legacy" in *The Nation November* 22, 1993. 635.

Rivera, Gilberto. Interview, spring 1991.

Rivera, Tomas. *...y no se lo tragó la tierra/and the earth did not devour him*. Evangelina Vigil-Piñon, trans. Houston: Arte Publico, 1987.

Roy, Arundhati. *Walking With the Comrades*. Penguin Publishing, 2011.

Russo, Ann. "'We Cannot Live without Our Lives': White Women, Antiracism, and Feminism" in *Third World Women and the Politics of Feminism*. Chandra Talpade Mohanty, Ann Russo and Lourdes Torres, eds. Bloomington & Indianapolis: Indiana University Press, 1991. 297–313.

Ruta, Suzanne. "Fear and Silence in Los Alamos." in *The Nation*., January 4--11, 1993. 9–13.

Said, Edward. *Orientalism*, New York: Vintage Books, 1979.

Saidullah, Jawahara K. "A Chipko Journey" in *The India Magazine of Her People and Culture*, Vol. 13 #8, July 1993. 30–41.

Salas, Mario. *The Alamo: a Cradle of Lies, Slavery and White Supremacy*. Sentia Publ., 2022.

Saldaña-Portillo, Maria Josefina. *The Revolutionary Imagination in the Americas and the Age of Development*. NC: Duke University Press, 2003.

Saldívar, José David. *The Dialectics of the America: Genealogy, Cultural Critique, and Literary History*. Durham N.C.: Duke U P, 1991.

Saldívar, Ramón. *Chicano Narrative: The Dialectics of Difference*. Madison: The University of Wisconsin Press, 1990.

Saldívar-Hull, Sonia. "Feminism in the Borderlands: From Gender Politics to Geopolitics" in *Criticism in the Borderlands: Studies in Chicano Literature, Culture, and Ideology*. Héctor Calderón and José David Saldívar, eds. Durham & London: Duke UP, 1991. 203–220.

Salleh, Ariel. "The Ecofeminism/Deep Ecology Debate: A Reply to Patriarchal Reason" in Environmental Ethics, Vol. 14, # 3, Fall 1992. 195–216.

Sathyamala, C. et al. "Effects of Bhopal gas leak on women's reproductive health." Bombay: IBCS, 1985.

Sathyamala,C. "The Medical Profession and the Bhopal Tragedy" 6:1/2 Lokayan Bulletin, 1988.

Seager, Joni. in Toxic Struggles: The Theory and Practice of Environmental Justice. Hofrichter, Richard., ed. Philadelphia, PA: New Society Publishers, 1993.

Seager, Joni. "Class, Race, and Gender Discourse in the Ecofeminism/Deep Ecology Debate" in Environmental Ethics, Vol. 15, # 3, Fall 1993. 225–244.

Sharma, Rajiv Lochan, Kim Laughlin, Satinath Sarangi, Arun Kumar Singh, Vinod Raina and Rex D. Rozario, Producers. Voices From Bhopal. Bhopal: Bhopal Group For Information and Action, 3-12-1990.

Sharpe, Jenny. *Allegories of Empire: The Figure of Woman in the Colonial Text*. Minneapolis: University of Minnesota Press, 1993.

Shiva, Mira. "Environmental Degradation and Subversion of Health" in *Close to Home: Women Reconnect Ecology, Health and Development Worldwide*. Philadelphia, PA: New Society Publishers, 1994.

Shiva, Vandana. "Foreword" in Peña Devon G., ed. *Chicano Culture, Ecology, Politics: Subversive Kin*. Tucson: University of Arizona Press, 1998.

Shiva, Vandana. Ed. *Close to Home: Women Reconnect Ecology, Health and Development Worldwide*. Philadelphia, PA: New Society Publishers, 1994.

Shiva, Vandana. *Staying Alive: Women, Ecology and Development*. London, U.K.: Zed Books, 1989.

Shiva, Vandana. in *IPAG Newsletter*, Vol. 3, # 2, October 1992. India Progressive Action Group, Austin Texas.

Shiva, Vandana. *Navdanya Vandana Shiva Seed saving website*. http://www.navdanya.org/

Sibal, Nina. *Yatra. (The Journey)*. London: The Women's Press, 1987.

Silko, Leslie Marmon. in *The Nation*, October, 1995. 414–416.

Silko, Leslie Marmon. *Almanac of the Dead*. New York: Simon and Schuster, 1991.

Spivak, Gayatri Chakravorty. "Can the Subaltern Speak?" in *Interpretations of Marxism*. Urbana: University of Illinois, 1988.

Spivak, Gayatri Chakravorty. "Draupadi" by Mahasveta Devi. In *Critical Inquiry*, Vol. 8, No. 2, Writing and Sexual Difference. Winter, 1981, The University of Chicago Press. 381–402.

Spivak, Gayatri Chakravorty. Translator and discussion. Imaginary Maps: Three Stories by Mahasweta Devi, New York: Routledge, 1995.

Spivak, Gayatri Chakravorty. *In Other Worlds*. New York: Routledge, 1988.

Spivak, Gayatri Chakravorty. *Outside in the Teaching Machine*. New York: Routledge, 1993.

Spivak, Gayatri Chakravorty. *The Spivak Reader*. Donna Landry and Gerald MacLean, eds. New York & London: Routledge, 1996.

Subramaniam, M. Arun and Ward Morehouse. *The Bhopal Tragedy: What Really Happened and What It Means for American Workers and Communities at Risk.* A Report for the Citizens Commission on Bhopal. Council on International Public Affairs, 1986.

Tactaquin, Cathi. "Environmental Justice Needs No Green Card" in *Crossroads*, November 1993, 13.

Tau Lee, Pam. "Pam Tau Lee speaks out against attempts to blame immigrants for the environmental crisis" in *Crossroads*, November 1993, 4.

Taylor, Verta and Nancy Whittier. "Collective Identity in Social Movement Communities: Lesbian Feminist Mobilization" in *Frontiers in Social Movement Theory.* A.D. Morris and C.M. Mueller, eds. Yale University Press, 1992. 104–129.

Torres, Lourdes. "The Construction of the Self in U.S. Latina Autobiographies." in *Third World Women and the Politics of Feminism.* Chandra Talpade Mohanty, Ann Russo and Lourdes Torres, eds. Bloomington & Indianapolis: Indiana University Press, 1991. 271–287.

United Farm Workers of America. *No Grapes.* Video narrated by Mike Farrell with Martin Sheen, Edward James Olmos and others, 1992.

United Farm Workers of America. *Wrath of Grapes.* Video narrated by Mike Farrell, 1986. 15 min.

Usher, Ann Danaiya. "After the Forest: AIDS as Ecological Collapse in Thailand." in *Close to Home: Women Reconnect Ecology, Health and Development Worldwide.* Vandana Shiva, ed. Philadelphia, PA: New Society Publishers, 1994.

Venkateswaran, Pramila. "When they hang a poet" in *L'Ouverture: The Black Marketplace of Ideas.* Atlanta, Georgia.

Vivek, P. S. *The Struggle of Man Against Power: Revelation of 1984 Bhopal Tragedy / P.S. Vivek.* 1st ed. Bombay: Himalaya Pub. House, 1990.

Viramontes, Helena María. *Under the Feet of Jesus: a novel.* New York: Penguin Group, 1995.

Wald, Sarah D., David J. Vázquez, Priscilla Solis Ybarra and Sarah Jaquette Ray, eds. *Latinx Environmentalisms: Place, Justice, and the Decolonial.* Philadelphia: Temple University Press, 2019.

Weber, Thomas. *Hugging the Trees: The Story of the Chipko Movement.* Penguin Books, 1989.

Weir, David. *The Bhopal Syndrome: Pesticide Manufacturing and the Third World.* Penang, Malaysia: International Organization of Consumer Unions (IOCU), 1986.

White, Hayden. "Historical Texts as Literary Artifact" in *The Tropics of Discourse: Essays in Cultural Criticism.* Baltimore: Johns Hopkins University Press, 1978.

Wilkins, Lee. *Shared Vulnerability: The Media and American Perceptions of the Bhopal Disaster.* ABC-CLIO, LLC, 1987.

Williams, Raymond. *Resources of Hope: Culture, Democracy, Socialism.* Brooklyn NY: Verso, (original from University of Michigan), 1989.

Wysham, Daphne. "Ten-to-one against: Costing people's lives for climate change." in *The Ecologist,* Vol. 24, # 6 November/December, 1994. 204–206.

Ybarra, Priscilla Solis. *Writing the Goodlife: Mexican American Literature and the Environment.* Tucson: University of Arizona Press, 2016.

Zald, Mayer N. and John D. McCarthy, eds. *The Dynamics of Social Movements: Resource Mobilization, Social Control, and Tactics.* Cambridge, Mass: Winthrop Publishers, 1979.

Zald, Mayer N. and John D. McCarthy. "Resource Mobilization and Social Movements: A Partial Theory." *American Journal of Sociology.* Vol 82. No 6, May, 1977. 1212-1241.

Index

https://doi.org/10.1515/9783111041575-018

www.ingramcontent.com/pod-product-compliance
Lightning Source LLC
LaVergne TN
LVHW050954080826
845145LV00006B/1495

* 9 7 8 3 1 1 2 2 1 4 9 6 1 *